PEDIGREE AND PANACHE

A History of the Art Auction in Australia

PEDIGREE AND PANACHE

A History of the Art Auction in Australia

Shireen Huda

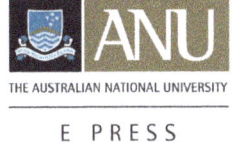

E PRESS

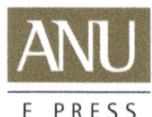

Published by ANU E Press
The Australian National University
Canberra ACT 0200, Australia
Email: anuepress@anu.edu.au
This title is also available online at: http://epress.anu.edu.au/pedigree_citation.html

National Library of Australia
Cataloguing-in-Publication entry

National Library of Australia Cataloguing-in-Publication entry:
Author: Huda, Shireen Amber.
Title: Pedigree and panache : a history of the art auction in
             Australia / Shireen Huda.
ISBN: 9781921313714 (pbk.) 9781921313721 (web)
Notes: Includes index.
             Bibliography.
Subjects: Art auctions--Australia--History.
             Art--Collectors and collecting--Australia.
             Art--Prices--Australia.
Dewey Number: 702.994

All rights reserved. No part of this publication may be reproduced, stored in a retrieval system or transmitted in any form or by any means, electronic, mechanical, photocopying or otherwise, without the prior permission of the publisher.

Cover design by ANU E Press
Cover image: John Webber, *A Portrait of Captain James Cook RN*, 1782, oil on canvas, 114.3 x 89.7 cm, Collection: National Portrait Gallery, Canberra. Purchased by the Commonwealth Government with the generous assistance of Robert Oatley and John Schaeffer 2000.

This edition © 2008 ANU E Press

Table of Contents

Preface ix
Acknowledgements xi
List of Figures xiii
Introduction 1

Chapter 1. The International Context for Art Auctions 7
    French Art Auctions 8
    English Art Auctions 9
    Dealers, Artists and Auctions 11
    Nineteenth Century American Art Dealers/Auctioneers 12
    Dealers' Rings 13
    The Reputation of Auctions 15

Chapter 2. The Major London Auction Houses 19
    Christie's 21
    Bonhams and Phillips 26
    Sotheby's 28

Chapter 3. Colonial and Early Australian Art Auctions 33
    Art Unions and their Role in the Art Market 35
    The Art Auction Market 37
    Early Auction Houses — Gemmell, Tuckett & Co. 38
    Thomas Sutcliffe Mort and Thomas Ware Smart: Two Collectors, their
    Agents and Auctioneers 40
    Carl Kahler's Studio Auction 43
    The Baldwin Spencer Collection 47

Chapter 4. Australian Art at Auction: the 1960s Market 55
    Lawson's 55
        The G. W. Eedy Sale 57
        The W. A. Little Collection 57
        The James T. Hackett Collection 58
        The William Barclay Collection 59
        The Norman Schureck Sale 60
    Leonard Joel 66
        The Charles Ruwolt Collection 67
        The George Page-Cooper Sale 68
    Trends in the Australian Art Auction Market in the 1960s and
    '70s 70

Chapter 5. Christie's Australia 77
    Christie's Autonomy 79
    Christie's Satellite and Telephone Link-up Sales 85

    Christie's First Auction in Australia 86
    The Como Sale 87
    The 1971 Dobell Sale 88
    The Major Harold De Vahl Rubin Sales 88
    Christie's Retreat, Re-establishment and Restructure 90
    The Trout Sale 92
    The Dallhold Sale 94
    The Mertz Sale 95
    In Recent Times 98

Chapter 6. Sotheby's Australia 103
    Robert Bleakley and the Establishment of Sotheby's in Australia 105
    Sotheby's First Australian Sale — The Webber Portrait of Captain Cook 108
    The Aboriginal and Torres Strait Islander Art Market 112

Chapter 7. Art Auction Practices and Innovations 123
    Buying-in 124
    Setting the Rhythm 125
    Referrals, Reserves and Estimates 125
    Art Auction Catalogues 127
    Art Education 130
    Guarantees of Authenticity 131
    Commissions/Buyer's Premium 132
        The Bath of Diana Sale 134
    Marketing and Glamorizing Art Auctions 136
    Buyers at Auction 139
        The *Mount Wellington and Hobart Town* Sale 140

Chapter 8. Other Major Art Auction Houses 149
    F. R. Strange 149
    Geoff K. Gray 150
    Lawson's/Lawson-Menzies 153
    Leonard Joel 157
    Phillips/Shapiro Auctioneers 161
    Goodmans/Bonhams & Goodman 163
    Deutscher-Menzies 163

Sources 173
    Interviews and Oral Histories 173
    Art Auction Catalogues and Brochures 175
        Christie's 175
        Deutscher-Menzies 176
        Gemmell, Tuckett & Co. 176
        Geoff K. Gray 177

      Hamilton & Miller 177
      Lawson's 178
      Lawson-Menzies 178
      Leonard Joel 178
      Phillips 179
      Sotheby's 179
Exhibition Catalogues 182
Electronic Sources 184
Media Releases 186
Newspaper and Journal Articles 188
Books 224
Unpublished Theses 232
Unpublished Papers 233

Index 235

Preface

While this study is the most comprehensive history of the art auction in Australia, it is not intended to be exhaustive or definitive. Written from the perspective of an independent observer, it necessarily possesses self-imposed boundaries. It would require writing a detailed history of Australian art — which was not my intention — to include the influences of major cultural institutions and their collecting policies and exhibitions, art publishing, the economy and the broader art market. These subjects are touched on in other works. Similarly, delving deeply into all the current machinery and machinations of the art market would require a separate study; other works, particularly international ones, provide this information. For this reason art crime is also essentially omitted and corporate collecting and philanthropy are only mentioned cursorily. *Pedigree and Panache* is thus only one of many potential histories.

While the art auction industry is permeated with sensationalism, this book is not written in the sensational style adopted in other books and journalism. I see *Pedigree and Panache* as a history based on empirical research with its genesis as a PhD thesis. It is written in the style of international auction histories and the periodic repetition of auctioneers' promotionalisms and the use of potentially loaded terms, such as 'quality', give a flavour of the language and marketing of the times, as well as the atmosphere surrounding particular art auctions. It was my hope in undertaking the research to tell a story, rather in the tradition of William Moore in *The Story of Australian Art*.

It is also not the aim of this study to provide advice on art investment or buying and selling at auction. However, *Pedigree and Panache* would be helpful in providing prospective users of the auction system or interested individuals with the tools necessary to analyse trends as they unfold and, perhaps, to make more informed opinions or purchases.

Although legislation, particularly in relation to trade, was of importance for the development of the art auction industry, little emphasis is given to the role and responsibility of public policy and regulation in this study. Sotheby's, and others, however, were instrumental in overturning trade restrictions in the post-World War II era in order to increase their business and turnover.

Events are often pieced together from various primary and secondary sources. It is possible that some inaccuracies may have crept in, for works of this nature are not infallible, relying as they do quite heavily on people's memories which are not always unbiased, or ephemeral material not always substantiated with further evidence. It has not always been possible or practicable to test every statement or anecdote. That said, the value of the book is that most of its information has not been recorded before and/or in this manner, using oral histories obtained from key stakeholders in the Australian art auction industry, contemporary news reports and auction catalogues. Assuming my readers will have a certain level of knowledge of or interest in art auctions, I have left it to them to draw their own conclusions from many comments made by informants or journalists.

It should also be noted that the prices for works are sometimes quoted with a buyer's premium and sometimes without, depending on available information. For the more recent decades I have generally used prices from the *Australian Art Sales Digest* which occasionally includes the buyer's premium. Other prices are taken from auction houses' media releases, news reports and other publications and, regardless of whether they include or exclude the buyer's premium and GST, still give an indication of whether prices were high or low. The same can be said of the different currencies used in different periods. There is also some difficulty in writing a work which covers a number of auction houses and auction practices over a long period of time in always stating conclusively when things stopped or started; by the time this is published, many things will have changed again. Imposing a cut-off of April 2006 allows a degree of hindsight and some perspective on events and practices. As a source book then *Pedigree and Panache* aims to be a broad and solid foundation stone to be built upon.

Acknowledgements

I would firstly like to pay homage to my friends, family and colleagues for their unwavering support and faith both during the course of my PhD research and the subsequent writing of this book. I am sure they are now collectively sighing in relief!

The Humanities and Creative Arts ANU E Press Advisory Board members must be thanked for their patience throughout the lengthy process of converting this from a thesis to a book. The peer reviewers they engaged also offered valuable advice. Barbara Holloway offered extremely constructive structural advice and provided a solid copy edit and I owe her a huge vote of thanks. The staff of the ANU E Press, especially Duncan Beard, were very helpful during the final publishing phase.

I also gratefully acknowledge the assistance of the following in providing important information either in the shape of interviews, correspondence, or sharing their own research with me: Richard J. Agnello, Anita Archer, Orley Ashenfelter, Carlos Barros, Robert Bleakley, Arthur Brooks, Timothy Richard Brown, Lisa Burkhill, Jane Clark, Roger Dedman, Chris Deutscher, Jenny Dickerson, Jon Dwyer, Mark Fraser, Victor Ginsburgh, Christopher Heathcote, Sue Hewitt, Robert Holden, The International Center for Art Economics (Venice), Kate Joel, Heather Johnson, Annette Larkin, Joan McClelland, Roger McIlroy, Myra McIntyre, Christopher Marshall, Geoff Maslen, Justin Miller, Andrew Montana, Michael Moses, Charles Nodrum, Benedict Pownall, Alain Quemin, Michael Reid, Enrique Saravia, Antonello Scorcu, Andrew Shapiro, Adam Shoemaker, Paul Sumner, David Thomas, Michele Trimarchi, Annette Van den Bosch, Olav Velthuis and Suzanne Watteau.

I would like to thank the following people for helping with my requests to reproduce images in my book, particularly those who let me have the images at the scholarly rate or for free: Carol Burns, Royal Holloway, University of London; Jacklyn Burns, The J. Paul Getty Museum, Los Angeles; Laura Fiser, Paine Art Center and Gardens, Oshkosh, Wisconsin; Holger Gehrmann, Artothek, Germany; Helen Harrison, State Library of New South Wales; Bruce Howlett, National Portrait Gallery, Canberra; Daragh Kenny, National Gallery, London; Tim Klingender, Sotheby's; Maddy Kortegast, Viscopy; Diane P. Naylor, Chatsworth Photo Library; Bill Neill, Sir William Dobell Art Foundation; Nick Nicholson, National Gallery of Australia; Margot Riley, State Library of New South Wales; Madeleine Say, State Library of Victoria; Lucy Scrivener, Tate Modern, London; Penny Tripp, Victoria Racing Club Ltd; and Anthony Wallis, Aboriginal Artists Agency Ltd. I would also like to thank Rohan Thomson for taking my photo for the cover.

Gratitude must be extended to the staff of the following institutions who provided assistance with my initial research: the National Library of Australia, the National Gallery of Australia's Research Library, the Library of the Art Gallery of New South Wales, the Mitchell Library and the State Library of New South Wales, the Schaeffer Fine Arts Library at the University of Sydney, the State Library of Victoria and the Baillieu Library of the University of Melbourne.

Lastly, I would like to thank those who provided support and advice during the course of my PhD research: Sasha Grishin, Robyn Maxwell, Andrew Sayers, Gino Moliterno, Margaret Brown and Paul Johns. I extend special thanks to Adam Shoemaker who has always believed in my research and provided encouragement throughout.

List of Figures

Figure 1: Jules Breton (French, 1827-1906), *Evening in the Hamlet of Finistere*, 1882, oil on canvas, 93.3 x 132 cm, Collection of the Paine Art Center and Gardens, Oshkosh, Wisconsin.

Figure 2: Edwin Long, *The Babylonian Marriage Market*, 1875, oil on canvas, 172.6 x 304.6 cm, From the Picture Collection, Royal Holloway, University of London. For a review of the Victorian Collection please visit www.rhul.ac.uk/picture-gallery/index.html.

Figure 3: Thomas Gainsborough (English, 1727-1788), *Portrait of James Christie (1730–1803)*, 1778, oil on canvas, 126 x 101.9 cm, The J. Paul Getty Museum, Los Angeles. Gift of J. Paul Getty.

Figure 4: Thomas Gainsborough (English, 1727-1788), *Portrait of Georgiana, Duchess of Devonshire (1757-1806)*, c.1785-7, oil on canvas, 123 x 96.4 cm, Collection: Chatsworth House, Derbyshire.

Figure 5: Carl Kahler, *The Derby Day at Flemington*, 1886, oil on canvas, 300 x 200 cm, Victoria Racing Club Collection.

Figure 6: *Artist Carl Kahler's studio, interior, Melbourne*, (west end), c.1890, gelatin silver photograph, 20 x 25 cm, State Library of Victoria.

Figure 7: Jack Hickson, *Auction of the Norman Schureck collection of art, including paintings by Dobell, James R. Lawson (auctioneers), Sydney*, March 1962, photonegative, 10 x 12 cm, Australian Photographic Agency Collection, State Library of New South Wales.

Figure 8: Jack Hickson, *Auction of the Norman Schureck collection of art, including paintings by Dobell, (here, Wangi Boy), James R. Lawson (auctioneers), Sydney*, March 1962, photonegative, 10 x 12 cm, Australian Photographic Agency Collection, State Library of New South Wales.

Figure 9: Gustav Klimt, *Portrait of Hermine Gallia*, 1904, oil on canvas, 170.5 x 96.5 cm, © The National Gallery, London (on loan to the Tate Modern, London).

Figure 10: Adam Elsheimer, *St Helena Questions the Jew*, c.1603–05, *Stadelsches Kunstinstitut* (Stadel Museum), Frankfurt. Image courtesy of Stadel Museum - ARTOTHEK.

Figure 11: John Webber, *A Portrait of Captain James Cook RN*, 1782, oil on canvas, 114.3 x 89.7 cm, Collection: National Portrait Gallery, Canberra. Purchased by the Commonwealth Government with the generous assistance of Robert Oatley and John Schaeffer 2000.

Figure 12: Johnny Warangkula Tjupurrula, *Water Dreaming at Kalipinypa*, 1972, synthetic polymer powder paint on composition board, 75 x 80 cm. Copyright the estate of the artist licensed by Aboriginal Artists Agency 2008.

Figure 13: John Glover (England 1767-1849 Australia), *The bath of Diana, Van Diemen's Land, 1837*, 1837, oil on canvas, 96.5 x 134.5 cm, National Gallery of Australia, Canberra. Purchased with the assistance of the National Gallery of Australia Foundation 1993.

Figure 14: John Glover (England 1767-1849 Australia), *Mount Wellington and Hobart Town from Kangaroo Point 1831-3*, 1834, oil on canvas, 76.2 x 152.4 cm, Tasmanian Museum and Art Gallery, Hobart and National Gallery of Australia, Canberra. Purchased with funds from the Nerissa Johnson Bequest 2001.

Introduction

> ... art auctions are to the twentieth century what watching the king was to the eighteenth, a place to be seen and a chance to see a spectacle: grown men and women spending more money than most see in a lifetime for something noone needs.
>
> Jeffrey Hogrefe[1]

Art auctions are fascinating affairs. Each one is different, a fresh contest played out in the saleroom, the arena in which art and money openly combine, separate and reconfigure. Art auctions are veiled in a mystique beyond their elitist overtones and functional reality. They are places where phenomenal — and well-publicized — sums exchange for works of distinction, while some works stay ignominiously, unexpectedly, unsold; for in the saleroom, 'while the good need not be expensive, the expensive must always be good'.[2] Fashionable people mingle at the previews, notable people are seen at the auction, dealers and consultants make conspicuous bids — auctions are an established part of the exchange of art, artists' reputations, individual fortunes and cultural history.

Have art auctions always had this role at the centre of cultural exchange? How and where were auctions first used to sell art? How did they get their glamorous veneer? What are the key art auction houses and how have they affected the market?

Pedigree and Panache was written to answer such questions, tracing art auctions all the way from their historical roots to their central and authoritative position in the Australian art market today. In the process a number of other questions are systematically addressed.

Did art and auction houses combine in colonial Australia? Why, how and by whom were Christie's and Sotheby's established in Australia? What has their impact been on the Australian art market and did their arrival result in the internationalization of this market? What trends or practices in the art auction market keep recurring? What do auctions reveal about tastes in collecting? Who were the protagonists to have shaped or participated in the Australian art auction industry? The profile of art in Australia is fleshed out in the process of following key players — auctioneers, artists and collectors — and key works through the course of sales and their later fate.

As art auctions developed in the Western world in the twentieth century, a number of recurring themes began to define the market as we know it today in Australia. Establishing the authenticity of individual works, coupled with an increasing emphasis on scholarship, became important. Art sales also evolved as spectacles and the social status of auctions and auctioneers changed. In tandem with these developments, the relationship that art dealers and artists maintained with auctions and auction houses often became more complex.

Art auctions have received extensive media coverage in recent years, not least over the manner in which the international auction houses, Christie's and Sotheby's, have conducted their business. Despite the fact that these firms have presented themselves as paragons of 'cultural and corporate professionalism', they have been vilified and/or penalized in the United States for colluding to fix commission prices.[3] Ironically, through attracting a wider public audience through the media, 'auction houses have [also] made themselves...more vulnerable to public scrutiny and demands for greater accountability.'[4]

Although some of these themes have been covered in international studies, including Learmount's *A History of the Auction*, Watson's *From Manet to Manhattan* and Cooper's *Under the Hammer*, such works make scant reference to Australia. Only one, Ruhen's *The Auctioneers*, has been written on an Australian auction house (Lawson's). *Pedigree and Panache* thus aims to add to the established international — and burgeoning body of national — work about the art market by providing the most comprehensive study of the development and role of art auctions in Australia to date.

Interest in the Australian art market has grown in recent years. *Art House*, for example (a documentary series I assisted with), was aired in 2004 for a general audience to take a look behind-the-scenes at art auctions at Christie's and Deutscher-Menzies.[5] It was warmly received by viewers. A number of published works, including Reid's *How to buy & sell art*, Van den Bosch's *The Australian Art World* and Anderson's *Art + Australia*, also address a fairly wide readership.

Pedigree and Panache begins by identifying the international background and context of art auctions. Chapter Two then documents the rise of auction houses, including Christie's and Sotheby's, in eighteenth century London and their twentieth-century expansion into the Australian market.

The art marketing system was relatively unstructured in colonial Australia and Australian collectors generally opted to buy and sell their 'quality' art in the international marketplace, particularly in London. Local auction houses often included copies of Old Master paintings and works of indeterminate quality as part of general sales and it was some time before specialized Australian art auction houses emerged from this unsophisticated market. However, key early art auctions had a great influence on the development of the local art market, as well as on the predilection for contemporary Australian, rather than European, art and on the perception that art provided opportunities for investment. Chapter Three traces these developments and provides a general discussion of colonial and early Australian art auctions, their influences and place in the art market.

Chapter Four focuses on the establishment and early development of two enduring Australian auction firms, Sydney-based Lawson's and Melbourne-based Leonard Joel, principally in relation to specific art auctions held in the 1960s and trends prior to the arrival of Christie's. By the early 1960s, interest in art investment and speculation in Australia was rising. This affected not only the local market and the value of Australian art, but also Christie's decision to open an Australian saleroom in 1969.

The establishment and development of Christie's and Sotheby's in Australia had an impact on the existing Australian art auction market, particularly in the rationalization which ensued from increased and sophisticated competition. Chapter Five explores the establishment of Christie's in Australia; its early sales; retreat from a saleroom presence around 1979; re-establishment in 1984 and subsequent withdrawal in 2006. The re-establishment of Christie's and the establishment of Sotheby's in 1982 also meant that 'auctions became more accessible'.[6] Christie's auctions were fairly 'low-key' in the early years but when Sotheby's arrived on the scene 'more fanfare' was injected into the Australian art auction market.[7] This is explored to some extent in Chapter Six, a history of Sotheby's in Australia.

Chapter Seven investigates the introduction of certain auction practices, innovations and marketing strategies to the Australian market by the multinational firms. Although there may be 'no historical precedent for the price structure of art in the late twentieth century', as Robert Hughes claims, there are historical precedents for some practices, such as the use of a buyer's premium, which may have been innovative for the Australian marketplace but are part of a firmly entrenched Western tradition.[8] Owing to its effective marketing strategies, in some ways the impact that Sotheby's had on the local Australian market is more noticeable and, therefore, more profound than that of Christie's.

Art and money, the sale of art at auction and the public interest generated by media coverage are interrelated, as the publicity given to prices realized at art auctions repeatedly emphasizes the importance of the monetary value of art as a key indicator of aesthetic value. Hence, auctions have become the most visible and effective barometer for defining a work's value. Hughes commented that:

> Sotheby's and Christie's have been flogging the benefits of art ownership to the rich on both shores of the Atlantic; art as investment, art as social elevation, art as confirmation of status, art as relic-hunting. The whole rigmarole has done more to debase the real values of art than anything else in our culture.[9]

The auction houses have been vehicles for the art/commodity transaction, which one could say is the 'fruit of a marriage between marketing and standardized demand'.[10] However, American art dealer and consultant, Ben Heller, differed:

'because of their immense power and brilliant marketing skills…we have made Sotheby's and Christie's scapegoats for the pressures and dislocations brought about by the radically increasing value attributed to certain kinds of art.'[11] Another American art dealer, Irving Blum, commented that 'An auction result is only one measure among many', yet its very visibility makes this a most important measure, particularly with regards to contemporary art.[12]

The arrival of Christie's and Sotheby's also had a marked impact on some major local Australian auction houses which had held important sales of art, including F. R. Strange, Geoff K. Gray, Lawson's/Lawson-Menzies and Leonard Joel. These firms either initially rallied to the challenge presented by the multinationals, only to surrender later by altering their business focus, and/or pared back their art sales in the wake of increased competition. Other firms for whom art sales formed a large component of their business, such as Phillips/Shapiro Auctioneers, Goodmans/Bonhams & Goodman and Deutscher-Menzies, are foundling firms, established only in recent times, possibly as a direct consequence of the pivotal role played by the multinational firms in the Australian art auction market. These firms are the subject of Chapter Eight.

Sir Alan Bowness, Director of the Tate Gallery in London from 1980 to 1988, argued that artists' success can be pre-determined and described by whether they conform to certain criteria or 'conditions of success'.[13] He claimed that each artist passed through four levels of recognition on his/her way to fame and success: peer recognition, critical recognition, patronage by dealers and collectors, and public acclaim, usually won over a period of approximately 25 years. Bowness also made a distinction between the artist who produces work for public art galleries or museums ('genius') and the artist who produces work for the marketplace ('journeyman'). According to Bowness, 'It is only the museum artists whose work begins to rise to exceptional prices, and of course it is the very rarity of such artists in a supply-and-demand market that accounts for the phenomenal prices achieved today [in 1989] in the auction houses.'[14]

Like it or not, the auction houses themselves are now, to varying degrees, involved in determining the progress of artists through Bowness' four stages. I would argue that it is only recognition by other artists which is not influenced by the auction houses. Public acclaim, by Bowness' reckoning the final stage, has become a main determinant in the process of legitimation through the assiduous marketing conducted by the auction houses.

The tension between the aesthetic and monetary value of art has long been of concern in art market analysis. According to the economist William Grampp 'from an economic point of view, most paintings have been durable consumer goods subject to obsolescence'; that is, the art that is discarded and the art that remains depends on the tastes and incomes of the buyers.[15] Art auctions are innately interesting because they are revealing about changing collecting tastes.

Auction houses play an important role in both reflecting collecting tastes through the stock they source and sell and cultivating collecting tastes when their standard stock is depleted.

In Australia, contemporary art has been fashionable at various points in time. It was auctioned in the colonial era, as is demonstrated by the sale of the contents of Carl Kahler's studio in 1890. However, it was not until early in the twentieth century that Australian art was considered a wise purchase, mirroring a decided shift in collecting tastes and habits. The auction in 1919 of some of the collection of Sir Walter Baldwin Spencer (perhaps best known as an anthropologist) created a demand for the art of contemporary Australian artists, greatly assisting the careers and markets for the likes of Sir Arthur Streeton. There was a renewed enthusiasm for Australian art and of art investment after the 1962 Norman Schureck sale, with auctions once again directly influencing taste and having an impact on living artists and art dealers. Such sales are discussed in early chapters of this study and represent precedents for the current penchant for auctioning contemporary art in Australia.

Australia is, in many ways, an insular marketplace and it is also an intriguing and dynamic marketplace. Furthermore, not all practices adopted overseas have been replicated identically in Australia. In the past, it was thought that one could only look at Australia as a derivative of London or New York — that is, its place in the international market — but it is in fact perfectly legitimate to study Australia as a 'centre' in its own right, while including international parallels or influences where appropriate. Thus, a perceptible undercurrent is the extent to which Australian art and collecting tastes have been internationalized, ostensibly through Christie's and Sotheby's.

Pedigree and Panache has centred on Christie's and Sotheby's as this enabled an examination of the Australian art auction market before and after the arrival of the international firms and provided a roughly chronological structure. This general history of the art auction in Australia narrows in to focus on the period from 1969 (when Christie's arrived in Australia) to April 2006 (when Christie's withdrew from conducting auctions in Australia). This has also necessitated concentrating on Melbourne and Sydney, as these are where the salerooms of the international firms were based and where the crux of the Australian art market has been located. The auction of paintings is the primary concern of this study, owing to the inordinate amount of publicity and high sales figures they generate, as well as representing the established pinnacle of the fine arts. Auction houses are publicly judged by their success with high profile art sales, as we shall see.

ENDNOTES

[1] Jeffrey Hogrefe, *'Wholly Unacceptable' — The Bitter Battle for Sotheby's*, Harrap, London 1986, p.13.

[2] Gerald Reitlinger, *The Economics of Taste — The Art Market in the 1960s*, Barrie and Jenkins, London 1970, vol. 3, p.10.

[3] Geoff Maslen, 'Final art auctions start under a cloud', *The Age*, 11 November 2000, p.14.

[4] Gertrude Prescott Nuding, 'Saleroom Practice', *Apollo*, July 1988, p.39.

[5] Made by Hilton Cordell Productions and aired on The Australian Broadcasting Corporation (ABC) in August 2004.

[6] Kathryn Chiba, *Dr Joseph Brown: Dealing in Cultural Capital*, MA thesis, University of Melbourne, 1999, 2 vols, vol.1, p.42.

[7] Roger Dedman, partially taped interview with the author, Melbourne, 2 October 2002.

[8] Robert Hughes, *Nothing if Not Critical — Selected Essays on Art and Artists*, Alfred A. Knopf, New York 1991, p.395. This was also quoted in the frontispiece of Peter Watson's book, *From Manet to Manhattan — The Rise of the Modern Art Market*, Random House, New York 1992.

[9] Quoted in Geoff Maslen, 'Final art auctions start under a cloud', *The Age*, 11 November 2000, p.14.

[10] Judith Benhamou-Huet, 'Buren, Richter, Christie's et Sotheby's — The Artist and the Auction House', *Art Press*, no. 241, December 1998, p.14.

[11] Ben Heller, 'The "Irises" Affair', *Art in America*, vol. 78, July 1990, p.53.

[12] Quoted in Carter Ratcliff, 'The Marriage of Art and Money', *Art in America*, July 1988, p.80.

[13] Alan Bowness, *The Conditions of Success: How the Modern Artist Rises to Fame*, Walter Neurath Memorial Lectures, Thames and Hudson, London 1989, p.7.

[14] Bowness, *The Conditions of Success*, p.11.

[15] William D. Grampp, *Pricing the Priceless — Art, Artists, Economics*, Basic Books, New York 1989, pp.74–5.

Chapter 1. The International Context for Art Auctions

Auctions have provided people with a means to conduct trade for aeons, with antecedents in the ancient world. The Greek historian, Herodotus, wrote the earliest extant account of auctioneering when he described a regular Babylonian marriage market of about 500BC. The ancient Romans were keen auction participants and the word 'auction' is actually derived from the Latin *auctio*, which means 'increase' or 'auction sale', and this definition confirms that the increasing, or ascending, system of auctioneering was used, as is the practice in Australian auctions today.

A number of the auctioneering practices and expressions identified in this chapter have helped to shape contemporary Western art auctions and demonstrate recurring aspects of the art auction market. In 146BC, after the Romans defeated the Achaeans, the consul Lucius Mummius ordered that a public auction be held in Rome to sell the paintings and sculpture which they had appropriated. According to Giorgio Vasari in the *Lives of the Most Eminent Painters, Sculptors and Architects*, Attalus, King of Pergamum, successfully bid an enormous amount, 6000 sesterces, for a painting of Bacchus by Aristides.[1] However, the Romans refused to grant it an export licence. They assumed that because it had attained a large price at auction that it was valuable and hence desirable. This is an early account of monetary value defining the aesthetic value of art and a contemporary example of this is discussed in Chapter Seven in relation to a John Glover painting.

Financial arrangements were employed in ancient Rome. We know the Pompeian auctioneer, Lucius Cecilius Iucundus, who operated during Nero's reign (AD54–68), took a one per cent commission and extended credit to buyers he was confident would sell through him in the future. There is also evidence that the Romans invented the buyer's premium, which was re-invented in modern times in the 1970s. Prior to Nero's reign, the buyer had been required to pay a tax, approximately two per cent half a century earlier in the reign of Augustus (27BC–AD14). Brian Learmount, an authority on the history of auctions, thinks it highly likely that the Romans held a pre-auction viewing, as occurs today.[2]

If auctions have a long history, so too do art auctions. Auctions were often the medium through which plunder including art was sold. Auctioneers followed in the wake of the Roman army and conducted *sub hasta* ('under the spear') sales of booty and slaves. The auction would be conducted where the soldiers pushed a spear into the ground; this was the early version of 'under the hammer'.[3]

French Art Auctions

Although art auctions in all major European cities appear to have shared parallel developments, it was not until the sixteenth century that systems of auctioneering were introduced to the major art markets of Paris and London.

Martin Shubik, an expert on the economics of art auctions, believes that the first mention of a public sale of art in Europe dates from 1550 in Paris, although it is not certain if auction or fixed-price sale was employed. Gilles Corrozet, a Parisian writer and bookseller, published a history of Paris in 1550, *Les antiquitez histoires et singularitez excellentes de la Ville, Cite, & Universite de Paris, capitale du Royaume de France*. In this Corrozet wrote that religious artworks were saved and smuggled out of English churches in a period when many images in Catholic churches were being destroyed and that art comprised the contents of early public auctions in Paris.[4]

In 1556, an Act was passed in France to legitimize the occupation of the *huissiers-priseurs*, or bailiff-auctioneers. They were given the exclusive rights to appraise and auction estate properties or properties 'taken in execution', including any art that formed part of an estate.[5] Their title was changed by Louis XIV in 1715 to their present one, *commissaires-priseurs*. A description of a *commissaires-priseurs* auction was provided in *Le Tableau de Paris* (*Panorama of Paris*, written 1781–8) by Louis Sebastien Mercier, one of the first French dramatists of middle-class eighteenth century Parisian urban life. This description captured the mood and practices of the auction, as well as reflecting the negative public perception of auctioneers as benefiting from the misfortune of others by profiting from forced sales:

> The business of the auctioneer...becomes every day more lucrative. As luxury grows the more numerous become the necessities; the quiet struggle between ease and poverty causes a multitude of sales and purchases. Losses, bankruptcies, deaths, all are to the benefit of the auctioneers when reverses, variations of fortune, or change of place or circumstance call for forced or voluntary sale...The stentor's hoarse cry of 'Silence' hardly rises above the confused murmur of the crowd, passing the articles from hand to hand, inspecting them or disdaining them according to fancy or requirement...This is how things are sold, from a picture by Rubens, down to an old coat out at the elbows...[6]

Mercier's writings also revealed that sales were held in the evenings and that auctions could be seen as democratic in that not only were articles of differing value sold in the same sale, but people from different social backgrounds mixed in the bidding audience. Until 2001, however, the French market was insular and highly regulated, with only French state-run auction firms permitted to conduct sales. Therefore, it was the success of English art auctions which led to the dominance of the private London auction houses and provided the paradigm for Australia.

English Art Auctions

By the seventeenth century, a number of auctioneering systems were already in use in England — sale by inch of candle (in use from at least 1490), 'outroping' (in use from at least 1585) and 'Mineing' (in use from 1691). These systems were originally used for selling a variety of goods, including furniture, land and books and appear to have been employed to sell paintings from the seventeenth century.

Sale by inch of candle (whereby the last bid placed as the candle went out was the successful bid) was one of the earliest forms of auctioneering in England and had become the main method by the seventeenth century. However, it was probably the slowness of the practice that led to the development of other approaches in the late seventeenth and eighteenth centuries. After various experimentations with the candle sale theme, the present system of increasing and successive bids triumphed and became known simply as the 'English Method'. Not much is known about 'outroping', other than that it was the only legal method of auctioneering in seventeenth century England, although other methods were tolerated. These include 'Mineing' described by Ralph James.[7] The auctioneer would begin by calling out a high figure and would consecutively lower the amount until someone shouted 'Mine!' and clinched the deal.

Public sales of art were conducted by Mineing in late seventeenth century London and appear to have been immensely popular. An advertisement for a Sale by Mineing at Mrs Smythers Coffee House in Thames Street from 12 to 14 March 1691 stated that it was 'a Method of Sale not hitherto used in England'.[8] Paintings were exhibited prior to the sale and catalogues were available for perusal in the Coffee House. According to the advertisement, the paintings for sale included ones by 'the most Famous, Ancient, and Modern Masters in Europe'; namely Titian, Rubens, Van Dyck, Dürer and Rembrandt.[9] Book and other auctions were often held in coffee houses, as well as taverns and stationers' shops and by the end of the seventeenth century some of these establishments, such as Tom's Coffee House, were beginning to specialize in either picture selling or book selling. It was from this increasing specialization that a structured art market began to evolve and painting auctions began to be associated with prestige and wealth.

Advertising has always played an important role in the promotion of auctions and as soon as newspapers were invented they were the primary medium for advertising sales. The *London Gazette* (no. 886) was used to advertise the first English painting auction on 18 May 1674 and the first open book auction, two years later. One assumes that, although books had been sold publicly for some time prior to the first painting auction, these sales had been fixed-price, so that the first open auction was actually that of paintings. There were twice as many advertisements in late seventeenth century London newspapers for painting auctions as for book ones, possibly reflecting the relative popularity and profitability of the two collecting areas.

There has been a continuous relationship between the selling of books and the fine arts. Many successful art auctioneers began their careers conducting book auctions. Edward Millington, one of the main late seventeenth century auctioneers, was a bookseller by trade, auctioning paintings when they became fashionable and returning to bookselling by 1693–4. He was renowned for using wit, psychology and a theatrical flair for display to his advantage by making auctions a source of entertainment; he used banter to encourage bidding and brilliant artificial lighting as a unique selling proposition. These tactics enabled him to charge a very large commission, probably between 15 and 20 per cent.[10] Samuel Baker, the founder of Sotheby's, also originally specialized in the sale of books.

By the late eighteenth and early nineteenth centuries, auctions were so numerous and so large in volume that the coffee houses no longer sufficed as temporary salerooms and permanent salerooms began to be used. Auctioneers began to reside in the fashionable environs around Covent Garden and the Royal Exchange. Samuel Paterson was one such bookseller and auctioneer located in the vicinity of Covent Garden in the late eighteenth century. Paterson was renowned for selling collections of books and prints and, according to E. G. Allingham, was the first auctioneer to produce scholarly catalogues with 'proper descriptions of the lots' both for himself and on behalf of other auctioneers.[11]

Other famous eighteenth century English auctioneers included Christopher Cock and Abraham Langford. Cock auctioned books but was better known for his art sales. According to records, Cock had a large company, produced catalogues and charged a five per cent commission up to £40 or £50, using a sliding scale thereafter.[12] Cock and Langford, who appear to have been partners from 1748–9, became experts in all aspects of disposing by auction, foreshadowing the development of large auction houses from the middle of the eighteenth century. Auctioneers such as Cock set estimates for paintings. This did not become a standard practice until 1973.

Auctioneering methods and the composition of stock underwent a change in response to the growing popularity of auctions and the need for a fast and efficient means of disposal. The subsequent streamlining of the method of auctioneering resulted in the emergence of the principal auctioneers and the establishment of the major auction houses in the late eighteenth century, some of which specialized in the sale of art.

Dealers, Artists and Auctions

While auctioneering methods and stock were evolving, so too was the relationship between dealers, artists and auctions. From the late seventeenth century, auctioneers such as Edward Davis, John Smith and Parry Walton capitalized on both the growing public interest in art and discerning taste by beginning to deal in better quality and authentic paintings. Walton was the official Surveyor of the King's/Queen's Pictures from 1679 to 1701 and a pupil of Sir Peter Lely, a fashionable artist and principal painter to Charles II. Walton auctioned works of unimpeachable quality, conducting about six auctions of paintings during the 1680s and 1690s from the collections of the Duke of Norfolk and the first sale of Lely's own paintings and drawings in 1682. He was not only knowledgeable about paintings, but was also an expert salesman, two essential qualities in the auctioneering trade then and now.

Lely's works were auctioned in two sales after the artist's death in 1680; April 1682 and April 1688.[13] These sales probably contributed to the manifold painting auctions in the 1680s, with many advertisements for auctions at this time promoting them as selling in the style of the Sir Peter Lely sale.[14] In fact, there was such a strong demand for paintings in England in the 1680s that a number of agents and artists became professional art dealers.[15] One of these was the landscape painter, Thomas Manby, who purchased a number of paintings while studying in Italy and auctioned them at the Banqueting House at Whitehall Palace when he returned to London in 1686.

Living artists have also been directly involved in the auction marketing of their own work in the past as in the present. The dealers Lodewyck van Ludik and Adrian de Wees said that the artist Rembrandt often overbid at auction in seventeenth century Holland.[16] Furthermore, there was a market in promissory notes written by Rembrandt, used by those who wished to ensure that he would indeed deliver the paintings he promised, and the artist also bought his own prints at auction in order to maintain high prices, another precursor of the future complexion of the auction market.

Jeremy Cooper, who based most of his overview of the early auction scene on Gerald Reitlinger's monumental work, *The Economics of Taste*, maintains that the art sales records for the late eighteenth century demonstrate that auction rooms played a tiny role in the sale of expensive fine art.[17] His analysis is based on the fact that most auction prices in the eighteenth century appear to be less than £1000, while connoisseurs or artists received much higher prices by dealing directly with collectors. For example, in one of the most prestigious sales of the eighteenth century, the Empress Catherine the Great of Russia paid £3500 in a private deal for the Houghton Guido Reni (probably *The Fathers of the Church Disputing the Christian Doctrine of the Immaculate Conception*) in 1779. The Empress purchased a number of works from Houghton Hall, the estate of Sir

Robert Walpole, onetime Prime Minister of Britain and an avid collector, for £40,555 and had them shipped to St Petersburg in 1779. They are now in the Hermitage Collection.

In the nineteenth century, a number of important dealers were intimately acquainted with auctions. In the latter part of that century, Agnew & Son was a dominant force in the art market, on par with the auction houses and possibly 'Christie's biggest customer'.[18] The nineteenth century French Impressionist and Barbizon dealer, Paul Durand-Ruel, believed that it was a dealer's responsibility to protect the prices of works by the artists in his stable. In order to do this, he bought as many of their works as possible in order to monopolize their market and 'bid up' the prices for his artists' paintings at auction to maintain their public monetary value. The latter practice also occurs today and is now known as ramping.

At the Courbet estate sale in 1881, Durand-Ruel was the expert appraiser. He used what was then a common saleroom tactic by selling in a different order from that listed in the catalogue. The expert would discuss estimates and works with possible buyers prior to the sale and then sell the ones that he considered to be the most popular first. If a work sold unpredictably well, the expert would change the order during the sale, putting up a similar work next in order to capitalize on the momentum. The dealer, Hector Gustave Brame, had a workable price-raising strategy where he would sell a painting for 5000 francs with a signed guarantee that he would buy it back in a year's time for 6000 francs.[19] This method ensured that he made sales and forced market prices up, rather like the stock market. With the painting appreciating in value, the collector would not wish to sell it back to him.

Nineteenth Century American Art Dealers/Auctioneers

There were also a number of important art dealers/auctioneers in New York in the mid-late nineteenth century who were prominent tastemakers and played a key role in shaping that influential art auction market.

Samuel P. Avery, of Avery's Art Rooms, was possibly the most influential player in the fledgling American art market between 1864 and 1880. In order to ensure the authenticity of his stock, Avery usually obtained art directly from contemporary artists. Moreover, he exhorted collectors to invest in art. Ernst Gambart was likewise one of the first specialist contemporary art dealers in the nineteenth century, patronizing living artists such as Bonheur, Holman Hunt, Millais, Alma-Tadema and Dante Gabriel Rossetti. He bought numerous works at auction, paying exorbitant prices — thus drawing attention to himself and pushing up prices.

The American Art Association (AAA) — a private company despite its name — launched in about 1882, aimed to encourage and promote local American art and opened to instant public accolade. The AAA combined art dealing and auctioneering, although after 1895 it focused on the auctioneering side of the business. Owing to good management and marketing strategies, Thomas Kirby, the proprietor, turned the AAA into the premier firm for the sale of art, one which was frequented by prosperous and notable men such as the railroad tycoon Collis P. Huntington. Both the display rooms and auction rooms were sumptuous and provided an atmosphere conducive to extravagant sales.

Though we know of the theatrical Millington in England, Kirby has been credited with creating the idea of the auction as a public spectacle owing to his handling of events surrounding the Seney sale in 1885. The *Evening Post* declared that ten of the paintings to be auctioned were fakes; however, this served only to intensify public interest. Kirby's (probably empty) threat to sue the paper for libel further increased publicity. The guards protecting the paintings at the auction wore silk gloves and an admission fee was charged, emphasizing the importance of the occasion. The atmosphere was flamboyant — 'The porters, now dressed in Second Empire livery, placed each picture in turn on an easel draped with crimson velvet' — and the sale was a resounding success.[20]

Not only did the notoriety of the sale assist the AAA to achieve superstardom status, but the contemporary artist, Jules Breton, also achieved great success. Breton's *Evening in the Hamlet of Finistère* (1882) sold on the third and final night of the auction for $18,200, then the highest price attained at an auction in the United States (Figure 1).

Dealers' Rings

According to records, dealers' rings (which are not exclusive to art auctions) also have antecedents in eighteenth century Paris and London. The aim of the ring, usually consisting of a group of dealers, is to reduce the competition and buy the intended work(s) for lower prices than would be achieved in a truly competitive marketplace; that is, beneath real market value. The members of the ring, rather than the original vendor and auctioneer, therefore reap the financial benefits.

Mercier provided illuminating commentary on an eighteenth century dealers' ring when writing about court-ordered auctions in his *Tableau de Paris*:

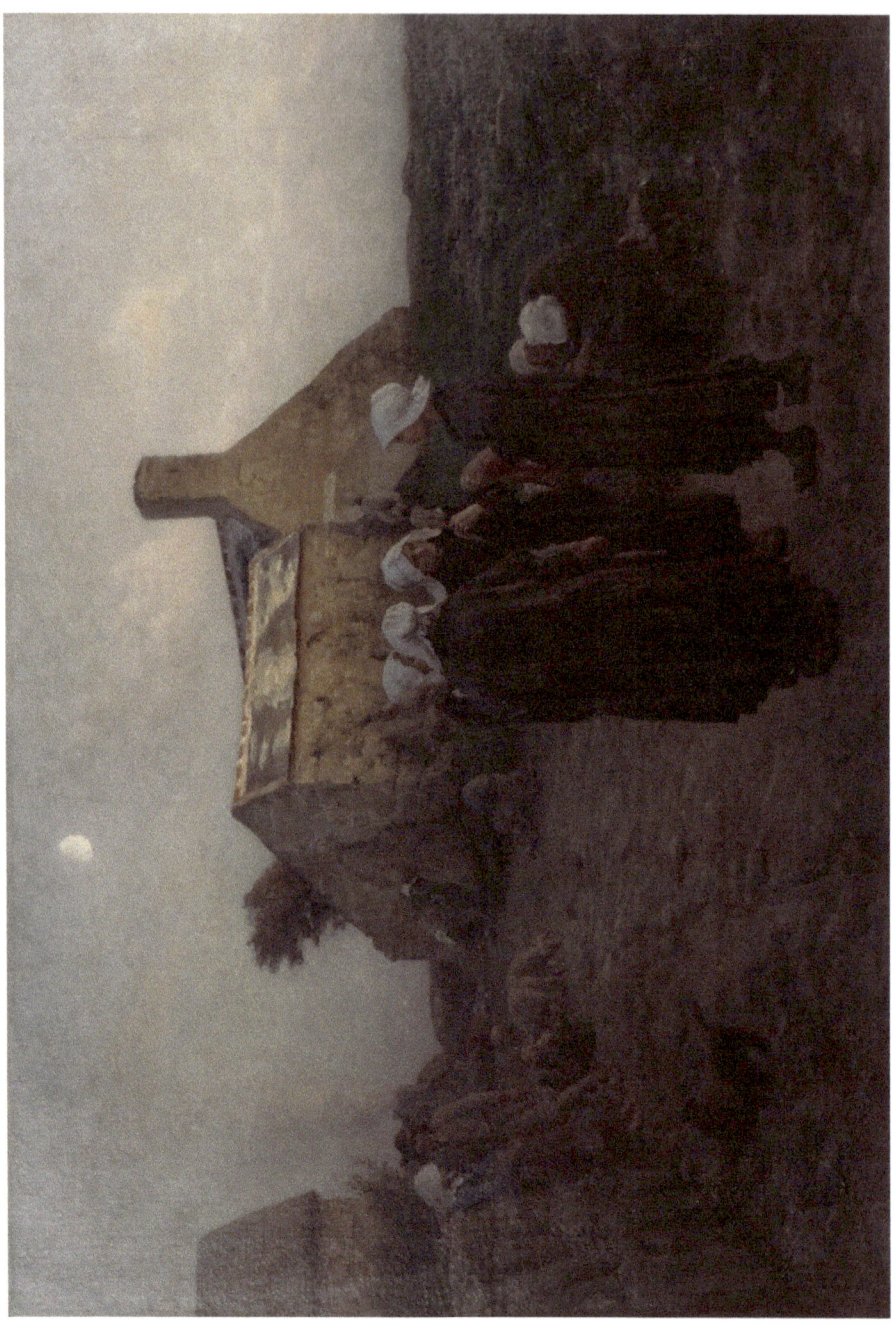

Figure 1: Jules Breton (French, 1827-1906), *Evening in the Hamlet of Finistere*, 1882, oil on canvas, 93.3 x 132 cm, Collection of the Paine Art Center and Gardens, Oshkosh, Wisconsin.

> In these auctions there is a private feature for which one must always be on the alert, this is called 'La Graffinade'. It consists of a 'ring' of dealers who do not outbid each other in the sales...These sharpers thus become masters of the situation, for they manage matters so that no outside buyer can bid above one of their own ring. When a thing has been run up sufficiently high to prevent any outside bidder making a profit, the ring meets privately, and the article is allotted to one of the members. This arrangement accounts for the high prices which surprise so many persons of experience. The ring does not wish the article to re-appear in the auction room, less it should fall to a lower price than that at which they pretend to have acquired it. This conspiracy against the purse of private persons has driven from the auction room a large number of buyers...[21]

Rings were also prevalent in the London art market and auctioneers attempted to curtail this practice through various means. In the 1920s, for example, Montague Barlow, one of Sotheby's partners, introduced some of the major art dealers to Sotheby's and based their consulting fees on the hammer prices so that it benefited them if works were not prey to rings and sold for high prices.[22] The greatest means at the disposal of auctioneers for combating rings was setting reserves and not declaring that lots were bought-in, thus casting speculation on their market value and whether they had actually sold. Nevertheless, Nicholas Faith, a London financial and economic journalist, argues that rings actually benefit auction houses on occasion, including during times when the demand for certain works is slight.[23]

Rings, although perhaps unethical, were not illegal in the United Kingdom until January 1928 when the *Auctions (Bidding Agreements) Act 1927* came into force. The Act was a result of a concerted campaign by the media and others taking umbrage at the practice of rings. Art rings became illegal unless the members of the ring informed the auctioneer in writing prior to a sale that they would be bidding as a group; this appears never to have been put into practice by dealers. The Act was amended in 1969 but it was not until 1980 that a successful prosecution was achieved.

The Reputation of Auctions

Against the background just painted, it is not surprising that auctions have been viewed in varying lights over the centuries. An address by the colourful auctioneer Millington included in an auction catalogue of *Paintings and Limnings* at the Barbadoes Coffee-House in London in February 1689 implied that art auctions were considered disreputable. However, there were galleries in this establishment set aside for the exclusive use of 'Ladies and Gentlewomen', implying that attending art auctions was a society occupation.[24]

> When I first essay'd this way of Selling Paintings and Limnings by Auction, I propounded to myself the obliging of the Gentry, Citizens etc and to bring it into esteem and reputation, to make it familiar and acceptable…And that I may remove the Prejudices of some, and the misapprehensions of others, as to the sincerity of the management, I have printed the Conditions of Sale with an additional one, that no Person or Persons shall be admitted to bid for his, of [sic] their own Pictures…[25]

The snippet by Millington demonstrates the use of conditions of sale and the exclusive sale of paintings and 'limnings' (which from the sixteenth century referred to miniature portraiture). It, more importantly, demonstrates that dealers' rings may have been widespread, with a practice of bidding up their own works, thus adding to the insalubrious reputation of auctions.

In the eighteenth century, those in the art auction trade, and the very trade itself, were satirized in political cartoons and the theatre by artists like William Hogarth. However, this satire does not appear to have focused on attempted fraud such as the dealers' ring, but rather on the mannerisms of the auctioneers. In the nineteenth century, an overriding stigma attached to the business of auctioneering because of its identification with the auction of slaves. Anti-auction sentiments were recorded in Paris, London and New York, the three most important markets for art. In these cases auctioneers were accused of malpractice including causing bankruptcy; providing an instrument for the sale of stolen or fake art; selling inferior goods; corruption, fraud and having a deleterious effect on the business of dealers.

An 1812 London pamphlet, *The Ruinous Tendency of Auctioneering and the Necessity of Restraining it for the Benefit of Trade demonstrated in a Letter to the Right Honourable Lord Bathurst, President of the Board of Trade*, chiefly complained about the perceived corruption of the auctioneers.[26] However, the author of the pamphlet heaped praise on the late Mr Christie, whom he called 'Gentleman Christie', while commenting on Sotheby's 'Ruinous as this system is to trade…', the auction houses of Squibb's, Robins's and Leigh & Sotheby's were 'not fit places for the professional classes'.[27]

It was not until government began to regulate the art trade and the frequency of art auctions, with their growing social cachet, increased that auctioneers and auctioneering began to cast off some of their former unsavoury image. The public perception of auctioneers began to change by the late eighteenth and early nineteenth centuries and some auctioneers, such as Christie and Leigh, were actually perceived to be stylish. Fluctuating social acceptability has permeated the history of art auctions.

ENDNOTES

[1] Giorgio Vasari, *Lives of the Most Eminent Painters, Sculptors and Architects*, translated by Gaston Du C. de Vere, introduction by Kenneth Clark, Harry N. Abrams Inc. Publishers, New York 1979, 3 vols, preface to Part 1, p.26. However, it is worth noting that translations do differ as to whether Attalus [Attala] bought the picture, probably at auction, or whether he commissioned it and whether the price was 600,000 or 6000 sesterces. Translations do seem to agree that Lucius Mummius then placed the picture in the temple of Ceres.

[2] Brian Learmount, *A History of the Auction*, Barnard and Learmount, Great Britain 1985, p.7.

[3] Learmount, *A History of the Auction*, p.8.

[4] Quoted in Martin Shubik, 'Auctions, Bidding and Markets: An Historical Sketch', in Richard Engelbrecht-Wiggans, Martin Shubik and Robert M. Stark (eds), *Auctions, Bidding and Contracting: Uses and Theory*, New York University Press 1983, pp.44–5.

[5] Octave Uzanne, 'The Hotel Drouot and Auction Rooms in Paris Generally, Before and After the French Revolution', *The Connoisseur*, vol. 3, May-August 1902, p.235.

[6] This is reproduced, to a large extent, in Uzanne, 'The Hotel Drouot', pp.236–8.

[7] Learmount mentions Ralph James in his *A History of the Auction*, p.20; however, no bibliographic information is provided, making it extremely difficult to trace the original article. We do know that the James article was based on rare catalogues of the day.

[8] This advertisement is reproduced in Giles Mandelbrote, 'The Organization of Book Auctions in Late Seventeenth-Century London', in Robin Myers, Michael Harris and Giles Mandelbrote (eds), *Under the Hammer: book auctions since the seventeenth century*, British Library, London 2001, p.17.

[9] Mandelbrote, 'The Organization of Book Auctions', p.17.

[10] On Millington see Iain Pears, *The Discovery of Painting: the growth of interest in the arts in England 1680-1768*, Yale University Press, London 1988, pp.60–1.

[11] See E. G. Allingham, *Romance of the Rostrum: being the business life of Henry Stevens, and the history of thirty-eight King street, together with some account of famous sales held there during the last hundred years*, compiled by E.G. Allingham; with a preface by the Right Honourable Lord Rothschild, F.R.S., London 1924, p.13.

[12] On Cock see Pears, *The Discovery of Painting*, pp.63–5 and Learmount, *A History of the Auction*, pp.23–8.

[13] Jeremy Cooper, *Under the Hammer: the auctions and auctioneers of London*, Constable, London 1977, p.16.

[14] The advertisements were presumably referring to the first Lely sale.

[15] On Manby see especially Pears, *The Discovery of Painting*, p.72.

[16] Peter Watson, *From Manet to Manhattan – The Rise of the Modern Art Market*, Random House, New York 1992, p.49.

[17] Cooper, *Under the Hammer*, p.17 and Gerald Reitlinger, *The Economics of Taste – the Rise and Fall of Picture Prices 1760–1960*, Barrie & Rockliff (Barrie Books Ltd) London 1961, vol. 1; Gerald Reitlinger, *The Economics of Taste – The Rise and Fall of Objets d'Art Prices since 1750*, Barrie & Rockliff, London 1963, vol. 2; and Gerald Reitlinger, *The Economics of Taste – The Art Market in the 1960s*, Barrie and Jenkins, London 1970, vol. 3.

[18] Watson, *From Manet to Manhattan*, p.72.

[19] Watson, *From Manet to Manhattan*, p.85.

[20] Watson, *From Manet to Manhattan*, pp.36–7.

[21] Louis Sebastien Mercier, *Tableau de Paris*, Amsterdam 1783. Quoted in Learmount, *A History of the Auction*, p.60 and Uzanne, 'The Hotel Drouot', pp.237–8.

[22] Cooper, *Under the Hammer*, p.88.

[23] Nicholas Faith, *Sold: the Rise and Fall of the House of Sotheby*, Macmillan, New York 1985, p.137.

[24] Harris, 'Newspaper Advertising for Book Auctions before 1700', p.6.

[25] Learmount quoted Ralph James in *A History of the Auction*, p.21.

[26] Part of this pamphlet is reproduced in Learmount, *A History of the Auction*, pp.93–8.

[27] Learmount, *A History of the Auction*, p.95.

Chapter 2. The Major London Auction Houses

The Victorian artist Edwin Long's painting, *The Babylonian Marriage Market* (1875), was inspired by Herodotus's account of the auction of women, but the painting quickly acquired an auction history of its own. In 1882 it was bought by Thomas Holloway at Christie's in London for £6615. Holloway (1800–83) was a millionaire whose fortune had been made from patent medicines and a great philanthropist, who had founded Royal Holloway College (now Royal Holloway, University of London), for women, in 1879. *The Babylonian Marriage Market* is both the largest work and a key painting in the Royal Holloway Collection, a collection of Victorian art endowed to the college by Holloway 'for the edification of the ladies'. Holloway, who was careful in his art acquisitions, purchased seventy-two of the seventy-seven paintings in his collection from Christie's London auctions. Holloway was accused of setting artificial benchmarks for artists' prices through his zealous pursuit of his chosen works and was thought to have been outbid only once. He believed implicitly in the importance of an impeccable provenance and believed this to be provided by Christie's and major art dealers, rather than private vendors. The Long purchase set a record price for a painting by a living artist.

Although the subject of Long's painting was inspired by Herodotus, its composition was inspired by contemporary painting auctions, particularly those at Christie's in London. The auctioneer depicted at the rostrum is thought to be Thomas Woods, a famous auctioneer of the period and presumably he of Christie's fame, and the prospective buyers scrutinizing each objectified woman were reminiscent of Old Master dealers (Figure 2).

There are four London auction houses that can trace their interrelated histories to eighteenth century Georgian roots – Christie's, Bonhams, Phillips and Sotheby's. Christie's was a fairly traditional upper class firm; Bonhams was originally a family business of print specialists; Phillips began as a firm of general auctioneers; and Sotheby's was initially a firm of book auctioneers which shifted its focus to fine art in the early twentieth century, bringing it into direct competition with Christie's. Their historical differences continue to be reflected, to some extent, to the present time.

Pedigree and Panache

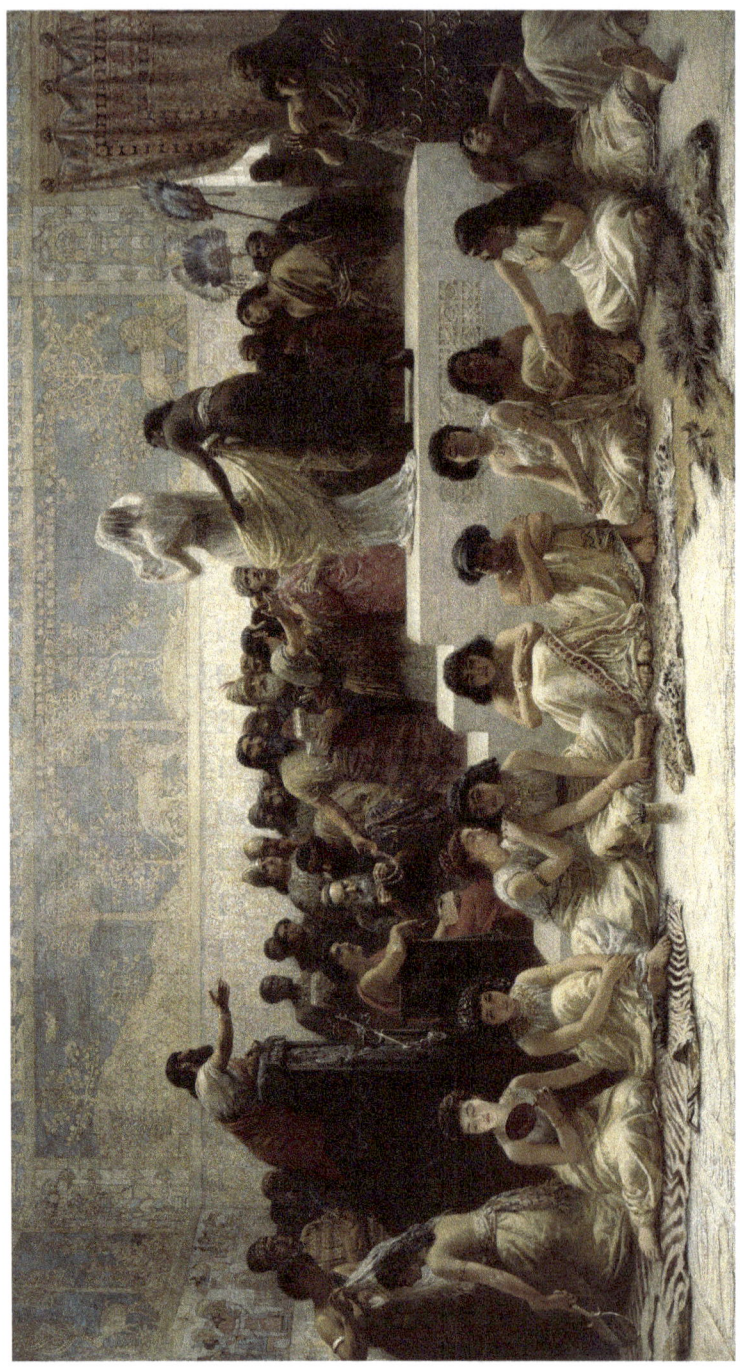

Figure 2: Edwin Long, *The Babylonian Marriage Market*, 1875, oil on canvas, 172.6 x 304.6 cm, From the Picture Collection, Royal Holloway, University of London. For a review of the Victorian Collection please visit www.rhul.ac.uk/picture-gallery/index.html.

Christie's

Christie's was established in 1766 and was to remain the key player in the London art market until after World War II. The founder, James Christie (1730–1803), had worked in the navy before being apprenticed as a sales clerk to Mr Annesley, a Covent Garden auctioneer, who shortly thereafter took Christie on as his partner. They parted ways after several years and Christie had set up his own rooms, the 'Great Room', in the Richard Dalton print warehouse in Pall Mall by 1766. Christie's first auction was a library sale on 5 December 1766 and his first painting sale was on 20 March 1767 (or 1766).[1] Christie took on various partners on occasion; the dealer, Robert Ansell, sourced valuable collections for Christie overseas and was so useful that he was taken on as a partner from 1777 to 1784.

Christie moved further down Pall Mall and into bigger rooms in 1770, where he became acquainted with the celebrated artist, Thomas Gainsborough, his next-door neighbour. Christie quickly established a good reputation and accumulated other useful and influential friends including the author, politician, and collector, Horace Walpole; the English Rococo painter, Sir Joshua Reynolds; the theatre star and theatrical manager, David Garrick; and Richard Tattersall, who founded the world's first bloodstock auction house in 1766. In fact, Gainsborough, Walpole, Reynolds and Christie dined together often enough to become known as 'Christie's Fraternity of God Parents'.[2] Christie himself acknowledged that the presence in his rooms of successful artists, such as Gainsborough, improved his commission by 15 per cent.[3]

The relationship with Christie also had a positive effect on Gainsborough's career. In 1778, Gainsborough painted *Portrait of James Christie, gratis*, on the proviso that it was hung in a prominent position in the auction rooms to advertise his skill. The portrait was exhibited at the Royal Academy in London along with twelve other paintings by Gainsborough that same year. It was thought to be a very good likeness of Christie and hung at the auction house in London until it was sold by his relatives in 1846. It now belongs to The J. Paul Getty Museum in Los Angeles. In this painting, Christie is depicted leaning against what was presumably one of Gainsborough's own landscapes, thus promoting the genre which he had found difficult to sell. Through portraying the auctioneer, Gainsborough was also drawing parallels between the Old Master paintings, which were usually sold at Christie's, and his own work, thus elevating or attempting to validate his position and authority as an artist (Figure 3).

Gainsborough may also have gained inspiration on his numerous visits to Christie; he had copied the copy of Murillo's *The Christ Child as the Good Shepherd* (1675–80). The Murillo copy had been awaiting sale at Christie's in 1778, probably at the same time that Christie was sitting for his portrait.[4] Another portrait of Christie, the etching, *'A Specious Orator', James Christie* by Robert Dighton, was published in 1794 and Christie's used this as the basis for its logo.

Pedigree and Panache

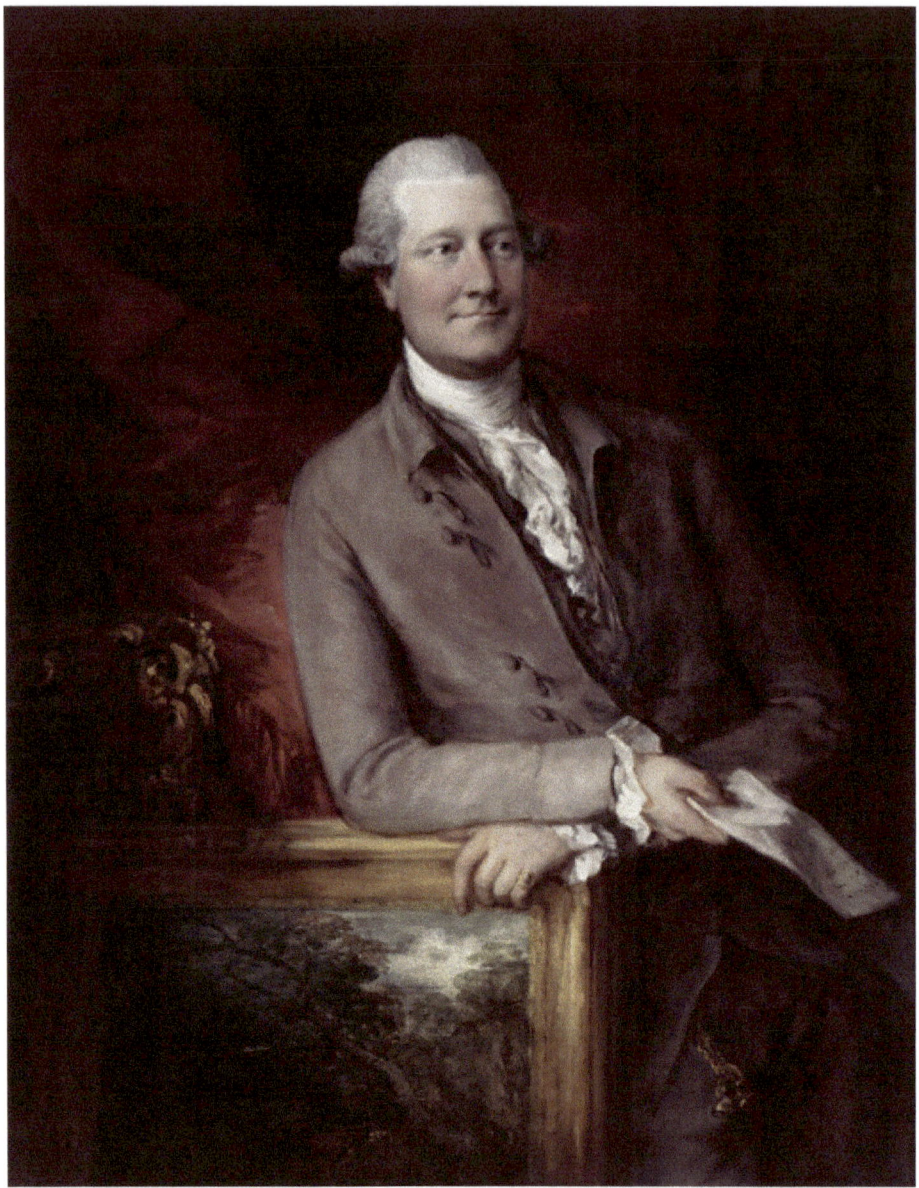

Figure 3: Thomas Gainsborough (English, 1727-1788), *Portrait of James Christie (1730–1803)*, 1778, oil on canvas, 126 x 101.9 cm, The J. Paul Getty Museum, Los Angeles. Gift of J. Paul Getty.

As the title of Dighton's etching affectionately suggests, James Christie was probably the first truly popular auctioneer and was chiefly responsible for launching art auctions in London as celebrity events. His success was due in a large part to his charming manners, which resulted in him being patronized by the upper classes, thus legitimizing fine art auctioneering as a socially acceptable activity. Furthermore, by virtue of being the auctioneers of choice for the British aristocracy, Christie's have always been the 'establishment auctioneers'.[5]

Christie's various business strategies ensured his continuing success. He used the media to his advantage, produced thorough and reliable catalogues and held private views and receptions in the evenings. These 'private views...[were] the natural antecedents to the prestigious evening sales at Christie's which are now covered by camera crews from three continents'.[6] A description of a Christie's auction from the 1887 *Graphic* highlights the ostentation associated with purchasing expensive works at the public spectacle of an art auction: 'and when the hammer falls at last to a lumping sum, there is a perfect uproar... for the Christie audience revels in high prices simply for money's sake, though of course some of the applause is meant for the picture'.[7]

Christie's famous Stowe sale took on biblical proportions when it lasted for 40 days. Beginning on 15 August 1848, it was so popular it placed Christie's at the very peak of auctioneers in London, a position that was not to change until Sotheby's began to sell Impressionist and modern paintings internationally in the 1950s. The public swarmed over Stowe House, reveling in the spectacle of the ruined aristocrat, the Second Duke of Buckingham and Chandos, and his fabulous art treasures. Despite the sale's popularity, it realized only £75,560, with many works failing to achieve even the original cost of acquisition. In another strange twist Thomas Woods, the gamekeeper's son at Stowe House, was asked to join Christie's after displaying his knowledge of the paintings in the collection. He eventually became a partner in 1859.

Another Gainsborough portrait was the star attraction at the Wynn Ellis sale at Christie's in 1876. *Portrait of Georgiana, Duchess of Devonshire* (c.1785–7) was knocked down to the dealer Agnew for 10,100 guineas, 'then a record price for any picture by any artist of any nationality'.[8] Agnew announced only three weeks later that he had sold it to the American banker and financier, Junius Spencer Morgan, who wanted to give it to his son, James Pierpont Morgan, as a gift. The publicity and the monetary value of the painting resulted in the work being viewed more cynically as a tangible commodity. The painting was stolen that very night and was not seen again for more than twenty-five years, when the thief contacted Agnew's from America just before the former's death. The painting was handed over to Agnew's in an hotel in Chicago and was then sold to James Pierpont Morgan for between £32,000 and £35,000, so that it was acquired by its intended owner (Figure 4).

In February 1882, Christie's conducted the first of two Hamilton Palace sales, auctioning a wonderful array including six Mantegnas, a Velazquez, a number of van Dycks and Rubens, a Botticelli, a da Vinci, Gobelin tapestries and Reisener furniture.[9] This sale entered the annals of auction history as one of the most amazing single collection sales ever and set a new taste for French furniture. The majority of the English paintings were not sold until the second Hamilton Palace sale in November 1919 when Americans were at their height of Anglophilia and the well-known dealer, Joseph Duveen, purchased a Romney painting for £54,600, making a sizeable profit by then reselling it for £70,000.

The original Hamilton Palace auction was the first to occur after pivotal legislation was passed in Britain in 1882. In simple terms, changing economic conditions in Britain in the late 1870s, owing to the flooding of the British market by cheap prairie wheat from America and the effects of industrialization on the rental income of estates, led to the need for the *Settled Lands Act*. The Act enabled the landed gentry to liquefy their heirloom assets, to break the trust of land, house and contents so that contents could be used to finance the land and house. Thereafter, aristocrats, who had been the largest buyers of art at auction, became the main suppliers of art (predominantly Old Master paintings) at auction. The dispersal of important art from established English collections then allowed mainly new collectors from Britain and America to form large collections of good quality. Naturally, the auction houses in general and Christie's in particular, with its aristocratic links, were inundated with superb collections.

Furnishings and paintings from Hamilton Palace were sold through Christie's, but the books were sold by Sotheby's, as it was the premier auctioneer of books, coins, prints, antiquities and stamps. There was 'an unwritten agreement' that it would pass any paintings, furniture and other art works on to Christie's and that Christie's would reciprocate by passing libraries to Sotheby's. It was normal for collections to be distributed between the two auction houses in this manner even until World War II. However, it was in 1913 that Christie's and Sotheby's first became rivals. The beginning of this inter-firm rivalry resulted from a serendipitous event. Montague Barlow, one of Sotheby's partners, literally stumbled upon some paintings stacked in the old Sotheby's premises in Wellington Street and decided to sell them rather than passing them on to Christie's. On 20 June 1913, Sotheby's auctioned a Frans Hals portrait on the same day Christie's auctioned two other portraits by Hals, placing the firms in direct competition. The Sotheby's Hals was bid up to £9000, enough to convince Barlow that there was a profitable market in paintings.

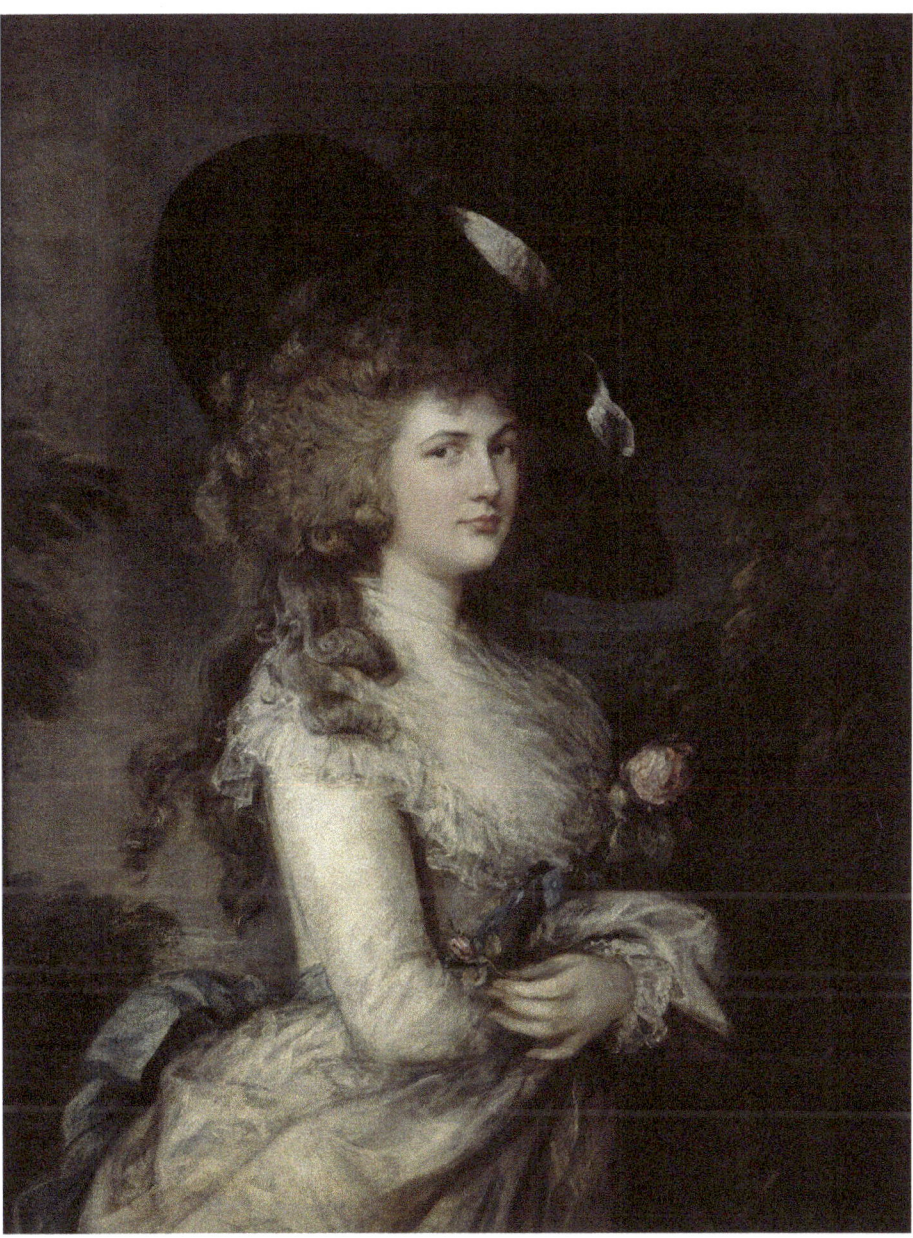

Figure 4: Thomas Gainsborough (English, 1727-1788), *Portrait of Georgiana, Duchess of Devonshire (1757-1806)*, c.1785-7, oil on canvas, 123 x 96.4 cm, Collection: Chatsworth House, Derbyshire.

Of crucial importance in Christie's more recent history has been the firm's emphasis on marketing and global expansion after World War II. In 1967, Christie's conducted reconnaissance missions overseas to assess where best to install offices. Christie's went in the first instance to Australia. (Its history there is discussed in detail in Chapter Five.) Christie's also assessed Tokyo because of the potential in newfound wealth after the War and the concomitant social changes. In 1968, Christie's opened its first French office in Paris (Sotheby's had opened one in 1967), an office in Montreal (Sotheby's had established an office in Toronto in 1967), and held its first sale in Geneva. 'Christie's International Year', however, was 1969, as it held its first auctions in Tokyo and Montreal, more auctions in Melbourne and Sydney, and a pivotal jewellery auction in Geneva.[10] The year 1970 was similarly international in essence with a number of auctions held in Montreal, Ottawa, Melbourne, Tokyo and Geneva. Christie's took over Edmiston's in Glasgow in 1979 and also Debenham Coe in about 1975 to form its immensely successful South Kensington saleroom which specializes in low value sales. Even if the international auctions were not always a financial success, they did help to generate the Christie's brand throughout the world.

Christie's opened in New York in 1977 and, as a result of astute publicity campaigns, managed to expand the New York market. John Herbert, Christie's Public Relations Director until he retired in 1985, believes that even before Christie's and Sotheby's employed public relations staff, they were favoured with extensive press coverage, resulting in their becoming household names and attaining a brand status.[11] Herbert noted that although sensational art auctions attract press coverage and public interest today, this was not the case in the late 1950s and 1960s and the newspapers' daily reportage of general auctions then did not reflect 'the public interest in art auctions'.[12] It was not until after the second Goldschmidt sale in London in 1958 that editors began to be selective in their auction reporting, allocating space in their newspapers depending on the relative importance of the sale.

By 1985, Christie's had offices in Amsterdam, New York, Los Angeles, Florida, Mexico City, Buenos Aires, Vancouver, Paris, Geneva, Zurich, Dusseldorf, Munich, Hamburg, Rome, Milan, Turin, Madrid, Vienna, Oslo, Stockholm, Brussels, Sydney, Melbourne, Venice, Tokyo and Rio de Janeiro. Christie's was purchased by Artemis, the holding company of Francois Pinault, in 1998 and was granted conditional amnesty for the well-publicized price-fixing scandal which saw Sotheby's take the brunt of the penalties. As of March 2006, Christie's had eighty-two salerooms and offices in thirty-seven countries.

Bonhams and Phillips

Bonhams, probably the first continuous fine art specialist in the auction world, was founded in 1793 by William Charles Bonham, a book specialist, and George Jones, although it evolved from a gallery founded a few years earlier by Thomas

Dodd, a well-known print expert and dealer.[13] Bonhams initially specialized in the sale of prints, when print collecting was at its pinnacle in the late eighteenth and early nineteenth centuries. The firm also appears to have been a reputable auctioneer of antiques in the nineteenth century, with advertisements for its sales given as much prominence in the London press as those of Christie's and Phillips. (Sotheby's, on the other hand, appears only to have advertised in journals that specialized in books at this time.)

In the 1820s and 1830s, Dodd collaborated with the dealer Martin Colnaghi to catalogue various collections. These included the famous print collection of Horace Walpole when it was put up for sale in the 1820s and the Douce Collection of 50,000 prints which Francis Douce bequeathed to the Bodleian Library. George Jones' son Henry joined his father in the firm and was to form a partnership with George Bonham in the 1850s, when the firm became known as Jones and Bonham. Although Henry Jones continued to auction print collections, some of which he obtained from the stock of insolvent or deceased print dealers, he had included paintings in Bonhams sales from the 1840s.

Phillips was established around the same time as Bonhams. Harry Phillips resigned as head clerk at Christie's to set up his own auction firm, holding his inaugural sale of household furniture on 23 April 1796. He gained standing as an auctioneer and utilized good marketing techniques — influenced by Christie's strategies — holding evening events full of pomp and ceremony. These events were frequented by a fashionable clientele, some of whom had followed Phillips when he left Christie's.

Phillips managed to secure a number of highly important collections and properties for auction, including some of the paintings of Sir Godfrey Kneller, the Baroque court portraitist, in 1822. Phillips must also be remembered as having conducted the only auction ever to be held at Buckingham Palace at the request of Queen Victoria in 1836, although his biggest triumph was the Fonthill Abbey sale in 1823. Christie had originally been engaged to conduct the Fonthill sale. However, the vendor, wealthy Gothic novelist William Beckford, eventually decided to sell most of the important pieces privately and sold all of Fonthill Abbey and the contents that still remained to John Farquhar, the gunpowder magnate, for £350,000. Farquhar, in turn, commissioned Phillips to auction the contents of Fonthill Abbey in a sale that lasted a marathon thirty days. An estimated 7200 people attended the viewing. It was rumoured that Phillips 'salted' or 'rigged' this auction by adding items, specifically books, from other properties. (This is a practice that obviously undermines the transparent nature of auctions but it indicates the prestige associated with particular single-owner sales.)

When Harry Phillips died in 1840, his son William Augustus took over the management of the firm. He auctioned the famous Lord Northwick collection which realized £95,725 in 1859. This auction was attended by two wealthy Australian collectors, Thomas Sutcliffe Mort and Thomas Ware Smart or their representatives, and was, as we shall see, to have an impact on taste in colonial Australia.

Sotheby's

As mentioned previously, Sotheby's was for most of its early history principally a firm of book auctioneers. Samuel Baker (1713–78), the founder, appears to have begun his career as an apprentice bookseller in about 1734, though his first extant catalogue of a fixed-price book sale, dated 19 February 1734, shows a professionalism suggesting Baker had probably been selling books for some time. Baker started his own business, possibly auctioning on a part-time basis for some years, as he was also a stationer and publisher. The firm got its distinctive name a generation later.

Baker's first book auction catalogue dates from 11 March 1744 (or 1745), when he auctioned Sir John Stanley's library in the Great Room in the Strand over ten evenings. Despite the agreement with Christie's not to include art, Baker had begun to include works of art in some of his auctions from as early as the 1740s, holding his first paintings auction in 1747. Baker's first auction in his new premises in Covent Garden in 1754 was the library of Dr Richard Mead which included prints, coins and manuscripts.

Auction houses not only followed the prevailing taste of the day, they also helped to create it, in the book world as much as the art one. In 1766, Baker and George Leigh became partners and the firm became Baker & Leigh. British collectors began to focus less on Greek and Roman classics at this time and, guided by Leigh, became more interested in early English and Elizabethan literature and manuscripts. When Baker died in 1778 he left the business to both Leigh and his nephew, John Sotheby. The firm was renamed Leigh & Sotheby, heralding the birth of an omnipotent auction house.

The next important instalment in the story of this firm was not until the twentieth century when a triumvirate, of John Carter, Peregrine Pollen and Peter Wilson, had the greatest impact on Sotheby's direction. However, it was Peter Wilson alone, the 'architect of the modern auction spectacle', who shaped Sotheby's, turning it into a sleek and well-marketed machine and taking it onto the 'global stage'.[14] Wilson joined Sotheby's in 1936 and was made a partner at the tender age of twenty-six in 1938, eventually becoming Chairman in 1958 as well as the main auctioneer, retiring in 1980.

Sotheby's really began an aggressive programme of self-promotion in the post-World War II era, under the visionary leadership of Wilson. It was Wilson who packaged the pedigree of Sotheby's, in the guise of prestigious paintings sales, selling it to the moneyed New York market. In the first half of the twentieth century, art dealerships were more successful than auction houses. After World War II, there was a distinct shift in the preferred method of acquiring art, with collectors opting for the ostentation of the saleroom at highly publicized and televised auctions, as opposed to the 'discretion' of the art dealer.[15] By the 1960s and 1970s international expansion made auction houses like Sotheby's the power brokers of the modern art market.

One of the first blockbuster auctions was the October 1958 Goldschmidt sale at Sotheby's in London of only seven Impressionist pictures. The sale lasted approximately 21 minutes and realised £781,000. Here the American philanthropist Paul Mellon bought Paul Cézanne's *Le Garçon au Gilet Rouge* (1888–90) for £220,000 (reserve £125,000), an auction record for a modern painting. It is now in the National Gallery of Art in Washington (Mr and Mrs Paul Mellon Collection). The Goldschmidt auction was also remarkable because it represented a return to night auctions, which had not been held since the eighteenth century, and evening attire was required.

Sotheby's instituted a number of further innovations that had a profound effect on the complexion of the international art auction market. These included opening a New York office in 1954, later buying Parke-Bernet in 1964 (and becoming known as Sotheby Parke Bernet) and holding specialized auctions of Impressionist and modern paintings from 1955 onwards. Sotheby's was chiefly responsible for the multi-million dollar Impressionist sales and for convincing wealthy Americans to buy and sell through London. At the important Weinberg sale in 1957 and the Goldschmidt sale in 1958, most paintings were bought by Americans. This expansion of an international art market, with London as the epicentre, and the public desire to purchase modern paintings even at high prices, resulted in art auctions attracting unprecedented media attention. Sotheby's cemented its position in the art market, hiring its first public relations person, Stanley Clark, in 1959 (Christie's had hired a full-time Public Relations Director, Herbert, in 1958). From the early 1960s, Wilson and other members of Sotheby's staff began to appear on television on a regular basis, including on current affairs shows, at the time of major auctions.

By launching a campaign of international expansion, Sotheby's effectively attained the flexibility of art dealers by being truly international. Sotheby's representative office in Melbourne was established in April 1968, a Canadian office in 1968, an Edinburgh office in 1969, and Beirut and Florentine offices.

From the end of the 1960s, Sotheby's had also begun to offer guarantees, otherwise known as 'special arrangements'.[16] These arrangements were used primarily to attract Impressionist paintings for sale, but resulted in many works being bought-in by Sotheby's. One of the biggest criticisms of this practice was that two different price lists were effectively in use, those that included and those that excluded the bought-in works. Sotheby's would guarantee the sale of collections and even resort to buying a whole collection if necessary, effectively ending its neutrality as an agent. This changing function of the firm was reflected in its conditions of sale as of April 1973 but by the late 1970s the practice of guaranteeing was rarely used.

From 1973, price estimates were habitually provided and/or included in auction catalogues. Sotheby's also introduced a five-year guarantee of authenticity in London in September 1975. In 1973 and 1977 respectively, Christie's and Sotheby's both went public and in 1975 they introduced a buyer's premium of 10 per cent and reduced the vendor's commission from 15 per cent to 10 per cent. The introduction of the buyer's premium resulted in the buyers, rather than the sellers, essentially funding the auction houses. Christie's was the first firm to introduce the buyer's premium, having observed that Continental firms charged the buyers a levy, and being keen to supplement its income without increasing the vendor's commission which had kept its London business competitive. Sotheby's introduced the premium two days after Christie's, claiming that the timing was coincidental.

In 1979, Wilson announced his retirement and takeover bids ensued. A. Alfred Taubman, the shopping mall magnate once described as Sotheby's 'White Knight' (who recently served a prison sentence owing to the Christie's/Sotheby's price-fixing conspiracy), eventually acquired Sotheby Parke Bernet in 1983 with his partners. At this time Taubman became Chairman, the firm was privatised and the name was changed to Sotheby's. Sotheby's was floated for a second time in 1988 and its headquarters are now in New York.

Taubman introduced a range of financial services to Sotheby's repertoire including providing instant advances, something that dealers had traditionally been able to provide and which had disadvantaged auctioneers. However, vendors were charged a rather high fee, approximately 3 to 4 per cent higher than the bank rate. Approved buyers were given credit for one year, with a similar fee attached. Sotheby's abolished this practice of advancing credit to clients in 1990, probably as a direct consequence of bankrupt Australian businessman Alan Bond's notorious failure to repay the Sotheby's loan used to purchase van Gogh's *Irises* in 1987. Taubman's development of Sotheby's financial services created 'the impression that art was bankable'.[17] Christie's was not initially interested in providing similar financial services, protesting that such services caused the market to be artificially inflated. However, as a result of losing clients to the ever-competitive Sotheby's, Christie's was reluctantly forced to introduce vendor guarantees in 1990.

Under Taubman's direction, Sotheby's placed an even greater emphasis on marketing strategies to help sell expensive works. In 1985, Sotheby's spent approximately $1 million on promoting the Gould Collection of Impressionist paintings by financing huge parties and travelling the works to locations such as London, Tokyo, Lausanne and throughout America, as well as hiring a theatre in which to stage the eventual auction on 24–25 April 1985 in New York. This signified a trend which was to dominate the 1980s of surrounding a sale with hype. Many of the bidders at this auction had their finance provided by Sotheby's and thus were not traditional auction-goers.

Auction houses changed their practices relatively little until after World War II, following in the traditions set by their Georgian forebears, which were also of course to influence Australian art auctions.

ENDNOTES

[1] There is some disagreement as to the first proper auction dates for both Christie's and Sotheby's. Frank Herrmann, in *Sotheby's: Portrait of an Auction House*, Chatto & Windus, London 1980, p.3, fn.5, explains that the confusion is owing to the difference between the beginning of the Julian calendar (used until about 1751 when the Gregorian calendar was adopted) and the date on which people popularly celebrated New Year's Day, on 1 January.

[2] Robin Myers, Michael Harris and Giles Mandelbrote (eds), *Under the Hammer: Book Auctions since the Seventeenth Century*, British Library, London 2001, p.231.

[3] According to W. T. Whitley, *Artists and their Friends in England 1700–1799*, London 1928, 2 vols, quoted in Jeremy Cooper, *Under the Hammer: the Auctions and Auctioneers of London*, Constable, London 1977, p.46.

[4] Michael Rosenthal and Martin Myrone (eds), *Gainsborough*, with contributions from Rica Jones et al., exhibition catalogue, Tate, London 2002, p.228.

[5] See Cooper, *Under the Hammer*, p.42 and numerous other sources, as this is widely quoted.

[6] Cooper, *Under the Hammer*, p.46.

[7] Quoted in Cooper, *Under the Hammer*, p.24.

[8] Cooper, *Under the Hammer*, p.58.

[9] H.C. Marillier, *Christie's 1766 to 1925*, Constable & Company Ltd, London 1926, p.55 and Frank Herrmann, 'The Hamilton Palace Collection', *The English as Collectors – A Documentary Chrestomathy*, Chatto & Windus, London 1972, pp.348–52.

[10] See John Herbert, *Inside Christie's*, St. Martin's Press, New York 1990, p.153.

[11] See Herbert, *Inside Christie's*, p.191.

[12] Herbert, *Inside Christie's*, p.191.

[13] According to Bonham's website, the firm was founded by Dodd and Bonham, not Jones.

[14] First quotation from Jeffrey Hogrefe, *'Wholly Unacceptable' — The Bitter Battle for Sotheby's*, Harrap, London 1986, p.13. Second quotation from Tribe, 'Household name turns 250', no pagination, probably taken from Sotheby's anniversary publication, *A Celebration of 250 Years*.

[15] Catherin Fisher, 'The hype and hope of auctioneering', *The Age*, 22 August 1994, p.17.

[16] According to Peter Watson, *From Manet to Manhattan – The Rise of the Modern Art Market*, Random House, New York 1992, p.336 and Herbert, *Inside Christie's*, p.162.

[17] Watson, *From Manet to Manhattan*, p.385.

Chapter 3. Colonial and Early Australian Art Auctions

Although auctions were commonly used for conducting art transactions from almost the inception of the Australian colonies in the late eighteenth century, there were also other vehicles through which art was bought and sold. These included retail stores, art dealers, art unions, Mechanics' Institutes, artists' exhibitions, artists' societies, private commissions, photographers selling on-site and black and white illustrations in periodicals and newspapers.

The lack of a structured art market in the colonial period meant that art was often relegated to non-institutional avenues for exhibition and sale and was also often a sideline to other retail business. Artists such as Eugène von Guérard and Nicholas Chevalier, for example, displayed works in the windows of music, framers', or other retail stores, in addition to their own studios. In May 1846, Robin Vaughan Hood opened possibly Australia's first art gallery, the Colonial Picture Gallery in Liverpool Street, Hobart. It too was next door to his framing shop.[1] In the 1850s, stationery shops, such as Mr Borthwick's Stationery in Collins Street, Melbourne were outlets for art, books, papers, prints and *cartes-de-visites*. Newspaper offices sold watercolours. Joseph Wilkie's piano store window at 15 Collins Street was actually a permanent exhibition space, with the artist E. Wake Cook commenting:

> I was a small boy when I landed in Melbourne in 1852, and there was an utter absence of visible art. Then on one memorable day, I saw in Wilkie's music shop window a little picture. 'Troopers, Mounted Police', admirably drawn and painted by William Strutt. Later on, a large painting, 'Fern Tree Gully,' by Eugène von Guérard, was shown, and was followed by a view of the Yarra, by Nicholas Chevalier. Shortly after this, drawings by S. T. Gill began to appear, the vestibule of the Theatre Royal being decorated with fifty of his sketches.[2]

There were only a handful of art dealers in the colonial period and they concentrated on marketing European art, as they could achieve 'better profits [between 50 and 100 per cent]…by buying indifferent English or foreign pictures at a small price, and selling them for a large one in this country…than by dealing with local productions, on which they take a simple 15 or 20 per cent'.[3] For major Australian collectors, Britain epitomised superior taste and it was for this reason that many sales were made through the London or European trade system.

Henry Wallis from the French Gallery, Pall Mall was a London dealer who exported a number of collections of both British and European works to Melbourne and Sydney in the late nineteenth century. Another art dealing firm,

H. Koekkek and Sons, who operated a gallery in Piccadilly, London also sold similar collections in Australia. For example, in April 1891, some works owned by this firm were auctioned by Gemmell, Tuckett & Co. after they had been exhibited in Australia and presumably not found sufficient ready buyers. The colonial businessman, Charles Raymond Staples, bought some of the stock at this auction, paying the top sale price when he purchased F. Baratti's *After the Bath* for £80.[4] Staples, a wealthy Melbourne businessman, was also the original purchaser of Streeton's *Settler's Camp* (1888), which is now in the Robert Holmes à Court Collection in Perth. According to art historian and Deputy Chairman of Sotheby's Australia, Jane Clark, this purchase by Staples enabled Streeton to relinquish his apprenticeship and concentrate on painting full-time.[5] Staples' own art collection was auctioned after he was declared bankrupt and convicted of fraud in the 1890s.[6]

The colonial Australian preference for Old Masters also resulted in the purchase of many 'potboilers'. ('Pot-boiling' refers to the practice of making a living by producing a body of literature or artwork for a specific audience. The expression seems to stem from the mid-eighteenth century and implies inferior or mediocre works.) The artist Sydney Long in his essay, 'The Trend of Australian Art Considered and Discussed', argued that:

> The figure painters find that the occasional portrait, and black and white work, crumbs that are to be garnered only in the city, lie more to their book than the uncertain masterpiece to be painted at some expense in the bush. We shall have to wait until the wealthy Australian buys his pictures here, instead of satisfying his artistic craving with imitations of the Old Masters, or potboilers by mediocre English artists imported for trade purposes.[7]

Many of the paintings sold at auction or in commercial galleries in Australia in the mid-nineteenth century were copies of Old Master paintings and although some were sold as such, others were marketed as originals by auctioneers and art dealers. However, it is quite likely that many collectors were unconcerned about the authenticity of their purchases, merely wanting 'wallpaper' and signifiers of culture and taste.[8] This desire for 'wallpaper' escalated with the rise of 'the overnight aristocracy of the boom period' following the Gold Rushes of the 1850s.[9] The press suggested Australia was seen as the perfect market in which to dump inferior European paintings; 'Artists were still complaining in 1899 of "wretched daubs" being imported and flooding the market, taking sales from Australian art'.[10]

The Australian colonial art market was thus inundated by European paintings, a practice which had a deleterious effect on the market for local paintings and the importance of authenticity and originality. The eventual dominance of original Australian paintings in the marketplace is partly attributable to the practices of art auction houses, which in turn were influenced by other cultural institutions, such as art unions.

Art Unions and their Role in the Art Market

Art unions were effectively lotteries with three aims: to make money for the organizers, to distribute contemporary artworks to the subscribers and to aid struggling artists.[11] Although they originated in Switzerland in the 1810s, they were emblematic of culture, civilization and education in Britain, America and the Australian colonies. They resulted in the industrial or decorative arts being married to the fine arts in a union which benefited all strata of society. The general population felt that it was now enjoying the fruits hitherto reserved for the upper echelons of society and they enabled Britain, for example, to be at the forefront of competitive luxury goods production.[12] This fostered a sense of national identity. There were also didactic motives for promoting art and 'By designating themselves as disinterested stewards of culture, Art-Union managers laid claim to aesthetic authority.'[13] It is this sense of 'aesthetic authority' that has been adopted by other cultural institutions, including modern auction houses.

The British government was supportive of art unions and passed the *Art Union Act* in 1846 in response to print-sellers and art dealers lobbying against art unions under the Lottery Acts. According to the *Report from the Select Committee into the Operation of Art Union Laws* Parliament exempted the art unions, 'For at that time, there was not a ready sale for pictures of a high and expensive class. With a show of reason therefore, Art Unions were encouraged, in order to create a market for the sale of high class pictures.'[14] This indicates that neither auction houses nor dealers provided such means and, interestingly, did not take into account the influence of institutions such as the Royal Academy of Arts.

The print-sellers and art dealers were outraged by the art unions because the London Art Union, established in 1837, was not only a morally-objectionable lottery, but also often functioned as a virtual dealership: it enabled access to art through its lotteries; it created demand for contemporary English paintings; its marketing practices helped to develop industries involved in the mass production of art, like electroplate printing; and its commissioning of sculpture promoted the print, bronze and pottery industries in Britain.[15]

Art unions permeated the Australian colonial art market. They were major vehicles for the sale of works by local artists and were also connected with other vehicles for art exchange, including the influential Mechanics' Institutes.[16] Before compulsory schooling in Australia, Mechanics' Institutes provided a means of public education, as well as training the necessary craftsmen to develop the colony. Australia's inaugural art union was held in Sydney by the artist Maurice [Morris] Felton on 15 December 1841.[17] Nonetheless, art unions did not really take root in Australia until 1845, with Melbourne's first art union and the establishment of the important Parramatta art unions. Dr Hill's art union in Parramatta in 1845–6 was the first Scottish-type art union in Australia and, although it provided a vehicle for art patronage in Sydney, it did not assist local artists to find a market, as most works were imported from Scotland.[18]

One of the chief complaints about the art unions in Australia, as overseas, was that they encroached on the traditional role and territory of the art dealers. In 1878, the Ballarat Gallery of Painting Art Union held a lottery for cash prizes. The organizers noted that 'if preferred, Messrs Bridges and Co. guarantee to find purchasers for pictures at the full amount for each prize, as stated, at the close of the drawing' and 'In Parramatta a special agent sold tickets to residents, receiving a 20% commission for his work'.[19] It is believed that many prize-winners preferred the cash to the art.

In 1848, the London Art Union, a prolonged and ostentatious affair, was conducted in Sydney by Messrs W. and F. Ford, art dealers and book-sellers based at 554 George Street. The Fords held the first art unions to contain art by colonial Australian artists such as William Nicholas, Frederick Garling, Conrad Martens, Joseph Fowles and W. J. Welch. When the soldier and avid collector of European and colonial art, Sir Maurice Charles Philip O'Connell, died in May 1848, the Ford art dealers took charge of most of the collection and sold it privately. Other works appeared in art unions until 1853, while the remainder were inherited by O'Connell's daughter, Elizabeth Somerset.

Australian artists who had not been able to sell their works through other avenues conducted a number of art unions. Eugène von Guérard sold sixteen oil paintings, some of which had been exhibited at the Melbourne Exhibition in October 1854, in a lottery in January 1855. These paintings included *Ballarat Flat in the Summer*, *Australian Sunset* and *Australian Aborigines on the Road to the Diggings*. However, art unions were not always profitable enterprises for aspiring artists, as promoters of the unions were occasionally known to abscond with the money and von Guérard actually found himself 'out of pocket' owing to an art union.[20]

Art unions began to have pejorative connotations after the mid-nineteenth century, as they became more associated with lotteries and gambling, with money as prizes instead of paintings. By the 1870s, the original intent of the art unions was lost, although Parramatta tried to preserve their original purpose. The last major art union in Parramatta was in 1876 when 50 works from America, England and Australia were included. In October 1911, the honesty and integrity of the art unions were severely undermined by the discovery of fraud in an art union in Perth. Their reputation was so dismal that by the end of World War I very few artists would associate with them and they had almost ceased to exist. The original art unions were dissimilar to those used today to raffle large houses or cars and have no cultural patronage role. Although questionable practices seem to have been their downfall, at their peak art unions contributed considerably to the promotion of art in Australia.

The Art Auction Market

Auctions were ubiquitous in colonial Australia, although it was not until around the 1830s that auctions of art became common, often as part of a general or furniture sale, or as part of a crate-load of works shipped from Europe. This gave rise to a bustling auction industry near Circular Quay in Sydney, owing to the need to sell the cargoes from ships expeditiously.[21] Damaged art also typified this era as a result of shipwrecks and mishandling.[22]

Terry Ingram, who has provided commentary on the Australian art market for the past four decades, says that 'serious fine art auctioneering would appear to have begun in Australia' on 15 October 1839 when C. H. Ebden from Middle Stores, Sydney offered at auction Poussin's *Woman Taken in Adultery* and Rembrandt's *Three Hebrew Children*, while writer Mary Holyoake says that the first reference to an art auction in Melbourne was in 1840.[23] As outlined previously, it is extremely unlikely that a real Poussin or Rembrandt would have been sent to Australia for auction. Such works were auctioned by small firms, often as part of a general or furniture sale, and they dominated auctions in Australia for most of the nineteenth century.

The auction sales were a reflection of the state of colonial society. There was an influx of goods to the auction market both during the 1842–4 depression and subsequently, if colonists left Australia and returned to their country of origin, unable or unwilling to cope with the harsh conditions of the new colony. In the 1850s, the Gold Rush resulted in the arrival of numerous people and the sale of homes and their contents decreased.

The perception of auctions and auctioneers appears contradictory, with specialist quality painting auctions being associated with high society and general auctions with the lower classes. Many general nineteenth century auctions were tainted by the lower-class and nefarious associations alluded to previously. An anonymous pamphlet from the 1840s, *Twice Round the Block, or A Visit to the Auction Rooms, of Sydney*, warned about the sales tactics used by auctioneers.[24] The pamphlet refers to auctioneers exploiting bidders' inexperience and claims they were ill-bred and lacked honesty and transparency in their business practices; that bullying tactics were used to drum up business; that catalogues were enhanced through 'rigging-in' (the inclusion of items not in the collection) and that auctioneers made huge profits, often by selling works they owned themselves.

Many of these negative perceptions are confirmed by the observations of nineteenth century travellers such as Lt. Colonel Godfrey Charles Mundy and Maturin Murray Ballou. While he was living and working in Sydney from 1846 to 1851, Mundy kept detailed diaries which included information on local auctions.[25] On 1 September 1846 he commented that people were often 'talked' into buying something by the wiles of the auctioneer or the aggression of the other bidders.[26] His discussion of the sales of the houses and household goods of people leaving the colony illustrates the general belief that auctioneers and buying at auction were ungentlemanly. Mundy's commentary on night auctions was particularly evocative of the shady reputation of auctions in 1852 and implies that they were probably the means through which stolen property was sold.[27] In the 1880s, the American traveller, Ballou, described the streets of Sydney, saying that 'the "going, going, gone", of the open sham auction rooms rings upon the ear'.[28] However, it should be noted that these comments referred to auctions generally, rather than art auctions specifically.

Early Auction Houses — Gemmell, Tuckett & Co.

By the 1840s, numerous auction rooms dotted Sydney and Melbourne. In Sydney, Walter Bradley & Co. offered a number of Old Masters from the collection of Sir Charles Nicholson, a physician and collector who was also instrumental in the establishment of Australia's first university (the University of Sydney), at auction in February 1854. These included portraits by Sir Peter Lely and works from the school of Rembrandt, Titian and Leonardo da Vinci.[29] Nineteenth century general auctioneers — the most eminent of whom included Samuel Lyons, W. J. Moore, Thomas Stubbs, Thomas Sutcliffe Mort and Charles Moore — were flamboyant characters.[30] Much of the nineteenth century flurry of auction activity in Sydney centred on the theatre as the object of, or venue for, sales or as an inspiration for auction strategies. Isadore Brodsky, a Sydney historian, described the ceremonial aspects of Sydney auctioneering in the nineteenth century, while commenting that this very drama had dissipated by the time he was writing in the late 1950s.[31] In nineteenth century Sydney, bell ringing in the street and the 'display of bunting' were used to lure the crowds into the auctions.[32] Sydney arguably had few amusements at this time and auctions fulfilled a broader role as free entertainment. This has recurred in the past few decades where art auctions have been referred to as 'free art shows'.[33]

The Melbourne Auction Company, located in Collins Street, was the main body of general auctioneers in colonial Melbourne. Other auctioneers, such as A. H.

Hart and Carfrae & Bland, were located in Queen Street and Little Collins Street. Carfrae & Bland advertised an auction of items belonging to Judge Willis, 'including several original sketches of distinguished persons by Sir Joshua Reynolds; also a number of pictures', in the *Port Phillip Herald* on 30 June 1843. After George Gilbert, who was involved in many facets of Melbourne cultural life, resigned from his position as Gold Commissioner in 1853, he attempted to pursue a career in auctioneering. He moved his auctioneering business to the Auction Mart Hall of Commerce in 1855, where he sold (unspecified) paintings, among other items. Beauchamp and Rocke became well known auctioneers of furniture and general goods in the 1860s, conducting auctions from their premises at 38 and 40 Collins Street East.

Gemmell, Tuckett & Co. was a very successful auction business in Melbourne from approximately 1870 to the early twentieth century and, while its core business appears to have been the sale of books, often entire libraries, it was entrusted with the sale of a number of important art collections. It was situated in the heart of Melbourne's business district, in Tuckett Chambers, Collins Street West, near banks and insurance agencies. The firm had earlier operated under the name of Gemmell, McCaul and Co. from about 1862 to 1870.[34] At some point in the late nineteenth century, the firm became known as the 'Art and Furniture Auctioneers'.

In the opinion of the *Argus* in 1868, the lighting and lay-out of Gemmell, Tuckett & Co.'s auction rooms were conducive to a good viewing.[35] Viewing the lots in person was encouraged as the firm accepted no responsibility for the authenticity of the paintings sold; according to its conditions of sale, 'No claim for damage or errors of any description will be entertained; purchasers are therefore particularly requested to examine the lots before purchasing.'[36] The company's art auction catalogues were representative of such catalogues in the mid-nineteenth to early twentieth centuries. In the 1840s, descriptions, particularly of the elaborate frames, medium and subject matter of the works, were often included in sales notices and catalogues, although artists' names and the titles of paintings were rarely provided. By the 1850s, the titles of paintings were often listed and catalogues at this time basically comprised a list of titles and artists, with a rare, brief description and the occasional photographic illustration.[37] By contrast some of Gemmell, Tuckett & Co.'s catalogues included critical reviews and a paragraph on the merits of each work to boost its sales appeal. Works were generally sold 'without reserve' or 'without any reserve' so that a sale at any price was the objective. Vendors' names were invariably included in catalogues, as by the end of the nineteenth century it was recognized that provenance added significant value to works. Estimates were still excluded from catalogues — their inclusion did not become standard practice until almost a century later.

Even Gemmell, Tuckett & Co. is not above suspicions of profiteering. On 27 October 1886 the firm auctioned the collection of oil paintings and watercolours belonging to Joseph R. Tuckett, one of the proprietors, who was obliged to make an extended stay in England owing to 'ill health'. It is unclear whether Tuckett was to retain any proprietary interests in the firm, for if so he would have had a doubly vested interest in the outcome of the sale.

Gemmell, Tuckett & Co.'s art auctions also included the sale of a number of works by living Australian artists. For example, an invitation was issued to a 'Private View' of works by Frederick McCubbin, Arthur Streeton and Tom Roberts on 3 December 1890, with the auction to be held two days later.[38]

Thomas Sutcliffe Mort and Thomas Ware Smart: Two Collectors, their Agents and Auctioneers

Serious colonial Australian art collectors participated in the international market. Many important citizens of Sydney, and later Melbourne, bought art while travelling abroad, often at Christie's auctions and sometimes through agents or dealers.[39] Not only did they generally make their major purchases overseas, but they also often sold their collections overseas. Had these collections been sold in Australia during the colonial period, perhaps specialized fine art auction houses would have been established at an earlier date and generated a flourishing market for so-called 'quality' art in Australia.

Both Thomas Sutcliffe Mort (1816–78) and Thomas Ware Smart (1810–81) resided in Sydney and bought at auction in London in the 1850s. However, they specialized in different areas: Mort's taste was for English watercolours, while Smart preferred Old Master paintings. Mort and Smart were neighbours as well as friendly rivals on personal and business fronts until 1866 when a bad investment in a mining company put an end to their association. Both opened their art collections for public inspection at their residences in Darling Point — Mort from 2 March 1861 at 'Greenoaks' and Smart from 13 July 1861 at the Mona Gallery — making them prominent philanthropists and tastemakers. Author and curator, Robert Holden, believes that the collections were unparalleled in the colonies in terms of quality and accessibility. He notes that it was not until 24 May 1861 that the first public art gallery, the National Gallery of Victoria, opened in Australia and that it initially only comprised casts and statues, with a picture gallery being added on 24 December 1864.[40]

Mort was born in Manchester and arrived in Sydney in 1838, founding an auctioneering business which prospered. He was a leading wool auctioneer but, as was the case with many other auctioneers of the period, accepted anything offered to him for sale. Incidentally, Mort became friends with Henry Parkes, the 'Father of Federation', when the latter was a toy-maker and he made the ivory hammer that Mort used in his auctions.[41] Mort did hold at least one auction of paintings:

> ...towards the end of the forties [1840s] he held a sale that would draw envious growls from a modern auctioneer: a consignment of paintings including works by Valesquez [sic], Bassano, Rembrandt, Canaletto, Vinkerboom, and Calvert. Of these articles, and of the general imports with which he had been dealing at Gosling & Browne's, Mort had sufficient experience to sustain his judgments on the rostrum.[42]

This having been said, one cannot assume that these works were genuine. It is probable, moreover, that this was Mort's sole specialist art sale.

Mort visited England from 1857 to 1859, while recuperating from an illness associated with a horse-riding accident sustained two years previously. He purchased art from a variety of sources including auctions, exhibitions, agents and studios. In July 1857, he attended the Earl of Shrewsbury's Alton Towers estate auction and acquired a large selection of arms and armour, traditional signifiers of wealth and nobility. He later purchased 112 works, mainly English watercolours, from other sales.

In Sydney, Mort frequently obtained new works for his collection from London, presumably from his agent/dealer. He obtained his bronzes from Elkingtons of London and purchased H. B. Willis' oil painting, *Oxen, Mid-Day Rest*, from the artist's studio.[43] Correspondence in the possession of Charles Mort, Mort's grandson, and perused by Holden, suggests that Mort's first London art dealer was White & Dalton, whom he engaged in 1858 after his arrival in London.[44] Edward F. White soon after became Mort's exclusive London agent, having left the partnership. He bid on Mort's behalf at Phillips' Northwick sale in 1859. As Mort rarely heeded the advice of White, it is likely that he chose the paintings at this sale himself, rather than leaving it to the discretion of his agent. Mort instructed White to send shipments of works on a regular basis back to him in Sydney, subject to his approval, in order to augment his collection of watercolours. In a letter to White, dated 21 January 1861, Mort informed him:

> I would prefer the works of rising young men to those of men who are at the maximum of their fame & prices. Now & then I shall not object to pay a good price for a really first class Drawing, etc., but as 'fashion' does not affect us in N. S. Wales I am not prepared to pay for great names.[45]

Mort's assertion that New South Wales was impervious to British collecting tastes appears to have been a minority one. As Mort was disinclined to pay large prices for art, White was obliged to source the work of living artists. However, in late 1861 and early 1862, Mort did purchase a number of works from White at high prices, including a Vicat Cole for £52 and a J.B. Pyne for £47.

After Mort's death in 1878, much of the collection passed to members of his family. Mort's second wife died in 1910 and the contents of 'Greenoaks' were put up for auction on 6–7 December 1910 by the auctioneers James R. Lawson & Little in conjunction with H. Y. Norton. Included in this auction were eighteen oil paintings, 35 watercolours, and bronzes and statues of classical subjects such as *Laocöon*, *Venus Rising from the Ocean* and the marble, *Good Samaritan*, which he had commissioned from Birch of London. It is significant that the *Sydney Morning Herald* reported on 7 December 1910 that the top price at the auction was for a watercolour of *Toolengen Park* by Conrad Martens, which sold for 105 guineas.[46] The auction catalogue emphasizes the English aristocratic provenance of the majority of Mort's collection, thus bestowing celebrity status on it:

> Catalogue of the Superb Collection of Early English and French Furniture — RARE ITALIAN AND FRENCH BRONZES PURE CARRARA MARBLE STATUARY EARLY ENGLISH AND ITALIAN ARMOUR and MEDIAEVAL IMPLEMENTS OF WAR also The Valuable Collection of Oil Paintings and water-colour Drawings. NOTE – The principal portion of the Furniture and Objets D'Art at 'GREENOAKES' [sic] was purchased at the Dispersal Sale of the LATE EARL OF SHREWSBURY'S EFFECTS at 'Alton Towers', England, and should specially appeal to Collectors and Connoisseurs.[47]

Australian-born Smart, a wealthy businessman and politician, who actually began his working life as an auctioneer in Sydney, also spent from 1855 to 1859 in England. There he purchased twenty-nine paintings, the bulk of his collection, from the Northwick sale through an agent for £3600. Lord Northwick had acquired a number of Old Masters, some of which were of doubtful origin. Smart probably purchased some of these works as he paid quite low prices for the alleged masterpieces.[48] Lord Northwick, in the great philanthropic tradition to which the likes of Mort and Smart ascribed, purchased both Old Masters as well as contemporary art and opened his two galleries to the public, *gratis*. He died intestate and his collection, which included more than 1400 paintings and *objets d'art*, was subsequently auctioned over twenty-two days from 26 July to 30 August 1859. The entire sale grossed £95,725.

It is probable that Smart relied heavily on the judgment and tastes of agents and dealers to purchase works appropriate for his station when building his collection of predominantly Old Master paintings suitable for 'public edification'.[49] The collection had 66 items including works purportedly by Giovanni Battista Tiepolo, Angelica Kauffman, Breughel and Gainsborough.[50] Two of the 16 English works in Smart's collection were acquired at the Northwick auction. Of these English works, the most important was the copy of Gainsborough's *The Market Cart* (1786), whose original is in the National Gallery in London. Smart purchased this for £73 and it was later sold at his auction in 1884 for £450.

Smart's collection was open for public inspection on the first Saturday of the month from 13 July 1861 until it was sold by auction after his death in 1884.[51] The auction was held on 26 June by the auctioneers Bradley, Newton & Lamb. Smart's picture gallery, the Mona Gallery, at his home at Darling Point, was presumably where the collection was exhibited for sale.

Holden notes that Mort was 'one of the extremely few colonials to be in regular contact with the London art world, being constantly apprised of the current exhibition scene there and the vagaries of fashion in the art market'.[52] That is, most Australian collectors did not purchase art regularly from London, but in Australia and thus by contemporary standards both Mort and Smart imported large quantities of art into Australia.

Carl Kahler's Studio Auction

Auctions were sometimes utilized to sell the contents of studios of artists, both living or deceased. These sales performed an educational role, as they presented a collection of an artist's work, rather like a retrospective, for both the public and collectors to view as a cohesive body. A number of artists who worked in Australia auctioned the contents of their studios before they returned overseas and their estates were ultimately sold in England. In reverse, John Glover auctioned the contents of his studio in London in 1830, prior to settling in Tasmania in 1831. Glover's children raffled off his paintings after his death in December 1849 in what is known as the 'most important dispersal of Glover's paintings in Tasmania'.[53]

Gemmell, Tuckett & Co. were the auctioneers in one notable instance. Carl Kahler (c.1855–1926?) was an Austrian painter and a celebrated artist in colonial Melbourne, where he worked from around 1885 to 1890.[54] Kahler mainly earned portrait commissions but also painted nudes.[55] He was most celebrated for his painting of the Flemington race meeting of 1886 entitled *The Derby Day at Flemington*, and two related works, *The Lawn at Flemington on Melbourne Cup Day* 1887 and *The Betting Ring at Flemington* c.1887–9. These works were influenced by William Frith's famous 1856–8 painting, *Derby Day*, which had travelled around Australia from 1864–5; it was exhibited in the studio of the sculptor Charles Summers at 92 Collins Street, Melbourne at the end of 1864.[56]

Kahler's three works on the running of the Melbourne Cup were immensely popular and photogravure reproductions were made by the lithographers Goupil of Paris and published by Carl Pinschof of Pfaff, Pinschof and Co. in Flinders Lane, who had purchased the reproduction rights. Carl Pinschof was the Consul-General for Austria and Hungary and Kahler's sponsor in Melbourne.

Pedigree and Panache

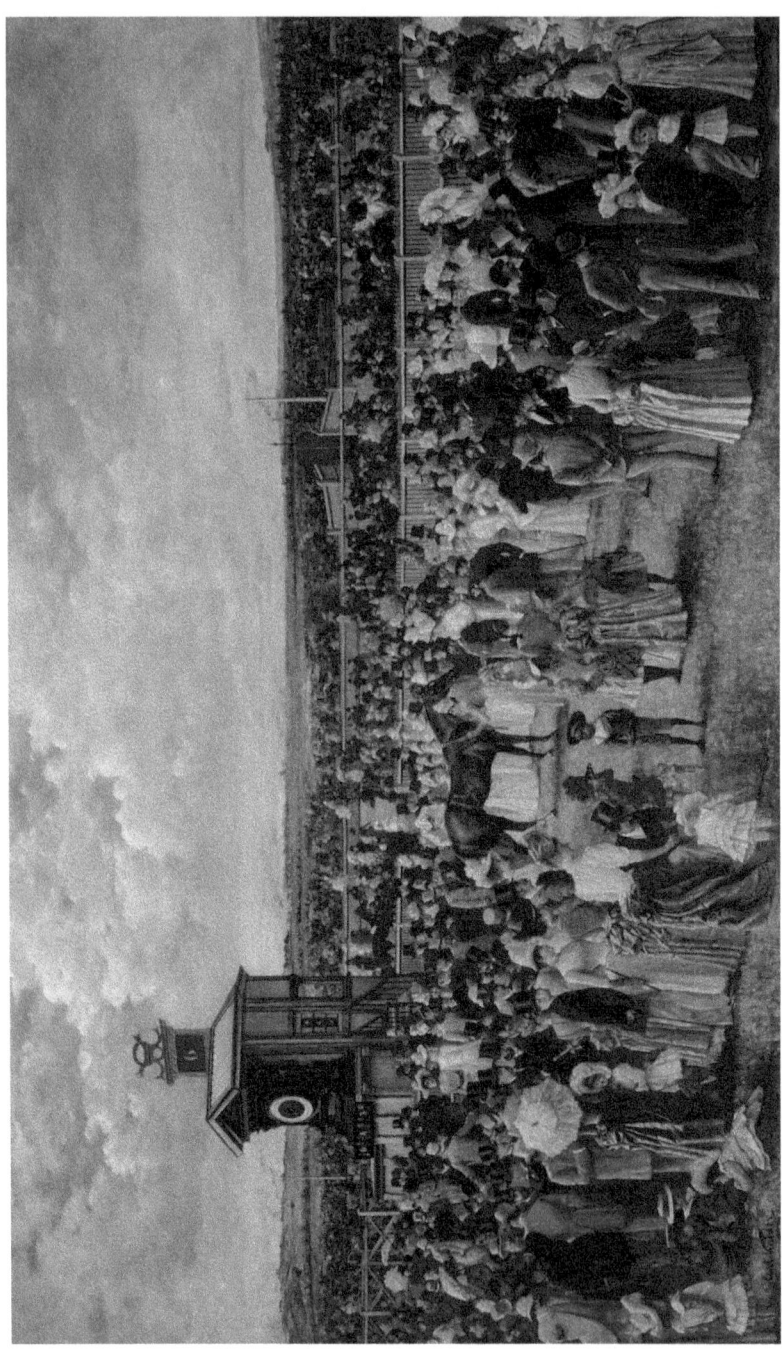

Figure 5: Carl Kahler, *The Derby Day at Flemington*, 1886, oil on canvas, 300 x 200 cm, Victoria Racing Club Collection.

Kahler's *The Derby Day at Flemington*, a group portrait as well as individual portraits, included a key which identified *la crème de la crème* of colonial Melbourne society including Kahler himself. It was generally thought that Kahler had charged Melbourne society figures five guineas to include their portraits in this work.[57] The fact that a number of people had to sit for their portraits explains why the painting was finished approximately two years after the race and indicates both the social validation to be acquired through inclusion in such a portrait, as well as Kahler's astute business mind. The painting was exhibited at the Athenaeum in Melbourne in January 1889 and numerous people attended, paying an admission fee of one shilling for the privilege (Figure 5). Kahler was so admired at the time that he 'was the subject of what is probably the first pamphlet, solely biographical, to be published on an artist working in colonial Australia'.[58]

Kahler's studio was auctioned over two sales in 1890 before he left Australia with plans to paint in Japan, China and India. (Although he did not reach Asia, he was in New Zealand by November 1890 and left for San Francisco on 1 December of that year.)[59] Gemmell, Tuckett & Co. conducted the first auction at Kahler's studio at 19 Elizabeth Street, Melbourne on 20 February and viewings were held on the five days prior to the sale. This auction has been described as 'a major event in the early annals of the Australian saleroom'.[60]

The auction catalogue, *An Artist's Sanctuary — Catalogue Raisonne' of the Contents of Herr Kahler's Studio…*, is a beautiful publication, and includes two original photographs of the east and west ends of the studio. These photographs show a sumptuous setting, including a multitude of paintings and props such as ornate and exotic items of furniture, bric-a-brac, luscious ferns, fabrics and wall hangings, the backgrounds for Kahler's nudes. As Holden notes, these photographs 'provide rare visual documentation of a grand aesthetic setting in late nineteenth-century Australia' (Figure 6).[61] Nevertheless, the catalogue foreword indicates that the studio appeared quaint even in the nineteenth century.

Kahler's pastels and paintings were later auctioned by Gemmell, Tuckett & Co. at their New Art Gallery on 7 May 1890, having been 'Removed from his studio for convenience of sale'.[62] The auction catalogue stated that *'every picture must be positively sold'* and indicated that some of the pastels were captured in the photograph of the studio. The pastels and paintings included works with such romantic titles as *Early Reveries*, *My Favourite Author*, and *An Odalisk, or Turkish femme de chamber [sic]*. The catalogue gives a short flowery description underneath most of the works, generally comprising details of what the subjects were wearing.

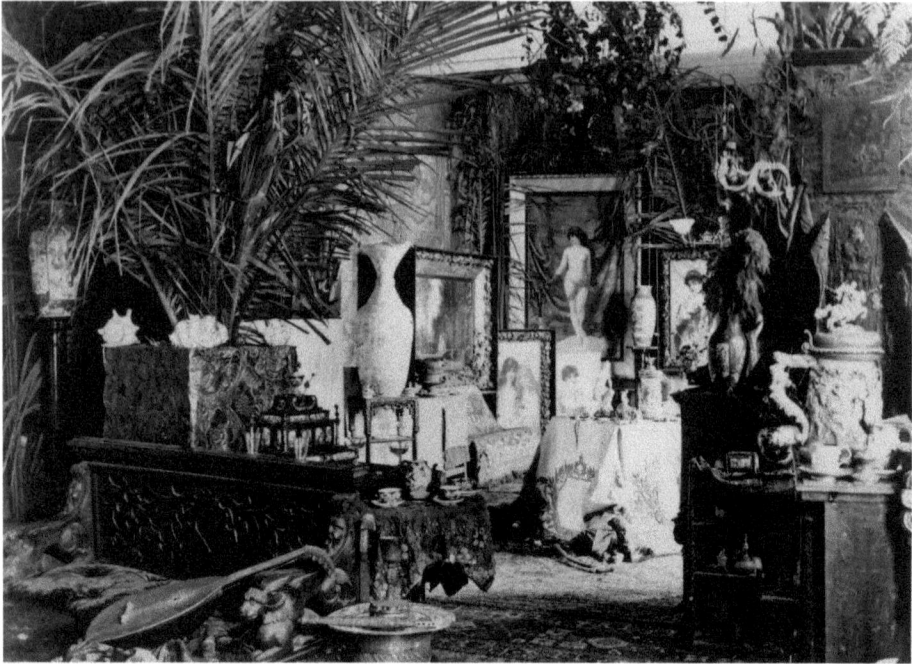

Figure 6: *Artist Carl Kahler's studio, interior, Melbourne,* (west end), c.1890, gelatin silver photograph, 20 x 25 cm, State Library of Victoria.

The first nine lots in this second auction catalogue are pastels, with twenty oil paintings and the two photographs of the studio following. This is interesting in itself, as today the oils would be presented first and the 'lesser' works reserved for the back of the catalogue. The catalogue is very elegantly presented and displays some of the current auction and commercial gallery catalogue traits, in that it 'talks' or 'puffs' up the works and includes references which would increase the value, mentioning the technical skill of the artist and including poetic references. For example, Lot 10, an oil painting, *The Munich Burgher's Daughter*, is described as 'A girl in the costume of the last century, with a bird perched on her shoulder. The costume consists of a grey satin robe, with a gold-embroidered bodice; her cap also embroidered in gold. *A most graceful and expressive work. The whole of the textures wrought out with conscientious fidelity.*'

The italicized annotation for Lot 13, *A Secret* (1884), claims '*This work, which is shown in the view of the artist's studio, has always been a great favourite with visitors to the latter*'. It is the most recent of Kahler's works to surface in an Australian saleroom, fetching $13,512 (estimate $12,000–$18,000) at Christie's November 2000 auction and resurfacing at a Deutscher-Menzies auction in September 2005, where it remained unsold (estimate $8000–$12,000).

The Baldwin Spencer Collection

A pivotal auction for the early twentieth century Australian art market was that of the Baldwin Spencer Collection on 19–21 May 1919. 'Both the building of the collection and its disposal at greatly inflated prices proved landmarks in the recognition of Australian art.'[63] Sir Walter Baldwin Spencer (1860–1929) was an academic and administrator, a well-known anthropologist and connoisseur. He was a trustee of the National Gallery of Victoria from 1895 and encouraged the purchase of Australian art. Baldwin Spencer was awarded the Medal of the Society of Artists, Sydney in 1926 for his contribution to art in Australia. His portrait by George Lambert is in the Museum of Victoria and portraits by W. B. McInnes are owned by the University of Melbourne and Exeter College, Oxford. There is another portrait of Baldwin Spencer by E. Phillips Fox, but its whereabouts is currently unknown.

Baldwin Spencer's biographers speak at length on his connoisseurship and patronage of local contemporary artists including Sir Arthur Streeton. They show that although he began to amass his collection of Australian art around 1906 when he inherited an annuity from his parents' estate, he was already immersed in the Australian market, purchasing his first Streeton in 1892. He sold more than 200 works at his auction in 1919, although he retained approximately half of the collection and began collecting more works soon after.

The auction in 1919 was held at Gill's Fine Art Society's Galleries in Alfred Place, Melbourne where it was first exhibited for six days. It was conducted by the Fine Art Society in conjunction with Arthur Tuckett & Son. The thirty-two-page catalogue contained 313 lots — 97 oil paintings followed by 70 watercolours and pastels, 59 black and white works (sketches, etchings), 9 items of glassware, 46 copper, pewter, brass and Sheffield plate, 19 Staffordshire cottage figures, and 13 items of furniture et cetera. It made special mention of the fact that it had been issued in plenty of time to allow country and interstate buyers to attend the viewing and that commissions could be left with the auctioneer.[64] By contrast with the Kahler catalogue, the works' dimensions were mostly included as was the occasional reference to reproductions in journals, such as *Art in Australia*, as well as to collections in which the artist was represented. Opinions of scholars were also included where appropriate and some of the entries for artists and individual works were quite lengthy. Baldwin Spencer personally supervised the compilation of the auction catalogue and Hans Heysen gave consent for his painting, *Sunset Haze*, to be reproduced in colour as plate 59.[65]

The collection was important because it comprised 'Australian Pictures and Works of Art', rather than European works, and it established a benchmark in the acknowledgement of the strength of Australian art.[66] The collection included works by artists who are still highly regarded today including W.B. McInnes,

McCubbin, George Lambert, Gruner, Streeton, David Davies, Hans Heysen, Walter Withers, E. Phillips Fox, Conder, Roberts, Sydney Long, Ambrose Patterson, Thea Proctor and Norman Lindsay.

The auction boosted the profile of living Australian artists, with Streeton's prices demonstrating the most dramatic increase. Thirty-two works by Streeton were put up for auction, including one that was not listed in the catalogue; they realised a total of £2341.[67] Streeton's fourteen oil paintings and twelve watercolours sold at a profit of £1748, a substantial sum when compared with the sale total of £4500. Baldwin Spencer had made a profit of almost 200 per cent on his original purchase price of £603. It is likely, based on the figures assembled by Mulvaney and Calaby, that Baldwin Spencer's entire collection, at 1919 prices, would have cost approximately £2500 to £3500.[68] The works which were passed-in realized another £209 at an additional sale held that December.

William Moore, author of *The Story of Australian Art*, agrees that the Baldwin Spencer auction was most noteworthy because of the value placed on Streeton's work. Baldwin Spencer had originally purchased Streeton's *The Centre of the Empire* (1903) at the Guild Hall Exhibition in 1907 for £100. This same work sold at his 1919 auction for 400 guineas, approximately four times the 1907 price.[69] Moore noted that 'While he realized a good profit from the sale of his collection in 1919, it has to be remembered that Sir Baldwin Spencer purchased Australian works in Melbourne at a time when the apathy of the public was rather appalling.'[70] Baldwin Spencer had bought at a time when prices were low and artists were undervalued, but sold at a time when apathy was dissipating and these same artists had gained in popularity.

Streeton capitalized on the prices set at Baldwin Spencer's sale by buying back *Golden Summer, Eaglemont* (1889), his *pièce de résistance* which inspired Jane Clark's famous 1985 blockbuster exhibition.[71] Streeton wrote to Baldwin Spencer on 29 August 1919 'I was glad...that my market is still good — one picture [*Sydney Harbour, Across Cremorne*] seemed quite an excellent rise...from £75 to £525 — quite a sound investment and not likely to go down either'.[72] Baldwin Spencer warned Streeton forthwith that if he continued to 'boil the pot' and churn out inferior work, the resultant flooding of the market would negatively affect the prices of his works. It was at this time of financial success that Streeton's relationship with Baldwin Spencer became strained and Streeton even encouraged speculation that it was mainly owing to Baldwin Spencer's influence that the National Gallery of Victoria had declined to acquire *Golden Summer*.

In addition to Streeton, Baldwin Spencer's patronage was extended to Hans Heysen, Norman and Lionel Lindsay, J. J. Hilder and W. B. McInnes. He was, in fact, one of the first people to buy the work of Lionel Lindsay and he owned more than forty works from Norman Lindsay's early career. Baldwin Spencer commissioned Tom Roberts to paint a portrait of his friend, A. W. Howitt. He also attended auction salerooms, although it is uncertain how frequently. By 1917, Baldwin Spencer's collection contained the work of around sixty artists, the majority of whom were living. His collection was hailed as a paradigm for an exemplary Australian collection. On two occasions, in the few years prior to its dispersal at auction, part of Baldwin Spencer's collection was exhibited at the Art Gallery of New South Wales as well as being included in the second edition of the influential *Art in Australia*.[73] Mulvaney and Calaby assert that the first exhibition of his collection at the Art Gallery of New South Wales represented 'one of the largest showings of a private collection in the history of Australian art'.[74]

Baldwin Spencer had purchased works by J. J. Hilder from 1907 and sold nine of Hilder's watercolours at his 1919 auction for £824, eight times their original price. In 1916, just prior to Hilder's death, Baldwin Spencer had been sent six works by Hilder's dealer/agent, Adolf Albers, from which he was to make a selection and return the rest. Baldwin Spencer bought all six works, forwarding two of them to other art collectors. In the interim, Hilder had died and his dealer, mindful that prices for his works would now increase, demanded that Baldwin Spencer return the works, to no avail. Albers placed his own interpretation on events, an interpretation which he appears to have passed on to Hilder's family, who felt that they had suffered an injustice. By the time of the auction in 1919, Hilder's works had increased in value substantially and confirmed for some that Baldwin Spencer was indeed a profiteer.

It was unfortunate that the success of this auction led to the general conclusion that Baldwin Spencer had exploited artists ruthlessly through using their works to attain a solid financial return. Baldwin Spencer had been in need of liquidity in 1919 and he had discussed his intentions and reasons for selling his collection prior to the auction with several of the artists concerned, including Heysen, McInnes, Norman Lindsay and Streeton.

After, Baldwin Spencer and Julian Ashton (the art teacher, artist and founder of the prestigious Julian Aston School in Sydney) agreed that prices of some Australian works, notably those of Streeton, were inflated. Ashton believed that this market inflation was directly attributable to Spencer's auction. He wrote on 18 September 1921: 'You complain of the high prices Australian artists are asking…well, you have yourself to blame. To no one in Australia have our artists more reason to be grateful…when you sold…that collection and realised a great rise in value…the artists raised their prices to meet the demand'.[75]

In April 1918, the Sydney art collector and friend of Streeton's, Leonard Dodds, had sold some of his collection of Australian art which fetched very high prices, possibly influencing Baldwin Spencer's decision to auction his collection.[76] Information on Leonard Dodds is scarce, we do know that he was involved in the mining industry and was also an art patron.[77] His wife, Winifred, was acquainted with Streeton and Roberts when they were living at Sirius Cove and the latter painted a lovely portrait of her c.1893. She may well have influenced her husband's tastes in art. There appear to have been a number of auctions of Dodds' collection after World War 1, in, for example, 1919, January 1922 and 1927.[78]

The Leonard Dodds auction on 31 January 1922 was one of Lawson's major art auctions, considered second only to that of the Baldwin Spencer auction in importance.[79] This Dodds auction contained sixty-one paintings and sixty prints by approximately thirty-six artists, most of whom were Australian. The artists included Blamire Young, Streeton, Lloyd Rees and Tom Roberts and the works were, in the main, landscapes and still lifes. Dodds also owned a number of modern works by Roy de Maistre and Roland Wakelin, possibly out of the desire to sell them at a profit when the artists had further established their reputations; his patronage of modern Australian artists was unusual for the time. The auction catalogue emphasized that Australian art was a profitable investment, although Australian artists still needed international validation:

> Twenty-five years ago there were no auction sales of Australian art. Australian pictures... were not worth their weight in copper. But with the great distinctions won for Australia by her artists overseas...And the one-man shows initiated by Streeton, in Melbourne, 1906–1907, have taken place...with continuous success...with the result that a good Australian picture is now a valuable asset and a good investment.[80]

The first assertion needs qualification as this chapter has shown that Australian art was sold in the nineteenth century, although European art was certainly most popular. Dodds had amassed his art collection over a period of twenty-five years and had purposely attempted to assemble a collection which was representative of Australian art history. The catalogue notes that Dodds' first art purchase was Streeton's *The Railway Station, Redfern* (1893) (currently in the collection of the Art Gallery of New South Wales). Dodds had bought it for £12, a price considered ludicrously high at the time, and it fetched 350 guineas at the Dodds auction.[81] Yet another auction of Dodds' collection was conducted by Lawson's in November 1927, indicating that either many works were passed-in at his previous auction or that he possessed a very large and ever-increasing collection. It could be said then, that the Baldwin Spencer and Dodds sales combined to set a new standard for the monetary, and hence aesthetic, value of Australian art.

As explained in earlier chapters, Australia had historically looked to England for guidance on taste and hence bought and sold many paintings overseas. By the early twentieth century, this 'cultural cringe' was beginning to lose its potency. Collectors began to deal with the local marketplace, thus contributing to the birth of enduring Australian auction houses. Besides this steady development, nothing of great significance for the purpose of this study took place until the 1950s. Australia was still sending 'quality' works for auction overseas and a number of locally-owned auction houses, with the capacity to conduct specialized art auctions, were beginning to emerge. This rise to dominance of art, especially Australian art, at auctions held by local general firms, some of which had their roots in the colonial era, is the subject of the following chapter.

ENDNOTES

[1] This gallery is sometimes cited as Robert Vaughan Hood's Picture Gallery. Alan McCulloch, *Encyclopedia of Australian Art*, Allen & Unwin, St. Leonards, New South Wales 1994 (3rd ed.).

[2] Quoted in William Moore, *The Story of Australian Art — From the Earliest Known Art of the Continent to the Art of To-day*, Angus & Robertson Ltd, Sydney 1934, 2 vols., vol. 1, p.51.

[3] Terry Ingram, 'Sales of the century: Sydney Harbour and the bush are tops', *Art and Australia*, 37(2) 1999, pp.270–275 and Terry Ingram, 'Artist, teacher, prophet', *Australian Financial Review*, 17 February 1972, p.11. Quotation from *Australasian Critic*, 1 May 1891, p.192.

[4] See *Table Talk* (no. 304), 17 April 1891, p.5.

[5] Jane Clark and Bridget Whitelaw, *Golden Summers — Heidelberg and Beyond*, exhibition catalogue, National Gallery of Victoria, Melbourne 1985, p.74.

[6] Here I should mention that Staples was my great-great-grandfather.

[7] From *Art and Architecture*, Sydney, January 1905 and included in Bernard Smith (ed.), *Documents on Art and Taste in Australia — The Colonial Period 1770–1914*, Oxford University Press, Melbourne 1975, p.266. Although this quotation is not strictly from the colonial period, but just after Federation, I thought that it was still relevant to include.

[8] See Tim Bonyhady, *Images in Opposition — Australian Landscape Painting 1801–1890*, Oxford University Press, Melbourne 1985, p.3.

[9] Mary Mackay, 'For a mere five guineas, Carl would paint you in next to the Governor', *Sydney Morning Herald*, 24 December 1983, no pagination.

[10] See Johnson, *The Sydney Art Patronage System*, p.63; and A. J. Daplyn, 'Art Notes', *Australasian Art Review*, 1 May 1899, p.14.

[11] McCulloch, *Encyclopedia of Australian Art*.

[12] See Shannon Hunter Hurtado, 'The Promotion of the Visual Arts in Britain 1835–1860', *Canadian Journal of History*, 28 (1) 1993, p.61.

[13] Rachel N. Klein, 'Art and Authority in Antebellum New York City: The Rise and Fall of the American Art-Union', *The Journal of American History*, 81(4) 1995, p.1541.

[14] See Hurtado, 'The Promotion of the Visual Arts in Britain 1835–1860', p.74. Taken from the *Report from the Select Committee into the Operation of Art Union Laws* 1864, p.577.

[15] Hurtado, 'The Promotion of the Visual Arts in Britain 1835–1860', p.77.

[16] On Mechanics' Institutes in Australia see Philip C. Candy and John Laurent (eds), *Pioneering Culture: Mechanics' Institutes and Schools of Arts in Australia*, Adelaide 1994.

[17] See *The Australian*, 7 October 1841, p.2.

[18] Robert Holden, *Aspects of Art Collecting and Patronage in Colonial New South Wales*, Honours thesis, University of Sydney, Sydney 1981, p.10.

[19] Rivett, *The Art Union Story and Old Parramatta*, p.21.

[20] See Ingram, 'Boil the pot and skin 'em alive', p.94.

[21] Carl Ruhen, *The Auctioneers: Lawsons — The First 100 Years*, Ayers and James Heritage Books and James R. Lawson Pty Ltd, Sydney 1984, p.27 and Ingram, 'Boil the pot and skin 'em alive', p.94.

[22] See Graham Abbott and Geoffrey Little (eds), *The Respectable Sydney Merchant — A.B. Spark of Tempe*, Sydney University Press, Sydney 1976, pp.78–9, entries under 19 and 20 May and 16 June 1837.

[23] Terry Ingram, 'From Rembrandt to Roberts — Great Saleroom Moments', *Australian Art Collector*, issue 3, January–March 1998, p.56 and Mary Holyoake, 'Melbourne Art Scene from 1839 to 1859', *Art and Australia*, 15(3) 1978, p. 296.

[24] This is reproduced in full in Ruhen, *The Auctioneers*, p. 24.

[25] Lt. Colonel Godfrey Charles Mundy, *Our Antipodes: or, Residence and Rambles in the Australasian Colonies, with a Glimpse of the Gold Fields*, Richard Bentley, London 1852, 3 vols., (2nd ed., rev.), pp.56–57.

[26] Mundy, *Our Antipodes*, p. 58, see also pp. 59–60.

[27] Mundy, *Our Antipodes*, pp.60–1.

[28] Quoted in Ruhen, *The Auctioneers*, p.26. See Maturin Murray Ballou, *Under the Southern Cross*, Houghton, Mifflin 1890, third ed.

[29] See Ingram, 'From Rembrandt to Roberts', pp.57–8 and the *Sydney Morning Herald*, 17 February 1854.

[30] Isadore Brodsky, *Sydney Looks Back*, Angus and Robertson, Sydney 1957, p.86 and Alan Barnard, *Visions and Profits – Studies in the Business Career of Thomas Sutcliffe Mort*, Melbourne University Press, Melbourne 1961, p.21.

[31] See Brodsky, 'Salesmen of Another Century', in *Sydney Looks Back*, pp.84–9.

[32] Brodsky, *Sydney Looks Back*, p.85.

[33] Justin Miller said that this had been reported in the press regarding the Sotheby's Fairfax auction in August 2002. Justin Miller, taped interview with the author, Sydney, 3 September 2002.

[34] These dates are estimates based on the holdings of auction catalogues at the State Library of Victoria.

[35] The *Argus* review was included in Gemmell, Tuckett & Co., *Catalogue of a Valuable Collection*, 22 May 1868.

[36] Gemmell, Tuckett & Co., *Catalogue of the Beautiful and Costly Art Furniture, Marble Statuary, Real Bronzes, Art Treasures, Oil Paintings, Water Colour Drawings, Fine Old Engravings, &c., Collected by Sir George Verdon, K. C. M. G, C. B.*, Melbourne, 1 June 1891.

[37] See, for example, Gemmell, Tuckett & Co., *Catalogue of Paintings in Water-Colour*, Melbourne, 26 August 1885.

[38] Gemmell, Tuckett & Co., Invitation to an 'Exhibition of Pictures By Fd [sic] McCubbin, Arthur Streeton, and Tom Roberts', Melbourne, 3 December 1890.

[39] Terry Ingram, 'Australia Goes To Auction…Offshore', *Australian Art Collector,* issue 4, April–June 1998, p.74.

[40] See Holden, *Aspects of Art Collecting and Patronage in Colonial New South Wales*, p.29.

[41] According to Barnard, *Visions and Profits*, p.21.

[42] Barnard, *Visions and Profits*, p.19.

[43] See *Sydney Morning Herald* 8 March 1861, p. 4. A photograph of the entrance hall of the Greenoaks Gallery, taken in the early 1860s, was reproduced in Holden, *Aspects of Art Collecting and Patronage in Colonial New South Wales*, as was an interior photograph of the gallery depicting the Willis painting on the wall.

[44] Holden, *Aspects of Art Collecting and Patronage in Colonial New South Wales*, p.43.

[45] Quoted in Holden, *Aspects of Art Collecting and Patronage in Colonial New South Wales*, p.43. Taken from 'Extracts from Mr. Mort's Letters — after a careful re-perusal —with remarks thereon', by Edward F. White pp.1–2. See also 'The Greenoaks Collection', *Sydney Morning Herald*, 5 August 1861, p.5. This appraisal of the collection continued in the *Sydney Morning Herald* issues of 13 August 1861, p.8; 19 August 1861, p.8; and 2 September 1861, p.2.

[46] Also cited in Ingram, 'Australia Goes To Auction…Offshore', p.74.

[47] Holden reproduces the catalogue of the sale of the Greenoaks collection in *Aspects of Art Collecting and Patronage in Colonial New South Wales*.

[48] See *Sydney Morning Herald*, 20 July 1861, p.8.

[49] Holden, *Aspects of Art Collecting and Patronage in Colonial New South Wales*, p.37.

[50] Smart's collection was described in the *Sydney Morning Herald* in the following issues: 13 July 1861, p.5; 17 July 1861, p.2; 20 July 1861, p.8; 23 July 1861, p.2; 26 July 1861, p.5; and 30 July 1861, p.5.

[51] See *Sydney Morning Herald*, 25 June 1884, p.15.

[52] Holden, *Aspects of Art Collecting and Patronage in Colonial New South Wales*, p.43.

[53] Bonyhady, *Images in Opposition*, p.9.

[54] Contrary to popular belief, it seems that Kahler did not actually die in the San Francisco earthquake of 1906, but was still painting in America in 1924. This is borne out by Holden, *Photography in Colonial Australia — The Mechanical Eye and the Illustrated Book*, Hordern House, Sydney 1988, p.73, as well as a number of American sources including Peter Falk, *Who was who in American Art*, Sound View Press, Connecticut, 1985.

[55] For more biographical information on Carl Kahler see *Table Talk*, 16 December 1887, p.1 and Robert Holden, *Photography in Colonial Australia*, pp.71–3.

[56] Engravings of these works (sometimes sold as a set) have appeared in Australian salerooms on about eight occasions in the last twenty years.

[57] See Mackay, 'For a mere five guineas', no pagination.

[58] According to Holden, *Photography in Colonial Australia*, p.72. See James Smith, *Herr Kahler's celebrated historical picture of 'The Lawn at Flemington on Cup Day' with a biographical sketch of the artist*, McCarron, Bird & Co., c.1889.

[59] See *Table Talk*, 14 March 1890, p.5 and 19 December 1890, p.2, Holden, *Photography in Colonial Australia*, p.73 and Peter Falk, *Who was who in American Art*, Sound View Press, Connecticut, 1985.

[60] Terry Ingram, 'A Purrfect picture', *Australian Financial Review*, 5 September 2002, p.56.

[61] Holden, *Photography in Colonial Australia*, p.71.

[62] See Gemmell, Tuckett & Co., *Catalogue of Herr Kahler's Beautiful Oil Paintings & Pastels, to be sold by Gemmell, Tuckett & Co. at their New Art Gallery Wednesday 7th May, 1890*, Melbourne, 7 May 1890.

[63] D. J. Mulvaney and J. H. Calaby, *'So Much That Is New' — Baldwin Spencer, 1860–1929 — A Biography*, Melbourne University Press, Carlton, Victoria 1985, p.335.

[64] Arthur Tuckett & Son and W. H. Gill's Fine Art Society, *The Baldwin Spencer Collection of Australian Pictures and Works of Art, Fine Art Society's Galleries, Melbourne, May 1919*, Melbourne, 19–21 May 1919. In the papers of William Henry Gill, Box ML MSS.285/13B – *Catalogues of exhibitions at the Fine Art Society 1898–1934*, the Mitchell Library, Sydney.

[65] See Mulvaney and Calaby, *'So Much That Is New'*, p.353. Despite the unillustrated catalogue at the Mitchell Library, the original must have included illustrations, at least one of which was in colour.

[66] In the words of the auction catalogue.

[67] See Mulvaney and Calaby, *'So Much That Is New'*, p.464, fn.29.

[68] Mulvaney and Calaby, *'So Much That Is New'*, p.347.

[69] See Moore, *The Story of Australian Art*, p.31.

[70] Moore, *The Story of Australian Art*, p.37.

[71] See Clark and Whitelaw, *Golden Summers*.

[72] Quoted in Mulvaney and Calaby, *'So Much That Is New'*, p.465, fn.72.

[73] Only one catalogue could be found, that of *Sir W. Baldwin Spencer's Collection at the National Art Gallery of N.S.W*, December 1916. This is held by the Art Gallery of New South Wales' library. Johnson implies in *The Sydney Art Patronage System*, p.23, that there was a 1918 exhibition of Baldwin Spencer's art collection at the Art Gallery of New South Wales.

[74] Mulvaney and Calaby, *'So Much That Is New'*, p.345.

[75] Quoted in Mulvaney and Calaby, *'So Much That Is New'*, p.465, fn.83.

[76] The 1918 auction catalogue, referred to by Mulvaney and Calaby, *'So Much That Is New'*, p.353, has remained elusive. Although they cite the collector as 'Dodd', it seems likely that it was Leonard Dodds. Ruhen, *The Auctioneers*, p.68, mentions a Leonard Dodds sale, which was almost as influential as the Baldwin Spencer one, leading one to believe that these sales were one and the same.

[77] Johnson, *The Sydney Art Patronage System*, pp.138–9.

[78] Extant catalogues include W. A. Little, *Catalogue: valuable collection of paintings, by order of a well-known Sydney connoisseur...*, Sydney, 18 November 1919; James R. Lawson, *Leonard Dodds' Collection*, 31 January 1922; and James R. Lawson, *Catalogue – Mr Leonard Dodds [sic] Collection of Valuable Pictures*, Sydney, 22 November 1927.

[79] James R. Lawson, *Mr Leonard Dodds Collection of Valuable Pictures*, Sydney, 31 January 1922.

[80] Foreword in James R. Lawson, *Leonard Dodds' Collection*, 31 January 1922.

[81] William Moore, *The Story of Australian Art*, p.27.

Chapter 4. Australian Art at Auction: the 1960s Market

A handful of influential art auctions held in Australia in the 1960s resulted in a boom in the purchase of Australian art for investment purposes and probably contributed to Christie's decision to establish a base in Australia. The most significant was the Schureck sale conducted by Lawson's in Sydney in 1962. Though Lawson's, like Leonard Joel in Melbourne, was a general auctioneering firm, art played a prominent role in the business from its establishment and together the two firms had arguably the greatest effect on the 1960s Australian art auction market. A number of other firms, such as Geoff K. Gray in Sydney and Decoration & Co. in Melbourne, also conducted art auctions in the 1960s. Beside renewed faith in Australian art's investment potential the decade saw broader trends appear in the Australian art market, particularly the interrelationship of dealers and auction houses. The story is best told in accounts of a number of auctions.

Lawson's

Lawson's is an old and dignified auction house in Australian terms. James Lawson Senior arrived in Sydney from Scotland in 1855; he was trained as a joiner and cabinet-maker and later became a furniture dealer in Sydney in the 1860s. The first reference to 'Lawson, James and Sons, Cabinet-Makers, Art Furniture Manufacturers and Carpet Warehousemen', appeared in the Sydney directories in 1884, the foundation date of Lawson's.[1] The eldest son, James Robert (1860–1926), was interested in auctioneering and joined the firm of Harris and Ackman (who owned the New Auction Mart at 190 Pitt Street, Sydney), presumably as an apprentice. James R. Lawson married Marie Rossiter on 20 January 1885 and they honeymooned in England, an apparent irrelevance except for the fact he could well have been inspired by visits to the London firms of Christie's and Sotheby's.

By 1886, Lawson had started his own auctioneering business and succeeded despite a number of partnership changes. Although established as a firm of general auctioneers, Lawson's conducted important art auctions from its earliest years. In 1887, when Lawson had only been in business for approximately 18 months, he conducted a sale so renowned that even in the early 1900s it was still being described as 'by far the most important sale of pictures ever held in Australia'.[2] The auction comprised the effects of the late Earl of Shannon from County Cork in Ireland and included works by Holbein, Canaletto, Gainsborough and Breughel. The collection had been sent to Sydney by Messrs. Burgess and Sons, proprietors of a Dublin warehouse. By about 1910, Lawson had acquired the title of 'national auctioneer' and Lawson's was credited with initiating the 'auction stage' in Australia.[3]

Lawson adopted a theatrical persona, following in the tradition of other great nineteenth-century auctioneers such as Christie, Stubbs and Lyons. He became famous for his attire, habitually wearing a top hat, frock-coat and pince-nez, with a carnation or red rosebud adorning his lapel, and gaining the appellation of the 'best-dressed auctioneer in Sydney'.[4] Lawson had humour and panache and his charismatic manner was satirized in the papers of the time. Carl Ruhen, who wrote a book on the history of Lawson's, concluded that 'James R. Lawson had brought a highly individual flair and showmanship to the auctioneering profession in Australia, which was to ensure for him a significant place…in the annals of the profession itself…'.[5] By 1918, Lawson's had strengthened its reputation for fine art auctions.

Max Lawson, James Robert's eldest son, rejoined the firm after World War I and obtained his auctioneer's licence in 1920, signalling the beginning of a long and illustrious career. The 'Man of the Week' article in *Smith's Weekly* on 27 November 1926 provided his father's obituary and concluded with comments on Max, referred to as the 'last of the auctioneers'.[6] Max Lawson continued the tradition of presenting himself impeccably, although he was 'more restrained' than his father.[7] He invariably wore a carnation or a pearl stickpin when auctioning and could adeptly sell 150 lots in an hour. He was charming, a great admirer of women and a popular after-dinner speaker. He not only paid attention to his own appearance and role as an auctioneer, but insisted that all his auctioneers be well trained, to the extent of having elocution lessons so that their enunciation was clear.

Views conflict on whether Max Lawson was himself an art collector. Ruhen said he was not, that he obeyed his father's edict that as an auctioneer one did not 'collect, deal or buy at auction'.[8] One newspaper article noted that Lawson began to collect in a minor way but William Ellenden, who worked for Lawson's from 1953 to 1973, maintained that Lawson was not a collector, but bid occasionally in order to purchase presents for others.[9] Like his father he believed in the differentiation between dealers, buyers and auctioneers and that one could be either an auctioneer or an art dealer, but not both.

Max Lawson contributed to the reinvention of the profession, endowing it once more with flair and making it newsworthy. For example, the *Daily Telegraph Pictorial* said of him that 'the auctioneer creates the atmosphere of a fairyland, and jauntily garbs himself with the mantle of a Santa Claus'.[10] *Smith's Weekly* claimed in 1920 that 'In the metropolis, which is the centre of Australia, the auctioneer of second-hand wardrobes and worn-out carpets has more immediate social importance than a Governor-General'.[11] This is interesting in terms of the changing social status of auctioneers. However, this comment seems to be anachronistic, as it was not really until much later that auctioneers became an integral part of high society. Furthermore, *Smith's Weekly* was a populist publication given to hyperbole.

The G. W. Eedy Sale

In 1921 James was still alive and Max was consolidating his career when Lawson's collaborated with James Tyrrell, a Sydney bookseller and art dealer, for the Eedy sale. They adopted innovative marketing techniques and set new standards for display. Porcelain from China and Japan, as well as other Chinoiserie and Japonisme were highly collectable at times. Tyrrell had a certain specialty in the field and after Captain G. W. Eedy, a collector of Oriental art, died Tyrrell collaborated with Lawson's to sell his collection on 11 October. Velvet drapes were used for the display of each lot, a practice which had been utilized overseas for some time but was an innovation for Sydney, and spotlights were employed. Tyrrell had catalogued the collection meticulously so that guarantees could be offered with each lot. Nevertheless, this cataloguing was criticized and was only vindicated after it was approved by London experts.[12] Tyrrell noted in his memoirs that Lawson had two reliable bidders in his saleroom; these were actually imaginary and conjured up only to stimulate bidding.[13] Thus even in the 1920s in Australia, taking pretend bids was already general practice, at least at Lawson's.

The W. A. Little Collection

William Augustus Little founded his own auctioneering business, specializing in furniture, fine art and general sales.[14] This was not unusual except that Little had become James Lawson's partner in March 1904. By October 1913, Lawson & Little was inviting people to private viewings, at least for art collections. The partnership ended in September 1915, however its fame endured. It was noted by a journalist in 1920 that Lawson had 'set a fashion in second-hand sales, which Mr Little himself has emulated'.[15]

It is uncertain whether Little was still in business as an auctioneer when Lawson's auctioned the collection of the firm's former partner over two sales in November 1926. Little had become enamoured of Europe and decided to sell everything in Sydney and move there permanently. It was presumably because of his ex-partner's reputation that Little chose to consign his collection to Lawson's and not his own or another firm. The works auctioned show that many Australians were still primarily collecting European art and that selling without setting reserve prices was still quite common practice in art auctions in the early to mid twentieth century.

Max Lawson provided good copy for the newspapers at the Little auction. According to *Smith's Weekly*:

> It was all an essay in the complete art of salesmanship. No bludgeoning; but it wasn't safe to meet Lawson's eye. No wheedling; but there was persuasion in every inflection of his voice. No fustian; but when he spoke of this 'bit' or that 'piece' not immediately to want it was to challenge the whole range of art values [and moreover] This last stage is accomplished so quickly, the inevitable impression is that the last bidder has got a bargain. Which again is salesmanship.[16]

The Little collection realised £10,000, with the highest price (425 guineas) paid for an Australian work, Hans Heysen's watercolour, *The Farm on the Hill*. Colour prints fared well at this sale and an illustrated catalogue was available for a small fee. The buyers were 'hard-headed dealers and knowledgeable amateurs', indicating that even in the 1920s, buyers at auction were generally either professionals or quite well educated laymen.[17]

The James T. Hackett Collection

Many salerooms held charity auctions for the War Effort during World War I, and Lawson's was no exception. One of its most auspicious auctions of this type was the James T. Hackett Collection in September 1918. Hackett, an Adelaide lawyer, had gathered his collection on overseas travels and decided against consigning it for sale in London because of the effects of the war on the market for collections of European art. He sent it to Sydney for auction because it was a 'better centre for buyers'.[18] This collection consisted mostly of European paintings, porcelain, bronzes and manuscripts and was marketed with the slogan, 'the finest art collection that has ever been dispersed in Australia'.[19] A note on page 3 of the auction catalogue said that 'In this Catalogue information or a detailed description of an object is given only where it seemed necessary...Paris, now as always, is the principal centre of the art world...'[20]

Most of the collection was sold without reserve prices, a practice often employed in the period, and it was announced that 25 per cent of the sales would be donated to the Red Cross. In fact, Hackett intended to donate most of the proceeds to various charities and war-related funds. He reiterated the difficulties of collecting European art, noting that:

> In this sale buyers have the great advantage of knowing that everything is genuine (unless otherwise stated). I, like others, had to purchase my experience at a high price. Over and over again I have had to weed doubtful things out of my collection, and these represented considerable sums of money. Anyone who buys at this sale is putting his money into the best of all investments.[21]

Despite the excellence of the collection, and the fact that collectors from throughout Australia attended, the sale did not achieve the prices Hackett hoped. Nonetheless, it was considered to be a milestone auction for some time afterwards.

The William Barclay Collection

By contrast, Lawson's auction of *Mr William Barclay's Collection of Magnificent Pictures* on 4 May 1937 raised issues regarding provenance and authenticity in a very public manner.[22] At this time, one of Lawson's conditions of sale was a veritable *caveat emptor* and made the auction house inviolable by making the buyer responsible for ascertaining the authenticity of a proposed purchase. The relevant condition of sale was number six:

> The lots to be taken away and paid for, whether genuine and authentic or not, with all faults and errors of description at the buyer's expense and risk, before 11am of day following sale, JAMES R. LAWSON not being responsible for the correct description, genuineness or authenticity of, or any fault or defect in any lot, and making no warranty whatever.[23]

The Barclay collection was touted as exceptional, mainly comprising works by European masters. The introduction to the auction catalogue was peppered with formulaic auctioneers' promotionalisms:

> Without doubt the finest of its kind to be offered by auction in Australia, this magnificent collection comprises works by some of the greatest English and Continental masters, each being a very fine and important example of the artist's best work…For the interest of collectors we have stated, wherever possible, the source from which they came, and where they have been exhibited…A unique opportunity…presents itself to all collectors and picture lovers to acquire paintings of rare merit and distinction at auction prices…[24]

The Sydney *Daily Telegraph* commissioned an art expert, Mr J. S. MacDonald, then Director of the National Gallery of Victoria, to analyze the paintings with particular emphasis on the accuracy of their catalogue entries. MacDonald's acid analysis was published by the paper on the day of the sale.[25] He claimed that most works were mediocre and that the authenticity of some, including Sir Joshua Reynolds' *Georgiana, Duchess of Devonshire* and Thomas Gainsborough's *The Coming Storm*, was highly questionable; furthermore, the *Daily Telegraph* pointed out no guarantees of authenticity were included in the conditions of sale.[26] It should be noted that MacDonald was renowned for being extremely conservative in his outlook and also condemned modern art in general. The resulting celebrity surrounding the sale ensured a huge crowd of voyeurs attended the auction.

The *Daily Telegraph's* umbrage at the auction practices displayed by this sale had a negative impact on its outcome although Max Lawson announced at the beginning of the sale that the vendor had declared that he would and could provide personal guarantees for the works.[27] Nevertheless, the sale result was dismal. Lawson was naturally livid and his comments were reproduced in the *Daily Telegraph* on the day following the sale. This article claimed that 'The auctioneer appears to have been annoyed, because, according to him, the public placed more reliance upon Mr MacDonald's expert opinions than on the glowing descriptions of the pictures printed in James R. Lawson's catalogue'.[28] The paper emphasized the lack of responsibility taken by the auctioneers and the claims in their catalogues were, therefore, worthless and without foundation.

Although the newspaper's and Mr MacDonald's motives for writing the exposé may not have been completely objective, the Barclay auction illustrates the unregulated nature of the art auction market and that auctioneers were presenting themselves as experts while rejecting the responsibility of guaranteeing authenticity. Legal writs were issued on behalf of the vendor, resulting in the eventual printing of a retraction by the *Daily Telegraph*, acknowledging that the catalogue had included information provided by the vendor and that the condition of sale accepting no liability for inauthentic works purchased 'was a usual condition inserted by reputable auctioneers at home and abroad'.[29] It was also clarified that the auctioneer had not deliberately intended to provide misleading information. Though this auction, like previous examples, illustrates developments and trends in the Australian art auction market, it was the Schureck sale in 1962 that was to have fundamental repercussions for this market.

The Norman Schureck Sale

It can be said that the sale of The Norman Schureck Collection held by Lawson's on 27 and 28 March 1962 stimulated an Australian art investment boom, with high prices notably attained for contemporary art. The value of the collection was estimated to be £30,000 but realized an amazing £81,858. It was, quite possibly, Lawson's most successful art auction and Max Lawson thought that it was 'one of the most interesting sales in 30 years'.[30]

Norman Schureck — who has variously been described as a professional importer of costume jewellery and textiles, an amateur painter and a cosmetics entrepreneur — has also been described as one of Australia's last major collectors of Australian art, amassing a collection of several hundred works spanning Old Masters and modern abstracts.[31] Schureck, in the tradition of Baldwin Spencer, was the patron of young Australian artists, especially William Dobell. He believed implicitly in Dobell's talent and frequented his nearby studio. Here he made a number of purchases of what Dobell thought of as lesser works or studies on the understanding that they would never be publicly exhibited.

Schureck was also a patron in the mediaeval sense of the word, inviting struggling artists around for dinner, buying their works and lending them money.[32] Schureck had loaned a number of works from his collection over the years, the most notable Loan Exhibition being that in 1958 at the (then) National Art Gallery of New South Wales. He had lived alone in his commodious fifteen-room apartment in Potts Point, which housed his art collection, as well as his collections of china, glass, ceramics, jade, Persian rugs and classical records. The highlight of the Schureck collection was undoubtedly Dobell's *Wangi Boy* 1948–9, which had been hung with pride over the fireplace in Schureck's drawing-room.

Schureck died suddenly. Just prior to his death he had been made a Trustee of the National Art Gallery of New South Wales and had expressed his intention to his solicitor to alter his will to allow for the donation of twelve paintings to the Gallery.[33] The Hebrew University, the major beneficiary of Schureck's will, donated one of Dobell's earliest works, *Saddle-my-Nag* (1941), to the National Art Gallery of New South Wales in order to honour Schureck's intentions.[34] Much of the collection was also given to Schureck's friends but a substantial amount was sent for auction by Perpetual Trustee Company Limited.

The Schureck sale contained 282 lots, the first 191 being oil paintings and the remainder watercolours, pastels, prints and lithographs. There were thirty-six works by Dobell, the largest collection of Dobells ever exhibited in Australia and the first time that works by Dobell had been offered, and thus tested, in the public marketplace. The auction house was thus functioning as a public gallery in a quasi-philanthropic role.

Most of the major galleries sent representatives to the auction and dealers were instructed to act as agents on behalf of both national and international clients. Approximately 750 to 1000 people attended the sale, with the saleroom full to overflowing. The press was in attendance, including society reporters. The hustle and bustle was too much for the distinguished silver specialist, Arthur Grimwade, one of Christie's London directors, who left early. Grimwade claimed that he did not intend to purchase anything but was there merely as a spectator; however, he was apparently very impressed by the prices attained at the auction, possibly paving the way for Christie's to establish an Australian office in 1969.[35] Roy Castle commented in the *Telegraph* that most people in Sydney seemed to have attended the auction and that it was the largest and most exciting art auction in Sydney in memory.[36]

Max Lawson skilfully marketed the collection. Desmond O'Grady and Vic Worstead from *The Bulletin* commented on the role of the auctioneer:

> The master of ceremonies was Max Lawson who conducted the sale with a combination of cheery business efficiency and corny-funny patter. Balding, bespectacled, black-suited, he alternately jolted and jollied the

audience with his barker's voice and amiable manner. If anyone raised a hand to his hair during bidding Lawson would rap out a warning: 'Don't do that or you'll finish up with a picture.' If bidding was slow he would offer to sit down and wait.[37]

While Lawson's role in assisting the escalation of prices through cajolery and repartee was widely reported by the press, *The Bulletin* appears to have retained the rather archaic opinion that auctioneers were not quite a respectable class, writing with what Ruhen described as 'patrician disdain'.[38]

The chief players of the auction, Sydney art dealers, Rudy Komon and Terry Clune and the millionaire Queensland pastoralist, Major Harold Du Vahl Rubin, waged an entertaining bidding war:

> Komon, standing near the auctioneer, in short sleeves and dark glasses, bid with a slight movement of the hand or even a nod of the head; Clune sat near the aisle towards the back of the room with a small group about him and bid with a determined salute; Major Rubin, dark-suited, small and restless, roved about the back of the room bidding from different spots by raising his catalogue to about chin level and waiting, with a puckish smile, until the opposition dropped out.[39]

The fact that Rudy Komon was also Dobell's agent suggests that he may have been manipulating the market by forcing prices for Dobells up through aggressive bidding. Clune purchased eight Dobells at a price of 14,605 guineas. Dobell's *Study for Woman in Restaurant*, one of his better-known paintings, had made £10 to £15 at its primary sale. On this secondary market it became a highly contested piece, eventually being knocked down to Clune for 4500 guineas with accompanying applause from the audience. This was cited as being an 'Australasian record' and was the highest price at the auction.[40]

Major Rubin already possessed the largest Dobell collection in the world, owning 63 paintings by the artist. Rubin was the auction's biggest buyer, purchasing 20 paintings in total for over 15,000 guineas, including five Dobells for 10,725 guineas. The Commonwealth Government purchased four paintings at the auction, including Dobell's study for the portrait of Dame Mary Gilmore, for 2100 guineas. Dobell believed that this work should never have been sold because it was only ever meant to be a rough study rather than an art work. The Australian Book Society, which had commissioned the work, gave the final portrait to Dame Mary Gilmore in 1957 and she, in turn, presented it to the National Art Gallery of New South Wales in December 1960.[41]

At the Schureck auction, prices for European works, traditionally the mainstay of the Australian art auction market, fetched prices that were diminutive in comparison to those for modern Australian works. Dobell was the highest selling artist. He was followed by the pre-Impressionist painter, Eugene Boudin, with his 15 paintings achieving almost 8200 guineas. A work by Courbet sold for just 420 guineas and *Rue à Montmartre* 1912 by Utrillo attained the paltry sum of 100 guineas.

The Dobell prices were incongruous, especially for a living artist, and bore 'no relation to the general market value of paintings either in Australia or Europe'.[42] However, the work of other artists, such as Sidney Nolan, Russell Drysdale and Leonard French, had also risen in status in recent years. It was suggested in the popular press that snobbery and ostentation played a major role in the high prices.[43] Schureck had originally paid between £500 and £600 for the Dobell paintings and they attained over £50,000 at the auction; this represented an investment return of 8000 per cent in under 25 years, exceptional by any standards. Dobell's painting palette was also included in the sale and sold for 15 guineas. This is a revealing commentary on the tantalizing lure and atmosphere of auctions and the desire for spectacle, coupled with the prospect of handsome investment returns (Figure 7).

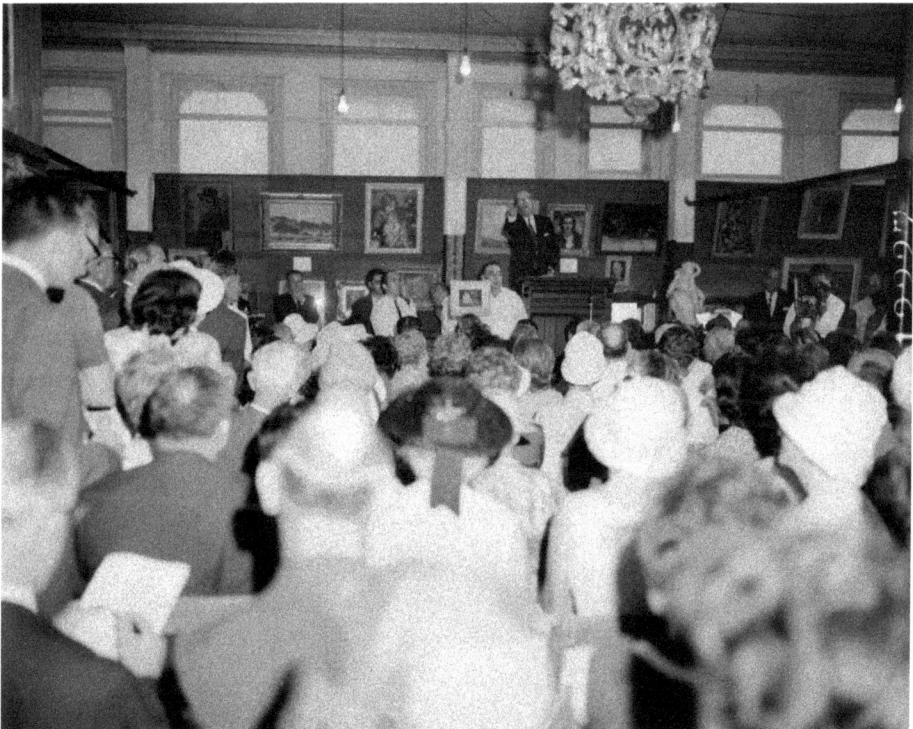

Figure 7: Jack Hickson, *Auction of the Norman Schureck collection of art, including paintings by Dobell, James R. Lawson (auctioneers), Sydney*, March 1962, photonegative, 10 x 12 cm, Australian Photographic Agency Collection, State Library of New South Wales.

The art auctions did seem to confirm to art dealers 'the nearly unlimited value of a star painter with a limited output'.[44] After World War II, dealers began to cement their territory in the market and from the late 1950s/early 1960s dealers like Rudy Komon introduced the 'stable system' to the gallery trade and advanced money to their artists.[45]

The Schureck sale signified a change in collecting tastes, with the works of contemporary Australian artists being highly prized. Though Ruhen claims that 'There had been nothing like it in the history of art auctions in Australia', the Baldwin Spencer auction had already demonstrated a keen awareness of and interest in contemporary Australian art in terms of both aesthetic and financial appreciation.[46] It appears, then, that this collecting taste had not been consolidated until the Schureck sale. It is claimed, in fact, that the sale of Dobells at the Schureck auction spawned a new emphasis on the reputation of artists, resulting in increasing numbers of solo exhibitions.[47] This can be contrasted with early colonial art auctions, where the name of the artist was often omitted.

The 1942 portrait of Norman Schureck by Dobell is just one of a number of paintings which demonstrate, through their subsequent travels through the marketplace, the effect that the Schureck sale had on market values. It sold to Major Rubin for 3000 guineas at the 1962 sale and was sold by Christie's for $11,000 in October 1972 at the first of Rubin's estate sales. *The Cockney Mother* sold in 1962 for 3000 guineas and fetched $27,000 at the Darrell Lea auction at Geoff K. Gray in February 1974. It is interesting to note that both these works were cited by Dobell as having been of some intrinsic value.[48]

Speculation that the sale was going to be phenomenal was rife for some time before the event, with rumours of syndicates of arbitrageurs being set up, intending to resell in London at a profit.[49] Prices for Australian art suddenly escalated and Dobell paintings became desirable currency. The *Sunday Telegraph* noted that a Sydney businessman had contacted an art dealer, saying, 'I want to buy a Dobell…I don't want to see the painting, and I don't care how much it costs. I just want to get in on this art racket'.[50]

Dobell himself seemed stunned by the prices paid for his paintings, thinking that the monetary values were inflated. He wryly commented after the auction that 'People have got more money than sense'.[51] He had originally sold all the paintings, except *Wangi Boy*, for no more than 15 to 20 guineas each. In Dobell's opinion, only five of his works in the auction were important pieces: *Wangi Boy* (purchased by Clune for 4000 guineas); *Saddle-my-Nag* (donated to the National Art Gallery of New South Wales prior to the auction); *The Cockney Mother* (purchased by Rubin for 3000 guineas); *My Lady Waits* (1700 guineas); and the portrait of Norman Schureck (purchased by Rubin for 3000 guineas).[52] These paintings had originally been sold for a total price of less than £230. Dobell was aghast that people would remember him by what he considered to be his inferior works, commenting that people could have bought far superior work at much cheaper prices by visiting him in his studio.[53] This is testament to the powerful aphrodisiac of the saleroom.

Dobell painted two versions of *Wangi Boy*, one with the boy lying down and another, which sold at the Schureck sale, with the boy standing near a boat. Reportage of these two works has been confused. According to Christie's and Sotheby's catalogues, the earliest version was of the boy standing; however, according to a news report, the depiction of the boy lying was the earliest painting and the one which Dobell had not liked.[54] The subject of the painting, Dobell's nephew, claimed that because Dobell was not convinced by the painting's merits, he later made another *Wangi Boy* painting, which Dobell thought to be one of his most important works.[55] The Schureck *Wangi Boy* later sold at Sotheby's on 26 July 1987 for $240,000 and again at Sotheby's Rivkin sale on 3 June 2001 for $200,000, against an estimate of $250,000–$350,000 (Figure 8).

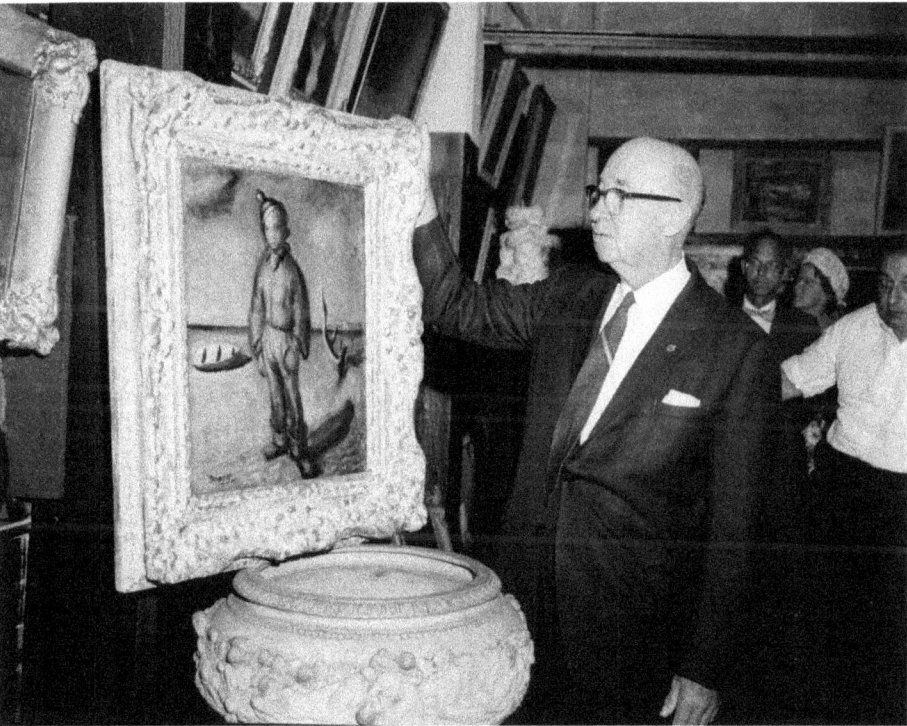

Figure 8: Jack Hickson, *Auction of the Norman Schureck collection of art, including paintings by Dobell, (here, Wangi Boy), James R. Lawson (auctioneers), Sydney*, March 1962, photonegative, 10 x 12 cm, Australian Photographic Agency Collection, State Library of New South Wales.

The auction had implications for the general Australian art market. Most importantly, it brought the concept of *droît de suite*, or art resale royalty, into the public arena, with Rudy Komon noting that in Europe artists would receive a commission when their works sold on the secondary market.[56] (An art resale royalty is back on the agenda under the new Labor Government.) A royalty was most pertinent to Dobell's situation, as he had sold his works for a paltry sum while the Schureck estate reaped huge rewards. In the wake of this sale, Australian dealers anticipated that the Australian art market would emulate the European one where paintings were quoted on an art exchange and auctions were glamorous multi-million dollar affairs.[57]

According to art historian Christopher Heathcote, the sale also directly informed the art collection policies of corporations and resulted in the injection of larger amounts of capital into art prizes sponsored by both governmental and corporate bodies.[58] Max Lawson, who had never seen anything like the mania surrounding the Schureck sale, noted that it would have a monumental effect on the market for Australian art.[59] It demonstrated the vast investment opportunities presented by collecting contemporary Australian art, particularly works by Dobell, Drysdale, Boyd and Nolan, who had arguably established minor reputations internationally.[60]

Leonard Joel

Leonard Joel, a Melbourne-based general auction house, was founded in the first quarter of the twentieth century and became renowned for its art sales, especially from the 1960s onwards. Three generations of two families shaped the firm; Leonard, Graham and Warren Joel and Tom, Paul and Jon Dwyer. Tom Dwyer worked at Gemmell, Tuckett & Co. from 1906, joining Leonard Joel in 1920 in its first year of operation. However, the Dwyers never had a controlling interest in the firm, which was completely owned by the Joel family. Leonard Joel held weekly general sales and three major art auctions each year, as well as estate sales and smaller specialist sales. Although a Victorian firm, Leonard Joel reached a national audience with people from around Australia regularly attending the art sales.

By the 1960s Leonard Joel was generally known as the major paintings specialist in the Australian auction world and thus virtually monopolized this market until the arrival of Christie's. One could argue that, notwithstanding Lawson's Schureck sale, Leonard Joel had no real competition for supremacy of the paintings market until the advent of Sotheby's in the 1980s. The paintings department was established around 1962 and was run almost as a separate business.[61] Their marathon art auctions at the Malvern Town Hall were a veritable Melbourne institution. Paul Dwyer had the reputation of being the pre-eminent expert in Australian paintings and fine art formed the nucleus of

Leonard Joel's business with jewellery and furniture a large part of the firm's general business.[62]

Leonard Joel's art auction catalogues were traditionally small and devoid of illustrations, except perhaps the occasional black and white one; they were basically stapled checklists without any estimates. The year of the auction was often not included in the catalogues, implying that no or little thought was given to posterity and the scholarship value of the publications. This was customary until the late 1960s. Later on, when catalogues were more lavishly illustrated, there was less need for prospective buyers to view the works in person, leading to more telephone bidding and a reliance on the authority of the auction house as embodied in the art auction catalogue. Leonard Joel changed its policy for the sales of the Charles Ruwolt and George Page-Cooper collections and these catalogues were of an exceptional standard for the 1960s.

The Charles Ruwolt Collection

Charles Ruwolt was an engineer and industrialist, as well as a prominent collector of Australian art. The art collection had adorned Ruwolt's New South Wales homestead. The Charles Ruwolt Collection of Australian Paintings was sold by order of The National Trustees, stalwart providers of estate sales for Leonard Joel, at Leonard Joel's rooms at 17 McKillop Street, Melbourne on 17 November 1966.

The sale comprised most of Ruwolt's collection of historical works, covering the Heidelberg School, late colonial and modernist paintings. The catalogue foreword noted that Charles and Emily Ruwolt built up the collection in the 1920s and 1930s and it is possible that they were inspired by the high prices obtained for Australian art at the Baldwin Spencer auction and may thus have had investment in mind from the outset. According to the catalogue:

> The unique offering of Streetons is in itself the most impressive that has been offered since the Baldwin Spencer Collection in 1919. All the pictures in this offering are outstanding works, and although some of the great names in Australian traditional art are missing, the Collection is the most important to have been offered for many years.[63]

In addition to Streeton, the collection included works by William Beckwith McInnes, David Davies, Elioth Gruner, Heysen, Blamire Young, Norman Lindsay, Louis Buvelot, McCubbin and Tom Roberts. The catalogue foreword also noted that the auction included a few works not from the Ruwolt collection.

Interestingly, the eight illustrations were not in any particular order but were dispersed at intervals throughout the catalogue. Most of the artists were marketed with a paragraph of biographical information, including life dates, training, prizes, exhibitions and gallery representation. The colour illustrations, which signified what the auctioneers considered to be the most significant works in the auction, were for two works by Streeton, *Coogee* (1890) and *Hawkesbury River* (1896). The presentation of the catalogue, the respect paid to local artists and the provenance of a single-owner collection made this art auction of considerable importance at the time.

The George Page-Cooper Sale

Another auction which assisted with establishing a taste for investing in Australian art, and was promoted with a comparatively sumptuous catalogue, was that of the George Page-Cooper Collection held on 21–22 November 1967. This estate sale was also Leonard Joel's first art auction in the Malvern Town Hall, which became the venue for the firm's art sales. It realized an impressive $141,000 from 404 works covering the gamut of Australian art from the colonial period to the contemporary era. Admission to the sale was 20 cents, with the proceeds donated to the Alfred Hospital Centenary Appeal. Over 500 people attended the auction, with collectors not limited to Victoria, but hailing from throughout Australia.

George Page-Cooper was Director of Tye's Gallery in Melbourne from about 1945 to 1954, as well as a keen collector of Australian and international paintings, drawings and documents. Page-Cooper had assembled his collection from the early 1930s until the mid-1960s and he was a visible presence at art auctions during that period. A contemporary news report commented:

> He was a familiar figure in the city's auction rooms, generally wearing a battered hat and an open neck shirt. Every so often he would bid for a picture and take it off to his home in Kew. But no-body ever was invited in to view his collection. It was rumored to be fabulous. Fuel was added to the rumors when, to settle an argument about an artist's style, Mr. Page-Cooper would bring a picture into the city from Kew and show it to the arguing parties. It might be a Burn, or a Gill or a Buvelot or any of a dozen famous Australian artists.[64]

Page-Cooper's collection had been crammed into his home at Kew, with four rooms filled to overflowing and paintings hanging on picture rails and occupying any available space on walls and floors. There was no order to the arrangement and, unfortunately, no catalogue of the collection made by Page-Cooper, although he did note on the backs of works from where he had acquired them. He had treasured his collection so much that when he had moved from Richmond to Kew, about six years prior to his death, he transported all the paintings himself in around two hundred car trips.

Page-Cooper sold a number of works during his lifetime. Most of his collection of international art had been sold over five auctions at the Melbourne Town Hall in 1926, indicating that he was presumably changing his focus to collecting

Australian art from this time onwards, after the success of the Baldwin Spencer auction had set a new trend for Australian art. Page-Cooper also disposed of a number of paintings in the early to mid-1960s, but none from his core collection of Australian art which he had obviously cherished. The last auction of his estate was that of his historical paintings of Australian art, especially nineteenth century art, by order of The National Trustees, Melbourne in 1967.

The auction, although named as being of paramount importance to the development of a taste for Australian paintings at auction in Australia, does not appear to have been covered widely by the press of the time. Sotheby's and Christie's in London were beginning to embrace the media in the 1960s. However, Australia was yet to follow suit. The scarcity of concrete, analytical information was still somewhat surprising, considering that it was reportedly 'the most expensive auction of Australian art held in Melbourne'.[65] Furthermore, Leonard Joel stated at the time that the 'auction was unprecedented in Australian history, both in importance and in prices paid'.[66]

Works by S. T. Gill, Louis Buvelot, Conder and Streeton attained some of the highest prices: Conder's *Figure in the Sun* achieved $6000 on the first day of the auction and Streeton's *Early Sydney Harbour Scene with Figures* sold for $5250 on the second day. The Australian artist, James A. Turner's, *Australian Pioneers* sold for $1200, signifying, according to Ingram, 'the rewards that can be made even when paintings are not selected with any consideration as to aesthetics'.[67] Furthermore, *Colonial Buildings, Hobart 1853* by the Norwegian-born artist and drawing teacher Knut [Knud] Bull, sold for $90 at the Page-Cooper sale and re-sold at Leonard Joel in 1991 for $77,000, reflecting both the quality of the painting and a dramatic rise in opinion of its monetary and aesthetic value.

The layout of the catalogue was fairly innovative, with short biographical entries on many of the artists in the collection compiled in an encyclopedic manner and including the general Australian art history references used to obtain the information. The conditions of sale and title page were followed by a biographical page on Page-Cooper by Graham Joel. Dispersed throughout the catalogue were ten illustrations, four of which were in colour: Buvelot's *Victorian Landscape*, (1872); Gill's *Night Concert, Main Road, Ballarat*, (1854) (sold for $2000); Henry Burn's *Old Punt Road*, (1869); and Frederick McCubbin's *Stone Crusher, Richmond Quarry* (1908). Each entry included the artist's name, title of the work, medium, dimensions and basic provenance where known. Including estimates in the catalogues in the next decade added another element to the spectatorship of auctions, so that one could compare the sales prices to the estimates at the time of the auction, intensifying the sense of awe and immediacy. Hearing the hammer fall, with no figure for comparison, was not nearly as exciting for the audience. However, it was generally known at the Page-Cooper sale that the prices were considered unusually high and it 'is now known as the foundation sale of historical Australian art'.[68] Even then, a couple of news articles focused on a provision in Page-Cooper's will that his dog, Darkie, be well cared for after his death. George Page-Cooper was thus known as much for his love of his dog as for the art collection.

Trends in the Australian Art Auction Market in the 1960s and '70s

O'Grady and Worstead said in 1962 that 'As middle-men in the art world...the dealers occupy a crucial position, particularly in Australia where art auctions are few. Overseas, auctions theoretically provide an index to market values but here dealers keep such information largely to themselves'.[69] This is revealing of the *status quo* in the Australian art market of the 1960s.

The broad art market (that is, the commercial dealers and the auction houses) prospered in the wake of the 1962 Schureck sale, with a rapid surge in interest in art as an investment. However, while the general art boom continued, the art auctions began to suffer because prices were too high at one extreme, pushed up by a handful of wealthy collectors like Major Rubin, or too low at the other, causing vendors to choose an alternative means of disposal, where their lots were given more prominence than they were in long-winded general auctions.[70]

Taste in the 1960s was conservative on the whole, but a growing emphasis on art education and awareness and scholarship became intertwined with market sophistication; major paintings auctions became eminently newsworthy, often attaining front-page status. The art market was also relatively sedate prior to the arrival of Christie's and Sotheby's, as the art market boom did not really begin until the mid-1970s. After the Schureck, Ruwolt and Page-Cooper sales in the 1960s, a number of important auctions were conducted in the early 1970s — the Major de Vahl Rubin sales at Christie's in October 1972 and October 1973, the Dobell sale at Sotheby's in November 1973 and the Sim Rubensohn sale at Lawson's in June 1973.

In the international context, Australian art had also been displayed in *Art of Australia, 1788–1941*, an exhibition which travelled in North America in 1941 sponsored by the Carnegie Corporation. While Australian art had been shown in London previously, the press at the time reported that the international interest in Australian art and its market could be pinpointed to three major events from the early 1960s: the exhibition of contemporary Australian art at London's Whitechapel Galleries in June 1961; The Tate Gallery's exhibition of Australian art previewed at the 1962 Adelaide Festival of Arts; and the Schureck sale in 1962.[71] These events, particularly the Whitechapel exhibition, which received critical acclaim from the British press, arguably made contemporary Australian art more visible and took it onto the world stage. This having been said, there appears to have been a difference between what the Australian press reported about the impact of Australian art on the international marketplace and the reality. Australian art, then and now, with the notable exception of Aboriginal and Torres Strait Islander art, has a comparatively minimal presence internationally.

The Australian auction houses appear to have made a decision to concentrate their business efforts on retailing to the private collector, a deviation from the traditional saleroom audience in London, which comprised mainly dealers.[72] This is substantiated by Ellenden who claimed that most buyers at auction in Australia in the 1960s and early 1970s were private collectors and not professionals.[73] Furthermore, Australian bidders at auction, unlike their international counterparts, had not generally been involved in forcing up prices at auction prior to the Schureck sale in 1962. The Schureck sale thus introduced a new breed of buyer to the art auction market, that of the investor/speculator, who was instrumental in the escalation of prices for the works of contemporary artists at auction. However, it was later emphasized in various news reports that Christie's began to woo the private collector when it arrived in 1969 and that this market had been underdeveloped prior to this, which seems to contradict earlier reports.

Some indeed maintained that despite the professed international interest in Australian art, Australia itself was insular:

> The extraordinary belief persists in some quarters that the 'sixties will go down in the world's art history as some sort of 'Antipodean' period, although it developed from, and is only part of, a general revival and broadening of interest in the Western world which began in the early 'fifties. The Australian art scene remains inbred, ingrown, a world and a law unto itself...[74]

This was concurrent with the general sophistication of the art world, an international phenomenon which began to permeate the Australian art market in a 'fragmentary fashion' in the 1960s, transforming painting into 'another slick branch of show business'.[75] However, auctions and auction houses in Australia differed from those overseas in the 1960s in terms of status within the art market. The Australian art world was 'fragmented' and 'disorganized' compared to that overseas, where large-scale, glamorous and vastly expensive art auctions would make the Schureck sale appear trivial.[76]

Expatriate Australian author and art critic, Robert Hughes, said in 1972 that the paintings market in Sydney was better than in New York and that 'New York is no longer the beginning and end of the art world'.[77] Earlier, in 1964, Hughes claimed, mainly in relation to Dobell, that 'No Australian painter has won an international reputation yet and there's no automatic cachet on Australian painters overseas. But they have to go if they want to become part of world art rather than a rather meaningless hero figure in Australian art'.[78] Moreover, 'Australian art had been briefly in vogue in London in 1961' and the only artists with any international recognition were Brett Whiteley and Clement Meadmore, with a burgeoning reputation in London for artists such as Arthur Boyd.[79] Hughes also said that the only reason that works by some Australian artists had sold for decent prices in exhibitions overseas was because the overseas' price-tags were lower than those placed in Australia and that most works sold to Australian dealers engaging in arbitrage.[80]

It was owing to what Annette Van den Bosch defines as the Australian buyers' general 'inexperience' that some Australian auction houses had offered guarantees on works purchased at auction, not only because of the lack of knowledge of the collectors, but also because huge amounts of inferior and forged works abounded in the salerooms in the 1960s.[81] Therefore, it was perhaps in opposition to the furore surrounding the lack of guarantees provided by Lawson's for the Barclay sale in 1937, that the money-back guarantee of authenticity was an attractive feature of the 1960s art auction market with Warren Elstub, from Geoff K. Gray's paintings department, pointing out the difficulty in obtaining accurate information on Australian artists, saying that 'Australian auctioneers…claim expertise only in auctioneering'.[82] However, O'Grady and Worstead thought that buyers would obtain a fairer deal by purchasing art through dealers in Australia rather than auctioneers, as Australian auctioneers were not required to provide guarantees of authenticity, unlike their European counterparts.[83]

Included in Geoff K. Gray's art auction catalogues from the 1960s was a 'special condition of sale', a three-week money-back guarantee of authenticity, which the firm was offering prior to the arrival of Christie's. In comparison, in the late 1960s, for example at the Page-Cooper sale in 1967, Leonard Joel stipulated that it offered no guarantees in its sixth condition of sale: 'No claim for damage, misdescription, genuineness or authenticity of or errors of any description will be entertained. Purchasers are, therefore, particularly requested to examine the lots before purchasing. All lots at the risk of the purchaser immediately on the fall of the hammer'.[84]

Australian art dealers criticized art auctions in the 1960s for being 'too tedious and too scruffy', saying that the bidders were mainly uneducated 'bargain hunters' and that catalogues often contained errors.[85] Hoad asserted in *The Bulletin* in 1968 that 'The weakness of the Australian auction system is really no more than a part of the general weakness in scholarship and discrimination, the lack of confidence and the madly fluctuating price structures that result'.[86]

Sotheby's began to have a presence in Melbourne in 1968 and Christie's was also in 1968 considering establishing an Australian office after the resounding success of its first telephone link-up sale with London. It is interesting that dealers were apparently delighted with the prospect that Christie's would hold proper auctions in Australia — that is, not telephone sales — and that, by contrast, one can therefore assume that they were dissatisfied with the *status quo*. Hoad believed that:

> …should Sotheby's and Christie's decide to set up art auctions here – and for the moment there is a note of caution in the air, a slightly bitter taste of money, markets, and material misjudged – knowledgeable entrepreneurs and a well-informed art public are two essential ingredients of a successful auction system which they cannot supply.[87]

However, this is arguably exactly what Christie's and Sotheby's did do.

ENDNOTES

[1] See the foreword by Leslie Walford, 23 August 1984, in Carl Ruhen, *The Auctioneers: Lawsons – The First 100 Years*, Ayers and James Heritage Books and James R. Lawson Pty Ltd, Sydney 1984, p.7, see also p.19.

[2] Ruhen, *The Auctioneers*, p.30.

[3] See, for example, Author unknown, 'Man of the Week — Knight of the Hammer', *Smith's Weekly*, 23 October 1920, p.2 and Ruhen, *The Auctioneers*, p.45, respectively.

[4] See James R. Tyrrell, *Old Books, Old Friends, Old Sydney*, Angus and Robertson, Sydney 1952, p.177.

[5] Ruhen, *The Auctioneers*, p.72.

[6] Author unknown, 'The Man of the Week — A King in his Kingdom', *Smith's Weekly*, 27 November 1926, p.2.

[7] Author unknown, 'A King in his Kingdom', p.2.

[8] See Ruhen, *The Auctioneers*, p.102.

[9] Author unknown, 'A King in his Kingdom', p.2 and William S. Ellenden, 'Reminiscences of an Auctioneer', *The Australasian Antique Collector*, 20th ed., 1980, pp.125–33.

[10] *Daily Telegraph Pictorial*, 22 February 1928, p.8.

[11] Author unknown, 'Knight of the Hammer', p.2.

[12] See Tyrrell, *Old Books, Old Friends, Old Sydney*, p.176.

[13] Tyrrell, *Old Books, Old Friends, Old Sydney*, p.177.

[14] He advertised in the *Sydney Morning Herald* on 21 September 1915, p.4. The dissolution of the Lawson & Little partnership was noted on the same page.

[15] Author unknown, 'Knight of the Hammer', p.2.

[16] Author unknown, 'A King in his Kingdom', p.2.

[17] Author unknown, 'A King in his Kingdom', p.2.

[18] See Author unknown, 'Hackett Art Collection', p.5. For daily newspaper updates of the sale's progress see *The Sun*, 17, 18, 19, 20 September 1918.

[19] Author unknown, 'Hackett Art Collection', *The Sun*, 17 September 1918, p.5.

[20] James R. Lawson, *Catalogue of J. T. Hackett's Art Collection*, Sydney, 17 September 1918 and following days.

[21] This note was made by Hackett on a copy of the catalogue which he sent to Lawson's and was reproduced in Ruhen, *The Auctioneers*, p.52.

[22] See Ruhen, *The Auctioneers*, chapter 14, 'A Matter of Provenance', pp.113-118.

[23] James R. Lawson, *Mr William Barclay's Collection of Magnificent Pictures*, Sydney, 4 May 1937.

[24] James R. Lawson, *Mr William Barclay's Collection*, 4 May 1937.

[25] On MacDonald see Patricia Anderson, *Art + Australia: Debates, Dollars & Delusions*, Pandora Press, Sydney 2005, pp.136–139.

[26] Author unknown, 'Art Critic Issues Warning to Buyers — Questions the Claims Made in Catalogue of Today's Big Sale — Doubts if Gainsborough and Reynolds Painted Pictures Credited to Them', *Daily Telegraph*, late edition, 4 May 1937, p.1, 6.

[27] Ruhen, *The Auctioneers*, p.116.

[28] Author unknown, 'Art Criticism Causes Stir — Public Heeded Our Expert's Warning — Auctioneer's Abuse of Critic Failed to Keep up Prices', *Daily Telegraph*, late edition, 5 May 1937, p.1.

[29] Ruhen, *The Auctioneers*, p.118.

[30] Author unknown, 'What price a Dobell?', *Woman's Day with Woman*, 26 March 1962, p.3.

[31] See Ray Castle, 'Norman Schureck dies — Australian art loses great patron', *Daily Telegraph*, 10 August 1962, no pagination and Terry Ingram, *A Matter of Taste — Investing in Australian Art*, William Collins Publishers, Sydney 1976, p.56.

[32] See Author unknown, 'He was among the first to recognise Dobell's talent', *Sun-Herald*, 11 February 1962, no pagination.

[33] Author unknown, 'Old Masters: New Plans', *Sydney Morning Herald*, 3 February 1962, no pagination.

[34] Author unknown, 'Early Dobell for Art Gallery', *Sydney Morning Herald*, 16 March 1962, no pagination.

[35] Author unknown, 'Art auction besieged', *Daily Mirror*, 27 March 1962, p.2.

[36] See Ray Castle, 'Goes to the Art Auction and Comes Away Musing: Money-wise, Dobell was not in the picture', *Daily Telegraph*, 28 March 1962, no pagination.

[37] Desmond O'Grady and Vic Worstead, 'Investment in Art — A Sound New Business', *The Bulletin*, 14 April 1962, p.13.

[38] Ruhen, *The Auctioneers*, p.130.

[39] O'Grady and Worstead, 'Investment in Art', p.13.

[40] Unspecified experts at the time made this claim, which was noted by Author Unknown, '£50,000 auction: artist got £600', *Daily Telegraph*, 28 March 1962, p.1 and Ruhen, *The Auctioneers*, p.129.

[41] Author unknown, '£50,000 auction', p.3, under the banner of 'Utrillo low price a surprise'.

[42] Author unknown, 'Snobs! — Dobell's in the fashion', *Daily Mirror*, 28 March 1962, p.3.

[43] Author unknown, 'Snobs!', p.3.

[44] See Author unknown, 'The Art Plantations', p.15.

[45] See Philippa Kelly, 'Women at Auction', *Art Monthly Australia*, no. 150, June 2002, p.5 and Author unknown, *The First Gallery in Paddington*. For a discussion of the wider Australian economy at this time see Annette Van den Bosch, *The Australian Art World: Aesthetics in a global market*, Allen & Unwin, Sydney 2005.

[46] Ruhen, *The Auctioneers*, p.130.

[47] See Kathryn Chiba, 'Dr Joseph Brown: Dealing in Cultural Capital', MA thesis, University of Melbourne 1999, 2 vols, vol. 1, pp.60–1.

[48] Author unknown, '£50,000 auction', p.3, under the banner of 'Utrillo low price a surprise'.

[49] See O'Grady and Worstead, 'Investment in Art', pp.13–16.

[50] Quoted in Barnes, 'An 8000 per cent dividend in 25 years', p.17.

[51] This was widely quoted, including in Ruhen, *The Auctioneers*, p.127; Barnes, 'An 8000 per cent dividend in 25 years', p.17; and Author unknown, 'Snobs!', p.3.

[52] See Author unknown, 'William Dobell chooses his favourite Dobells', *Sydney Morning Herald*, 20 June 1964, no pagination.

[53] See Ruhen, *The Auctioneers*, p.132.

[54] Christie's, *Australian and European Paintings*, Sydney, 17–18 August 1998; Sotheby's, *The Collection of Mr and Mrs René Rivkin*, Sydney, 3 June 2001; and Author unknown, 'Dobell "disliked" his Wangi Boy', *Sydney Morning Herald*, 15 February 1974, p.3.

[55] Author unknown, 'Dobell "disliked" his Wangi Boy', p.3.

[56] See Castle, 'Goes to the Art Auction and Comes Away Musing', no pagination.

[57] See Barnes, 'An 8000 per cent dividend in 25 years', p.17.

[58] Christopher Heathcote, *A Quiet Revolution – The Rise of Australian Art 1946–1968*, Text Publishing Company, Melbourne 1995, p.157.

[59] See, for example, Author unknown, 'Art auction besieged', p.2.

[60] See Annette Van den Bosch, 'The Art Market since 1940 – A Model of the Relationships between Key Players and the Interactions Between Aesthetic and Financial Values', PhD thesis, Department of Fine Arts, University of Sydney, June 1989, 2 vols, vol. 2, p.6.

[61] Jon Dwyer, taped interview with the author, Melbourne, 23 October 2002 and Kate Joel, taped interview with the author, Melbourne, 25 October 2002.

[62] Author unknown, 'Graham and Warren Joel will sell your jewels or your junk', *Sydney Morning Herald*, Good Weekend, 9 November 1985, pp.76–81.

[63] Leonard Joel, *The Charles Ruwolt Collection of Australian Paintings*, Melbourne, 17 November 1966.

[64] John Hamilton, 'Briefing', *The Age*, 14 September 1967, p.4.

[65] See Author unknown, 'Record city art sale', p.3.

[66] See Author unknown, 'Record city art sale', p.3.

[67] Ingram, *A Matter of Taste*, p.83.

[68] Leonard Joel, 'Twenty Years at the Malvern Town Hall', 4-5 November 1987, no pagination.

[69] O'Grady and Worstead, 'Investment in Art', p.15.

[70] See Author unknown, 'The Art Plantations – How gallery directors cultivate the boom', *Nation*, 16 October 1965, pp.15–16.

[71] Author unknown, 'Interest from Overseas', *Sydney Morning Herald*, 16 July 1962, p.58.

[72] Terry Ingram, 'Australia Goes To Auction...Offshore', *Australian Art Collector*, issue 4, April–June 1998, p.70.

[73] See Ellenden, 'Reminiscences of an Auctioneer', p.126.

[74] Brian Hoad, 'Playing the Art Market', *The Bulletin*, 27 July 1968, p.28.

[75] Hoad, 'Playing the Art Market', p.29.

[76] O'Grady and Worstead, 'Investment in Art', p.15.

[77] See Derryn Hinch, 'Robert Hughes rampant – New York, he says, is not America', *Sydney Morning Herald*, 1 July 1972, p.18.

[78] Ron Saw, 'No longer a boom at the top – Artists now share the jackpot', *Mirror* (Sydney), 5 June 1964, no pagination.

[79] This was stated by Robert Hughes when he was interviewed on the ABC's Guest of Honour programme and summarized in various articles, including Author unknown, 'Australian flavour "hopeless" factor in art', *Sydney Morning Herald*, 31 July 1972, p.12.

[80] Terry Ingram, 'Robert Hughes on local art – The high cost of chauvinism', *Australian Financial Review*, 31 July 1972, p.7.

[81] Van den Bosch, *The Art Market since 1940*, vol. 2, pp.5–6. See also Annette Van den Bosch, *The Australian Art World: Aesthetics in a Global Market*, Allen & Unwin, Sydney 2005, p. 45.

[82] Hoad, 'Playing the Art Market', p.33.

[83] O'Grady and Worstead, 'Investment in Art', p.15.

[84] Leonard Joel, *The George Page-Cooper Collection*, 21–22 November 1967.

[85] See Hoad, 'Playing the Art Market', pp.32–3.

[86] Hoad, 'Playing the Art Market', p.33.

[87] Hoad, 'Playing the Art Market', p.33.

Chapter 5. Christie's Australia

The commercialization and global expansion of Christie's and Sotheby's post-World War II laid the foundation for many methods and practices adopted in art auctions in Australia, particularly after the arrival of Christie's in 1969.

The key figure in establishing an Australian branch of Christie's was the Australian-born William Spowers, who essentially co-founded it with Len Voss Smith in April 1969. Spowers had been educated at Geelong Grammar in Victoria and joined the Army in 1942, transferring to the British Army the following year. While serving in the army overseas, he subsidized his pay by buying books and manuscripts and selling them in London. This is how he first encountered Christie's, which he joined after leaving the Grenadier Guards in 1960. In 1970, he was Director of the Department of Books and Manuscripts at Christie's in London, as well as a Director of Christie's Australian branch. Herbert described Spowers as 'Immaculately dressed in his black suit, stiff collar and exciting striped shirts and with a diamond-mounted pin keeping his tie in place, he did not appear suited to the world of antiquarian books. Although somewhat small of stature he looked far more of a dashing blade'.[1] Spowers was an extraordinarily colourful figure — while cataloguing the Northwick Park library, Spowers had brought his mono-ski with him tied to the top of his Rolls Royce and proceeded to water-ski on the lake at Northwick Park.

Spowers had close family ties with Australia and his relationship with his godfather the then Governor-General, Lord Casey, was instrumental in the appointment of Christie's initial Australian representatives; Sue Hewitt and Joan McClelland, were approached on the recommendation of Casey's wife after Spowers consulted her.

Spowers believed that a Sydney branch of Christie's could provide a service to Australian collectors by securing Australiana (Australian art, books and manuscripts) in Europe and auctioning them directly in an Australian saleroom. Half the books and manuscripts in Christie's March 1970 auction, for example, were obtained from Britain. Christie's aimed to provide the means for these Australian items to return to Australia at minimal cost to the buyer, bypassing the involvement of art dealers, who had built up a lucrative business in sourcing items at auctions in England for sale in Australia at often double their auction price.[2] This was an innovation for the Australian art auction market and placed Christie's in competition with some dealers and the existing regime, despite the fact that many dealers had reportedly initially welcomed the firm's arrival.

Len Voss Smith, Spowers's co-founder of Christie's in Australia, was a Melbourne businessman, dealer, publisher and collector of Australian and European art. According to Ingram, 'Monocled, blazered and with a moderately intimidating air, Len Voss Smith was very much the image of a Christie's gentleman, except that this very thin man tended to hold his trousers up with string even in the office'.[3] Christie's London Directors — Spowers, Jo Floyd (Chairman) and Guy Hannen (Deputy Chairman) — approached Voss Smith to gauge his interest as soon as they decided to open an Australian saleroom. Joan McClelland was chosen as Christie's first Melbourne representative and Sue Hewitt as the Sydney representative.

McClelland had taken over the running of the Joshua McClelland Print Room in 1956, following the death of her husband. She left Christie's at the end of 1972 to concentrate on running the Print Room, partly owing to the increasing difficulty in separating sourcing stock for the Print Room and for Christie's.[4] McClelland's and Hewitt's work involved garnering paintings for auction and liaising with Voss Smith, who was the overall Australian representative and who established the main office in Sydney.

Voss Smith also had strong ties with England where he had gone to live in the early 1960s, returning to Australia in 1969, when he established Christie's. Voss Smith had been the Australian representative for Hutchinson publishers and in this capacity was instrumental in convincing his London office to publish Alan McCulloch's mammoth *Encyclopedia of Australian Art* in 1968. (He was also involved in commissioning one of the most famous Australian paintings, Russell Drysdale's *The Cricketers*, which was commissioned in 1948 for Sir Walter Hutchinson. Sir Walter was reportedly dissatisfied with the work.)

Voss Smith only managed Christie's until about 1970, when he returned to live in London, operating as Christie's consultant on Australian art until about 1979; he then returned once more to live in Sydney. John Henshaw then became the Australian representative of Christie's, running the picture department both in Melbourne and Sydney. Prior to this, Henshaw was the editor of art books at Lansdowne Press, art critic for *The Australian* and an art teacher at East Sydney Technical College.

As an aside, some of the Voss Smith collection was sold by Sotheby's and not by Christie's as one might have expected, in November 1988. The $5.7 million estate sale included, as its star attraction, Arthur Boyd's *The Little Train* (1950) which sold for $250,000, its upper estimate. *The Little Train* is named as the greatest of Boyd's work during the period and has been hung in numerous exhibitions including in The Whitechapel Gallery in London in 1962, the Boyd Retrospective at the Art Gallery of South Australia in 1964 and at an exhibition of Australian paintings and tapestries at New South Wales House in The Strand in London in 1972. It was also later sold at Sotheby's in Melbourne in 1998 for $200,500 (estimate $180,000–$220,000) and was passed-in at Deutscher-Menzies in Sydney in 2004 (estimate $340,000–$380,000). Approximately 100 other works from the Voss Smith Collection were later sold by Sotheby's in August 1997.

Although the items offered in 1988 were predominantly European, Sotheby's decided to auction them in Australia, hopeful that their celebrated provenance would convince Australian collectors to purchase international art, as Voss Smith himself had attempted to cultivate a taste in Australia for such works at an earlier date.[5]

Sue Hewitt was approached by Christie's Directors Jo Floyd and Guy Hannen who were visiting Australia in early 1969 while she was working at Government House, Canberra. She agreed to join Christie's when she finished her job in September 1969, prior to the inaugural auction. Her initial role was as Office Manager of the Sydney operation, assisting first Voss Smith and then Henshaw. She held various high positions at Christie's over the years, appointed as the Manager of Christie, Manson & Woods (Australia) Ltd in 1975 and a Director in 1977. She left Christie's in 1991 and is currently a Sydney-based art consultant.

Sue Hewitt was Christie's first female auctioneer worldwide. She was thrust into taking her first sale unexpectedly at a specialist print auction at the Hilton Hotel in Sydney probably in September 1976.[6] Up until that time, Hewitt had clerked at the sales, maintaining the auctioneer's books and noting the reserves and bids. On this occasion, Spowers had conducted a book auction in the afternoon and, on their return for the evening session at 8pm, informed Hewitt that she would be taking the sale. Evelyn Barlow, Montague's sister, had conducted auctions for Sotheby's in the 1920s and was probably the first female auctioneer ever at a major auction house. Hewitt noted in an interview in 1987 that Clara Hewitt (no relation) was the first woman licensed as an auctioneer in Melbourne in 1899.[7]

Christie's Autonomy

In the early 1970s, Christie's obtained a new rostrum, a replica of that made for James Christie by Chippendale, the English carver and cabinet-maker, for use in its Australian sales. The replica reinforced not only the pedigree of Christie's, but also the fact that it was part of a multinational company with an English provenance. Christie's Australian office retained a reasonable amount of autonomy in terms of its day-to-day affairs, although the London office was naturally very interested in its progress, demanding regular reporting on accounting and sales figures, which had to be transmitted manually by telex. It took some time before the new Christie's was able to report a profit though, as with most businesses, this was expected and allowed for in the set-up costs.[8]

The expense of running Christie's Australian operation was fairly high because it was standard practice to fly one of the London directors to conduct the sales in Australia. The absence of an Australian auctioneer in the early years was very much in keeping with a centre and periphery attitude. For the first sale in September 1969 Jo Floyd was the auctioneer. Spowers was the auctioneer at the second sale in March 1970 and in September 1970 Floyd returned. It would have been much more practical and cost efficient to train local auctioneers, as is the case today, although many of the top auctioneers – including Roger McIlroy – have still undergone London training and grooming. Nonetheless, Christie's London auctioneers were reportedly exceptionally good and brought what has been dubbed the 'London style' or the 'international style' to Australia.[9]

Prior to Christie's presence in Australia, Australian auctioneers had employed a more 'rappy' style, similar to that used at furniture sales in suburban auctions.[10] The London style of auctioneering, which has been described as 'slightly stiff and sparing', had actually evolved into the international style after it was taken to New York by Sotheby's when it took over Parke Bernet in 1964.[11] Some have credited Robert Bleakley with introducing the London style to the Antipodes when he established Sotheby's in Australia in 1982, bringing the 'rather urbane manner which has effectively conquered the world…a very important cultural shift'.[12]

Expense and difficulty also took a less expected form. Once again, catalogues feature. By the time that Charles Nodrum was running the Melbourne branch (end of 1975 to 1978), the catalogues were collated in Sydney, but still had to be printed in London.[13] This practice was the main reason that Christie's lead-time for sales was so long, as the local firm was required to have its works ready two months in advance of an auction to allow for printing in London and delivery to Australia. All Christie's printing was done by the London firm of White Bros, also owned by Christie's, who saw the advantages of vertical integration. Catalogue production was problematic if the Australians could not oversee their own printing. This desire to control Christie's Australian operations from head office resulted not only in lack of autonomy, but also in the inability of Christie's to realise its full potential in Australia, something which Sotheby's was arguably able to achieve. Catalogues these days are often distributed shortly before the auction; changes to printing processes and printing locally have enabled auctions to be organized very quickly, giving the auction houses more flexibility and greater precision in setting reserves and estimates.

Christie's Australian office sent a large volume of goods to London for sale. Although it was 'accredited' with these works, it did not receive money for them.[14] This policy was in keeping with the Australian office's role as a peripheral supplier of lucrative sleepers for the central London salerooms. (A 'sleeper' is a work which is usually a serendipitous discovery and attains a much higher price than expected, as it may be a hitherto unidentified work by a master artist.) The frequency with which sleepers have made it into the saleroom have decreased over time, concurrent with advances in scholarship and access to expert advice, most notably though multinational networks such as that utilized by Christie's. Most of the sleepers sent were European and would realise their full sales potential in London, where they could be assured of ready buyers.

One of the most important items sent to London by the Australian office was Gustav Klimt's *Portrait of Hermine Gallia* (1904), sold by Christie's in London in 1972 for around AUS$50,000. The portrait was commissioned by Moriz Gallia, Hermine's husband, and had hung in their stylish apartment in Vienna. The Gallias had five rooms in their apartment designed by Josef Hoffmann, the Viennese Secession furniture designer, in 1913 including all the furniture, wallpaper and even beaded evening bags. In 1936, after the death of Hermine (Moriz had died earlier), the contents were divided in half; one half was distributed to the son, Ernst, and the other half was shared by the daughters, Margarete and Kathe. The children fled Vienna for Sydney just prior to World War II. The goods were shipped to Australia separately and it was only the sisters' belongings that arrived, as the brother's shipment was lost. Soon after arriving in Sydney, the sisters sold at auction some items which did not fit into their new abode, including chandeliers and furniture. Christie's Australian office was later instructed to sell the portrait, which was shipped to London in 1971 for sale. It was later purchased by the National Gallery, London in 1976 and is currently on display at the Tate Modern, London. There was no market for the Hoffmann furniture and decorative arts in Australia in the early 1970s. With Margarete and Kathe no longer alive, most of the remaining collection was acquired by the National Gallery of Victoria in 1976. The Gallery held an exhibition in 1984, for which it borrowed the Gallia portrait from the National Gallery in London (Figure 9).

In 1981 another important work was discovered by Christie's in Australia and sent to London for sale. It was a small picture by the sixteenth century German painter, Adam Elsheimer. The vendor had purchased it from Spencer, an antique dealer in Edgecliff, Sydney, who purchased most of his stock from London. Sue Hewitt sent a photograph of the work to London for appraisal. The London office telexed immediately that it thought it was a long-lost Old Master by Elsheimer. Hewitt confirmed that the work was by Elsheimer by ascertaining that it was executed on silvered copper, a medium preferred by the artist.[15] The picture found in Australia belonged to an altarpiece commissioned by the Grand Duke Cosimo II de' Medici. The altarpiece, originally consisting of seven small pictures depicting the Finding and Exaltation of the True Cross, had been dismantled over time and the panels sold separately. Here was the second piece of the tabernacle located on the bottom left, identified as *St Helena Questions the Jew* (Figure 10).

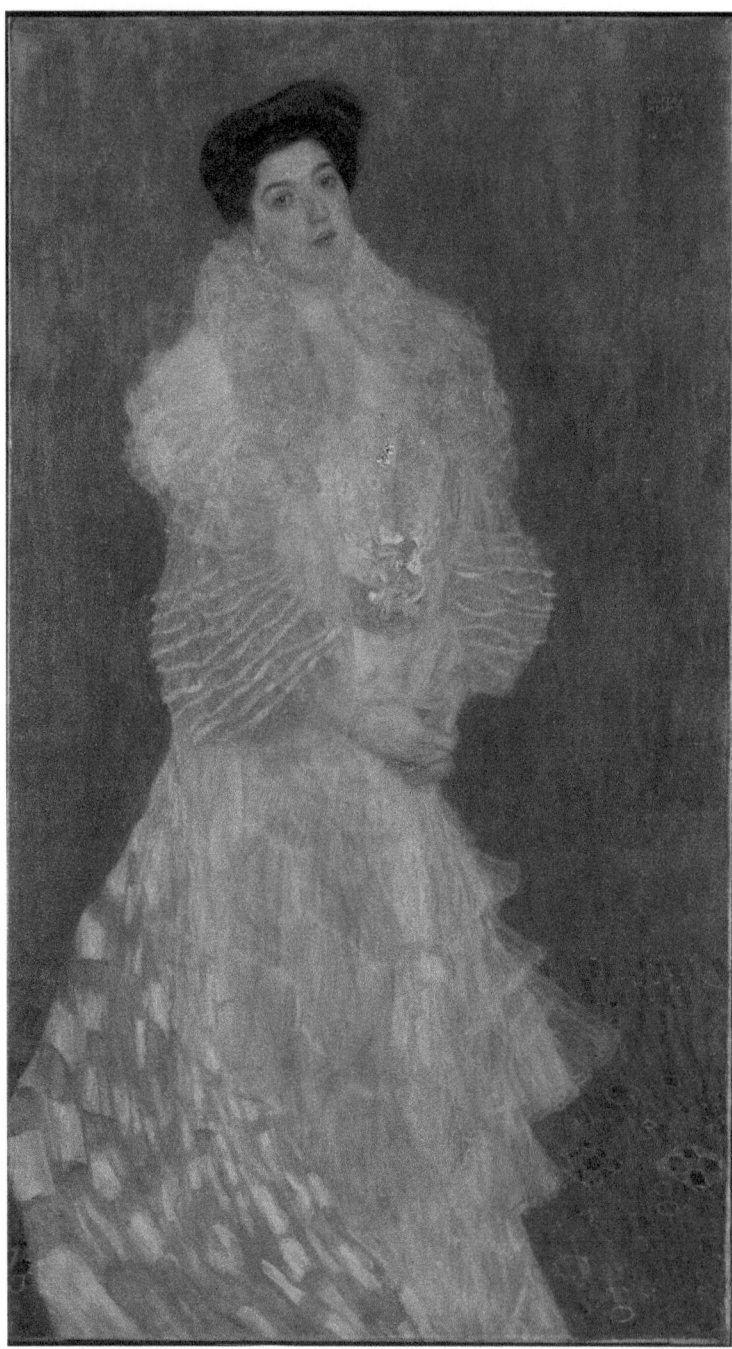

Figure 9: Gustav Klimt, *Portrait of Hermine Gallia*, 1904, oil on canvas, 170.5 x 96.5 cm, © The National Gallery, London (on loan to the Tate Modern, London).

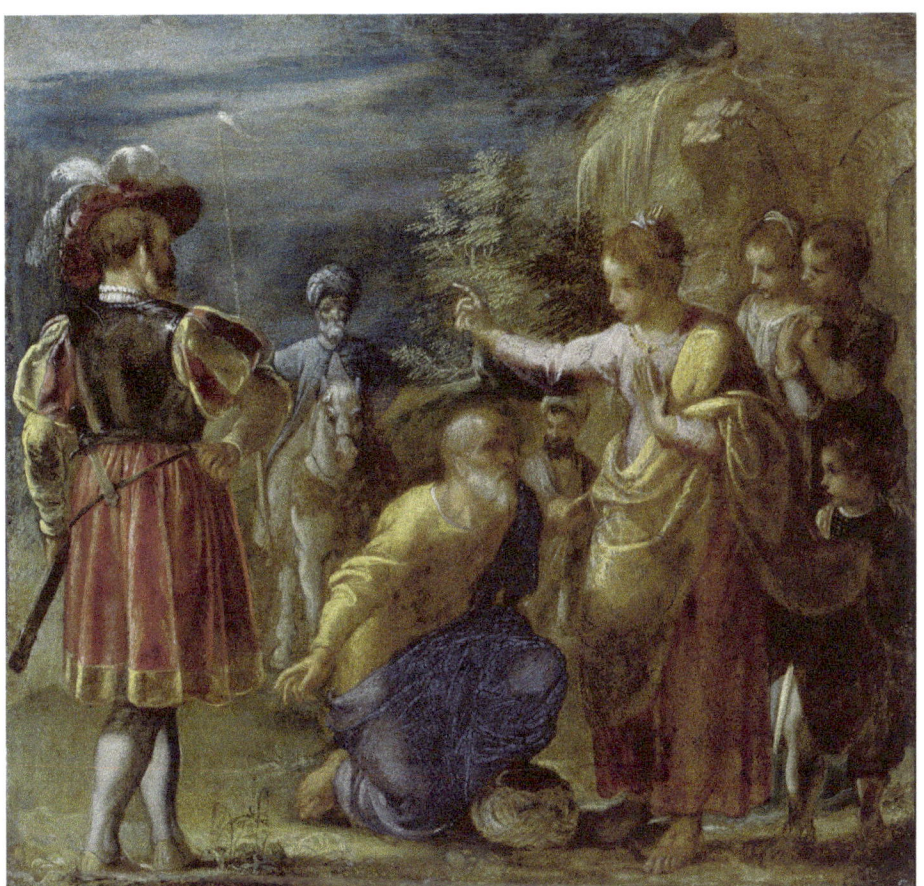

Figure 10: Adam Elsheimer, *St Helena Questions the Jew*, c.1603–05, Stadelsches Kunstinstitut (Stadel Museum), Frankfurt. Image courtesy of Stadel Museum - ARTOTHEK.

The London sale of the Australian Elsheimer picture raised the issue of an auction house's role, as well as emphasizing the importance of an international network for sourcing and identifying valuable stock. The *Stadelsches Kunstinstitut* in Frankfurt had all but reassembled the altarpiece, having managed to acquire the other six pictures, and was obviously intent on purchasing the final picture. However, as it is the responsibility of the auction house to protect the interests of the vendor, Christie's was not at liberty to place a low reserve. At the same time, there was a distinct possibility that the *Stadelsches Kunstinstitut* could rig the sale, making their desire to acquire the picture known and advising Old Master dealers to refrain from bidding. The Australian panel did sell to the *Stadelsches Kunstinstitut* for £110,000. These examples not only illustrate Christie's access to buyers and markets all over the world, but also the lack of a market in Australia for European items, in contrast to the preference for European works among colonial collectors.

Christie's made an attempt to stimulate interest in European works. Its first move was Voss Smith's promotion of French Impressionism in the firm's early sales. Secondly, it was hoped that the establishment of the West German branch of Christie's in the early 1970s would generate fresh interest in nineteenth-century German Romantic artists, such as Eugène von Guérard who had worked in Australia from 1852 to 1882. This West German office afforded an opportunity for branches of Christie's around the world, including Australia, to source and send such works to Germany for sale.

Prices for von Guérard in the decade from 1960 to 1970 show a market reassessment of the artist was taking place, in conjunction with an impending monograph on the artist and a reappraisal of the German Romantic School. In December 1960, Leonard Joel had sold von Guérard's *Cabbage Tree Hill* for 25 guineas and Christie's sold (much larger) works by von Guérard in March 1970 for between $4000 and $8500.[16] However, on the whole works by modern artists commanded higher prices at auction with Drysdale and Dobell two of the most popular artists in the saleroom in the early 1970s. The highest price in this period was $30,000 for Drysdale's *Emus in a Landscape* (1950), bought by the National Gallery of Australia in September 1970. It was noted later, in 1989, that 'through their offices all over the world, Christie's and Sotheby's are bringing batches of Australian art from overseas owners who are steadily becoming aware of the almost avaricious appetite for good Australian art of the colonial, impressionist and modern period'.[17] In the 1980s, a lot of Australian art was repatriated owing to this 'avaricious appetite'.

Christie's early Australian sales highlight the fact that the Australian art auction market was in a state of flux, adjusting to new demands and competitors. Their sales introduced a more sophisticated approach to auctioneering and intensified the competition between local auction houses, dealers and the international firm, thus irrevocably altering the shape and dynamics of the Australian art auction market. Nonetheless, it is clear that in some respects Christie's in its first incarnation in Australia never really became much more than a representative office.

Christie's Satellite and Telephone Link-up Sales

Prior to the first Australian sale in September 1969, Christie's had attempted to hold a satellite auction in June 1968. When this attempt failed, Spowers succeeded in conducting two sales by telephone on 2 July 1968 and 18 March 1969, with buyers in Melbourne and Sydney linked to the London saleroom. This meant that, strictly speaking, they were London and not Australian sales, although they did contain Australian works and involved Australian bidders.

Sotheby's had held a satellite auction simultaneously in London and New York in about 1965, using the Early Bird satellite system to avoid any delay; previous link-up sales had also been simultaneous, but had only been conducted via the telephone. The reported success of these Sotheby's telephone and satellite sales may have been the inspiration behind Christie's preliminary sales in Australia in the late 1960s.[18] Spowers visited Australia in February 1968 to ascertain whether it was practicable to hold Australiana auctions in Australia rather than in London. However, he decided that it would be easier to conduct the auction via satellite, as Sotheby's did. He then endeavoured to arrange this satellite auction in Australia for June 1968. The sale would have been an opportunity for Australian collectors to purchase valuable works of Australian origin without having to pay the commissions of American and British art dealers.

Despite the fact that Christie's had offered to pay the rental expenses of the satellite (estimated at $5000), the Australian Broadcasting Corporation (ABC) claimed that the auction of Australian paintings would not be of interest to the public and refused to televise it.[19] This demonstrates the relatively low profile of art auctions in Australia in the late 1960s, prior to the establishment of Christie's and Sotheby's. It is a stark contrast to the situation today, where art auctions make headlines and are analyzed in saleroom sections of newspapers and specialist art, business and finance magazines.

Setbacks of a proposed satellite sale notwithstanding, Spowers succeeded in orchestrating a telephone link-up sale a month later. Renting a suite at the Wentworth Hotel, Sydney, with a glass of champagne in one hand and a telephone with an open line to Christie's in London in the other, he relayed Australian bids. An amplifier broadcast the auction throughout the suite. The London-Sydney telephone link-up was open only for the twenty-nine Australian paintings on sale, from approximately 8:30–9:10pm. Buyers in Australia could telephone their bids to the hotel and be transferred directly to Christie's in London. There were also 242 books and related material to be auctioned the following day, but a telephone link-up was not viable for this sale because of the expected duration of over three hours.

Spowers also had logistical difficulties with this auction. The auction catalogues, valued at £500, were detained by Customs, which insisted that they were liable for duties because they were classed as advertising. Spowers was concerned that not enough people had heard of the auction, partly owing to the Customs hold-up of the catalogue distribution, and feared no-one would attend, commenting that 'The Australian market is very small beer to Christie's, after all, and if Australians want their own paintings and books they'll just have to show a bit more interest'.[20] An absence of serious bidders on the night would have resulted in him returning to London and Christie's dropping the idea of establishing a branch in Australia. However, results at the July auction were solid; Sidney Nolan's *Central Australian Landscape* (1950) sold for 2200 guineas, Sali Herman's *The Black House* (1940) sold for 320 guineas and the highest price for an Arthur Boyd work at this sale was 950 guineas for *Figure in a Landscape*. A second link-up sale was apparently held between Christie's London, Sydney and Melbourne.

Christie's telephone link-up sales were successful enough to encourage Christie's to establish offices in both Melbourne and Sydney, with Floyd saying in early 1969 in Sydney that 'Australia is going to become another America. This country, I think, is at that dramatic stage of development similar to the American boom days around 1880 and 1890'.[21]

The physical location of Christie's offices and salerooms had an impact on the firm's success and demonstrated its desire to appear more sophisticated than the local firms. It was Christie's policy that all its representative offices be located in a prestigious and central position. Christie's held two paintings auctions per annum initially, one in Sydney and the other in Melbourne. Its Melbourne offices were firstly located in Collins Street, with auctions held at *The Age Gallery* or in the ballrooms of major hotels. Despite Christie's policy of a city location for representative offices, there was some feeling that the Collins Street location had a negative impact on business; in purely practical terms, parking was extremely difficult.[22] The Sydney offices were located in Double Bay, with early auctions held at the Bonython Gallery in Paddington and leading Sydney hotels. This emphasis on the location was important in establishing Christie's pedigree in Australia. The idea of capitalizing on the chic ambience of the major hotels was to be explored to the full by Robert Bleakley of Sotheby's in the 1980s.

Christie's First Auction in Australia

Christie's first 'real' auction in Australia was held at the Bonython Gallery in Paddington, Sydney on 24 September 1969. Voss Smith had begun gathering paintings on his return to Sydney in April, desirous of obtaining a variety of works with a strong historical strain, including Heidelberg and contemporary works, with modern artists such as Boyd, Nolan, Dobell and Drysdale. Christie's initially sourced stock with facility, as the publicity from each sale resulted in a flurry of inquiries about possible consignments, with Christie's representative, Henshaw, describing it as 'a self-perpetuating phenomenon'.[23] There was also no need to go to tender for major collections, as it was the vendor who approached the auction houses for comparable propositions, attracted by the 'certain glamour' of Christie's, and not the responsibility of the auction houses to approach the vendors and attempt to sway them with competitive offers and counter-offers, as tends to be the case today.[24]

Two advances most visible at this first auction were the introduction of a seating system and glamour. At major London auctions it was essential to book seats and tickets were issued (as one would expect in the theatre). Only the Big Buyers gained admittance to the inner sanctum of the main saleroom – the system was highly formal and organized, whereas seating at auctions in Australia had traditionally been of an informal nature. Christie's Australian office based the seating system at its inaugural auction on the London one — to instil some order in the process — taking bookings for seats, but not issuing tickets. However, at the first sale people were not *au fait* with seating systems and sat wherever they chose, resulting in pandemonium. Hewitt recalled that it was still a very glamorous social event, with dealers bringing their most important clients clad in fur coats, thus making it an unusually up-market auction.[25]

The Como Sale

On 11–12 March 1971, Christie's held an auction of Australian paintings at Como, a National Trust property in South Yarra, Melbourne. This was advertised as the 'most valuable auction held in Australia'; a familiar catch-cry, but also showing the constant up-swing of the market.[26] Most of the 248 lots on offer were, in fact, imported from London, Switzerland, Rome, Paris and New York, as overseas collectors were beginning to see the benefits of repatriating Australian works. However, a number of the paintings were from the Margaret Carnegie collection (Property of Mr and Mrs Douglas Carnegie, Holbrook), including Drysdale's *Old Larsen*, which obtained the top price at the Como auction when it sold for $26,000 (estimate $25,000–$30,000). Nonetheless, most of the works sold for $1000 or under.

This sale was a rather inauspicious beginning to Christie's involvement in the Australian art auction market because of a number of mishaps: the art students who had been engaged to assist with the sale decided to demonstrate (having earlier attached a note to the back of an Albert Namatjira painting demanding that the artist be paid a few pounds); the gates to the property were locked prior to the sale; and one of the major buyers rushed off in the middle of the sale, never to be traced.[27] Nevertheless, the sale was considered a glamorous and popular occasion. The auction opened on the Thursday night with a formal affair; 750 guests, most of whom were not bidders, attended the $3 per person event for love of the spectacle. Spowers commented that 'Melbourne people seem to look upon auctions as more of a social occasion than in Europe or England'.[28] His view is consistent with comments by Brodsky mentioned earlier, that auctions were considered to be a great form of entertainment as early as the nineteenth century. Spowers' remark also reflects the fact that European and English bidders were predominantly art dealers, attending auctions in their official capacity, and not private collectors.

The 1971 Dobell Sale

On 5–6 October 1971, Christie's auctioned works from the studio of the late Sir William Dobell in the Grand Ballroom at the Wentworth Hotel in Phillip Street, Sydney. Christie's had been awarded the sale after fierce competition from Geoff K. Gray, Lawson's and Sotheby's. Charles Lloyd Jones, one of the Sir William Dobell Art Foundation's trustees and the subject of a riveting portrait by Dobell now hanging in the National Portrait Gallery in Canberra, had encouraged other auction houses to express an interest in conducting the sale, as he believed that auctioning the works would be 'most suitable' and that the trustees envisaged 'a most spectacular auction'.[29] Moreover, it was the responsibility of the trustees to ensure that the paintings achieved the best results possible and this was most likely to be achieved from committing them to auction rather than private treaty sale, reflecting both the positive auction climate and the high prices achieved for Dobell paintings in the early 1970s.

The Dobell Foundation had attempted to 'avoid swamping the market by selling off only a small group at once'.[30] Therefore, only six drawings and nine paintings were consigned, mainly studies for renowned works such as *Sketches of Dame Mary Gilmore* ($1300) and *Sketch for the Street Singer* ($450). The most important piece was Dobell's late work, *The Night of the Pigs* (1970), which sold to the Art Gallery of New South Wales after the sale for $10,000 (estimate $10,000–$15,000).

The Major Harold De Vahl Rubin Sales

The colourful Queensland collector Major Harold De Vahl Rubin has already made an appearance in these pages, not least as purchaser of a number of works at the Schureck auction in 1962. Rubin's patronage of Australian art was invaluable and his 'old robber baron tactics' buoyed the local market, contributing substantially to the art boom in the early 1960s.[31] He 'elevated Australian art-collecting to serious status and splashed it all over the front pages of the popular press along with his five wives, his fabulous philanthropies and his appetite for live goldfish'.[32] At the time of his death, Rubin had 25 works by Dobell in his collection, reputedly the finest collection of Dobells. These works were sold over two consecutive years so as not to flood the market and fetched approximately $86,000 at auction. On 4 October 1972, Christie's auctioned the first half of the Rubin Collection at the Wentworth Hotel in Sydney, with a huge 96 per cent of the paintings selling, including the Dobell portrait of Schureck.

Christie's October 1973 sale also featured another thirty Dobell works, mostly from the Rubin estate, though Dobell's *The Dead Landlord* (1936), consigned by Gerald Leroy-Terquem of Paris, was the star attraction. (Leroy-Terquem is presumably the psychiatrist, photographer and art collector who co-founded Galerie Gérald Leroy-Terquem, Paris in 2003.) *The Dead Landlord* was considered to be 'the most important modern Australian painting to be offered at auction' and was the inspiration for Patrick White's play, *The Ham Funeral*.[33] The painting was originally purchased for less than 25 guineas, but sold at the 1973 auction for the staggering amount of $60,000, against an estimate of $30,000–$40,000. It was also considered to be more important than any of the Dobells on offer at Sotheby's Dobell sale at the Opera House in November 1973. Prices for Dobells had virtually stagnated soon after the Schureck sale in 1962, as it was noted in 1973 that Dobells were selling for similar prices to those attained at that pivotal auction.[34] However, collectors were keen to acquire Dobells once more after the death of the artist in 1970.

Art auctions had already gained the appellation of a 'spectator sport' by the early 1970s.[35] The popularity of art auctions was demonstrated by the fact that at the 1972 Rubin sale only people who had purchased a catalogue for $4.50 were given admittance. Fewer than 200 out of the 1000-strong audience actually intended to place bids.

The mainstream appeal and success of the Rubin and other auctions at Christie's in 1972 revived the notion that the Australian art market was over-inflated, a notion mainly promulgated by Robert Hughes, who thought that the Australian art market was unique in its ridiculously high prices at auction.[36] Hughes joked in 1974 that he believed Peter Wilson, Sotheby's International Chairman, had strategized to equate art with gold as a solid vehicle for investment in the public imagination.[37]

The uniqueness of Australia's high prices is something which Henshaw denied, believing this to be the case worldwide, where local artists who were well-known and depicted familiar scenes, for example, would naturally achieve higher prices in their home country than in an overseas market where they were anonymous.[38] Moreover, some local Australian art critics argued prices for some of the works, such as Drysdale's *Man in a Landscape (Young Man)* (1953) (sold for $9000) and Dobell's *Study for the Cypriot (Aegeus Gabriell Ides)* (1934) (sold for $14,000 to Sydney art dealer, Barry Stern) and *Donkey and Cabbage Cart* (1934) (sold for $6000 to a buyer called Keswick), were actually below expectations.[39]

Hughes disagreed, but laid the blame mainly on 'the sham which speculative art dealers in this country have perpetrated on local collectors'.[40] He said that dealers were responsible for 'the main transmission belt between art and the public in Sydney, and in Melbourne' and that even the Power Bequest and other internationalizing activities had not overcome Australia's parochialism.[41]

Christie's Retreat, Re-establishment and Restructure

By 1972–3, Christie's Australian painting sales were deemed to be successful, according to Herbert.[42] However, Christie's began to decrease its involvement in the Australian art market from the mid-1970s, closing its paintings saleroom around 1978–9. Christie's cited a variety of reasons, including that Spowers had become jaded by the incessant travel involved in the venture by 1974 and that the Australian branch was not making enough money and was costing too much to maintain. Christie's also claimed that it had wound down its Australian operation because it believed that the 'market was drying up', as it suffered a downturn in 1974.[43]

Christie's final regular sale of paintings appears to have been held in June 1978, after which it was demoted to the status of a representative office, collecting works to send to London for sale. Hewitt remained as Christie's representative in Australia, assisted by a part-time secretary. In 1984, Sue Hewitt was offered the collection of Dr John Raven, a Perth haematologist and art collector, which was valued at more than $500,000.[44] At the core of the 145-lot Raven collection was Conrad Martens' paintings of Sydney Harbour which were rich in historical narrative. Raven had been a passionate collector of colonial Australian paintings for two decades and his collection was ranked as 'one of the finest private collections in the country'.[45] This sale in the ballroom of the Regent Hotel, George Street, Sydney, according to Hewitt, catapulted Christie's back into the Australian market.[46]

In the interim, Sotheby's had entered the local market with its inaugural auction in 1983. While Christie's was decreasing its involvement with the Australian market in the late 1970s, Sotheby's was preparing its Australian presence. Christie's withdrawal worried Sotheby's London directors when Bleakley first approached them about setting up in Australia.[47]

According to some, Sotheby's arrival on the scene in November 1982 propelled Christie's into action.[48] According to others, when Sotheby's arrived Christie's London management was not interested in fiercely competing with Sotheby's in Australia as it was conducting a programme of expansion in other parts of the world, where it was able to achieve better returns; for example, the Hong Kong branch could turn over £11 million in a single night.[49] However, Roger McIlroy felt that Christie's needed to 'combat' Sotheby's dominance of the market and it seems likely that Sotheby's arrival did force Christie's directors to reassess the Australian office.[50]

Christie's Australian operation was reorganized in 1989–90 when McIlroy came out from London as Managing Director. Kathie Sutherland, who made the transition from Sotheby's, replaced Hewitt about 1991 at Christie's when the firm was revamped. As head of Christie's paintings department, Sutherland was attributed with helping Christie's to return to a position where it could rival Sotheby's virtual monopoly of the top end of the paintings market.[51]

Christie's felt that Australia represented a 'promising market' in 1989, despite the fact that it provided less than 1 per cent of its sales throughout the world.[52] Christie's became a fully-fledged subsidiary company, rather than a branch, in May 1990 when it purchased premises at 1 Darling Street South Yarra in Melbourne. In late 1988, McIlroy, Lord Carrington (Chairman of Christie's International) and Christopher Davidge (Christie's International Managing Director) had visited Australia with a view to purchasing property for an Australian operation. Melbourne was chosen because it was the centre of the Australian art market and where it was possible to charge a buyer's premium. These premises were purchased for $1.9 million and a further $400,000 was spent on renovations to create Christie's first Australian on-site saleroom. Christie's also expanded its Double Bay storage and office space in Sydney twofold.

It was at this time that Christie's changed from being Christie, Manson & Woods (Aust) Ltd to Christie's Australia Pty Ltd. This was a key change and reflected a shift in perception and priorities. Perhaps as proof of Christie's optimism, the new company was formed under the chairmanship of local Australian, James B. Leslie, A.O., M.C., from Qantas. As previously mentioned, McIlroy was appointed as Managing Director and Hewitt became Deputy Chairman. Christie's announced that it would 'now offer a comprehensive service to clients throughout Australia and New Zealand, similar to our most important locations in Europe and America'.[53] This renewed emphasis on its Australian operations was part of a general programme of expansion within the Pacific region.

McIlroy's success as Director and auctioneer at Christie's had a lasting impact on the Australian art auction world. Sydney-born McIlroy returned to Australia in October 1989 and began in his official capacity in March 1990. He had spent more than a decade working for Christie's in London and Scotland and was intending to expand Christie's business in Melbourne. McIlroy gained his entrée to the art auction industry c.1973 while in his teens, when Thelma Attwood, 'one of Australia's first female auctioneers', came to value his family home for probate.[54] Attwood gave him an introduction at Lawson's, as well as his prized rosewood gavel. McIlroy spent five years at Lawson's learning every facet of the business from the bottom; he had been, ironically, aggrieved by Christie's 'intrusion' in 1969.[55]

McIlroy went to London in 1977, where he worked at Phillips for six months, after which he was offered a job in Christie's ceramics department in 1978. He ran the ceramics department in King Street, London for around eight years before moving to Scotland, where he was given the temporary position of Managing Director for two years. It was during this period that McIlroy was asked to be the secondary auctioneer for the famous auction of Van Gogh's *Sunflowers* in 1987. He then returned to King Street as the assistant to the group Managing Director.

By 1998, Christie's 'new businesslike' image led to McIlroy being invited to join the Presidents Club of fifteen of the country's leading executives.[56] This demonstrated a major change in the social status of auctioneers. McIlroy's approach has been described as 'a little bit more laid back' than his Sotheby's counterpart, Bleakley.[57] The forceful personalities of these two men have done much to shape the Australian art auction market as we know it today.

The Trout Sale

Christie's first major auction after its return to the Australian market was of Sir Leon and Lady Trout's collection, conducted by McIlroy and Hewitt in Brisbane on 6–7 June 1989. It fetched over $7 million (estimate $6–$10 million) and was 'the third largest house sale ever conducted by Christie's' worldwide and succeeded in re-establishing Christie's position in the Australian art auction market.[58] The Trouts began to collect seriously in the 1940s and 1950s and most of their art was collected on annual jaunts to London and Europe in the 1960s and 1970s, often purchased from Christie's and Sotheby's. All 1082 lots sold, with John Peter Russell's *Belle Ile* 1900 selling for $700,000. This work was later sold as part of The Farrow Collection by Leonard Joel in 1991 for $242,000 (estimate $450,000–$550,000) and again at Sotheby's in 2000 for $552,500 (estimate $500,000-$800,000).

The collection was offered by Christie's in conjunction with Philip Bacon, the respected Brisbane art dealer, who was also an adviser for the Trout estate. Bacon withheld 47 paintings from the auction, later holding his own exhibition, *Aspects of the Trout Collection*. This exhibition toured Australia, included 15 works by Charles Conder and 13 by John Peter Russell, and earned more than $3 million. The European works from the Trout collection were also withheld from this sale and auctioned separately at Christie's in London in April 1989. This is a novel example of an auction house and art dealer sharing a collection and was evidently brought about as a result of Bacon's connections with Sir Leon and Lady Trout. It was also apparently a deliberate ploy to maintain high prices and therefore obtain the greatest profits for the Trout estate.[59]

The Trout collection had been carefully constructed over a period of 30 years and the works, apart from having an enviable provenance, were fresh to the market. Little wonder it was heralded as 'the most important auction of traditional Australian' art since the sale of Baldwin Spencer's collection in 1919.[60] Another factor in the popularity of the Trout sale was that it was a Queensland sale and it was heavily supported by Queenslanders. Sir Leon and Lady Trout had been the largest patrons of art in Queensland in the 1970s and 1980s and enjoyed celebrity status within Brisbane. The sale attracted people who were not ordinarily collectors and resulted in a bidding frenzy, with someone even paying $150 (estimate $40–60) for 'A large quantity of Garden Hose'. Joseph Brown was commissioned to act as agent on behalf of the Queensland Art Gallery, with funds of $2 million at his disposal, although a news report commented that the Queensland Art Gallery spent around $1 million on works of merely average quality.[61] The gallery had expected to be left the Trout collection in Lady Trout's will.

It was, in Hewitt's experience, the first time that Christie's had to go to tender, to compete with the other auction houses for the rights to auction the collection; this has since become common practice.[62] This sale, although a coup for Christie's, was a blow for Sotheby's, which had been basking in the glory of consecutive record-breaking sales. Negotiations for the Trout sale were presumably intense; Christie's flew in 'a whole team' including an executive vice-president from its New York office to assist Hewitt with its winning submission. Executives from Christie's in New York and London supervised the auction, highlighting the importance placed on this sale and the need for the Australian arm to succeed, especially considering the heavy investments made by the London headquarters. A whole 'team of people' were also imported from the New York and London salerooms to assist with the sale, which is still remembered by some for the efficiency with which it was conducted.[63]

Bleakley stated that, although Sotheby's advocated the adoption of an aggressive marketing stance, Christie's had actually 'cut...[their] own throats' and been forced to accept a 'ridiculous' commission in order to obtain the Trout collection.[64] Bleakley claimed, moreover, that Christie's was 'seeking to buy a market share no matter what the cost'.[65] McIlroy countered with the claim that Christie's won the sale because its proposal was a comprehensive sixty-four pages, as opposed to Sotheby's one-page proposal. He further claimed that Christie's 'asked for a commission similar to what we would charge in NSW for a single-owner collection'.[66]

Christie's advertised the Trout collection in West Germany, France, Japan and America as well as in Australia, feeling that it was an appropriate vehicle to launch its revamped firm. The sale was also marketed on the international circuit because many of the artists represented in the collection, including John Peter

Russell, had associations with artists who were enjoying stellar performances at auction overseas, such as Vincent van Gogh and Claude Monet.

For the 1988/89 financial year, Christie's Australian sales had risen by 165 per cent to $13.9 million, primarily as a result of the Trout sale. Prices for traditional paintings peaked at this sale and have not reached the same or similar levels since then.[67] Ingram stated that the Trout sale represented 'the last hurrah of an art boom based largely on impressionist and colonial paintings' and following the stock market crash.[68] This auction was the most successful single-vendor sale in Australian history. The paintings fetched 'exceptional' prices, as the recession did not really hit until after that sale, with McIlroy describing the Trout sale as an 'anomaly'.[69] The art boom in the 1980s coincided with an increasing interest in Australian history in general and Australia's Bicentennial in 1988 coincided with the peak of the boom.[70]

The Dallhold Sale

Christie's auctioned the collection of Dallhold Investments, the private company owned by Alan Bond, on 28 July 1992 and Sotheby's held an auction of Bond items on 23 August 1992. The liquidator, John Lord, had sought submissions from Christie's, Sotheby's, Leonard Joel and Nevill Keating Fine Art (the London firm which acted as Bond's agent). However, Christie's convincing success with its April 1992 sale, as well as the reportedly very low commissions, clinched the deal for the firm.[71] It was even suggested that Christie's would not charge the liquidator any commission and that, apart from the 10 per cent buyer's premium, Christie's only reward would be the national and international attention the auction would certainly engender.

Christie's advised Lord to create hype around the Dallhold sale and to market it at an international level.[72] Although there was a general expectation that buyers would essentially be limited to Australian collectors, there was great interest from Japan, Hong Kong and the United Kingdom and moderate interest from the United States, possibly owing to Bond's international business connections. Within Australia, the Dallhold collection was toured to Sydney, Brisbane and Melbourne prior to sale.

The collection sold for $5.7 million, despite the fact that nine of the colonial paintings by William Lewin had been withdrawn owing to doubts about their authenticity. The sale total was the best one in Australia for three years. The dealers, Lady Angela Nevill (from Nevill Keating Fine Art), Dr John Buttsworth and Joseph Brown, were major buyers. The top price at the sale was $715,000 paid by Buttsworth for von Guérard's *Sydney Heads* (1866) (estimate $450,000-$600,000). This had originally been purchased at a Sotheby's auction in 1985 for $700,000, which could indicate that some colonial works had maintained their value into the early 1990s or that the provenance contributed to the value being retained. The estimate suggests that Christie's felt that interest in colonial works had peaked.

The first major work Bond had bought, just prior to the art boom, was *View of Lake Illawarra* (1860) by Eugène von Guérard for $100,000 (estimate $50,000–$150,000) from a Leonard Joel auction in 1980. This was the first work at an Australian auction to obtain a six-figure sum. When it was sold at the 1992 Dallhold sale it fetched $352,000 (estimate $250,000-$300,000). Frederick McCubbin's iconic *Feeding Time* (1893) had been purchased by Bond — who, along with a number of others had favoured collecting colonial works around the time of the Bicentenary — in 1986 at a Sotheby's auction for $693,000 (estimate $380,000-$450,000). It was sold at the 1992 Dallhold auction for $462,000 (estimate $350,000–$450,000), demonstrating the general downturn in the market and the fact that the inflated prices in the 1980s for Australian colonial works could not be sustained.[73]

Many potential buyers of Dallhold works were concerned, owing to Bond's bankruptcy for corporate fraud, about the possibility of becoming involved in leasing arrangements or lack of clear title. Nevertheless, Bond's notoriety also acted in favour of the sale and the Dallhold brass business plate actually sold for $2600. It was owing to the celebrity of Bond that the Christie's and Sotheby's auctions were popular and collectors favoured auctions as the medium for buying rather than the comparative anonymity of the commercial gallery.

The Mertz Sale

The Harold E. Mertz Collection of Australian Art was auctioned by Christie's in Melbourne on 28 June 2000. The sale realized approximately $16 million (estimate $5–10 million), an auction record for a single-owner collection in Australia. The 153 lots took four hours to auction, a long time considering the relatively diminutive size of the offering. Numerous record prices were set, some of which — notably for Charles Blackman's oil painting *Patterns of an interior* (1964–65) (sold for $299,500 against an estimate of $100,000–$150,000) and Albert Tucker's *The Last Days of Leichhardt* (1964) (sold for $662,500 against an estimate of $120,000–$160,000) — still stand today.[74] John Perceval's *Scudding Swans* (1959) set a record for a living Australian artist when it sold for $552,500 (estimate $220,000–$300,000), outperforming Sotheby's record of $486,500 for Johnny Warangkula Tjupurrula's *Water Dreaming at Kalipinypa* (1972), set two nights previously.

Over the years, the Mertz collection had been mythologized, as it was known to be the superlative collection of Australian art held overseas with works from the collection frequently loaned to Australian galleries. It was thus not necessary to embellish its provenance. The auction catalogue was an art form in itself, a 172-page, full-colour publication, with most illustrations large or full-page and including short, curatorial-style essays by Patricia McDonald and the Adelaide dealer who had originally assembled most of the collection, Kym Bonython. Showing the collection in Australia's major capital cities attracted more than 12,000 viewers to the works. The Mertz sale was covered extensively on television and by major newspapers and journals. This may have accounted for its popularity with private collectors on the night of the auction and resulted in it being a truly national auction of unprecedented success.

Bonython had gathered the works on behalf of the American millionaire, Harold E. Mertz, the proprietor of a publishing business, who had become enamoured of Australian paintings during a visit to Australia in 1964. The collection was put together from 1964 to 1966 and cost approximately $500,000. Bonython acquired the works from various quarters, including other dealers, directly from artists, from his own collection and direct commissions. Mertz was, therefore, seen by living Australian artists, during that short period of time, as a great benefactor, with Brett Whiteley apparently coining the slogan, 'Mertz Means Marvellous'.[75]

Mertz had hoped to build a representative collection comprising the best examples of Australian painting by living artists from a specific point in time. The only previous collection of Australian paintings shown in America was the one which was sponsored by the Carnegie Corporation in 1941. *Legends and Landscape in Australian art: a selection of paintings from the Harold E. Mertz collection* was exhibited at the Adelaide Festival in 1966 before it was sent to Washington, opening at the Corcoran Gallery of Art, from 10 March-16 April 1967. It was then exhibited at minor American museums in 11 locations in 1967, sponsored by the American Federation of Arts. Mertz eventually donated his collection to the Jack S. Blanton Museum at the University of Texas in 1972, where it was virtually warehoused until it was deaccessioned in order to finance the acquisition of Baroque works of art. The Mertz auction, a 'failed cultural ambassador', could also be said to exemplify another failed attempt by multinationals to create a market for Australian art overseas.[76]

Mertz's bequest to the University of Texas, while primarily motivated by tax benefits, also stemmed from a genuine philanthropic desire to create a taste for contemporary Australian paintings in America. However, the University lacked the context in which to place the bequest and it was viewed as a 'white elephant'.[77] Mertz died in 1983 and his ex-wife, LuEsther, died in 1991, so it is unknown what their opinions may have been on the sale of the collection. Barbara Blackman, formerly married to the artist, Charles Blackman, who was represented in the Mertz collection, believed that the collection should have remained intact and not have been dispersed at auction. Blackman thought that it should be sold, as a body, to a public institution in Australia.[78]

The greatest appeal of the Mertz collection was its freshness to the market. Having been cloistered for a period of three decades, it was a 'time capsule'.[79] It also purported to comprise the best examples of works by some of Australia's most talented artists, rather than works which had necessarily had the most public or commercial appeal. However, Ingram claims that not all the works were the artists' best examples and that it was the celebrity status of the collection which had ensured the astronomical prices, prices which would not have been achieved had the works sold through an avenue other than the saleroom.[80]

The majority of buyers at the Mertz auction were private bidders, many through agents utilizing mobile telephones. Institutional bidders included the Queensland Art Gallery, which was outbid for Jon Molvig's *The Lovers* (1955) by the art dealer, Martin Browne, who paid $134,500, more than four times its upper estimate (estimate $20,000-$30,000) and the Art Gallery of New South Wales, which purchased Brett Whiteley's *Woman in Bath IV* (1964) for $332,500 (estimate $350,000–$550,000). Sydney dealer, Michael Nagy, was the biggest buyer at the Mertz sale, acquiring eight works, including Sidney Nolan's *Death of Constable Scanlon* (1954) for $1,322,500 (estimate $800,000–$1.2 million).

Art historian Tim Bonyhady said that the auction 'was not just a triumph of art marketing. It also involved a striking instance of market failure'.[81] This was in relation to the distinct lack of competition for John Brack's *Self-Portrait* (1955), 'Mertz's one great painting', with only Denis Savill and the National Gallery of Victoria (represented by an anonymous telephone bid) entering the bidding fray. The latter was the successful bidder, paying $442,500 (estimate $350,000–$450,000). This lack of institutional competition was owing to an agreement between major public institutions not to bid against each other at auction. This agreement will be further explored in Chapter Seven.

Christie's obtained a commission of between 10 and 15 per cent on this sale from the buyer's premium and vendor's commission. The University of Texas made a financial contribution towards the sale costs. The collection had been hotly contested by the major Australian auction firms, Deutscher-Menzies, Christie's, Sotheby's, Goodmans, Lawson's and Phillips. The fierce rivalry in the tendering process would have meant that Christie's would have offered a highly competitive vendor's commission, lower than the norm of 5 to 10 per cent. Art dealers reportedly did not offer to purchase works directly from the University prior to auction, equipped with the knowledge that Christie's, with its marketing machine, could obtain the best possible prices at a public auction, rather than a private sale.[82] However, it is rumoured that Australian dealers had approached the University of Texas in the hope of acquiring the Mertz works in previous years.

The Mertz sale was the last major auction before the introduction of the Goods and Services Tax (GST) in July 2000. The GST of 10 per cent applies to the sale of all new paintings and to the sale of works on the secondary market in some circumstances; it can also be applicable to commissions. The exceptional success of the sale prompted many collectors to consider offering their works for auction, in order to capitalize on the high prices and the new benchmarks, some of which were set for artists relatively new to the saleroom.[83] These new artists possibly included Kenneth Reinhard, whose *The Séance* (1964) sold for $9775 and Charles Reddington, whose *Season in Hell* (1964) sold for $10,925. Reinhard's slightly smaller mixed media pieces sold for less than $1000 in the late 1990s and Reddington had made no auction sales in the few years prior to the Mertz sale. The sale's success also propelled Christie's to the top position in the Australian art auction market for 2000, as well as boosting the sales figures for the overall market.

In Recent Times

Christie's held a number of successful sales after the Mertz auction until it withdrew from the Australian market in April 2006. Single-owner sales included the Estate of Frederick D. Bladin in 2003 ($1.6 million); the BHP Billiton Collection in 2003 ($2.6 million); the Collection of John Schaeffer in 2004 ($1.8 million); the Coles Myer Collection in 2004 ($1.3 million); the Bleasel Collection in 2005 ($1.8 million); the Dr Joseph Brown Collection in 2005 ($3.2 million); and the hugely successful sale of the W.R. Burge Collection in 2006 ($4.8 million). However, its Australian paintings sales had peaked in 2000 at $31 million which represented 40 per cent of the total art auction sales for that year.

Christie's final Australian sale was on 10 April 2006 when Fred William's *Upwey Landscape* (1965) sold for $1.8 million (estimate $500,000–800,000), a record for a modern Australian painting. Christie's continues to have a representative office in Sydney and Melbourne, as in the past, but discontinued its saleroom as the Australian arm reportedly still provided only 1 per cent of the firm's revenue worldwide — placing the Australian market in perspective — in an environment of increasing competition for diminishing stock of saleable quality.[84] It intends to concentrate on the burgeoning and wealthy markets in the United Arab Emirates, India and China. The firm's twenty-odd staff were obliged to find other positions after this sale. Most notably, McIlroy joined Lady Angela Nevill to form Nevill Keating McIlroy, an arts consultancy to manage private art sales in Australia and Asia, further emphasizing the current direction of the global market.[85] The largest inference from Christie's withdrawal from the Australian market — international considerations notwithstanding — is that increased competition for less marketable stock took its toll and that the Australian market has arguably not been fully integrated into the international one. As Christie's arrival had a substantial impact on homegrown firms, so too did Deutscher-Menzies' arrival have a substantial impact on Christie's. Gathering stock became increasingly difficult owing to competition from other firms, meaning that there was an oversupply of auction houses and, consequently, an undersupply of vendors and stock. This led to firms diversifying, branching out into carving new markets, such as contemporary art and Indigenous art, and to Christie's reverting to a representative office in 2006.

Christie's and Sotheby's 'duopoly' in the British art market in the late 1960s/early 1970s had already begun to spread its tentacles throughout the global environment. In 1967, these firms sold $105 million worth of art, the majority of Britain's art sales. Furthermore, they had begun to appreciate the potential and importance of overseas locations, such as Australia, for sourcing stock.[86] This was partly as a result of the interest of London dealers in the Australian market and the concomitant attractiveness of Australia owing to the increase in investment in Australian art in the wake of the Schureck sale in 1962. The increasing globalization and commercialization of the art market in the 1960s were also contributing factors in Christie's decision to found an Australian outpost at that juncture. However, as John Herbert noted, Christie's 'Expansion overseas was done in a circumspect way, only when there was sufficient cash to do it'.[87] There was a prevailing perception that Christie's and Sotheby's would make Australia an integral part of the international art market. *The Advertiser* observed in February 1968 that Christie's and Sotheby's sending representatives to Australia was a very positive manoeuvre and that 'The links with London's Big Two will put us on the map in the fine art world'.[88]

However, Robert Hughes was vocal about his belief in Australia's parochialism, saying in 1972 that Australia's 'isolation from the world market is almost complete and in this case Australian dealers have managed to drive up prices of the local heroes to quite incredible levels'.[89] These 'local heroes' included William Dobell, Russell Drysdale and Arthur Boyd and, although some Australian artists were attaining a modicum of success overseas, Australian art was largely unrecognized in the international marketplace. Others, like Kathryn Chiba, believe that 'The establishment of Christie's in Sydney, 1969, effectively brought the international art market to Australia, which in turn became more attuned to overseas trends'.[90] Chiba's view is something of an exaggeration.

Christie's actually had minimal impact on the Australian market initially. Moreover, some Australians were already participating in the international market and, although some international auctioneering practices may have been adopted in Australia, the establishment of Christie's did not create a taste for Australian art overseas.

ENDNOTES

1. Herbert, *Inside Christie's*, p.92.
2. John Hay, 'Our man at Christie's', *The Herald* (Melbourne), 16 February 1970, p.4.
3. Terry Ingram, 'Art market pioneer, Len Voss Smith, dies', *Australian Financial Review*, 10 March 1988, no pagination.
4. Joan McClelland, taped interview with the author, Melbourne, 2 October 2002.
5. Ingram, 'Art market pioneer, Len Voss Smith, dies', no pagination and Ingram, 'Sotheby's wins war of the "widow's mite"', p.41.
6. Terry Ingram, 'Appointment to fine art auction firm', *Australian Financial Review*, 9 February 1977, p.7.
7. Geoff Maslen, 'The art of the auction', *The Age*, 18 November 1987, p.3.
8. Author unknown, 'How Christie's builds an art market', *The National Times*, Money Talks section, 2-7 October 1972, p.45.
9. Charles Nodrum, taped interview with the author, Melbourne, 24 October 2002.
10. Charles Nodrum, taped interview with the author, Melbourne, 24 October 2002.
11. Peter Coster, 'The lost art of profit', *The Weekend Australian*, 14-15 April 1990, p.23.
12. Charles Nodrum, taped interview with the author, Melbourne, 24 October 2002.
13. Nodrum later set up Charles Nodrum Gallery in 1984, specializing in abstract works from the 1950s and 1960s.
14. Sue Hewitt, taped interview with the author, Sydney, 2 September 2002.
15. Sue Hewitt, taped interview with the author, Sydney, 2 September 2002.
16. Terry Ingram, 'A German romantic in a hostile land', *Australian Financial Review*, 13 January 1972, p.27 and Christie's, *Christie's Australian Art Sales Index 1969–1974*, Christie, Manson & Woods (Australia) Ltd, Double Bay c.1974.
17. Terry Ingram, Untitled, *Australian Financial Review*, 14 March 1989, p.10.
18. See Nicholas Faith, *Sold: the Rise and Fall of the House of Sotheby*, Macmillan, New York 1985, p.113 and Jeremy Cooper, *Under the Hammer: the Auctions and Auctioneers of London*, Constable, London 1977, p.106.
19. Jan Smith, 'Auction by satellite fails to get off ground', *The Australian*, 27 June 1968, p.4.
20. Smith, 'Auction by satellite fails to get off ground', p.4.
21. Adams, *Portrait of an Artist*, p.305.
22. Charles Nodrum, taped interview with the author, Melbourne, 24 October 2002.
23. Author unknown, 'How Christie's builds an art market', p.45.
24. Joan McClelland, taped interview with the author, Melbourne, 2 October 2002.
25. Sue Hewitt, taped interview with the author, Sydney, 2 September 2002.
26. Author unknown, 'Auctioneer loses at his own game', *Sunday Australian*, 14 March 1971, p.3.
27. Sue Hewitt, taped interview with the author, Sydney, 2 September 2002 and Kelly, 'Women at auction', pp.5–7.
28. Author unknown, 'Auctioneer loses at his own game', p.3.
29. Author unknown, 'Auctioneers compete to sell Dobells', *Sydney Morning Herald*, 19 March 1971, p.8.
30. Author unknown, 'Dobell's Dobells', *Australian Financial Review*, 12 August 1971, p.32.
31. According to Robert Hughes in Ron Saw, 'No longer a boom at the top — Artists now share the jackpot', *Mirror* (Sydney), 5 June 1964, no pagination.
32. Marion MacDonald, 'The New Spectator Sport', *The Bulletin*, 14 October 1972, p.40 and Martin Warneminde, 'The truth about Picasso and the goldfish', *The Bulletin*, 19 November 1991, pp.42–6.
33. Barry Pearce and Hendrik Kolenberg, *William Dobell: the painter's progress*, The Art Gallery of New South Wales, exhibition catalogue, 1997 and Terry Ingram, 'Price and prejudice interest in mammoth Dobell sell-out', *Australian Financial Review*, 13 September 1973, p.36, 39.
34. Terry Ingram, 'Who wants a dead landlord, even if it is a Dobell?', *Australian Financial Review*, 3 September 1973, p.10.
35. MacDonald, 'The New Spectator Sport', p.41.

36 Author unknown, 'How Christie's builds an art market', p.45.
37 Dennis Minogue, 'Hughes attacks our myths', *The Age*, 7 December 1974, p.15.
38 MacDonald, 'The New Spectator Sport', p.41.
39 See MacDonald, 'The New Spectator Sport', p.41.
40 Terry Ingram, 'Robert Hughes on local art – The high cost of chauvinism', *Australian Financial Review*, 31 July 1972, p.1.
41 Ingram, 'Robert Hughes on local art', p.1.
42 Herbert, *Inside Christie's*, p.208.
43 Annette Sampson, 'Rising Stars — Sotheby's bids up', *Australian Business*, 11 November 1987, p.96.
44 On Raven's art collection and trial for art fraud see Geoff Maslen, 'Bond's art remnants sold off', *Sydney Morning Herald*, 24 August 1992, p.4; Mairi Barton, 'Little-known trader who rivaled the high-flyers', *The West Australian*, 4 September 1997, p.3; and Mairi Barton, 'Crown attacks extra privileges', *The West Australian*, 4 September 1997, p.3.
45 Peter Menadue, 'Art cleaned out collector, and now he'll clean up', *The Australian*, 13 September 1984, p.3.
46 Sue Hewitt, taped interview with the author, Sydney, 2 September 2002.
47 Sampson, 'Rising Stars', p.96.
48 Libby Lester, 'Christie's vs Sotheby's', *Sunday Herald*, 18 November 1990, no pagination.
49 Peter Cochrane, 'Dueling Gavels', *Good Weekend Magazine*, 18 November 1989, p.60.
50 Roger McIlroy, taped interview with the author, Melbourne, 21 October 2002.
51 Peter Ward, 'Christie's v Sotheby's — A very civil war', *The Australian Magazine*, 4-5 July 1992, p.18.
52 Russell Baker, 'Record year for auction houses', *Australian Business*, 16 August 1989, p.31.
53 Baker, 'Record year for auction houses', p.31.
54 Cochrane, 'Dueling Gavels', p.57.
55 Cochrane, 'Dueling Gavels', p.57.
56 Terry Ingram, 'New auction house makes its D-mark as era comes to an end', *Australian Financial Review*, 12 February 1998, p.43.
57 Elizabeth Fortescue, 'The *fine art* of rivalry', *The Daily Telegraph*, 23 November 1996, p.34.
58 Quoted in Baker, 'Record year for auction houses', p.31. Also from Roger McIlroy, taped interview with the author, Melbourne, 21 October 2002.
59 Don Petersen, 'Heritage Lost', *The Courier-Mail*, Great Weekend, 3 June 1989, p.1, 2.
60 Ingram, Untitled, 14 March 1989, p.1.
61 Cochrane, 'Dueling Gavels', p.60. See also Paul Lynch, 'Lone collector nets choice of Trout sale', *The Australian*, 7 June 1989, p.3.
62 Sue Hewitt, taped interview with the author, Sydney, 2 September 2002.
63 Sue Hewitt, taped interview with the author, Sydney, 2 September 2002.
64 Cochrane, 'Dueling Gavels', p.58.
65 Quoted in Cochrane, 'Dueling Gavels', p.60.
66 Cochrane, 'Dueling Gavels', p.60.
67 Terry Ingram, 'Shoot-out of the Ned Kellys as auctioneers go gangbusters', *The Weekend Australian Financial Review*, Smart Money, 10–11 August 2002, p.35.
68 Terry Ingram, 'When AM means "after Mertz"', *Art and Australia*, 38(2) 2000, p.288.
69 Sue Hewitt, taped interview with the author, Sydney, 2 September 2002 and Roger McIlroy, taped interview with the author, Melbourne, 21 October 2002.
70 The broader stock market and real estate booms and busts also had an impact on the art market; see works such as Van den Bosch, *The Australian Art World*, for these influences.
71 Terry Ingram, 'Christie's wraps up Alan Bond collection', *Australian Financial Review*, 15 May 1992, p.9.
72 Ward, 'Christie's v Sotheby's', p.25.
73 Geoff Maslen, 'Bond paintings come back on the market', *Sydney Morning Herald*, 21 November 1995, p.15.

[74] Blackman's overall auction record for *The Mad Hatter's Tea Party*, which sold at Deutscher-Menzies for $430,000 (estimate $380,000-450,000) in May 2001, is listed under the category of 'other media and drawings' in Australian Art Sales Digest. *Patterns of an interior* was still the auction record price for a Blackman oil painting at the time of writing.

[75] According to Bonython, who was with Whiteley when he made the statement. Kym Bonython, introductory essay, Christie's, *The Harold E. Mertz Collection of Australian Art*, Melbourne, 28 June 2000. David Brearley, 'Raiders of the lost art', *The Australian*, 4 April 2000, p.14, claimed that Whiteley said 'Mertz Means Money'.

[76] Brearley, 'Raiders of the lost art', p.14. Also according to Christopher Marshall, interview with the author, Melbourne, 22 October 2002.

[77] The context remark was made by John McDonald, then Head of Australian Art at the National Gallery of Australia, in 2000 and the quotation was from Robert Hughes. Both from Brearley, 'Raiders of the lost art', p.14.

[78] See Brearley, 'Raiders of the lost art', p.14.

[79] Roger McIlroy, taped interview with the author, Melbourne, 21 October 2002.

[80] Terry Ingram, 'Mertz may have done better with Sydney real estate', *Australian Financial Review*, 15 July 2000, p.38.

[81] Tim Bonyhady, 'Buying power under the hammer', *Sydney Morning Herald*, 19 August 2000, Spectrum, p.9.

[82] Terry Ingram, 'Mertz may yet fund Old Masters', *Australian Financial Review*, 2 March 2000, p.36.

[83] Christie's, 'More Mertz for your money in Melbourne at Christie's August Australian & International Paintings Auction', Christie's, media release, 8 August 2000.

[84] 'Christie's Australia reverts to representative office', *State of the Arts*, 20 March 2006, <www.stateart.com.au/sota/news/default.asp?fid=4052> [4 April 2006].

[85] Katrina Strickland, 'Odd Lots', *Australian Financial Review*, 10 August 2006, p.45.

[86] Terry Ingram, 'Christie's explores new areas', *Australian Financial Review*, 13 January 1972, p.24.

[87] John Herbert, *Inside Christie's*, St. Martin's Press, New York 1990, p.244.

[88] Author unknown, Untitled, *The Advertiser* (Adelaide), 28 February 1968, p.4.

[89] See Robert Hughes in Terry Ingram, 'Robert Hughes on local art — The high cost of chauvinism', *Australian Financial Review*, 31 July 1972, p.7.

[90] Kathryn Chiba, *Dr Joseph Brown: Dealing in Cultural Capital*, MA thesis, University of Melbourne, 1999, 2 vols., vol. 1, p.62.

Chapter 6. Sotheby's Australia

Sotheby's was not formally established in Australia until November 1982, although it did have an Australian presence prior to that. Reginald Longden, a collector and dealer of Oriental art, was Sotheby's representative in Australia and New Zealand (based in Melbourne) from early 1968 and was responsible for sourcing stock to be sent to London for sale and conducting valuations. His purview included Australia, the Philippines, Japan and Hong Kong. Longden resigned after only one year because he found the job to be 'most frustrating'.[1] Sotheby's next representative was Bruce Rutherford who owned a jewellery and antiques firm in Collins Street, Melbourne. Rutherford's role was similar to that of Longden and was defined as simply distributing catalogues to 'local collectors, with the aim of generating material for consignment abroad'.[2] This was also essentially the same manner in which Christie's operated when it was a representative office. Ingram noted that Sotheby's intended to conduct auctions in Australia in the early 1970s, saying 'Sotheby's (which has had a branch here for more than two years shuttling works of art [to] or from its auctions in London) has disclosed that it is in the market to conduct auctions locally'.[3]

Sotheby's held a sale of paintings and drawings from Sir William Dobell's studio on behalf of the Sir William Dobell Art Foundation on 19 November 1973 at the Sydney Opera House. The auction was originally scheduled for March 1973, but Sotheby's delayed it in order to include more works to make it 'a presentation of the artist's work'.[4] Despite the success of the sale of Foundation paintings at the Christie's auction in 1971, the Foundation decided to consign the remaining works from Dobell's studio to Sotheby's, as the firm agreed to hold what was ostensibly a single-owner collection sale, thereby giving the works the greatest possible prominence. This was not only Sotheby's first sale in Australia, it was also expected to be the largest art auction ever held in Australia, as well as Sotheby's third ever single-artist sale.[5]

Works sourced in Australia and sold in London were generally by British or European artists, rather than Australian ones. The Dobell works were exhibited in New York, Los Angeles, London (at the Qantas art gallery in Piccadilly), Melbourne and Sydney prior to the sale, in order to generate interest on the part of potential international buyers. This sale represented the first occasion on which Sotheby's had travelled a collection around the world and commission bids were accepted for works at each of the exhibition venues. However, as this collection comprised the remnants of the artist's studio, it was not a true reflection of his *oeuvre* and ability and, therefore, perhaps not the most appropriate collection to introduce his work to the international market. Sotheby's had only ever auctioned one Dobell drawing in London before and this sale was thus a real test of the international interest in Dobell specifically and Australian art more broadly.

There were only a handful of international collectors who owned Dobell works at that time, including the Klebergs from the Texan ranching dynasty, who had acquired at least six. One of these, *Boy Sunbathing*, had been purchased for the princely sum of 1350 guineas at an unidentified Sydney auction in 1962. Yet, despite these collectors and the international release of James Gleeson's book on Dobell (revised by Thames & Hudson in 1969), it was felt in 1973 that 'Dobell's international esteem…[was] negligible, largely because of the absence of an Australian identity and the lack of any machinery overseas for promoting an 'international' Australian artist'.[6]

The Dobell estate sale was held at the Opera House before the landmark building had been officially opened. It was conjectured that the sale may have been booked for the Opera House because of the Dobell Art Foundation's strong links with the building, which included having recently commissioned John Olsen to paint its mural, *Salute to Five Bells*.[7] (The funds for this commission [$35,000] were part of the proceeds obtained from the Dobell sale at Christie's in 1971.) The auction was conducted by 'the persuasive voice' of Peter Wilson, Chairman of Sotheby's, to an audience of more than 1000 people packed in the concert hall.[8]

The most important work in the sale was *The Sex Kitten (Kitten on a Balcony)* (1970) from Dobell's later body of work. This was expected to fetch $30,000, but realized only $22,000. The purple chalk *Study for The Irish Youth* (1935) sold for a comparatively respectable $10,500 and Dobell's pencil drawings doubled their accepted market value, with *Sailor and Girl* — a pen and red ink and wash over pencil work — selling for $2400. Denis Gowing, a Melbourne-based car dealer who had purchased *The Dead Landlord* at the 1973 Christie's sale for the remarkable price of $60,000, made a number of purchases at the Sotheby's sale, including *Study for The Dead Landlord* for $1600 and *Study for The Sex Kitten* for $4100.

These remnants of Dobell's studio works had been valued at $130,000 in 1970, but were expected to fetch $200,000 at the 1973 sale. In actuality, the works reaped $381,650 for the Dobell Art Foundation, demonstrating a dramatic increase in prices. This increase caused havoc with the original valuations for the works and Dobell's market suffered. Works had almost certainly been purchased at over-inflated prices and a 'mini-depression' occurred in the following year.

Many of the buyers at the sale were reputed to have been new to the market, inspired to attend by Sotheby's astute publicity campaign, the glamour of the occasion and the fact that it was in aid of a charitable cause, as under the terms of Dobell's will, money raised from the sale of the works in his studio was to be used for the promotion of art in New South Wales. The buyers' determination to make a purchase reportedly resulted in 'the uneven relationship throughout of prices and artistic merit'.[9] Ingram, while noting that the catalogue was superb, pondered 'It is questionable whether the auction will in fact say anything relevant about the state of taste in today's saleroom', owing to the unusual amount of publicity and the social cachet of the auction.[10] Nonetheless, the success of this sale probably contributed to the decision to allow Robert Bleakley to establish Sotheby's Australia in 1982.

Robert Bleakley and the Establishment of Sotheby's in Australia

Robert Bleakley began to collect so-called 'Tribal Art' in 1965 while still a child, inspired by nineteenth century novels set in exotic places. He began to study arts at the University of New England in Armidale, leaving partway through the course when he enrolled in Sotheby's London art appreciation course in 1972–3. Bleakley was employed by Sotheby's antiquities department in about 1974. The traditionally-named 'Primitive Art' department was formed in 1978 and Bleakley became its director, Sotheby's youngest director, at the age of twenty-eight. His directorship coincided with a surge of interest in collecting Indigenous art. Bleakley remained working in London until he established Sotheby's in Australia at the end of 1982 and he thus trained as an auctioneer in the London salerooms. His auctioneering style differed from that used by Australian auctioneers and he was credited with bringing the London auctioneering style to Australia, as mentioned previously.

While working in the London antiquities department, Bleakley had particular success with the Ortiz sale of Tribal Art on 29 June 1978. This sale was the result of the kidnapping of Ortiz's daughter by the Italian Red Brigade terrorists in 1977. Ortiz was forced to sell his beloved collection, one of the world's most spectacular Tribal Art collections, to repay the US$2 million loan he had taken to pay the ransom. Although the girl was returned unharmed, the kidnappers disappeared with the ransom money.

The Ortiz auction was a phenomenal success, breaking all records for Tribal Art and achieving an auction total of approximately US$2 million.[11] An Hawaiian figure which had been collected by Captain Cook and was Ortiz's personal favourite broke a world record, selling for approximately $250,000. David Nash, who worked for Sotheby's for 35 years, said of the Ortiz sale that 'PCW [Peter Wilson] discussed prices way above the market, I thought he'd lost his judgment, he was putting crazy reserves onto the lots. But he said simply, "I thought I knew the market", and of course he was right.'[12] The success of the Ortiz auction enabled the separate 'Primitive Art' department to be established. The auction made newspaper headlines, was featured on the cover of *Newsweek* and created Bleakley's reputation.

Bleakley's proposal to establish an Australian office was twice rejected. However, he was finally able to persuade the directors of Sotheby's in November 1982, primarily through offering to fund around half of the endeavour personally, and he was given a corresponding amount of equity in the firm. Bleakley commented that the directors had been very 'reluctant' because they had just been forced to close their Los Angeles office owing to the 1981–2 recession.[13] This was the first time that Sotheby's had suffered an annual loss and the firm was interested in contracting rather than expanding. Moreover, in early 1983, Sotheby's New York was beginning to retrench two hundred members of staff.

One could make a number of assumptions regarding Sotheby's decision to allow Bleakley to open the Australian branch at that time, especially given the fact that Christie's had withdrawn its saleroom presence in the 1970s and did not reopen until 1984. The Australian market may have been considered to have been under-represented or an Australian branch may have been seen as a means to gain access to the Asian market. As noted earlier, the Dobell sale in 1973 was hailed as a great success and may also have contributed to Sotheby's parent body eventually being amenable to opening a permanent office and saleroom in Australia. According to Max Germaine, a founding Director of Sotheby's Australia, the main reason was that Sotheby's new Chairman, A. Alfred Taubman, saw 'investment potential in Australian art' that the former Chairman, the Earl of Westmorland, regarded as 'inconsequential'.[14]

Bleakley had researched the Australian art market carefully for at least a year before establishing Sotheby's Australia; dealers Charles Nodrum and Chris Deutscher recalled being approached about giving their assistance to the venture in about 1981.[15] This research demonstrated that Sotheby's could fulfil a role at the top end of the market and Sotheby's therefore planned to cater to the top 10 per cent of the population. Bleakley said of the 1982 market, 'The performance of local auction houses was very poor, in terms of marketing and presentation. Guarantees of authenticity, if they existed at all, ran to a couple of weeks'.[16] He said more recently that, through his visits to Australia, he had perceived that the art auction industry could be injected with a greater degree of professionalism, based on the London system, that this would be 'an interesting challenge' and that this was the main prompt for his proposal to establish a permanent Sotheby's presence in Australia.[17]

It was generally expected that Sotheby's venture would be unsuccessful even though Christie's had 'seriously stimulated' the Australian auction system in the 1970s.[18] In 1982 the market was at a low point; there had been a recession in 1981 and Christie's had withdrawn from conducting Australian paintings sales. According to one report, 'When Sotheby's arrived other Australian auction houses were somewhat underwhelmed [sic]' and took bets on how long it would stay.[19] However, Bleakley's timing was perfect. Sotheby's establishment actually created or coincided with a swell in the Australian art market. The firm's advanced and professional marketing techniques assured its immediate success and predominance. Sotheby's worked extremely hard and 'very effectively, to the extent that they tempted Christie's to come back' to the Australian marketplace.[20]

Sotheby's initially had to 'dispel the image of toffy-nosed Poms coming in, telling Australians what they should be buying and selling', because, as one would have expected, there was some local resistance to this perceived invasion.[21] Some collectors, however, were already used to dealing with Sotheby's London and were less resistant to Sotheby's setting up an Australian branch and competing with local firms.

Bleakley thought it was 'lunacy' that no auction house had had a substantial presence in both Sydney and Melbourne, despite the fact that the market appeared to be 'evenly distributed' between the two.[22] He set up salerooms in both cities, with the Melbourne representative office a subsidiary company answering to the Sydney headquarters. Establishment costs were $200,000, with half paid by Bleakley himself. Initial costs for Sotheby's office in York Street, Sydney were very low, essentially confined to renting a small office space, hiring a basic staff and utility expenses. Although it budgeted to operate at a loss for three or four years, Sotheby's began to turn a profit immediately. This profit was directed into marketing as the firm 'wanted to create an appearance of substance, of having been here all the time'.[23]

Auctions were held in various venues, including a number of Sydney hotels and commercial galleries, such as the Macquarie Galleries. Bleakley developed a good relationship with the management of The Regent Hotel in Sydney, as the hotel benefited from the patronage and Sotheby's received reduced hire rates.

Approximately two years after its establishment, Sotheby's Sydney branch leased the ground floor of 13 Gurner Street, Paddington. By 1987, about twenty members of staff were employed. Sotheby's underwent a programme of expansion in the late 1980s, which included installation of a computer system. This not only assisted with general administration, but also provided a valuable resource, with databases of works and clients. In early 1997, the Sydney office relocated to Queens Court, on the corner of Queen Street and Moncur Street in Woollahra. This move enabled some auction previews to be held on the premises and situated Sotheby's in the heart of the auction and antiques district.

Sotheby's Melbourne representative, Ann Roberts, originally worked from home. After the first year, she moved into a Queen Street office in Melbourne's Central Business District and Sotheby's later moved this office to a terrace in High Street, Armadale. Later still it moved to the old art deco picture theatre at 926 High Street, Armadale, where it remains today. Acquiring its own salerooms in

Melbourne was cost-efficient, as transport fees did not have to be paid for moving objects between viewing and auction venues. By 1988, the Bicentenary year, Sotheby's had become one of the country's largest art auction houses, selling approximately 60 per cent of Australia's top end art.

Bleakley's partial ownership of the company made Sotheby's Australia unique, as all other offices were wholly owned by the parent company. Although Sotheby's had to conform to the practices and standards set by the parent body, to follow rigorous reporting procedures and to maintain the reputation, quality and style associated with Sotheby's, Bleakley could manage the firm on a day-to-day basis as he saw fit.[24] This gave Sotheby's the degree of independence to tailor itself to the peculiarities of the Australian arena that Christie's had not enjoyed. Moreover, all Sotheby's auctions were conducted by Australian auctioneers and the printing of catalogues was generally done locally in either Sydney or Melbourne.

Bleakley sold his portion of the company to Sotheby's in the late 1980s/early 1990s. The Australian firm became fully integrated into the multinational network and with this came contemporary business practices with 'internal regulations', including target setting, business transparency, corporate compliance and corporate governance with regards to ethics and collusion.[25] Bleakley began to decrease his involvement with the firm from about 1992 and became a Senior Director and Chairman of Sotheby's real estate company.

Sotheby's First Australian Sale — The Webber Portrait of Captain Cook

The inaugural sale of Sotheby's incorporated Australian company was held on 23 March 1983. This auction of Australian and European Paintings and Oriental Ceramics and Works of Art was held at The Regent Hotel, 25 Collins Street, Melbourne. The Property of the Corporation of The Hull Trinity House, *A Portrait of Captain James Cook RN* (1782) by John Webber, was the star attraction of this so-called first Australian sale. The portrait was honoured with a full-page colour illustration in the catalogue and an extensive three-page essay. It was also the only work listed as 'estimate on application' and, although it was given the most prominence in the catalogue, it was not featured until page 28 as lot 45; this is owing to the structure of the sale as pre-ordained by Sotheby's to set the rhythm. It sold for $506,000 (including the buyer's premium) against a reserve of around $220,000, tripling the highest price ever paid at auction for an Australian work.[26]

The painting is significant because it was the only portrait painted of Cook by an artist who actually knew him, even though it was painted posthumously. Webber sailed with Cook on his third voyage (1776–80) on the ship *Resolution*, survived the massacre in Hawaii, which claimed the life of Cook, and completed drawings and engravings from the voyage on his return to England in October 1780. There are two other extant portraits of Cook by Webber, one in the National Portrait Gallery, London and one in the National Art Gallery, Wellington.

Christie's had auctioned Webber's estate on 14–15 June 1793, when this Cook portrait was probably sold to William Seguier, the first Keeper of the National Gallery in London. On Seguier's death in 1843, his paintings were sold by Christie's on 4 May 1844. However, the Cook portrait was not listed in the catalogue. The Hull Trinity House — a charitable trust founded in the fourteenth century for infirm seamen — acquired the portrait in 1844, possibly from a private treaty sale. There it remained until the early 1980s when Bleakley was in England prior to Sotheby's first Australian auction. He had heard from a colleague that The Hull Trinity House was interested in deaccessioning the portrait in order to raise funds, approached the Trust and was able to secure the painting.

The vast majority of lots at Sotheby's auction were sold to art dealers, either in their own capacity to use as stock or as agents acting on behalf of clients.[27] Lady Angela Nevill purchased Webber's portrait of Cook on behalf of notorious businessman Alan Bond. The Mitchell Library in Sydney and Canada's National Archives had been underbidders for this work, but were unable to compete with Bond's buying power. The National Library of Australia had also been interested in acquiring the portrait but could not obtain the additional funding it required from the Government. The Australian National Gallery (now the National Gallery of Australia) had not been interested in bidding for the work.

The journey of this portrait then became even more intriguing. After Bond's company, Dallhold Investments, collapsed the portrait was sold by Bond Corporation Holdings to George Way (a friend of the Bond family) at the High Street Gallery in Fremantle in 1990, after which it was effectively missing until it was found in Switzerland in 1993.[28] A Sotheby's staff member attending a function in New York was asked whether his firm would be interested in a portrait of Captain Cook, as the lady's father had reportedly received the portrait from Bond as part of a debt settlement.[29] In Bleakley's second brush with this particular painting, he retrieved it and was intending to give the Australian National Gallery the option to buy the work through a private treaty sale for about half the asking price of $3 million. The portrait appeared to have been exported illegally from Australia — no export licence was ever requested or received — and it was claimed at the time that this may have made the anonymous vendor, represented by Nevill Keating Pictures, lenient on the asking price.[30]

Bleakley had tried to establish title to the painting, but there were no title deeds. He did ascertain to his satisfaction that it no longer belonged to Bond so the vendors would be liable to any claims if their statement of title proved false.

Interestingly, Bond claimed in July 1993 that he had never owned the portrait.[31] Despite his assertions, the portrait had toured with the Bicentennial exhibition, *Terra Australis: the Furthest Shore*, in 1988 and was listed in the catalogue as belonging to Bond. Moreover, the portrait had been hung in pride of place in Bond's boardroom at Dallhold Investments, Perth and Bond had often been photographed standing in front of it. Betty Churcher, then director of the Australian National Gallery, in a glowing testament to the business credentials of Sotheby's said that 'she believed the title would be secure because the work was being sold through Sotheby's'.[32] However, as clear title was unable to be obtained on this occasion, arrangements to purchase the Cook portrait ended in 1993–4.

Attempts were made from 1994 to 1996 to sell the portrait to others. Lady Nevill wrote to Sotheby's with instructions that the work was no longer for sale and to cease all attempts to sell it, as the Bond liquidator had put a stop on the sale of all assets.[33] From March 1996, the painting was held in secure storage by Christie's in London, 'pending litigation'.[34] The South Australian Supreme Court ruled in June 2000 that the Cook portrait be given to Bond's liquidator.

The National Portrait Gallery, Canberra bought the portrait for $5.13 million in August 2000 with funds from two patrons — Rosemount Wines' Oatley family and Tempo Cleaning Services' John Schaeffer — and $2.8 million from the Australian Government. This deal was brokered by Lady Nevill in conjunction with Christie's. McIlroy commented that 'It is a tribute to the discretion of Christie's private sales department that our involvement was not indicated prior to the conclusion of the transaction'.[35]

Lady Nevill had approached Andrew Sayers, Director of the National Portrait Gallery, in September 1999, asking if his institution would be interested in acquiring the Cook portrait. Sayers went to London to view it in November 1999 and was amenable to the purchase, having previously seen the work in *Terra Australis*. Arranging an export permit for the painting from London was a tiresome and protracted affair, despite Sayers originally being informed that it was a formality.[36] Clandestine negotiations went on until 2000 and the painting was finally unveiled at the National Portrait Gallery by the then Prime Minister, John Howard, in August 2000 (Figure 11).

Sotheby's Australia

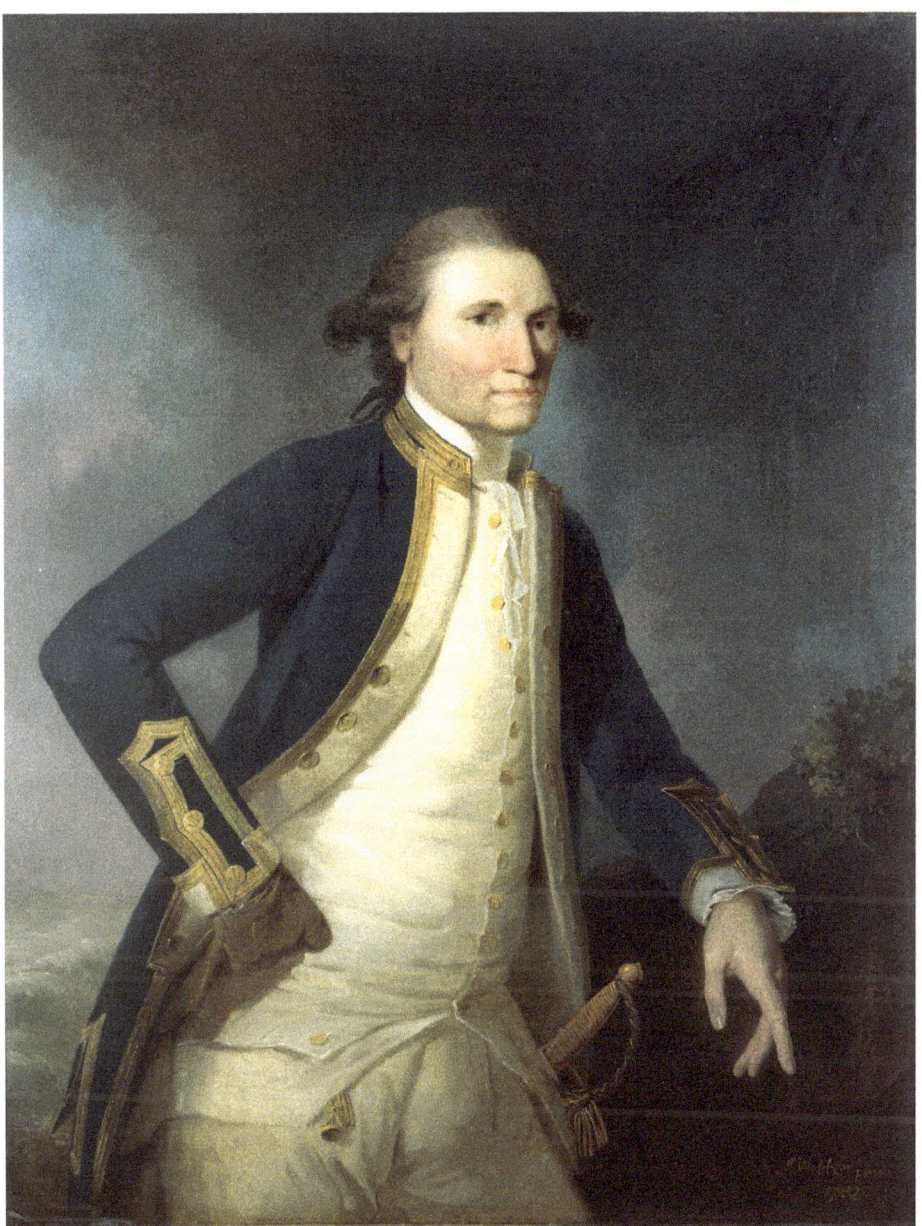

Figure 11: John Webber, *A Portrait of Captain James Cook RN*, 1782, oil on canvas, 114.3 x 89.7 cm, Collection: National Portrait Gallery, Canberra. Purchased by the Commonwealth Government with the generous assistance of Robert Oatley and John Schaeffer 2000.

In addition to the Cook portrait, Sotheby's literally had good fortune at its inaugural auction with Nicholas Chevalier's *Mount Zero and Lake Taylor, Victoria* (1862), which sold for $176,000 against an estimate of $50,000–$70,000. This was a successful launch into the Australian market. Sotheby's first Australian auction became known as the first sale of the Australian art boom and greatly assisted Sotheby's to establish its credibility in the Australian marketplace.

The Aboriginal and Torres Strait Islander Art Market

It is generally acknowledged that Sotheby's made a substantial contribution to the development of the international market for Aboriginal and Torres Strait Islander art (hereafter known, in Sotheby's terminology, as 'Aboriginal art', as this term is an international signifier). Bleakley's background and interest in the 'Tribal Art' spectrum meant that it featured in Sotheby's auction schedule from the beginning of its operation in Australia, with the auction of the Holt Collection in October 1983. There was not a lot of international participation in this sale, but enough interest was shown to indicate that the expansion and development of an international market for Aboriginal art might be possible.[37]

Sotheby's held annual Aboriginal artefacts and contemporary art auctions from the mid-late 1980s onwards, when Aboriginal works were still very much viewed as ethnography, rather than art. The catalogues for these early sales were inexpensive because Aboriginal art did not command huge prices at auction and it was therefore unnecessary to garnish the catalogues with illustrations. From the mid-1990s Aboriginal art grew into a very 'substantial part' of Sotheby's business, and sale prices escalated rapidly.[38]

Aboriginal art had monumental exposure in the United States in the late 1980s, with more than a dozen major exhibitions held in a two-year period in locations including Chicago, Los Angeles, St. Louis and New York.[39] *Dreamings: the Art of Aboriginal Australia*, arguably the most important of these exhibitions, was organized by the New York-based Asia Society Galleries and the South Australian Museum, travelling to the University of Chicago, the Museum of Victoria (Melbourne) and the South Australian Museum (Adelaide) in 1988–90. The American John Kluge, one of the world's wealthiest men, was influenced by the *Dreamings* exhibition and assembled an exceptional private collection of Aboriginal art. He gifted The Kluge-Ruhe Aboriginal Art Collection to the University of Virginia in 1997.[40] According to the latter's website, Ruhe actually began to collect Aboriginal art in 1965 while he was in Australia as a Fulbright Scholar and exhibited his collection in America from 1965–77.[41]

Other American commercial galleries that promoted Aboriginal art included the Caz Gallery (Los Angeles) and the John Weber Gallery (New York). It was estimated that American and European buyers accounted for 50 per cent of Aboriginal art and craft purchases — totalling $14.1 million — in the period from 1987 to 1988.[42] In 1989, the *Magiciens de la Terre* exhibition opened in Paris, cementing the presence of Aboriginal art in the international marketplace and as art, rather than ethnography. Also in 1989, Lauraine Diggins, a Melbourne dealer, attained record prices for works by Clifford Possum Tjapaltjarri and Michael Nelson Tjakamarra on the secondary market.

A lucrative private treaty sale for Sotheby's was that of forty-seven early Western Desert paintings to the National Gallery of Australia from the Peter Fannin collection in 1998 for $1.27 million, which included *Warrana* (c.1960) by Mawalan Marika. Sotheby's earnings in 1998 were attributed, in the main, to its sales of Aboriginal art and its Aboriginal art expert, Tim Klingender, was thus appointed as a director of the company.[43]

Klingender joined Sotheby's in 1990 and was to be given the task of developing the firm's sales in Aboriginal and contemporary art. He was ubiquitous in 1995, making two heavily publicized trips through Western Australia and the Northern Territory to scout for Aboriginal works for auction.[44] Approximately 100 works were discovered on these trips, including Clifford Possum Tjapaltjarri's *Love Story* (1972). This work was auctioned by Sotheby's on 18 June 1995, as part of a record-breaking auction of contemporary and Aboriginal art. The sale realized a total of approximately $600,000 with ten works, including *Love Story*, passing their high estimates. *Love Story* sold for $50,600 against an estimate of $15,000–$25,000; even the upper estimate would have been a record price, but the hammer price was actually a world record and thus obtained international media attention.

In June 1996, a number of important pieces were purchased by international buyers, confirming the belief that contemporary Aboriginal art is truly international in its appeal and outlook.[45] In October 1996, Sotheby's auctioned 820 lots over two sessions, 399 of which belonged to the Christensen Fund Collection of Oceanic and African Art. The Christensen Fund was established in 1957 by the American collector and founder of Utah Mining and Construction Company, Allan Christensen. Christensen had also founded Texas Mines in Carnarvon, Western Australia in the late 1960s and had been a big buyer of art at Christie's early auctions. The works had been on loan to the Art Gallery of Western Australia and the Queensland Art Gallery. Other works included in the auction were those deaccessioned from the Glenbow Museum, Calgary, Canada; from the Collection of the Late Major Alex Wynyard Joss; from the Collection of the Late Dr Douglas Burns; and from the Collection of Sir William Dobell. The sale was the 'largest of its type ever held in Australia'; it had grown in size because, as it contained a number of significant pieces, it had attracted the consignment of other items.[46] The success of these auctions paved the way for Sotheby's first specialized Aboriginal art auction in Melbourne on 30 June 1997.

Sotheby's well-publicized success with its previous auctions of Aboriginal art had resulted in works of great quality being consigned. The quality of the material persuaded Sotheby's to exhibit forty of the choice pieces at Sotheby's in New York for the first time in juxtaposition with the major Contemporary and Tribal Art sales. The New York auctions were the principal location in the world for show-casing art and the display of Sotheby's Australia's works generated a huge amount of international interest in the Melbourne auction.

The auction included deaccessioned works from the Holmes à Court Collection (culled owing to over-representation or duplication), the Tim Guthrie Collection of Early Western Desert Paintings and the Tom and Adi Barnett Collection of Bark Paintings and Sculpture, which had been on loan to Columbia University, New York for approximately thirty years.

At the June 1997 auction, 800 people squeezed into Sotheby's Armadale rooms — as both spectators and bidders — with the sale realizing $2.7 million. The high prices attained set a benchmark, with the auction representing a crucial moment in the development of the fledgling Aboriginal art market. Johnny Warangkula Tjupurrula's *Water Dreaming at Kalipinypa* (1972) sold to a Californian buyer for the record sum of $206,000 against an estimate of $50,000-$80,000 (Figure 12). Aboriginal art was increasingly being viewed as a positive flagship for Australia and three Aboriginal artists — Emily Kame Kngwarreye, Yvonne Koolmatrie and Judy Watson — were even chosen to represent Australia at the 1997 Venice Biennale.

The undoubted quality and provenance of the works, the wide catalogue distribution and Sotheby's heavy promotion of the sale internationally, all contributed to the auction's success. In America, the arts programme on CNN, *Visions*, aired a one minute story about the auction every four hours over a period of one week to 220 different countries. The BBC, the London *Sunday Observer*, the *Wall Street Journal* and *The New York Times* ran stories on it. Sotheby's own magazine included an article on the sale, the first occasion on which Sotheby's Australia had received press in its international magazine.

Sotheby's Australia

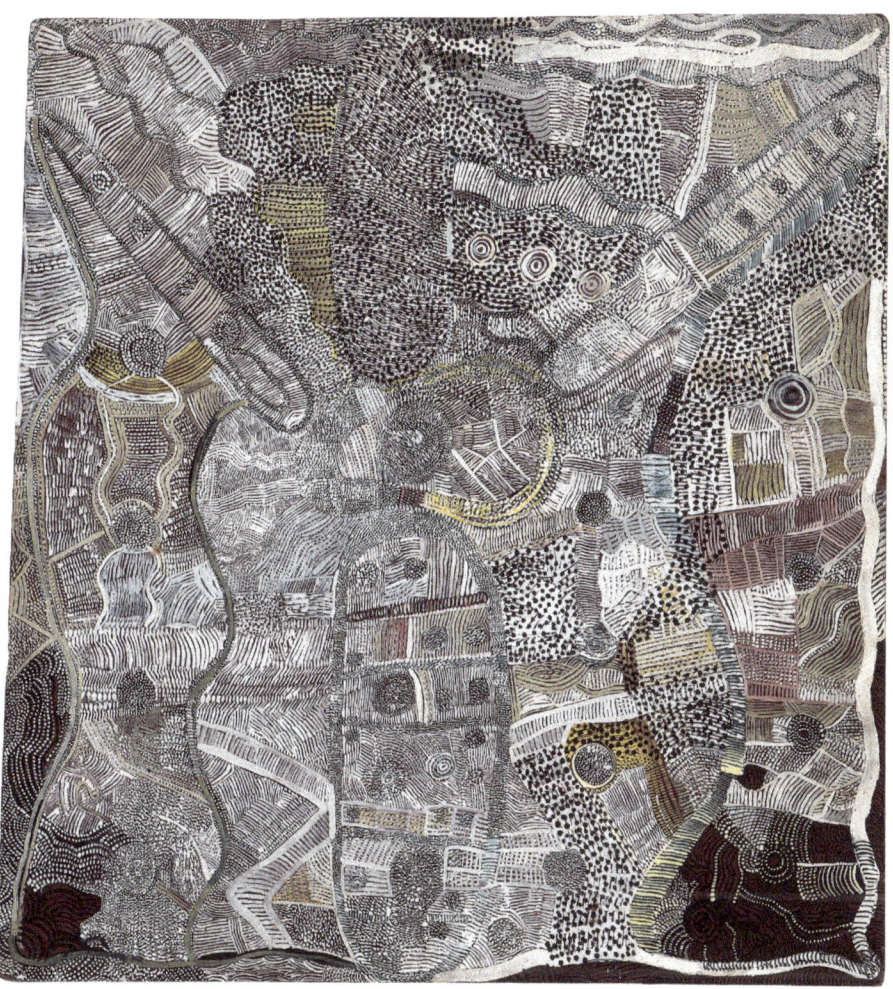

Figure 12: Johnny Warangkula Tjupurrula, *Water Dreaming at Kalipinypa*, 1972, synthetic polymer powder paint on composition board, 75 x 80 cm. Copyright the estate of the artist licensed by Aboriginal Artists Agency 2008.

It was primarily the New York and London collectors (both institutional and otherwise) who were responsible for the high prices and thus defining the Aboriginal art market. The Australian collectors could not compete with the international ones, who had begun to lodge telephone bids, on an unprecedented level, weeks prior to the auction. Thirteen people manned the telephones on the night, taking bids from Australia, North America, Europe and Asia. Thirty per cent of the lots, including half of the ten highest prices, were purchased by overseas collectors, mainly from America. Approximately 95 per cent of the works sold, compared to an auction average of 70 to 80 per cent. Although the quality of the auction was exceptional, it set a precedent. It was anticipated that future Aboriginal sales would prove as fruitful and Sotheby's decided to tour its next major Aboriginal art auction overseas.

Sotheby's auction of *Important Aboriginal Art* in Melbourne the next year, on 29 June 1998, followed along similar lines, with half of the top ten lots again going to overseas collectors. Billy Stockman Tjapaltjarri's *Wild Potato Dreaming* (1971) sold for $200,500 (estimate $20,000–$30,000) to a Los Angeles buyer. This work was included in the American preview of the auction and illustrated in the *Architectural Digest* magazine. Ingram claimed that there were two primary motivations for the frantic bidding at the auction: that collectors were concerned firstly about the scarcity of quality early works and secondly, that the *Protection of Movable Cultural Heritage Act 1986* — which regulates the export of works deemed to be of great cultural significance to Australia — once amended, would make it difficult to export the works and hence greatly reduce the number of international bidders.[47] Sotheby's lobbied against amendments to the Act which, according to it, would increase the burden of paper-work, restrict its increasingly lucrative international business in Aboriginal art and damage the Aboriginal art market.[48] In 1998, Sotheby's Aboriginal art turnover increased to rival the success of its other Australian art auctions.

Sotheby's auction of *Important Aboriginal Art* in June 1999 was notable for the interest shown by American investors, with seven out of the top ten works purchased by Americans, prompting one reporter to comment that 'The result proves the success of Sotheby's overseas marketing campaign. The top 10 selling works were among the 42 paintings previewed in Cologne and New York.'[49] The Melbourne dealer, William Mora, observed that 'This represents the first time we have had an art movement with an international market, [sic] that is certainly driving prices'.[50]

Deutscher-Menzies attempted to enter the market for contemporary Aboriginal art on two occasions, in June 1999 and June 2000, but was unable to compete with Klingender's superior network, reputation and international client base. Anita Archer, Deutscher-Menzies' auctioneer, admitted that 'Domestic demand is not so great that it warrants a separate catalogue. If we were marketing to the international market we could justify continuing with stand-alone sales but we don't have the infrastructure to sell overseas'.[51]

Nonetheless, 2004 witnessed fresh competition for Sotheby's supremacy of the Aboriginal art auction market with Bonhams & Goodman, Christie's and Lawson-Menzies holding specialized Aboriginal art sales. This resulted in some high prices but also flooded the market. Since that time Bonhams & Goodman has sold some works for high prices but has integrated Aboriginal art into its general Australian and International art sales. Christie's was able to source some important works, such as Rover Thomas's *Lundari (Barramundi Dreaming)* (1985), an early and significant work by the artist and one with the desirable provenance of The Holmes à Court Collection. This was widely expected to fetch more than $1 million, but Christie's was unable to sell it in August 2005. Christie's actually withdrew from the Australian market altogether (although this was not related to its Aboriginal art sales). Lawson-Menzies has achieved some success with, for example, Maggie Watson Napangardi's *Digging Stick Dreaming* (1995) attaining $216,000 (estimate $200,000–$300,000) at its November 2005 auction. This was an auction record for the artist. Lawson-Menzies' market share has grown from $1.5 million in May 2004 to $3.4 million in May 2006.[52]

The Hallinan Collection of New Guinea Art, at the time the largest collection of tribal art offered in Australia, was auctioned by Sotheby's at the Powerhouse Museum on 28 November 1993. Peter Hallinan was a Brisbane art dealer suffering from financial difficulties and therefore in need of liquidity. He had collected the pieces over a twenty-five-year period, during more than twenty visits to Papua New Guinea. Ninety per cent of the lots sold for a total of $400,000 (double the expected total) to a bidding audience comprising numerous collectors of contemporary and modern art, prompting one dealer to remark that 'Primitive has arrived'.[53]

Aboriginal art dealers were reportedly pleased with the high prices and publicity produced by Sotheby's; however, dealers in Contemporary art were less than pleased, as Sotheby's set its prices lower than retail ones to ensure a positive outcome.[54] Whether this is also a positive outcome for the Contemporary dealers and living artists is debatable.

As previously mentioned, Sotheby's had been holding combined auctions of Aboriginal and Contemporary art since the 1980s. However, Sotheby's had earlier conducted Australia's first specialized Contemporary art auction in Melbourne in June 1991 of paintings and sculpture from the collection of the Museum of Contemporary Art in Brisbane. Many of the works sold below their estimates, doing little to set respectable benchmarks for the works of Contemporary Australian artists. Sotheby's stand-alone Contemporary sales were not a resounding success overall and were later discontinued.

The importance of international buyers of Aboriginal art was once more highlighted by Sotheby's *Aboriginal Art* auction on 26–27 June 2000, where an interpreter was employed to aid European buyers bidding on the telephone. This was yet another record sale which realized $4.4 million; 62 per cent of the lots (by volume) went to American and European buyers, with private museums purchasing approximately 50 lots.[55] Forty-five of the star attractions had been previewed in Paris and New York, making the catalogue, photographs and condition reports of prime importance in attracting sales. Johnny Warangkula Tjupurrula's *Water Dreaming at Kalipinypa* (1972) was resold at this auction, again attaining the top sale price. It sold for $486,500 to the Melbourne art dealer, Irene Sutton, on behalf of a New York client and further demonstrated the degree to which Aboriginal art had infiltrated the international marketplace. This sale also raised the issue of the potential need for an art resale royalty again, as Johnny Warangkula Tjupurrula was originally paid only $150 for the work and was living in poverty.

Sotheby's 2003 auction of Aboriginal art was held over two evenings on 28–29 July at the Museum of Contemporary Art in Sydney. The sale, estimated at $6.5–8.5 million, realized $7.46 million. The collection of Kimberley Art which had been assembled by American anthropologist, John McCaffrey, in the mid-1960s was featured in the sale and favoured with its own museum-standard catalogue. The top bids, yet again, hailed from overseas, mainly Europe and America, with an estimated 70 per cent of works selling to international collectors. Klingender noted that 'It's fabulous that indigenous art is appreciated somewhere, if not in Australia, then internationally'.[56] This makes an interesting point about the comparative lack of interest in Aboriginal art by Australians.

The star attraction of the sale, *Ngurrara Canvas I* (1996), a collaborative work by artists represented by the Mangkaja Arts Resource Agency, sold for only $210,000 (estimate $300,000–$500,000), to a Perth businessman, Paul Naughton. This work had been marketed extensively to Americans, having been travelled in an Aboriginal art exhibition in 1999 and featured on television and in the print media, including the front cover of the Arts Section of *The New York Times*. According to Ingram, 'This week's sale was a triumph of slick marketing and stage management with even a potential disaster [sic] the aesthetically challenging star lot turned to great advantage…The work's dismal performance after the hype came too late for most newspaper deadlines.'[57]

The key works from Sotheby's eighth annual auction of Aboriginal art on 26–27 July 2004 were previewed at Sotheby's galleries in London for the first time. They had also been shown in Paris alongside Sotheby's auction of African and Oceanic Art. However, the auction's signature painting, *Uluru (Ayers Rock)* (1987) by Rover Thomas, failed to sell amid concern regarding the subject matter (it seemed unlikely that a Kimberley artist would be painting Uluru) and the high estimate of $700,000–$1,000,000. The work was passed-in at $675,000. It would have set a world record if it had reached its top estimate. At the time of writing in October 2007, the highest auction price for an Aboriginal painting is for Clifford Possum Tjapaltjarri's *Warlugulong* (1977), which sold at Sotheby's in July 2007 for $2.4 million.[58]

Increased competition resulted in Sotheby's halving its usual offering of Aboriginal art in July 2005. A large proportion of the works in this auction were sold to international buyers at a value of $2.04 million, almost half of the sale total of $4.83 million (estimate $6 million–$8.5 million). These included two works by Clifford Possum Tjapaltjarri: the first painting he created, *Emu Corroboree Man* (1972) (estimate $150,000–$250,000), which set a record for the artist when it sold to an American via the dealer Irene Sutton for $411,750 (including commissions) and *Man's Love Story* (c.1993) which sold to a French buyer also for $411,750 (estimate $40,000–$70,000).[59] However, auction turnover was much lower than anticipated. Sotheby's Aboriginal and Oceanic Art auction in Melbourne on 15–16 November 2005 — its second Aboriginal art auction for that year — achieved $1.4 million, with many works selling beneath the lower estimate or being passed-in.

The Aboriginal art auction market was worth $666,000 in 1988; by 2006 this figure had risen to a staggering $14,325,000 and the value of the Aboriginal art market as a whole was estimated to be upwards of $200 million.[60] According to Klingender, Australians began to collect Aboriginal art seriously in the late 1980s.[61] In the early 1990s, international buyers had only accounted for around 10 per cent of buyers at Sotheby's Aboriginal art sales.[62] Sotheby's sold $288,086 worth of Aboriginal art in 1994. This figure increased to $893,318 in 1995, followed by $1.2 million in 1996. In June 1996, less than 20 per cent of works from Sotheby's June Aboriginal art auction were purchased by international collectors; this figure had increased to 30 per cent by volume in 1997 and 50 per cent by volume in 1998.[63] Justin Miller commented at the time that Sotheby's achieved its highest annual turnover in 1998 because of the weak Australian dollar and the popularity of Aboriginal art, accentuating the importance of said art for the firm.[64] This success has had a flow-on effect to Australian dealers of Aboriginal art, with Gabrielle Pizzi estimating that her international sales of Aboriginal art doubled from the late 1980s to the late 1990s.[65] International dealers, such as Stephane Jacob in Paris, have also been promoting Aboriginal art for several years. Aboriginal art has now attained such status at an international level that it has been included in the collection of the Musée du Quai Branly in Paris.

ENDNOTES

[1] Reginald Longden, *An Antiques Saga*, R. Longden, Adelaide 1991, p.111.

[2] Peter Cochrane, 'Dueling Gavels', *Good Weekend Magazine*, 18 November 1989, p.60.

[3] Terry Ingram, 'UK art dealers scent Aust pay dirt', *Australian Financial Review*, 26 July 1971, p.5.

[4] Author unknown, 'Dobell art auction cancelled', *The Northern Territory News* (probably), 2 November 1972, p.5.

[5] Brian Adams, *Portrait of an Artist: A Biography of William Dobell*, Vintage, Milson's Point, New South Wales 1992, p.318.

[6] Terry Ingram, 'Price and Prejudice interest in mammoth Dobell sell-out', *Australian Financial Review*, 13 September 1973, p.36.

[7] Terry Ingram, 'Where there's a will there's a way — Dobell's Opera House auction', *Australian Financial Review*, 1 November 1972, p.1, 11.

[8] Adams, *Portrait of an Artist*, p.319.

[9] Terry Ingram, 'Dobell prices uneven', *Australian Financial Review*, 22 November 1973, p.42.

[10] Ingram, 'Price and Prejudice interest in mammoth Dobell sell-out', p.36.

[11] Michael Fitzgerald, 'Urban man heeds call of the tribal', *The Age*, 25 July 1990, p.3.

[12] Quoted in Nicholas Faith, *Sold: the Rise and Fall of the House of Sotheby*, Macmillan, New York 1985, p.94.

[13] Ava Hubble, 'Robert Bleakley: Dealer with a Difference', *Australian Art Collector*, issue 4, April–June 1998, p.37.

[14] Margaretta Pos, 'Van Gogh record makes investors hungry for a share of art market', *Hobart Mercury*, 4 April 1987, no pagination.

[15] Charles Nodrum, taped interview with the author, Melbourne, 24 October 2002 and Chris Deutscher, taped interview with the author, Melbourne, 3 October 2002.

[16] Cochrane, 'Dueling Gavels', p.66.

[17] Robert Bleakley, taped interview with the author, Canberra, 28 November 2002.

[18] Charles Nodrum, taped interview with the author, Melbourne, 24 October 2002.

[19] Fran Hernon, 'Selling "snobbism" at Sotheby's', *Daily Telegraph*, 31 October 1987, p.31.

[20] Charles Nodrum, taped interview with the author, Melbourne, 24 October 2002.

[21] Bleakley in Cochrane, 'Dueling Gavels', p.67.

[22] Bleakley in Cochrane, 'Dueling Gavels', p.66.

[23] Bleakley in Cochrane, 'Dueling Gavels', p.66.

[24] Charles Nodrum, taped interview with the author, Melbourne, 24 October 2002 and Justin Miller, taped interview with the author, Sydney, 3 September 2002.

[25] Mark Fraser, taped interview with the author, Melbourne, 21 October 2002 and Jane Clark, telephone conversation with the author, 2 August 2002.

[26] The approximate reserve was obtained from Robert Bleakley, taped interview with the author, Canberra, 28 November 2002.

[27] Terry Ingram, 'Art trade discovers life after Sotheby's', *Australian Financial Review*, 13 August 1987, p.32.

[28] Marshall Wilson and Jamie Fawcett, 'Family Bond', *Courier Mail*, 25 March 2000, p.23.

[29] Colleen Ryan and Kate McClymont, 'Bond's trail leads the art world to the first of our missing explorers', *Sydney Morning Herald*, 18 June 1994, p.34.

[30] Ava Hubble, 'Switzerland discovers our missing Captain Cook', *Sydney Morning Herald*, 29 July 1993, p.1.

[31] Terry Ingram, 'Cook portrait on convoluted voyage', *Australian Financial Review*, 12 August 1993, p.28.

[32] Terry Ingram, '$1.5m agreed for Cook portrait', *Australian Financial Review*, 3 August 1993, p.2.

[33] It should be noted that I had to piece this together from often conflicting news reports.

[34] Terry Ingram, 'Art — Even a trained eye can't pick fact from fiction', *Australian Financial Review*, 6 March 1999, p.36.

[35] Quoted in Terry Ingram, 'Rites of passage', *Australian Financial Review*, 31 August 2000, p.21.

[36] Andrew Sayers, unpublished floor-talk, National Portrait Gallery, 11 August 2002.

[37] Robert Bleakley, taped interview with the author, Canberra, 28 November 2002.

[38] Justin Miller, taped interview with the author, Sydney, 3 September 2002.

[39] Tony Fry and Anne-Marie Willis, 'Aboriginal Art: Symptom or Success?', *Art in America*, July 1989, pp.108–16, 159–163. See also Fred R. Myers, *Painting Culture: The Making of an Aboriginal High Art*, Duke University Press, London 2002.

[40] Susan Owens, 'From the outback to Manhattan', *The Weekend Australian Financial Review*, the fin, 30 September–1 October 2000, pp.4–5 and Terry Ingram, 'Mobile phone king makes an Aboriginal connection', *Australian Financial Review*, 4–5 October 1997, Smart Money, p.37.

[41] <http://www.virginia.edu/kluge-ruhe/index.php?p=about> [24 January 2007].

[42] Roger Benjamin, 'Aboriginal Art: Exploitation or Empowerment?', *Art in America*, vol. 78, July 1990, p.79.

[43] Terry Ingram, 'Sotheby's doubles earnings', *Australian Financial Review*, 13 August 1999, no pagination.

[44] Susan McCulloch, 'Body of origin', *The Weekend Review*, 18–19 November 1995, no pagination.

[45] Terry Ingram, 'Black Market', *Art and Australia*, 35(1) 1997, pp.126–7.

[46] Peter Fish, 'Primitive Urges', *Sydney Morning Herald*, 2 October 1996, p.5.

[47] Terry Ingram, 'Obsessions with rarities', *Art and Australia*, 36(2) 1998, p.251 and Michael Reid, 'Aboriginal collection comes home', *The Weekend Australian*, 20–21 June 1998, p.4.

[48] Terry Ingram, 'Sotheby's warns against heritage changes', *Australian Financial Review*, 16 April 1998, p.44; Susan McCulloch, 'Exports caught in the Act', *The Australian*, 26 June 1998, p.15; and Michael Reid and Susan McCulloch, 'Art dealers puzzled by 20-year rule', *The Australian*, 25 January 1999, p.17

[49] Gabriella Coslovich, 'Art sails off to USA', *The Age*, 30 June 1999, no pagination.

[50] Quoted in Coslovich, 'Art sails off to USA', no pagination.

[51] John Kavanagh, 'A collage of art successes', *Business Review Weekly*, 12 January 2001, no pagination.

[52] Lawson-Menzies, 'Emily Masterpiece From Holt Collection Unveiled for the First Time In Lawson~Menzies $4.8M Aboriginal Art Auction', undated, <http://www.lawsonmenzies.com.au/EmilyMasterpieceFromHoltCollectionUnveiled.html> [08/02/07].

[53] Peter Cochrane, 'Old patter sells tribal lots', *Sydney Morning Herald*, 29 November 1993, p.2.

[54] McCulloch, 'Body of origin', no pagination.

[55] Peter Fish, 'Foreign buyers go dotty over Aboriginal art', *Sydney Morning Herald*, 18 August 2000, Money, p.6.

[56] Jamie Berry, 'Aboriginal art at record highs', *The Age*, 30 July 2003, <www.theage.com.au/articles/2003/07/29/1059244620062.html> [08/08/2003].

[57] Terry Ingram, 'Big works lose out', *Australian Financial Review*, 31 July 2003, p.57.

[58] Much of this was first published in Shireen Huda, 'Over-priced, Under-appreciated', *Australian Art Review*, issue 6, November 2004–February 2005, p.25.

[59] Geoff Maslen, 'Aboriginal art heads overseas', *The Age*, 27 July 2005, <http://www.theage.com.au/news/arts/art-heads-overseas/2005/07/26/1122143839680.html> [08/02/2007].

[60] Katrina Strickland, 'As the 10th anniversary of indigenous art auctions looms…', *Australian Financial Review*, Australian Financial Review Magazine, 30 June 2006, p.26.

[61] Matthew Russell, 'Aboriginal art weaves magic prices on world stage', *Sydney Morning Herald*, 20 June 1997, possibly p.10.

[62] John Kavanagh, 'Dream time to the big time', *Business Review Weekly*, 18 August 2000, p.57.

[63] Rowena Stretton, 'Art and artifice: the pitfalls and pleasures of Aboriginal paintings', *The Weekend Australian Financial Review*, the fin, 29–30 August 1998, p.3.

[64] Bruce Atherton, 'FED – Weak dollar aids Aboriginal art boom', *Australian Associated Press*, 18 January 1999, no pagination.

[65] Brook Turner, 'An authentic market', *The Australian Financial Review Magazine*, undated, possibly 1999, p.15.

Chapter 7. Art Auction Practices and Innovations

Robert Bleakley said in 1993 that 'The role of the auction house is to create the situation where everyone is offered the chance to set a price. The auctioneer is adjudicator. He's there for the buyer and seller'.[1] The auction house acting as buyer, vendor, dealer, even curator — an all-encompassing agent — has been attributed to initiatives by Peter Wilson three decades ago.

Christie's and Sotheby's introduced numerous innovations or modifications in the local marketplace which reflect, to some degree, the institutional *personae* of the two firms. These innovations included buying-in, bidding numbers and referrals, reserve and estimate setting procedures, setting the rhythm of the sale, a five-year guarantee of authenticity, and commissions, such as the buyer's premium. The international firms also made a substantial revision to accepted standards for art auction catalogues and placed greater emphasis on educating their clients. Sotheby's prioritized marketing and added a veneer of glamour to auctions through the introduction of a black-tie dress code. These initiatives resulted in the greater sophistication of standard auction practices and the marketplace as a whole.

Over the past decade, some auction houses — in Australia and internationally — have once more ventured into selling contemporary art. Many believe that only well established artists can successfully compete in the auction arena and that contemporary artists with little exposure can have their careers irrevocably damaged by poor public sales. Furthermore, auction houses have traditionally not developed sustainable reputations for artists as art dealers do. However, Stuart Purves, then President of the Australian Commercial Galleries Association and National Director of Australian Galleries, noted in 2002 that 'The immensely high profile the auction houses have given Australian art has done more than the galleries could do on their own in 100 years. They are responsible for tripling prices and bringing them up to the reality that enables new, living artists to make a living'.[2]

Sotheby's was the first major art auction house in Australia to attempt to create a market for contemporary art at auction, holding specialized contemporary art auctions in the early-mid 1990s, mainly as a result of the economic recession. Its mixed-vendor stand-alone contemporary art sales were not particularly profitable and were discontinued in the mid-1990s, as works by modern artists were preferred by collectors and were still reasonably affordable in this period. Christie's had usually included contemporary art at the beginning of its general paintings sales and established a contemporary art department in 2000 to hold stand-alone contemporary art auctions, mostly focussing on works by artists who had already achieved a certain level of recognition. Art auction houses will continue to respond to changing circumstances and collecting tastes, while also influencing or creating new markets.

This chapter does not, therefore, attempt to provide a complete and current picture of all auction practices, but an overview and background to some of the more common practices; i.e. where they started and why, if known. Many questionable or unethical practices and forms of art crime are mentioned only briefly, because they warrant detailed and concentrated investigation in their own right. This is particularly so for art fraud as the establishment of Australia's first course in art authentication at Melbourne University Private in 2005 is testament to the growing concern about counterfeit works, purportedly by artists who have recently died or whose prices are increasing, including Aboriginal and Torres Strait Islander artists.

Buying-in

In the early 1970s, Christie's was fairly open about methods it used to ensure that sales achieved good results. The company had developed, through its network and access to expert advice, means to lessen the chances of bargains or 'sleepers' appearing. Imaginary bidders might be also used to assist a work to reach its reserve. This practice was known as bidding 'off the wall' or 'puffing the bid' and resulted in works being 'bought-in' or withdrawn discreetly if their reserves were not reached. John Henshaw maintained that the practice of buying-in was employed by both Christie's and Sotheby's during the late 1960s and early 1970s. According to Henshaw, buying-in maintained realistic market values for works and avoided the bad press associated with a work publicly failing to sell.[3] Christie's claimed that it did not, however, give permission for the vendor of a work to bid it up at auction and denied running up bids after the reserve had been reached. A concerned buyer was entitled to be given, upon application, the name of their underbidder to ensure that they were not bidding against a fake buyer.[4] This was referred to in the popular press in October 1974 as Christie's 'buying-in charade', as the practice had the effect of creating uncertainty as to whether works had actually sold.[5]

Indeed, from the prices supplied in *Christie's Australian Art Sales Index 1969–1974*, bought-in works were indistinguishable from works which really did sell. Edward D. Craig, compiler of *Australian Art Auction Records*, noted in his first edition in 1973 that the practice of buying-in a work when the reserve was not reached was common. The bought-in work was included in the published price list as a true sale price. However, Craig believed that as the bought-in price 'is usually only one bid above the last genuine offer, it does constitute a fair indication of the value of the particular work'.[6]

Fake buyers' names were most notably used by Spowers, who was inventive in his choice of names when he introduced this practice to the Australian salerooms in the late 1960s/early 1970s. In those days, the auctioneer was expected to know who the major buyers were and a successful bidder would announce his/her name. This was the precursor of the registration/paddle system at auctions, where fake bidding numbers were often employed. Bidding numbers were introduced because of a growing desire for anonymity.[7]

Sotheby's employed the registration (paddle/numbered) system from its foundation in Australia for 'accuracy' and 'clarity'.[8] Telephone and commission bidding were also employed from the beginning and were used extensively by bidders. The international firms were convinced to stop buying-in, partly from pressure brought to bear by lobby groups in New York. They began to declare a work was unsold by calling out 'thank you', without mentioning a bidding number. In 1991, legislation was introduced in New York making it obligatory to declare whether a lot was indeed unsold at the time of the auction. It was not until April 1998 that Christie's and Sotheby's main offices in both London and New York made it compulsory for their auctioneers to state at the time of sale if a lot went unsold. The practice of buying-in was thus outlawed.

Setting the Rhythm

Sotheby's, like other auction houses, has consistently paid attention to the minutiae of the mechanics of art auctions. It has also devoted much time to organizing the structure and order of the sale to maximize the possibility of an exceptional outcome by controlling the auction rhythm, thus capitalizing on the psychology of the event.

Lots are arranged so that some items are placed in key positions where they will create peaks of bidding excitement, leading to escalating prices. The structure of the sale — the orchestration of 'crescendos' — is principally responsible for an auction's success or failure.[9] Before each auction conducted by Bleakley, for example, he would sketch a floor plan from the rostrum in order to gauge where most of the bids were likely to come from, allowing him to concentrate on certain areas of the saleroom and encourage reticent bidders.

Referrals, Reserves and Estimates

The system of 'referrals', whereby the auctioneer states that he will consult the vendor when the reserve has not been met to ascertain whether he/she is willing to sell, has been utilized extensively by Sotheby's Australia. Christie's, on the other hand:

> Tends to adopt the more gentlemanly posture of suggesting that the unsuccessful bidder visit the auctioneer afterwards to 'see what can be done'. At all the multinational auctions, a price called above the lower

estimate should mean the lot has found a buyer as the auctioneer insists reserves are set below the lower estimate.[10]

This is indicative of, firstly, the differing styles of Christie's and Sotheby's, and secondly the fact that in the past reserves were not always set below or equal to the low estimate.

In 1976, although art auctions were a popular means of buying and selling art in Australia, buyers were becoming disenchanted with 'referrals'. Since late 1974 auction costs had risen while turnover had declined, effectively inhibiting the auctioneers' ability to haggle with the vendor prior to sale on reserves. Auction houses were also charging buying-in fees — 'commissions on works which do not meet reserve and go unsold' — and catalogue fees.[11] Christie's started charging the buying-in fee in its Australian office and Associated Auctioneers began to charge buyers a one per cent handling fee.

Christie's difficulties with setting reserves and estimates were considered in the mid-1970s to be owing to the fact that it only held two paintings auctions each year, meaning that paintings for sale would be gathered up to six months prior to a sale. This long lead-time made it extremely difficult when estimating market value, as market and economic fluctuations could have a deleterious effect by the time of the auction, and related to Christie's printing the catalogues in London.

Christie's introduced the practice of printing estimates in catalogues in 1983. Estimates, a key factor in art auction practices, were originally in the hands of staff and potential buyers were required to ask for the estimate on the lots that interested them, thus enabling 'the auctioneers to get a rough indication of the sort of interest that would be generated in the work by the number of inquiries'.[12] Access to auction estimates evolved from the mid 1970s to the early 1980s from asking staff to view estimates; to looking at printed estimates pinned on the wall; to their being made available at auction viewings (a practice similar to that used by art dealers); to finding them included in the rear of the catalogue (from the late 1970s); and finally, to reading them alongside each lot in the catalogue in 1983. Once Christie's introduced publicly available estimates, the clientele began to demand this initiative of other auction houses. It represented a huge change in the collective psyche of the art market, making the public increasingly educated about market values and practices and demanding certain inclusions or standards.

In the early 1970s, there was a perception that Christie's reserve prices were unrealistic and generated by the desire to attract quality works to its sales in order to boost the firm's prestige. Henshaw claimed that 'the greatest difficulty is getting a realistic reserve in relation to the market – and unless it is realistic it just doesn't sell'.[13] Christie's also said that it insisted on vendors putting up 'realistic' reserves so that the works would sell and that it was placing greater emphasis on accepting only quality lots for sale.[14] Generally, buyers would accept paying the true market value for works at auction, having some idea of what that value might be. This held especially true for art dealers. Astronomically high prices were the exception rather than the rule and usually the result of a couple of bidders desperately wanting the work and willing to acquire it at any cost.

Sotheby's introduced printed estimates in its art auction catalogues internationally in 1986. Bleakley said that Sotheby's differed from other auction houses in Australia in that it did not permit the reserve prices to be above the low estimates, aiming for its estimates to be 20 to 30 per cent lower than what it believed to be the market value.[15] This ensured that it acted 'ethically' and could 'establish market credibility'.[16] Many dealers and collectors had found that, although their bids had exceeded the low estimate, they still could not purchase the work because it had not reached the reserve. This was naturally a point of contention and resulted in a bad reputation for auction houses. Some reports have suggested that Sotheby's purposely gave works low estimates so that the sale prices would far exceed the estimates.[17] Sotheby's reserve policy worked as a positive marketing mechanism, increasing confidence in the professional standards of the new firm.

Art Auction Catalogues

The cachet of being included in a professional publication increases the monetary value of the work. Nonetheless, Christie's catalogues were becoming more anonymous, with many vendors concerned about the possible tax implications of publicly announcing that they were selling or buying art.[18] Only one vendor's name was included in Christie's October 1975 catalogue, that of James O. Fairfax, a desirable provenance.

Justin Miller, then Managing Director of Sotheby's Australia, said in the mid-1990s that the art auction catalogue is 'the most important marketing tool we have'.[19] An auction house, like Sotheby's, utilizes the quality and distribution of its catalogues to lure prospective clients, stressing not only the pedagogic nature of the presentation, but also the academic qualifications of its staff. Auction houses project an 'atmosphere of reliability'.[20] Their catalogues are thus presented as — and can be — reliable sources of information; they 'possess an aura of authority' through their very packaging.[21]

Roger Dedman confirmed that 'One conclusion worth repeating is the unquestionable value of an illustration in a catalogue'.[22] One can ascertain whether a work that seems to be appearing repeatedly at auction is indeed the same work and whether it is possibly the victim of 'ramping' — where prices are artificially boosted at auction by those who have a vested interest in increasing the value of an artist's works — or warehousing — where works are purchased with a view to storing them until they are resold for a profit. Even more significant is the fact that an illustrated work invariably demonstrates a substantial increase in sales price over an unillustrated one. Moreover, a work illustrated in a catalogue can claim a desirable provenance. The majority of lots are now illustrated in colour, accompanied by a detailed description, provenance, exhibition history, bibliographic references and estimates.

In the early years of Sotheby's Australia, the firm projected images of lots as they were sold onto a large screen next to the rostrum. This worked well and permitted everyone in the saleroom to see each lot clearly. The advent of new technologies and the decrease of printing costs which enabled auction catalogues to be more lavishly illustrated, revolutionized the Australian art auction market, enabling catalogues to be taken to a new level of professionalism, thus transmogrifying what had become a practical tool — a checklist — into an opulent vehicle for self-promotion. According to Cochrane, 'The art of cataloguing is a relatively recent development, mirroring the surge in painting values'.[23] Moreover, art auction catalogues are so well-illustrated that people do not have to attend viewings of the works or even the auction itself, relying on commission or telephone bidding. This is more labour-intensive and expensive for auction houses.

Although provenance is often included in auction catalogues in order to imbue the work with integrity and historical merit, there are occasions when an auction house may choose not to publicize the origin of a lot. It may be owing to the vendor's desire for anonymity; a lack of time in which to conduct research; because the auction house does not wish to advertise the source of stock; or perhaps because the work had a past best forgotten.[24] When works are described as belonging to a 'Private Collection' — a useful and all-embracing expression — it could in fact mean that it belonged to a dealer. Very recent provenances may be deliberately overlooked, as selling soon after purchasing does not enhance the saleability of a work, especially if it has recently sold for a sum considerably less than the current asking price. However, if the work sold on a previous occasion for a breathtaking amount, accompanied by fanfare, the auction house can capitalize on this in the hope of attracting a similarly spectacular bid.

Since Sotheby's arrival in Australia, art auction catalogues have placed less emphasis on a small selection of quality lots and a greater emphasis on quantity, owing to the need for a high turnover. Reitlinger prophesied in 1970 that 'As the good things vanish, sales get skimpier and catalogues bigger and more luxuriously illustrated. Non-art, the collector's substitute and second line of defence, is promoted with greater and greater assiduity. Everything portends the day when all that has been collected must become institutionalised.'[25]

In the late 1980s, at the height of the art boom, the number of lots on offer at auction ballooned from 100 to 200, to almost 600, including a number of lesser works. Sotheby's first catalogue from March 1983 contained only 54 paintings, with the Cook portrait as the highlight. Chris Deutscher, when he was still an art dealer, commented that auction houses, such as Sotheby's, should concentrate on quality rather than on high turnover and that 'Sotheby's should not be promoting the market but letting it find its own level'.[26] However, his opinion presumably changed once he was an auction house principal, as Deutscher-Menzies' catalogues often contained a couple of hundred lots, with the Australian + International Fine Art Sale in March 2006, for example, containing 325 lots.

In the 1990s, the multinational firms placed more weight on attracting expert staff to improve the quality of their research and catalogues. Jane Clark joined Sotheby's in April 1994 as Director of Paintings in Melbourne, leaving her twelve-year position as Curator of Australian Painting at the National Gallery of Victoria and taking with her a reputation for high academic ability. Patricia R. McDonald (no relation to Patricia McDonald, formerly of Christie's), was the research coordinator of the Arthur Boyd retrospective which toured Australia in 1994, and joined Sotheby's at the same time as Clark. McDonald was appointed to the position of Manager of Sotheby's paintings department in Sydney.

Bleakley commented at the time that 'The curatorial experience of both Jane and Patricia will bring new dimensions to fine art auctioneering in Australia'.[27] These appointments were part of a strategic plan to transform Sotheby's auction catalogues into something comparable to exhibition catalogues produced by major public institutions, in quality of research and presentation (although it should be noted that the depth of research completed is restricted by more stringent timeframes than in public galleries).

Since Christie's was established in Australia in 1969, business affiliations, commercial prowess and celebrity status have grown in importance. This is reflected in the appointment of 'opinion formers' as auction house staff.[28] Directors, too, were initially recognized experts in their arts-related field and intimately involved in the art market. Looking at Christie's catalogues from the 1960s onwards, one can see the augmentation of the list of Directors from three in 1969 to nine (including Associate Directors) at the time of the last auction in 2006, with an Advisory Board of eight. Over time, as each department of an auction house, such as Christie's, 'expanded and divided and specialized, you had a proliferation of directors'.[29] However, directors today are often engaged for their business kudos or social standing; prestige has become of paramount importance.

Art Education

The advent of publicly available art auction records, as well as serious attention given to art auctions by journals and the wider press, had repercussions for the market as a whole, not least the ability of the collector to do his/her own research. *Australian Art Auction Records* was, as noted, first published from 1973 and Christie's published its own art index from about 1974, covering sales held by Christie's and Sotheby's in Australia, as well as sales of Australian art in London. Before the readily available records it was much easier for people — dealers or collectors — to buy at auction, perhaps interstate, and sell again within a short timeframe in order to make a quick profit. Art auction records provided objective information, including whether works were passed-in. Although the transparency of the auction system is extremely important, there is no denying that any work which has been passed-in publicly is stigmatized to some extent.

The *Australian Financial Review* began a regular saleroom column on 4 July 1969, with Terry Ingram as its saleroom correspondent providing a consistent voice for almost four decades. The saleroom column began after Christie's and Sotheby's established a presence in Australia, implying that the finance newspaper did not take art auctions seriously when they were being conducted by local firms, but an increasing awareness of the investment potential of art and the interest of international firms turned art auctions into a more important and newsworthy enterprise. Geoff Maslen and Michael Reid have also made a substantial contribution to art market analysis in more recent years, with Maslen writing for *The Age* in Melbourne and latterly for the *Sydney Morning Herald*, and Reid the art market analyst for *The Australian*. The art market has also been assimilated into art history and curatorship, with most art journals today including regular reports on art auctions. *Australian Art Collector*, a specialised art magazine which has been providing coverage of the Australian art market since it was first published in 1997, exists in response to a market which has been substantially created by the auction houses.

By the 1960s, state galleries were increasingly interested in education and scholarship and talented young art curators like Bernard Smith, Ursula Hoff and Daniel Thomas were employed. Educating collectors about art has also been on the agenda of auction houses. Robert Lacey maintains that the forerunner of Sotheby's Works of Art Course, later known as Sotheby's Education, was conducted in 1969 and the actual course began in the early 1970s. He refers to it as 'the world's most prestigious finishing school'.[30] In the late 1990s, the major auction houses, Christie's, Lawson's, Phillips and Sotheby's, offered educational courses in order to expand and educate their client base, developing 'market awareness' and 'brand loyalty'.[31]

From 1990, Sotheby's introduced art history courses run by Lloyd Pollak, first in Melbourne, then Sydney and based on those taught in London. Sotheby's ran a full-time education course focusing on antiques with designated full-time staff from around 1990-93. McIlroy also introduced art education courses at Christie's and these courses have been renowned for their calibre. McIlroy discovered that, although there were more people buying at Christie's in the 1990s, they were not knowledgeable. People who completed Christie's art education courses would not only be more aware of works and artists in the comparatively narrow domain of the art market, but would also effectively be 'walking ambassadors for Christie's'.[32] Christie's Education, established in 1978, provides courses in art history, connoisseurship and the art market, offering degrees at University College in London and the University of Glasgow. Sotheby's Institute of Art in London, New York and Singapore also offers courses, degrees and various public programmes in art history, the business of art and connoisseurship.

Guarantees of Authenticity

In the early 1970s, most Australian art auction houses still offered little, if any, guarantee that the works they were selling were indeed executed by the professed artist or offered any recourse if found to be otherwise. Christie's and Sotheby's introduced guarantees that if works were proved to be forgeries they could be returned. Dealers had offered a similar money-back guarantee for some time. However, these guarantees differed in that they placed a time limit on returns. Sotheby Parke Bernet had first introduced a three-week guarantee in 1962 for its *Impressionist and Modern* and *Modern British* sales, in order to persuade private buyers to purchase art at auction themselves, rather than relying on art professionals.[33] The firm introduced the five-year guarantee of authenticity in September 1973.

In Australia, Sotheby's provided a guarantee of authenticity from its first auction in 1983. Although Sotheby's guaranteed the authorship of a work for five years from the date of the purchase, the provenance and exhibition history were not guaranteed, merely included to supplement the catalogue entry.[34] Although Christie's included a three-week guarantee (against 'deliberate forgery') in its auction in 1969, according to Bleakley Sotheby's generally 'made it very apparent that...[it] guaranteed authenticity'.[35]

Geoff K. Gray and Christie's, the latter under orders from its London headquarters, offered to rescind a sale and refund the money within twenty-one days of the sale if the work was found to be a forgery. Leonard Joel, Lawson's and Hamilton & Miller all refused to provide any refunds or guarantees of authenticity except in the most extraordinary of cases. Relatively few fakes and forgeries existed in the 1970s' Australian art market. In the absence of guarantees of authenticity, cheated buyers could rely on the threat of negative publicity to obtain a refund or they could take the vendor to court.

With the possible exception of Aboriginal art (the authorship of which is a sometimes complex issue), fakes and forgeries are thought to be less problematic now than in the past (for example the 1980s), owing to expert staff and consultants, a more aware and educated buying public, and the standard set by the multinationals of accepting culpability for incorrect attributions and a money-back guarantee. According to Ingram, 'The fantastic success of auctions as a medium for selling and marketing fine art was cited as the factor making the introduction of the guarantee possible'.[36] The auction houses were not only willing to claim that they were professional organizations, but to act in a professional manner.

Commissions/Buyer's Premium

In 1972 Christie's generally charged 15 per cent commissions. These paid for any catalogues printed or publicity and associated costs. Catalogue illustrations were usually paid for by the vendor. The commission could be negotiable, depending on the volume offered (a large estate for example), and out of that 15 per cent, 3 per cent might be given to a dealer who introduced a client who then made a purchase at auction. This implies that Christie's, at least initially, was working in tandem with the local art dealers, relying on their goodwill to attract clientèle.

For a substantial period of time, charging a buyer's premium had been illegal in New South Wales, but permitted in Victoria, accounting for both international houses conducting most of their auctions in Melbourne. The relevant New South Wales legislation, clause 30 in schedule 22 of the *Auctioneers and Agents Act 1941*, made it illegal for licensed auctioneers to obtain commissions from any party other than the vendor. This was to ensure that the auctioneer always acted in the best interests of the client (the vendor). Charging both buyer and vendor a commission would mean that the auctioneer would be acting on behalf of two principals.

Although Christie's also wanted the laws repealed, it was Bleakley at Sotheby's who was instrumental in having the New South Wales legislation amended, petitioning the Government for around nine years to enact changes allowing them to charge a buyer's premium and hence increase the number of auctions in Sydney. Other advocates for repealing the regulation included the Auctioneers and Valuers Association of Australia, also arguing that Sydney was disadvantaged because auction houses could not charge a premium and hence refrained from holding sales there.

As part of his campaign, Bleakley argued that buyer's premiums had been charged at art auctions in both London and New York since 1975 and in Melbourne from 1983, when Sotheby's held its inaugural Australian auction.[37] The ancient Roman buyer's premium, described in Chapter One, was reinvented in 1975 by both Sotheby's and Christie's in the same week. Allegations of collusion were made and then dropped, at the end of 1981, owing to costs.

Brian Learmount believes that the reinvention of the buyer's premium changed the complexion of international auctioneering.[38] It enabled Sotheby's and Christie's to lure vendors with their attractive rates and this resulted in the expansion and pre-eminence of the two auction houses. Ingram claimed that the introduction of the buyer's premium in Australia 'reflected the difficulties in obtaining consignments' when Sotheby's was first founded in late 1982.[39] Sotheby's claimed that it simply was not viable to conduct art auctions in Sydney unless it could charge a buyer's premium.[40]

The *Auctioneers and Agents Act 1941* was finally amended, allowing the auction houses to levy a buyer's premium in New South Wales from 1 March 1993. The Act became the *Properties, Stock and Business Agents Act* and was backdated to 1941. Ted Craig from Australian Art Auctions was the first of the Sydney auctioneers to charge a buyer's premium on 8 March 1993, with Goodmans and Lawson's following suit. What amounted to a deregulation of the Australian market was considered by some to have a positive effect on the trade, not only of the large international firms, but of the small, local ones.[41] Others could argue that a deregulated market enables auction houses, such as Sotheby's and Christie's, to operate unchecked.

The initial buyer's premium was 10 per cent and enabled the vendor's commission to be lowered in Melbourne to 10 per cent, as it was offset by the premium. Vendors in Sydney were generally charged a commission of 17.5 per cent. The net profit for Sotheby's (and most auction houses) is very slim, therefore it is essential for them to attract quality works for sale in order to increase their turnover. This is why they are willing to negotiate on vendors' commissions, choosing sometimes to rely on the buyer's premium. The buyer's premium was primarily responsible for Melbourne first becoming the centre of Australia's art auctions. According to Sotheby's Justin Miller, a side-effect of the buyer's premium is that it essentially buys a guarantee of authenticity for five years.[42]

From 1993, shortly after the introduction of the buyer's premium to the Sydney market, Sotheby's planned to increase it from 10 to 15 per cent, based on a head office directive and following a global rise. Dealers claimed that an increase would be disastrous, as it had taken a long time for clients to adjust to paying a commission at all.[43] Despite many of Christie's offices in other countries increasing their premium to 15 per cent, Christie's Australia was given an exemption so that it could gain ground on its international rival, Sotheby's. In response to Christie's refusing to increase the premium, Sotheby's was also granted an exemption from its reporting superiors. However, Sotheby's was forced to increase the buyer's premium on the first $50,000 to 15 per cent with

10 per cent thereafter in November 1993 because business had not been particularly profitable.

At the same time, Sotheby's continued to pursue the retail market by 'wooing' the private buyers, worrying dealers.[44] This having been said, dealers would not wish art auction sales to be unsuccessful, as the public failure of art sales 'would reflect on their own market' and they obtained much stock from auctions.[45] Owing to their public nature, and aggressive marketing campaigns, Sotheby's, and to a lesser extent Christie's, had increased confidence in their ability to source and sell major pieces of art and attract new and major clients, while diminishing confidence in the ability of dealers to do so. By March/April 2006, Christie's buyer's premium in Australia had jumped to 19.5 per cent on the first $200,000 with 12 per cent on the amount above $200,000. Sotheby's and Deutscher-Menzies both charged 20 per cent. GST is payable in addition to this.

The Bath of Diana Sale

The buyer's premium has facilitated auction houses offering competitive vendor's commissions, in conjunction with beguiling estimates, thus attracting valuable, high profile stock. This was the case in Melbourne in 1989, when Leonard Joel and Sotheby's competed for the honour — and commission — of auctioning John Glover's *The bath of Diana, Van Diemen's Land* (1837). Sotheby's was the successful contender, with the Glover attaining $1.76 million at its 17 April 1989 sale, demonstrating the quite phenomenal increase of 300 per cent in just four years. It was rumoured that Bleakley won the right to auction the work after offering a low vendor's commission and estimating that it would achieve more than $1.5 million at auction.[46]

However, both the work and its auction at Sotheby's were steeped in controversy. *The bath of Diana* had been purchased by David Waterhouse, of the horse racing dynasty, from Sir Andrew Grimwade in 1985 for $580,000 and Waterhouse had loaned it to the Art Gallery of Western Australia from 1986. The Art Gallery of Western Australia had been interested in acquiring the work permanently after it became apparent that it was not possible for Waterhouse to obtain any tax benefits from donating the work.

An American, Christopher Condon, who was acting on behalf of an unspecified client, placed the winning bid at the 1989 auction. The Australian Government, in an unprecedented decision, banned the export of the work under the *Protection of Movable Cultural Heritage Act 1986* on 4 October 1989. An export permit was again applied for on 11 July 1991 and refused on 4 February 1992. A review of the decision by the Administrative Appeals Tribunal was sought and referred to the Full Federal Court because constitutional concerns were raised.

The purpose of the Act is to protect movable objects of cultural significance and to 'see that those objects the export of which would constitute an irreparable loss to our cultural heritage remain in Australia'.[47] The National Heritage Control List separates 'cultural heritage' into either Class A (Indigenous heritage) or Class B (including objects of fine art and objects of social history). Under Section 8, Class B objects are assessed on a case-by-case basis against criteria such as age, rarity, quality and monetary value.[48] Class B objects, of which the Glover was one, could only be exported if a permit or certificate were awarded.

Condon had apparently said after the sale that his purchase of the painting depended on the granting of an export permit; however, Bleakley said that the sale was unconditional and that Sotheby's would take legal action to obtain the funds.[49] Condon was unknown to the Australian art auction world and had not consulted with Sotheby's regarding the conditions of sale prior to placing the successful bid.

Condon refused to pay for the painting, denying Sotheby's its $160,000 commission. The auction house retained the work and did take legal action resulting in Sotheby's agreeing to release *The bath of Diana* only after Waterhouse consigned Arthur Streeton's *Bathers, Killarney* to its April 1991 auction. Waterhouse eventually sold his Glover to the National Gallery of Australia in October 1993 for a mere $780,000. The art auction record set by the sale of this work was thus dwarfed by events surrounding the auction. Almost certainly as a result of this affair, Sotheby's amended its conditions of business so that a buyer would receive a refund if an export permit were declined.

This case also raised questions about how committed the Government really was to making such objects accessible to the Australian public. The National Cultural Heritage Fund did not have any funds at its disposal to provide assistance (perhaps to cultural institutions) to purchase culturally-significant items that had been denied an export permit. In *Waterhouse v Minister for the Arts and Territories* 119 ALR 89, 1993, Waterhouse argued that refusing to grant an export permit for *The bath of Diana* constituted an acquisition of property under the Constitution (Section 51 xxxi). The Court disagreed.[50]

The painting is undoubtedly significant. It is atypical of Glover's *oeuvre* because it depicted the Tasmanian landscape and Indigenous Australians within the context of classical mythology. Previous works by the artist were usually landscapes, populated by the occasional kangaroo or solitary traveller. The painting makes reference to the ancient Roman myth of Diana who, observed bathing by Actaeon, transformed him into a stag who was then devoured by his own hunting dogs. It depicts an idealised scene imbued with symbolism of the Fall and the descent into violence from an idyllic life which eventuated from colonization by European settlers.

The bath of Diana had first been purchased by Henry Bridges in Melbourne in 1869. He loaned it to the important *Art and Art Treasures Exhibition* that same year at the Melbourne Public Library and Museum. By 1991 the Tasmanian Aboriginal Centre thought that the painting was so significant it asked the Australian Government to buy it when it became available once more. The ensuing legal story of *The bath of Diana* is fascinating and raises a number of issues about the roles of individuals and organisations in the custodianship of culturally-significant objects. It is fortunate that in this case the public was the eventual beneficiary with the work at the nation's major art gallery (Figure 13).

Marketing and Glamorizing Art Auctions

Sotheby's was probably the first auction house in Australia to employ a full-time public relations person. Bleakley had been 'convinced of the importance of having a full-time PR person through…[his] time in London'.[51] The Australian media greatly assisted Sotheby's success, as it embraced the arrival of the illustrious firm and was pleased to provide extensive coverage. Bleakley, in turn, embraced the advantages of the media, saying in 1989 that 'We entered the market with the aim of promoting ourselves and our sales in a way that had not previously been done, putting a great deal of emphasis into marketing'.[52]

Sotheby's was fortunate in its timing, as news coverage of art sales had begun to increase in the late 1970s, just prior to the company's arrival in Australia. Rae Price was its first publicist, followed by her protégée, Jan Batten, who later became the publicist at the Art Gallery of New South Wales. Batten was viewed — universally — as being exceptional at her job. She operated on a *quid pro quo* principle and used the media brilliantly to give Sotheby's consistent and glowing press coverage. Batten's personal ability to obtain press coverage of particular works and sales helped to turn the art auction into a celebrity event, as well as increasing public awareness of and confidence in Sotheby's.

Bleakley has always denied that Sotheby's used hype to promote auctions. He maintained that selling paintings for absurdly high prices at auction represented 'distasteful elitism' and compared auctions to lotteries where you had to attempt to 'stack the odds in your favour'.[53] However, he was also quoted as saying that people like to buy at auction because it is 'conspicuous consumption' and that Sotheby's was openly selling 'snobbism'.[54]

Art Auction Practices and Innovations

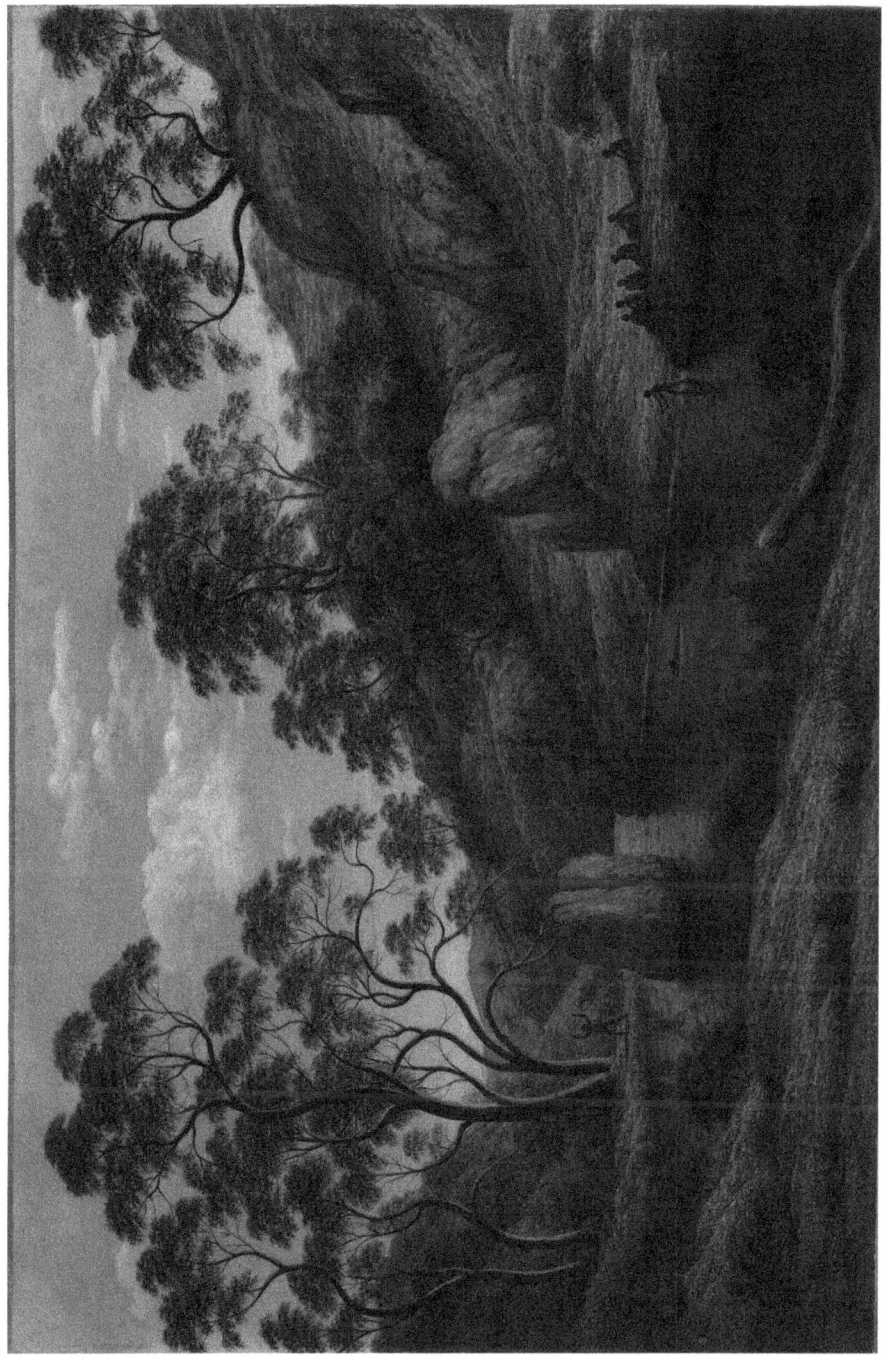

Figure 13: John Glover (England 1767-1849 Australia), *The bath of Diana, Van Diemen's Land, 1837*, 1837, oil on canvas, 96.5 x 134.5 cm, National Gallery of Australia, Canberra. Purchased with the assistance of the National Gallery of Australia Foundation 1993.

Sotheby's reinforced its reputation by promoting star artists. Bleakley said in August 1987 that he never planned to hold a sale that would not realise more than $1 million and that this meant 'concentrating on art stars', such as Fred Williams, Arthur Boyd, Sidney Nolan and Brett Whiteley.[55] In July 1987, Sotheby's reputation as Australia's premier art auction house had been cemented with the $3.85 million sale at Melbourne's Southern Cross Hotel, attended by around 1000 people. The firm had held eight out of the ten most financially successful Australian art auctions. Sotheby's Australia had become the most profitable firm in the Sotheby's group, owing in the main to its potent formula of hype and marketing. Bleakley responded:

> we've...gone for an aggressive marketing strategy, and we've attempted to develop new buyers and collectors. That's probably the biggest difference between us and the rest of the group. In Europe and North America, there is such a well-established group of buyers that the main push is getting material to sell, rather than getting people to buy it.[56]

Auction houses have long sought to develop new markets. Bleakley prophesied in 1988 that by 1993 Sotheby's would have grown fivefold and diversified into such fields as publishing and real estate, claiming also that art auctions would comprise only half of its income.[57] In this vein, Sotheby's began a prestige realty company in 1992, which provides a reasonable proportion of its total revenue. As with its art sales, only the top end of the real estate market (properties over $750,000) has been targeted. The realty company enables Sotheby's to increase its annual sales figures when art sales are flat; offers clients a more complete service, with the one firm able to sell both house and contents as was common in the colonial era; and provides publicity for Sotheby's, in this case paid for by the vendors.

The idea of marrying dazzling social events with art has been a consistent historical thread. The *conversazione* held in Australia from the 1850s combining ballad singing, 'picture-gazing', conversation and good food, was the precursor of today's exhibition openings.[58] They were held by fashionable society and received extensive coverage in the newspapers; they were an early and effective marketing technique. The Victorian Artists' Society in Melbourne, for example, held regular *conversaziones,* 'artists' smoke nights', dinners, and 'gentlemen's evenings'.[59]

Sotheby's has always held select previews or viewings before sales and often travelled them to other major cities, such as Perth. Auction previews were invitation-only and became exclusive social occasions, frequented by the *crème* of Australian high society and business; 'The wives and girlfriends of the entrepreneurs, merchant bankers and corporate lawyers came kitted out in Armani, Ferragamo and Fendi to be photographed against a backdrop of expensive paintings'.[60] The auction attendees also contributed to both Sotheby's and Australian art making headlines, thus creating the reputations of the auction firm, as well as certain Australian artists.

Bleakley introduced the wearing of black-tie evening clothes at auctions, infusing Australian art auctions with an 'element of panache'.[61] Sotheby's entertained regular and prospective clients on a grand scale and often asked celebrities to introduce auctions. The glamorous environments of new hotels were utilized to stage sales. This use of an appropriate stage setting contributed greatly to creating a certain mystique and flair surrounding the Sotheby's name. The black-tie dress code was discontinued around 1989, when the decade of outrageous wealth and the art boom were drawing to a close, and at the same time the auction venues were moved from the ballrooms of large inner city hotels to on-site or more low-key locations. However, in 1993, dealers were bemoaning the ordinariness of sales, wishing for a return to the glitzy hotel venues.[62] Interestingly, in 1997 national General Manager Paul Sumner commented that 'We have what the new generation wants, but our tradition of aiming for the best, our strength, is also a hindrance. It means too many people are a bit intimidated by us.'[63] Sotheby's thus wanted to demystify art auctions when it became necessary to develop new markets and new collectors.

Buyers at Auction

In the early 1970s, Christie's relied upon a small group of knowledgeable collectors and dealers and it was the firm's intention to build this core collecting group. Around 20 per cent of the bidding audience at Australian art auctions in the early years of Christie's Australian presence were dealers, with the remainder mainly private collectors. In the early years, the large proportion of private collectors bidding at auction meant, among other things, Australian auctions took longer to conduct than their London counterparts because non-professional bidders were more indecisive and less familiar with auction practices. This situation was in contrast to Christie's and Sotheby's auctions in London where, as noted earlier, the majority of buyers were art dealers. By 1987, the proportion of art dealers buying from Sotheby's Australia had jumped to 70 per cent.[64] In 1993, Sotheby's claimed that 80 per cent of its business was from dealers, either buying at auction for themselves or on behalf of clients.[65] This would seem to indicate that the international firms increased their client base by expanding the role of the dealer into that of agent at auction for corporate, institutional and private clients.

As early as 1972 speculation was regaining popularity in the art market; there had been a lull in art investment in the wake of the 1962 Schureck sale. Increasingly sophisticated and educated collectors were more aware of what was happening at an international level and of prices fetched. This new attitude was evident at Christie's three-day paintings auction in Sydney in October 1974, where only 50 per cent of lots sold. Careful consideration was displayed for the first time in about eighteen months, during which time vendors had had over-optimistic notions about the market value of their works; dealers had been making considerable profits by buying and reselling at auction with celerity; and collectors had been swept away on a tide of indiscriminate bidding frenzy.[66]

It would be natural to assume that the local auction houses and dealers would not have been pleased at what they probably saw as a foreign intrusion into their domain. However, contemporary newspaper evidence suggests the opposite, that dealers (at least) initially welcomed the arrival of Christie's and that they worked closely with both Christie's and Sotheby's in the early years.

More recently, many dealers have been quite vocal about feeling besieged. For example, Joan McClelland, the early Christie's representative in Melbourne and now herself a dealer, reflected in 1998:

> I don't like to think I helped set up a monster. It would have happened anyway and you have to say it's a much more animated scene than it used to be. But it has affected all our businesses – anything run on that scale would have to affect us – but I think we have all had to learn to adapt to it, and use the situation to our own advantage when we can.[67]

However, facts would seem to indicate the contrary, that dealers, for the most part, became larger players in the art auction market in Australia only after Christie's arrival. One could draw three conclusions — that auction houses were so successful in sourcing stock that dealers preferred to purchase their stock at auction, rather than directly from collectors, that buying at auction was a profitable and convenient enterprise for dealers, with the possibility of reaping large rewards by on-selling to clients at inflated prices, and that there was an increased demand for their services as agents. Despite evidence indicating that in Christie's early auctions in Australia private collectors dominated the saleroom, the general perception still persisted that collectors were introduced to buying art at auction by Christie's and Sotheby's, thus detracting from the trade that was once the sole realm of the dealer.

The *Mount Wellington and Hobart Town* Sale

The arrival of Christie's and Sotheby's not only affected dealers, artists and existing auction houses, but also had an impact on public institutions. Edmund Capon, Director of the Art Gallery of New South Wales, commented in 1988 that the ruthlessness, competitiveness and presence of Christie's and Sotheby's had forced the prices of many works up to such an extent that public galleries had difficulty in acquiring works.[68]

The highest auction price in 2001 was obtained for John Glover's *Mount Wellington and Hobart Town from Kangaroo Point 1831–3*. It was sold by Christie's on 27 November of that year for $1.76 million (including commissions) against an estimate of $1.5–$2.5 million. The Australian Competition and Consumer Commission (ACCC) began investigating claims of 'price-fixing, bid-rigging and exclusionary boycotts in the Australian art market' after allegations of anti-competitive behaviour were printed on the front page of *The Australian* newspaper on 8 December 2001.[69] The allegations concerned the joint sale of the work to the National Gallery of Australia and the Tasmanian Museum and Art Gallery for what was reportedly the painting's reserve price and low estimate of $1.5 million. Greatest furore was caused by the fact that the institutional partnership had no competition for the painting, despite the significance of the work, with no other bidders on the night (Figure 14).

The Australian alleged that at a meeting of the Australian Art Museum Directors Council in Melbourne on 7 November 2001, followed by a number of telephone calls, it was effectively agreed to fix the price of the Glover painting. Two private collectors who had been interested in acquiring the painting, and who had associations with the National Gallery of Australia, were allegedly persuaded that it was in the public interest that the gallery partnership should acquire the work. The National Gallery of Victoria was apparently similarly convinced to refrain from involvement in the auction.[70] It seems that one of the participants in the Council meeting confided to the newspaper that what occurred resembled a Dutch auction, where 'The gallery directors said "well, I can buy it for this much", and someone comes in at a lower price. Then everyone decided that they'd like Tasmania to have it anyway so (they) pulled back'.[71]

Gallery directors had reportedly signed an agreement during the 1980s not to compete with each other at auction if one party were extremely interested in acquiring a particular work.[72] This arrangement would not only reduce the possibility of public institutions competing with each other and forcing prices up in the process, but would also, to all intents and purposes, place a limitation on the price attainable at auction, unless other interested parties entered the bidding. The art auction system has been manipulated by various forces over the centuries, as we have seen. The Glover affair is a prime example of how the auction process can be manipulated by those other than auction house principals, dealers and artists.

Pedigree and Panache

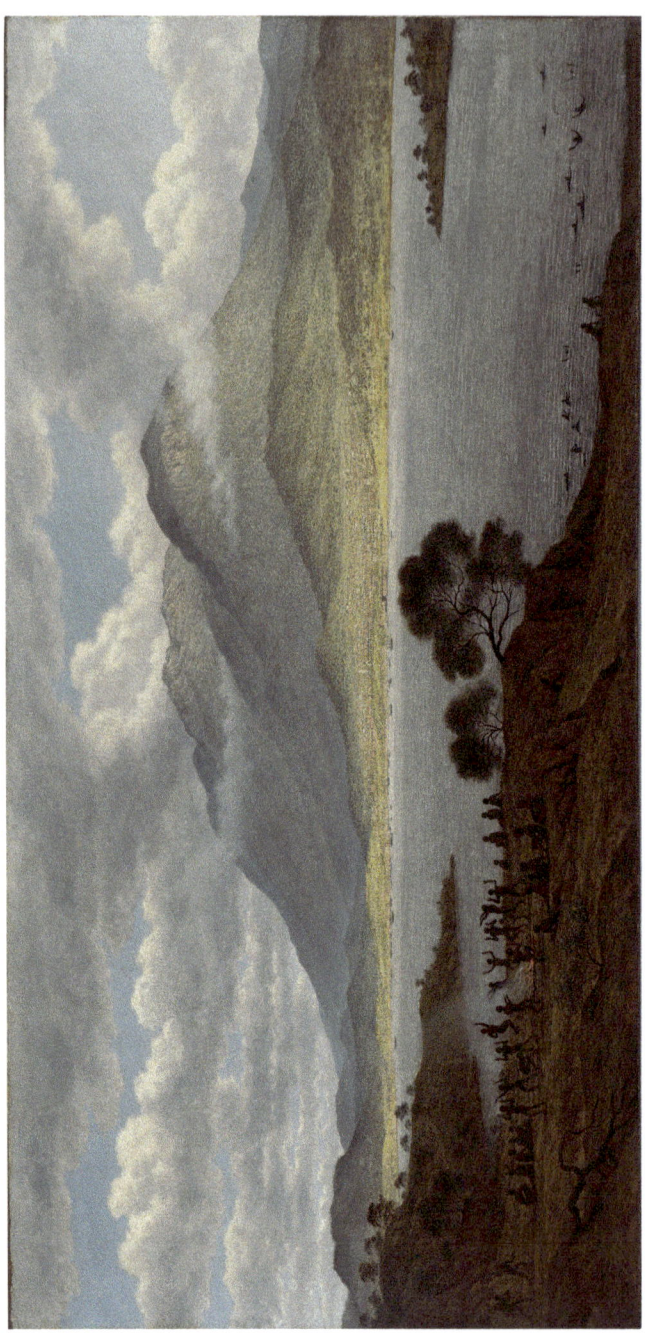

Figure 14: John Glover (England 1767-1849 Australia), *Mount Wellington and Hobart Town from Kangaroo Point 1831-3*, 1834, oil on canvas, 76.2 x 152.4 cm, Tasmanian Museum and Art Gallery, Hobart and National Gallery of Australia, Canberra. Purchased with funds from the Nerissa Johnson Bequest 2001.

The ACCC investigated whether the galleries were employing 'unlawful behaviour' as 'From initial discussions, the Trade Practices Act 1974 appears to apply to the buying and selling of art, including where public galleries owned by government buy or sell.'[73] Anti-competitive behaviour is illegal under the Act, unless prior immunity or exemption was granted. The ACCC further decreed that 'Art markets are as subject to the law as any market. Vendors have the right to get a fair price for their product — in this case art — free from "understandings" between potential bidders.'[74] The art galleries maintain that they are not acting in an illegal manner and are saving the government money, with David Thomas, formerly Director of the Art Gallery of South Australia and later a consultant for Deutscher-Menzies, saying that 'The forming of rings by the trade is illegal, 10 dealers cannot get together, then bid on something and all divvy it up, but when it's public money and it's in the public interest, the expenditure is being wisely controlled.'[75] Many would concur; however, some would possibly argue that anti-competitive behaviour is still unethical, no matter what the reasons and who the offenders.

Such deals between public institutions, although rarely documented, are unlikely to be unusual in the realities of the marketplace. Deutscher, who was probably unaware of the so-called agreement from the 1980s, thought that the practice of public galleries colluding probably resulted from the sale of John Brack's *The Bathroom* (1957) to the National Gallery of Australia in November 1998 at Christie's for $497,500 (estimate $120,000–$150,000).[76] The National Gallery of Australia had been forced to pay a premium price after competing for the work with the Art Gallery of South Australia.

A comparison was also made between the Glover sale and that of John Brack's *Self Portrait* (1955), which the National Gallery of Victoria had acquired for $442,500 (estimate $350,000–$450,000) at Christie's celebrated Mertz auction in June 2000, as no other public institutions placed bids for this work and the only other bidder was a private collector.[77] In order to avoid competing with another gallery, the Art Gallery of New South Wales negotiated with Sotheby's to purchase Grace Cossington Smith's *Centre of a City* (c.1925), which had been on loan to the Gallery since 1996, prior to the Fairfax auction in November 2002. The Gallery purchased the Cossington Smith for the price of $350,000 (including the buyer's premium), against an auction estimate of $250,000–$350,000. It had unsuccessfully bid against the Queensland Art Gallery for Roland Wakelin's *The Bridge Under Construction (In the Botanical Gardens verso)* (1928), which sold at the Sotheby's auction in August 1994 for $160,000, against an estimate of $80,000–$100,000.

Christie's had anticipated that Glover's *Mount Wellington and Hobart Town* would exceed the $2.3 million record price for an Australian painting at auction, which had been set by Frederick McCubbin's *Bush Idyll* (1893) in 1998.[78] It was the perceived failure of the work to make the expected record price that contributed to concern about possible collusions.[79] Nevertheless, it was still the fourth most expensive Australian painting to be sold at auction, as well as a record for the artist himself. The painting had been carefully marketed prior to the sale in the hopes of breaking the record set by McCubbin and was given its own special, glossy, well-illustrated brochure. It was also toured to London, New York, Hobart, Perth and Sydney before being displayed and sold in Melbourne.

Patricia Sabine, then Director of the Tasmanian Museum and Art Gallery, was naturally extremely pleased with the acquisition, saying that not only would it be a key piece in the Museum's collection, but that her Gallery could not possibly have afforded to buy the painting without the assistance of the National Gallery of Australia.[80] It has been suggested that the Tasmanian Museum and Art Gallery had used credit on the expected deaccession of one of its most expensive European paintings, William Adolphe Bouguereau's *Cupid and Psyche* (1899), to assist with finance for the Glover.[81] The sale of the Glover painting also represented a partnership, possibly unprecedented, between two public institutions collaborating to purchase a work jointly. As early as the 1980s, when the directors of major public galleries had reportedly agreed to limit competing with one another, a template was also drawn up for prospective joint purchases.[82] The Glover sale was apparently the first occasion this plan had been successfully used.

Under the *Trade Practices Act 1974*, if found guilty of collusion by the ACCC the galleries could have been fined up to $10 million and individuals involved charged a potential $500,000. On 10 December 2002, a year after it began its investigations, the ACCC announced that although it had completed its current investigation and was not taking any legal action, it did not rule out the possibility of so doing in the future if further evidence surfaced.[83] The ACCC concluded that the *Trade Practices Act* does indeed apply to public institutions when said institutions conduct business; however, the main problem in pursuing the investigation had been 'reticent witnesses' and the fact that, as much discussion had taken place via telephone conversations, it had not been documented.[84]

This case highlights both sides of what has become a major argument about the role of art auctions. That is, have art auction houses been responsible for encouraging prohibitively high prices in their salerooms, placing works out of the reach of individual public institutions? Do the works justify such prices? Who are the victims in such instances? What would a general consensus have been if the agreement had been between private collectors? Furthermore, are the galleries effectively engaging in 'rings' and 'knock-outs'? Vendors might be tempted to retain their treasures, fearful that they would not obtain a fair price, or perhaps convinced to sell privately. What impact does this then have on the public and public access to art?

Both Christie's and Sotheby's have had a marked impact on the Australian art auction market specifically and on the wider art market generally, making a viable and ostentatious alternative to buying from dealers. They have contributed to the greater sophistication and professionalization of the market, most especially with regards to the introduction of new mechanisms for the conduct of auctions and more emphasis placed on exploiting various avenues of marketing. Moreover, Christie's and Sotheby's have substantially and conclusively altered the social status of auctioneers, cementing them within the upper echelons of society.

Don Cornes, a major dealer in the 1980s, said that 'when you couldn't sell a painting Sotheby's created the flagship Australia lacked. It has taken what were regional sales and created a visible, national market.'[85] A writer from 1989 claimed that 'Sotheby's has sourced and flushed out more material than was ever available before and has created the impression that auctions are the only way to buy and sell art' through canny marketing.[86] According to Bruce James, after Sotheby's conducted its first auction in 1983:

> Domestic firms of the longevity and habitualness of Melbourne's Joel's and Sydney's Lawson's were suddenly forced to up the ante on their own auctioneering strategies, and a then-dormant Christie's, which had enjoyed a privileged but desultory presence in Australia since 1969, was thrown a startling antipodean gauntlet by its major international rival.[87]

The response of the major local art auction houses is the subject of the final chapter.

ENDNOTES

[1] Bruce James, 'Sotheby's eyes the future', *Australian Business Monthly*, February 1993, p.86.

[2] Quoted in Louise Bellamy, 'The new collectors', *The Age*, 25 November 2002, The Culture, p.3.

[3] Author unknown, 'How Christie's builds an art market', *The National Times*, Money Talks section, 2–7 October 1972, p.45.

[4] This is all noted in Marion Macdonald, 'The New Spectator Sport', *The Bulletin*, 14 October 1972, p.41.

[5] Terry Ingram, 'Christie's sale not quite an "unmitigated disaster"', *Australian Financial Review*, 10 October 1974, p.29.

[6] Edward D. Craig, *Australian Art Auction Records 1973–75*, Ure Smith, Sydney 1975, preface.

[7] Terry Ingram, 'Things are not always as they seem in the auction room', *Australian Financial Review*, 24–28 December 1998, p.33.

[8] Robert Bleakley, taped interview with the author, Canberra, 28 November 2002.

[9] Peter Cochrane, 'We have ways of making you *spend*', *Sydney Morning Herald*, 15 August 1995, Arts, p.15.

[10] Ingram, 'Things are not always as they seem in the auction room', p.33.

[11] Author unknown, 'Auction gamble starts again', *Australian Financial Review*, Fine Arts Feature, 5 April 1976, p.4.

[12] Charles Nodrum, taped interview with the author, Melbourne, 24 October 2002.

[13] Author unknown, 'How Christie's builds an art market', p.45.

[14] According to Sue Hewitt in Author unknown, 'Auction gamble starts again', p.5.

[15] Jill Rowbotham, 'The art dealer who is not bound with tradition', *The Herald*, 6 November 1989, p.13.

[16] Robert Bleakley, taped interview with the author, Canberra, 28 November 2002.

[17] For example, Rowena Stretton, 'The art of making money', *The Bulletin*, 8 January 1990, pp.88–91.

[18] Terry Ingram, 'Christie's: no Grosz expectations', *Australian Financial Review*, 16 October 1975, p.14.

[19] Cochrane, 'We have ways of making you *spend*', p.15.

[20] Nuding, 'Saleroom Practice', p.39.

[21] Nuding, 'Saleroom Practice', p.39.

[22] Roger Dedman, *Christie's Australian Art Market Movements Handbook*, Christie's, Victoria 2002, p.29.

[23] Cochrane, 'We have ways of making you *spend*', p.15.

[24] Terry Ingram, 'If history is missing you may not get the full picture', *Australian Financial Review*, 9 October 1999, p.38.

[25] Gerald Reitlinger, *The Economics of Taste – The Art Market in the 1960s*, Barrie and Jenkins, London 1970, vol. 3, p.12.

[26] Peter Cochrane, 'The art of market "correction"', *Sydney Morning Herald*, 18 August 1989, p.18.

[27] Simon Plant, 'At her bidding', *Sun*, 6 May 1994, no pagination.

[28] Michael Reid, taped interview with the author, Sydney, 30 August 2002.

[29] Charles Nodrum, taped interview with the author, Melbourne, 24 October 2002.

[30] Robert Lacey, *Sotheby's – Bidding for Class*, Little, Brown and Company, London 1998, p.170.

[31] Michael Reid, 'Budding connoisseurs bid for knowledge', *The Weekend Australian*, 11–12 January 1997, p.63.

[32] John Herbert, *Inside Christie's*, St. Martin's Press, New York 1990, p.268 and Roger McIlroy, taped interview with the author, Melbourne, 21 October 2002.

[33] See Robert Wraight, *The Art Game Again!*, Leslie Frewin of London, 1974 (rev. of 1965 publication), p.185.

[34] Terry Ingram, 'New York auctioneer offers five-year guarantee', *Australian Financial Review*, 27 September 1973, p.36.

[35] Robert Bleakley, taped interview with the author, Canberra, 28 November 2002.

[36] Ingram, 'New York auctioneer offers five-year guarantee', p.36.

[37] Rowena Stretton, 'The art gulf war', *The Bulletin*, 19 March 1991, no pagination.
[38] Brian Learmount, *A History of the Auction*, Barnard and Learmount, Great Britain 1985, p.163.
[39] Terry Ingram, 'Levy gap stirs art sale rivals', *Australian Financial Review*, 5 January 1993, no pagination.
[40] Elizabeth Fortescue, 'Fee squabble hits auctions', *The Daily Telegraph Mirror*, 11 May 1991, p.112.
[41] See, for example, Fortescue, 'Fee squabble hits auctions', p.112 and Bob Evans, 'Making a bid for the arts market', *Sydney Morning Herald*, 22 November 1991, p.4.
[42] Andrew G. Frost, 'Hammer Heads', *Australian Art Collector*, issue 2, October-December 1997, pp.26–9.
[43] Geoff Maslen, 'Sotheby's raises auction buyer's commission to 15 per cent', *The Age*, 4 November 1992, p.5.
[44] Terry Ingram, 'Sydney art sale defies gravity, says big spender', *Australian Financial Review*, 1 December 1993, no pagination.
[45] Ingram, 'Sydney art sale defies gravity, says big spender', no pagination.
[46] Geoff Maslen, 'Glover Intrigue', *The Age*, 11 October 1989, no pagination.
[47] Hansard, House of Representatives, 27 November 1985, p.3740.
[48] Cheryl Simpson, 'Cultural Heritage on the Move: Significance and Meaning', *Law in Context*, 14(2) 1996, p.50.
[49] David Washington, 'Plug pulled on Diana's Bath export', *The Advertiser* (Adelaide), 5 October 1989, p.1.
[50] Simpson, 'Cultural Heritage on the Move', pp.65–6, note 7 and Jacklyn Marett Leiboff, 'Reconstructing the Role of Cultural Significance in the Protection of Movable Cultural Heritage Act 1986 (Cth)', unpub. PhD thesis, Griffith University, November 2004, pp.109–113.
[51] Robert Bleakley, taped interview with the author, Canberra, 28 November 2002.
[52] Quoted in Rowbotham, 'The art dealer who is not bound with tradition', p.13.
[53] Huck, 'Robert Bleakley', p.40.
[54] Fran Hernon, 'Selling "snobbism" at Sotheby's', *Daily Telegraph*, magazine, 31 October 1987, p.31.
[55] Huck, 'Robert Bleakley', p.39.
[56] Nikki Barrowclough, 'The art of the marketplace', *Belle*, August/September 1987, p.26.
[57] Geoff Maslen, 'Growth of a super salesman', *The Age*, 26 March 1988, p.6.
[58] Mary Holyoake, 'Melbourne Art Scene — Part 2: Introduction to the 1850's', *Art and Australia*, 17(2) 1979, pp.138–9.
[59] See Bonyhady, *Images in Opposition*, p.18 and *Table Talk*, no. 207, 7 June 1889, p.5, col.1.
[60] Ava Hubble, 'Robert Bleakley: Dealer with a Difference', *Australian Art Collector*, issue 4, April-June 1998, p.39.
[61] Robert Bleakley, taped interview with the author, Canberra, 28 November 2002.
[62] Ingram, 'Sydney art sale defies gravity, says big spender', no pagination.
[63] Rowena Stretton, 'Sotheby's targets the designer generation', *Australian Financial Review*, 22 August 1997, p.16.
[64] Hernon, 'Selling "snobbism" at Sotheby's', p.31.
[65] Bruce James, 'Sotheby's eyes the future', *Australian Business Monthly*, February 1993, p.86.
[66] Ingram, 'Christie's sale not quite an "unmitigated disaster"', p.29.
[67] Quoted in Geoff Maslen, 'Queen of the auction room', *The Age*, 2 December 1998, p.20.
[68] Michael Robotham, 'Claws out in bitter art feud', *Sunday Telegraph*, 20 November 1988, p.44.
[69] Australian Competition and Consumer Commission (ACCC), 'Allegations of Unlawful conduct in Art Markets', media release, 8 December 2001, <http://203.6.251.7/accc.internet/media/search/view_media.cfm?RecordID=539> [11/11/2002] and Georgina Safe, Susan McCulloch-Uehlin and Michael Reid, 'A masterpiece undercut', *The Australian*, 8 December 2001, pp.1–2.
[70] Margaretta Pos, 'Prime purchase under investigation', *Hobart Mercury*, 15 December 2001, p.38.
[71] Quoted in Safe, McCulloch-Uehlin and Reid, 'A masterpiece undercut', p.2.
[72] Geoff Maslen, 'Public Interest?', *The Age*, 12 December 2001, no pagination.
[73] ACCC, 'Allegations of Unlawful conduct in Art Markets', no pagination.
[74] ACCC, 'Allegations of Unlawful conduct in Art Markets', no pagination.

[75] Quoted in Safe, McCulloch-Uehlin and Reid, 'A masterpiece undercut', p.2.
[76] Safe, McCulloch-Uehlin and Reid, 'A masterpiece undercut', p.2.
[77] Tim Bonyhady, 'Buying power under the hammer', *Sydney Morning Herald*, 19 August 2000, Spectrum, p.9.
[78] Susan McCulloch-Uehlin, 'Galleries ecstatic at art bargain', *The Australian*, 28 November 2001, p.3.
[79] Terry Ingram, 'Colonial Art Find Fetches Just $1.79m', *Australian Financial Review*, 28 November 2001, p.3.
[80] McCulloch-Uehlin, 'Galleries ecstatic at art bargain', p.3.
[81] Ingram, 'Colonial Art Find Fetches Just $1.79m', p.3.
[82] Geoff Maslen, 'ACCC inquiry into Glover painting sale', *The Age*, 16 September 2002, p.4.
[83] Australian Competition and Consumer Commission (ACCC), 'ACCC concludes investigation into allegations of unlawful conduct in art markets', media release, 10 December 2002, <http://203.6.251.7/accc.internet/digest/view_media.cfm?RecordID=896> [02/04/2003].
[84] Quotation from Penny Brown, 'Gallery in clear on Glover buy', *The Australian*, 11 December 2002, p.2. Also according to Michael Reid, taped interview with the author, Sydney, 30 August 2002.
[85] Quoted in Jan McGuiness, 'There's an art in buying art', *The Bulletin*, 11 July 1989, p.40.
[86] McGuiness, 'There's an art in buying art', p.40.
[87] James, 'Sotheby's eyes the future', p.84.

Chapter 8. Other Major Art Auction Houses

There are numerous auction houses in Australia, many of which deal in art. *The Art Newspaper — Guide to Art Auctions Worldwide* listed only a handful of Australian auction houses in 2002 — in Melbourne, Christie's, Deutscher-Menzies, Leonard Joel and Sotheby's, and in Sydney, Christie's, Deutscher-Menzies, Goodmans, Lawson-Menzies, Sotheby's and Shapiro Auctioneers.[1] The list helps to provide the framework for this chapter, which looks at a number of active and inactive art auction houses; namely, F. R. Strange, Geoff K. Gray, Lawson's/Lawson-Menzies, Leonard Joel, Phillips/Shapiro Auctioneers, Goodmans/ Bonhams & Goodman and Deutscher-Menzies.

Developments in the Australian art auction market in the early 1970s demonstrated that any major new competitor will have a substantial impact on the established firms; that is, changes wrought by one firm will ripple through the others. The immediate response of local Australian firms to the arrival of Christie's in 1969 was decisive. By 1971, competition was fierce and the positioning of the firms which sold art reshuffled.

F. R. Strange

F. R. Strange was a general Sydney-based auction house founded in 1912. It developed a fine art department for the first time in the wake of Christie's arrival in the hope of exploiting the increasingly lucrative art auction market, partly through its unexpected side specialty in the sale of the furnishings, including the art, of hotels and theatres. Strange held two fine art auctions in 1971 and planned to hold at least four *per annum* thereafter. In July 1974, it auctioned 137 paintings at the Wentworth Hotel, with prices ranging from $50 to $8500 and the sale total a respectable $108,000. Strange also began to place greater emphasis on the presentation of its premises around this time, renovating its salerooms at The Rocks.

Strange, with Lawson's, was one of Australia's oldest auction houses and owing to an amicable rivalry between the two firms, as well as the success of its general business, Strange had not previously moved into the auctioning of art as a serious enterprise. Strange bowed to pressure from associates of its valuations business to make fine art auctions part of its core business, although Ingram noted that 'F. R. Strange is entering a field that is steadily growing more competitive'.[2] The Sydney auction firm of Hamilton & Miller had also been holding auctions of quality fine art. Yet despite more auctioneers moving into the field, art sales were in a trough and many firms were consolidating their business in the early 1970s at the time of the economic recession.

Despite the presence of Christie's, it was Strange who became notable in the early 1970s for introducing a London auction practice to the Australian market. Max Germaine, best known for his dictionary, *Artists and Galleries of Australia*, was one of the directors of Strange (and also a founding Director of Sotheby's). He introduced the use of closed circuit television to Sydney auctions, the practice he had observed while at Sotheby's in London completing a decorative arts course in 1967. Closed circuit television had proved invaluable for the auction of hotels, as in practical terms, it meant that bidders could view all the lots on a large screen in the room designated as the saleroom, instead of moving throughout the hotel premises. This practice was common in fine art auctions in London.

Mason Gray Strange now focuses on conducting industrial auctions for companies, institutions and Government departments. The phasing out of Strange's art auctions could be a result of Lawson's 'more aggressive' initial response to the 'challenge' posed by Christie's, discussed presently.[3]

Geoff K. Gray

Together F. R. Strange and Lawson's shared the majority of the general and art auctioneering business in Sydney. This duopoly was overturned when Geoff K. Gray began to compete with Lawson's for the fine art trade. Gray's usurped the paintings market for works worth less than $2000 and was still considered to be the dominant player in Sydney in 1971, even with Christie's as a contender.

Geoff K. Gray, which described itself in 1969 as 'the largest industrial and fine art auctioneering organization in Australia', also responded quite aggressively to the advent of international competition, channelling further resources into its art division and appointing a full-time manager.[4] Gray's had actually proposed to enter into a joint venture with Christie's in early 1969 in an attempt to improve facilities for the auction of the fine arts in Australia; however, Christie's refused. This possibly explains the apprehension with which the local firms viewed the arrival of Christie's and apparent desire for a monopoly.

Since 1959, Gray's had held regular sales of furniture, paintings and other fine arts, coins, jewellery and stamps. It also held pledge auctions of items from pawnshops four times a week in its auction rooms in an old warehouse at 196 Castlereagh Street, Sydney. Most of Gray's business — about 95 per cent — was from its general and pawnbroking business, so the decision to place emphasis on the art side of the business in the early 1970s reflects the growing importance and prominence of art auctions.

Gray's style had reflected the more basic style of art auctioneering endemic in Australia. The old rooms lacked professional presentation and practices; collectors were often waylaid *en route* to the upstairs fine art saleroom by workmen moving furniture and other items out of the ground floor. At paintings auctions, Warren

Elstub, Manager of the Fine Arts Division in the early 1970s, auctioned an average of eighty works each hour, engaging the audience through age-old tactics of showmanship and allowing them time to decide whether to bid or increase bids. The shortage of art professionals at paintings auctions made this practice essential.

In 1971, Gray's left its Castlereagh Street warehouse, after eighty-nine years, and moved into a newly renovated carpet warehouse in Riley Street, Surry Hills. The old premises were to be demolished and although the new site 'cannot be compared to a Christie's or Sotheby's of London…it has its own special Australian charm'.[5] The new premises were luxuriously furnished in earthy tones of chocolate and orange, with the gallery featuring carpeted floors, subdued lighting, a good quality hanging system and a tasteful and intimate atmosphere. Gray's was now able to put on a higher quality preview than others at the time. Gray's new premises were the first in Australia to have been purposely designed as auction rooms, all others having adapted existing buildings, thus making Gray's the most sumptuous auction house in Australia. As part of this revamping, Gray's had observed trends and practices used in international auction houses to improve its business and attract a larger clientele. It reigned supreme in the middle market of works valued between $200 and $2000 in the Sydney paintings market and hoped to attract a more up-market clientele with its modish premises.

Gray's had actually been influenced by American auctions, rather than London ones, and the distinction between the two approaches is important in understanding the influences that have incrementally pervaded the Australian art auction market since the late 1960s/early 1970s. Most American fine art auction houses were purpose-built, as the majority of their bidding audience were collectors, rather than dealers, and the collectors had to be wooed with an appropriate ambience and setting. The Parke-Bernet, Astor and Plaza Galleries in New York were purpose-built, while Christie's and Sotheby's in London were not, reflecting their respective predominant clientele. The art dealers dominating London auctions were affiliates in the art trade, and did not need to be seduced by an opulent environment.[6]

Gray's had introduced the use of an easel on which to display paintings at its auctions and intended to improve on this technique by having each lot carried into the saleroom and placed on a special velvet picture rest. This had, in fact, been used by the American Art Association in New York in the late nineteenth century and by Lawson's for the sale of the Eedy collection in Sydney in 1921.

It was possibly Gray's who was responsible for the introduction of lavishly illustrated art auction catalogues to Australia, as well as specific and well-planned newspaper advertisements.[7] Gray's art auction catalogues in the 1960s were usually encased in glossy covers and had a number of colour illustrations, making them atypical. Gray's held, according to Charles Nodrum's recollections, the first important art auction in Australia in memory in about 1960; he was perhaps thinking of the Voss Smith collection auctioned on 14–15 November 1962.[8]

On 13 February 1974, Gray's auctioned the outstanding Darrell Lea collection of fourteen Dobell paintings in the ballroom of the Chevron Hotel, Potts Point, having won the right to auction the collection over other firms by offering very competitive terms. Darrell Lea was a Sydney businessman with interests in the footwear industry in America and Europe, as well as being a leading Australian confectionary manufacturer. The catalogue — familiarly — described the Dobell paintings as 'possibly the finest single collection to appear on the market for many years…'[9]

The resounding success of the Dobell Foundation sale conducted by Sotheby's at the Opera House the preceding year led to hopes that the collection would sell well, even though the works had been collected very recently — over a period of three years — and many had been obtained publicly at auction. Of the collection's star works, *The Charlady* realized $37,000 at the Darrell Lea auction, *The Tattooed Lady* $31,000 and *The Cockney Mother* $27,000. However, the sale of *Wangi Boy* (c.1951) for $70,000 to car salesman, Ron Hodgson, was 'the highest price at which any painting has gone under the auctioneer's hammer in an Australian saleroom'.[10]

The foreword for the auction catalogue noted that 'Among the offering, making its first appearance at public sale, is Sir William Dobell's "Wangi Boy", the version held in the collection of the artist and purchased privately from the Dobell Foundation after his death. This fine work has been named as at least the equal of its famous predecessor…'[11] Hodgson was offered, and rejected, $85,000 for the painting a few days after the sale. This monumental price prompted other collectors to pay more than $100,000 for Australian paintings in subsequent sales.[12] This version of *Wangi Boy* later sold at Geoff K. Gray's Darrell Lea auction in February 1974 for $70,000 and then at Christie's in August 1998 for $450,000, against an estimate of $400,000–$600,000.

Ingram noted that 'a more settled and discriminate art market [had been] established over the past two years…[that is, from 1969–71],' since the arrival of Christie's.[13] By the time of Christie's re-establishment and revamp in the mid-late 1980s, the business of Gray's had suffered. In the 1980s, Gray's was perceived to be akin to Lawson's, the 'people's auction rooms', but Gray's art sales decreased and by about 1989 had virtually ceased.[14] Gray's, currently Grays Auctions, no longer conducts specialist art auctions and focuses on auctioning commercial, industrial and consumer goods. However, the firm founded GraysOnline in 2000 and in 2006 appointed Amanda Benson, the biggest vendor of original art works on eBay in Australia, as its art specialist, and now holds regular online art auctions.

Lawson's/Lawson-Menzies

Bill Ellenden, a senior employee of Lawson's, compared the different auctioneering styles of Lawson's and Christie's at the latter's Dobell sale in 1971, describing Lawson's as an 'auctioneer' and Christie's as only a 'bid-taker'.[15] Ellenden noted that Christie's London auctioneer did not make special mention of the artist, as he considered all the works to be mere lots, rather than works of importance or interest, and that Australian auctioneers were enthusiastic as opposed to 'clinical'.[16] However, the more objective approach to auctions employed by Christie's, as well as Sotheby's, was to be more effective than the low-key Australian paradigm.

When Christie's arrived on the scene in 1969, Lawson's was actually the 'biggest auction house in the Southern Hemisphere' according to a news report.[17] Lawson's initial response to the arrival of Christie's was immediate and fundamental. The Australian market was changing in the late 1960s and early 1970s and Lawson's recognized that it had remained static. A number of changes occurred at Lawson's from the early 1970s, including the employment of new, key staff and the reorganization of the firm. Max Lawson's health worsened and, after Bill Ellenden resigned in 1973 to found his own auctioneering firm (William S. Ellenden), Peter Groth, an experienced businessman, was employed in July of that year to reinvigorate the organization. Henry Badgery, whose family had been involved in the auctioneering firm of Pitt, Son & Badgery, joined in October 1973 and became a member of Lawson's Board in August 1977. The Badgery family was linked with Lawson's until late 2002, when James Badgery resigned.

The engagement of personnel, such as Groth and Badgery, in the early to mid-1970s was part of a conscious attempt to modernize the firm and equip it to meet the new challenges of the era. Groth decided both to diversify and specialize, establishing, for example, a jewellery department in 1974, as well as an industrial division. Lawson's realized that it was no longer practicable to rely on its fine art sales now that the list of dedicated competitors had increased and accepted the option of diversification.

In 1981, Lawson's premises were deemed inadequate for the size of the crowds and it was decided to centralize its premises, moving to Cumberland Street in December 1981. Lawson's embraced the 'trend towards specialisation' and paid particular attention to the saleroom, organizing the gallery spaces in its new building so as to enable auctions to be held concurrently in three individual salerooms.[18] Groth and Badgery bought controlling interests in Lawson's and the Board was restructured at this time. It was decided to expand and from early 1983, Lawson's embarked on a programme of horizontal integration, with the acquisition of the venerable firm of James R. Newall Auctions (founded in about

1914) and, in April 1984, of Robert L. Godfrey Auctions, a firm of industrial auctioneers.

Lawson's 1973 Sim Rubensohn sale, 'one of the largest private art collection sales on record in Australia', also demonstrated the attempted modernization of the firm in the face of growing opposition.[19] Rubensohn was Chairman of Hansen Rubensohn-McCann Erickson, an advertising firm responsible for the successful 'It's Time' advertising campaign for the Australian Labor Party at the 1972 election. His home and garden were famous and were auctioned on 17 May 1973 by Raine and Horne Pty Ltd, presumably because Rubensohn's first job in Australia was as an office clerk at Raine and Horne. The Rubensohn sale of paintings, antique furniture, silver and porcelain that followed on 26–29 June 1973 used a closed-circuit colour television system for the first time in the history of the firm. However, Ellenden, the auctioneer, was concerned that the television would slow the pace of the proceedings and distort the size of the objects so that people who had not attended the viewings may have had an unreal perception.

The auction was held at the vendor's home, Kelvin Park at Dural, with the numerous onlookers seated outside in a 600-seat marquee. An average of 500 people was present each day of the sale, many from interstate. Rubensohn said that many buyers were also from America, Hong Kong, Singapore and New Zealand, possibly because the sale included Oriental art.[20]

This sale contributed to the professionalization of the Australian market through the quality of pieces auctioned, the standard of the catalogue and the use of closed-circuit television. Ellenden said that the Rubensohn sale had a similar impact on the Australian art market to Lawson's 1962 Schureck sale.[21] The sale realized over $500,000, almost $300,000 of which came from the third day's sale of the paintings, where the top price was $28,000 for Drysdale's *Black's Camp at the Outstation* (1965). The work of Norman Lindsay witnessed a dramatic increase in market value, with Lindsay etchings of comparable excellent quality selling for around $100 prior to the Rubensohn sale and up to $1500 afterwards. Rubensohn commented after the sale that 'I have never hoarded anything, and I have never bought anything with profit in mind, only the pleasure we could derive from it. It's just a matter of good fortune that our collection has proved an excellent investment.'[22] It would be interesting to substantiate this statement and to discover how long Rubensohn had been collecting for and whether the success of a particular sale inspired him, for example.

Lawson's still had a high profile in the early 1980s, winning prestigious art and estate sales. It also continued to hold regular weekly general auctions, monthly Fine Art auctions, small, specialized auctions and the large Fine Art auctions. For example, at Lawson's centenary sale in June 1984, the Charles Wymark house sale, Norman Lindsay's *Out of the Dawn* sold for $31,000. This was apparently regarded by Lindsay himself as his finest watercolour and was at the time the highest price for one of his watercolours sold in Australia.[23]

The Margolin estate sale at 'Barford', Bellevue Hill in August 1980 and the auction of the Charles Lloyd Jones collection at 'Rosemont', Woollahra in April 1981, were two noteworthy auctions conducted by Lawson's, which attracted thousands of viewers and bids were placed by collectors from major international cities. The Margolin collection was offered in conjunction with Leonard Joel, as Graham Joel had had many dealings with the Margolins in the past and they had also made purchases, for example, at the Ruwolt sale. Ruhen claims that auction firms at an international level had tried to win the Lloyd Jones sale, but that Lawson's had been the successful contender.[24] It was a hugely popular and prestigious sale of four days' duration; 7000 people attended the viewings and it realized over $1 million.

Ruhen's book on Lawson's, which was published in 1984 and thus appeared too soon after the establishment of Sotheby's and the re-establishment of Christie's to incorporate an analysis of the impact of these firms, emphasized that Lawson's was a quality auctioneer, focusing on quality art. However, Lawson's was state-based and arguably did not have a national reputation for excellence in the 1980s. The same might be said of Leonard Joel, the premier art auction house in Victoria until the supremacy of Sotheby's, Christie's and, more recently, the arrival of Deutscher-Menzies.

The multinationals gradually began to infiltrate the Sydney marketplace from 1993, after restrictions on charging the buyer's premium were lifted, with a dampening effect on the business of firms such as Lawson's. Lawson's was forced to compete with a number of auction houses in the late 1990s, including Goodmans, which had been becoming more aggressive in approach, as well as Christie's and Sotheby's. Lawson's also suffered because of its historical focus on more traditional works of art, with the increasing interest in contemporary works by collectors and other auction houses. Perhaps as part of a belated attempt to strengthen its position through international affiliations, Lawson's became the Australian representative of the International Association of Auctioneers in 1996. This association was reportedly 'capable of effective competition to the two world leaders, Christie's and Sotheby's'.[25] It enabled major auction firms of an independent nature, such as Butterfields (San Francisco, Chicago and Los Angeles), to be marketed internationally. However, Lawson's business had suffered to such an extent that the firm was ripe for a take-over by the Menzies Group of Auction Companies in 2001.

Henry and Peta Badgery retired in 2001 and sold their share of Lawson's to Rod Menzies, who had wanted to move into the field of general sales in order to compete fully with the national and international firms. Rod Menzies is an Australian by birth and was based in America for a number of years, returning to Australia in 1989. He owns a successful contract cleaning services and security company. James Badgery and his sister, Sally Hardy, initially stayed on with Lawson-Menzies, but both have subsequently left and are now involved in Badgery's Auctioneers and Appraisers in Chatswood, Sydney. In fact, most of Lawson's specialists left the firm after it was taken over by Menzies. The new management was in place as of 1 September 2001, with a commentator hoping that 'the pleasures of Lawsons [sic] don't disappear into a corporate slick'.[26]

Lawson's revival as Lawson-Menzies and its upmarket overhaul placed it in direct competition with the multinationals, as well as its sibling company, Deutscher-Menzies. The original plan had been for Deutscher-Menzies to deal in the top end of the market and for Lawson-Menzies to deal in the lower end, or 'everything else'.[27] However, after due consideration, it was decided that there was no reason why Lawson-Menzies could not confront the top end of the art market. Initially, there was much staff sharing between Deutscher-Menzies and Lawson-Menzies, which could have caused some confusion. A management board of Paul Sumner, Rod Menzies, Chris Deutscher and Mark Helps (Menzies' Chief Operating Officer) was formed with the purpose of avoiding conflicts of interest.

Most Australian auctioneers are not required to state at the time each lot falls whether it was actually sold or passed-in, although it is now a requirement of international firms, such as Christie's and Sotheby's. Rod Menzies encouraged the adoption of many international auctioneering practices and the auctioneer at Lawson-Menzies' July 2002 auction did clearly state the fate of each lot. Menzies' appreciation of these international practices may have been one of the reasons Paul Sumner was a desirable choice for Chief Executive Officer of Lawson-Menzies, with his vast experience and knowledge of both the London and Australian art auction markets.

Sumner, a decorative arts specialist, had commenced his career in the auctioneering business at Lalonde Brothers and Parham Fine Art Auctioneers (now known as Phillips) in Bristol, England in 1981, where he had been obliged to take his first auction at the age of seventeen when the scheduled auctioneer became ill. He then worked as saleroom manager at Michael Newman Fine Art Auctioneer in Plymouth and arrived in Australia in 1988 when he was employed at Rushton's Auctioneers in Sydney. Sumner worked for Christie's Australia from 1990 to 1994, followed by various positions at Sotheby's Australia, including General Manager in 1996 and Managing Director in 1999. In 2001, Sumner became Managing Director of Sotheby's Olympia in London and returned to Australia in 2002, taking up the position of Chief Executive Officer of Lawson-Menzies in September of that year. It was said that Sumner had been 'keen to return [to Australia] because of the more attractive Australian lifestyle and the freedom to get things done under an entrepreneurial owner rather than the corporate hierarchy at Sotheby's'.[28]

Lawson-Menzies' 'primary objective' under Sumner was to make the firm 'Australia's No. 1 integrated auction house for art, decorative arts, wine and jewellery'.[29] Under the new regime, sales were colour-coded and split into green for Lawson's and red for Lawson-Menzies, with green sales including all the furniture and household contents and industrial sales — which provide the company with consistent cash flow — while the red sales included art, antiques and collectables. This distinction was presumably made in order to attract new, more sophisticated clients to Lawson-Menzies, while attempting not to alienate existing clients of Lawson's. Sumner intended Lawson-Menzies to obtain national consignments and a national brand established on the basis of smaller, high value sales.

Lawson-Menzies held its final large-volume paintings auction in October 2002, featuring the Charles Blackman painting, *Suddenly Everything Happened* (1956), which had been sold after Deutscher-Menzies' auction the previous November for $336,000. It sold at Lawson-Menzies for $307,950 (estimate $260,000–$300,000) to a telephone bidder and set a record for the company. This sale demonstrated Lawson-Menzies' new emphasis on marketing and signature works, with the most expensive works having been well advertised prior to sale. The issue of transparency also arose after the sale of this work in such a short space of time by the two related firms.

As the movements and fortunes of auction houses have a domino effect, restructuring the existing hierarchy, Christie's and Sotheby's success with art sales effectively forced auctioneers of art, such as Lawson-Menzies, to prioritize their top-end paintings sales by taking an upmarket stance. In mid-2003, Lawson-Menzies entered into a consultative relationship with Martin Gallon, formerly managing director of Sotheby's Australia and a British art specialist, to develop the international paintings market in Australia. Messum's Fine Art also became affiliated with Lawson-Menzies to facilitate an exchange of European art between Australia and London. In November 2003, Lawson-Menzies' art department was merged with Deutscher-Menzies, with both firms to source art, but only the latter to conduct major art auctions. Sumner left Lawson-Menzies in 2004 and established Mossgreen Auctions soon afterwards, specialising in single-owner sales.

Leonard Joel

Leonard Joel also responded strongly and immediately to competition from Christie's, although Jon Dwyer felt that Sotheby's was Leonard Joel's first 'real' competitor, especially given Christie's intermittent presence in Australia until the late 1980s.[30] Leonard Joel's clearance rates in the late 1980s were higher than those of Christie's and Sotheby's, 'possibly as a result of the large number of cheap, unreserved lots offered by Joel's during their daytime sessions'.[31]

At this time, Leonard Joel retained the reputation of being the 'scarcely rivalled' experts in traditional Australian paintings.[32] Leonard Joel was also the dominant auction house for a while in the 1980s. It has been suggested that this may have been because traditional and colonial works were favoured by collectors and, as Melbourne was the epicentre of this market — a market controlled by Leonard Joel — it was able to capitalize on its conservative collecting base.[33] This is further substantiated by the fact that Leonard Joel sold the first million dollar Australian painting when it auctioned Rupert Bunny's *Une Nuit De Canicule* to Alan Bond in November 1988 for $1.25 million.

Leonard Joel is the Melbourne equivalent of the original Lawson's in that it is renowned for having an unpretentious auctioneering style and prides itself on its Australian origins. In 1989, Leonard Joel declared that it had 'no intention of changing…[its] style, which is to 'Christoby's' what Cinderella's ball is to the local hop. It's an advantage for…[us] to retain a bargain basement ambience' and a low-key brand.[34]

The style of Leonard Joel's auctioneers has been described:

> The pace at a Joel auction is steady. Graham's gaze flicks across the room skilfully identifying bids, eliminating the early bidders until only two or perhaps, three remain…Father and son trade jibes as one takes the gavel from the other. Warren constantly feigns politeness, invariably addressing his father as 'Mr Joel'.[35]

Leonard Joel has, therefore, usually attracted a different clientele to that of the more upmarket firms which exude finesse. Its art auctions were perhaps even more democratic than those of other firms in so far as a more representative body of the general public attended, from families and curiosity seekers to curators and art dealers. The customary clients of its art auctions in the late 1980s tended to be over sixty years of age and preferred historical, traditional art, because of which contemporary art was rarely offered. According to the — slightly biased — art critic, journalist and artist, Robert Rooney, 'Anything more recent [than the 1970s] is most likely offered for resale at one of the newer dealers' galleries, rather than at auction. As I discovered a few years ago…to the average auction-goer contemporary art is still a source of outrage and ridicule'.[36] This was probably a contributing factor in Leonard Joel relinquishing its dominant position to the multinational auction houses, which began to focus increasingly on contemporary art, in line with a shift in collecting taste.

Leonard Joel's Hans Heysen estate sale in June 1970 was one of its most significant art auctions, as it re-established an appreciation of Australian art not seen since earlier sales like the Baldwin Spencer auction of 1919 and the Schureck sale of 1962. For:

> In scenes not witnessed before or since, the Heysen auction attracted more than 4000 people and caused a panicky Malvern council caretaker to lock the town hall doors to prevent the crowds still outside from forcing their way through. Here, for the first time, was clear evidence that ordinary, middle-class Australians were interested in collecting their own artistic heritage.[37]

The Malvern Town Hall, the site of Leonard Joel's National Art Auctions, was described by Rooney in the late 1980s as almost anachronistic; 'As I pass through the dimly lit Victorian interior, with its heavy wooden panelling and ghostly marble statues, I know from past experience that the multitude of exhibits, on the over-crowded maze of temporary partitions in the main hall, are also relics from the past.'[38] Art auctions at the Malvern Town Hall were legendary, marathon events, with an average offering of a few thousand lots. Graham Joel claimed that 'Paul [Dwyer] started the art department when no one in Australia had ever heard of an auction-room having one and it grew out of nothing'.[39] In the mid-1960s, Leonard Joel had little competition and art sales provided the main avenue for its revenue until the early 1990s. The art department, established about 1962, was almost a distinct business, based separately from the general auction business, for around fifteen years, such was the prominence and importance of the art auctions.

Auctioning art had become an increasingly lucrative business. Graham Joel said in 1985 that 'In earlier days, you couldn't sell a pound note for 15 shillings at some stage of the auctioneering business and your percentage of goods not sold was astronomical.'[40] Turnover for Leonard Joel increased from approximately $7 million in the mid-1970s to $12 million in 1988, but by 1991, turnover was down to $10 million, probably partly as a result of the economic recession. In the 1980s, when traditional works were in vogue, fuelled by a growing appreciation of Australiana, demand far outweighed supply, increasing auction prices once again.

Leonard Joel's art staff, Paul and Jon Dwyer, made fairly regular interstate trips in order to source stock in the 1970s, but evidently not as early as the 1960s, signifying that the increased competition represented by Christie's sent them further afield. Despite being a state-based firm, Paul Dwyer 'travelled extensively both nationally and overseas from 1970 until about 1986 for Leonard Joel' and Jon Dwyer travelled on stock sweeps from 1982 until 1996, including regular trips to Sydney.[41] On one of these trips, in 1989, Jon Dwyer unearthed some Jessie Traill pictures in a farmhouse, including *The Tea Gardens*, which fetched $135,000, against an estimate of $45,000–$60,000, when Leonard Joel auctioned it in April 1989. However, in the 1990s, Christie's and Sotheby's began to compete with Leonard Joel's specialist auctions at the top end of the art market and sourcing stock became increasingly difficult.

It was in the 1990s that the business of the multinationals really began to eclipse that of long-standing family-owned auction firms, such as Leonard Joel. Leonard Joel began to modernize its business, as did others; its records were computerized by 1988 and in the mid-1990s a fairly comprehensive website was instituted. After profits began to decrease in the late 1990s, Warren Joel brought in his wife Kate, a management consultant, to restructure the business. Warren Joel started to make improvements to the operational side of the firm and Kate Joel focused on overhauling human resources, including the introduction of annual performance reviews, policies and systems.

In June 1998, both staff members of Leonard Joel's paintings department, Jon Dwyer and his assistant, Alexandra Wilcox, quit. Dwyer left to oversee valuations with Christie's, drawing to a conclusion the three-generation association of the Dwyer family with Leonard Joel, and Alexandra Wilcox defected to manage part two sales at Deutscher-Menzies. Dwyer took to Christie's twenty years' experience with Victorian Public Trustee companies, Leonard Joel's traditional strength and an essential tool for supplying stock. After Dwyer's departure, the art department lost its greatest art expert.

One of the eventual effects of the multinational competition was that Leonard Joel effectively closed its volatile art department in November 2001, although the clinching factor may have been the intensification of competition after the establishment of Deutscher-Menzies. Kate Joel confirmed that Deutscher-Menzies had had a 'significant impact' on Leonard Joel, as well as Christie's and Sotheby's.[42] Six members of staff were dismissed, including Treena Joel, Warren Joel's sister, who had worked with the firm for about two decades. This signified the demise of the three-day, thousand-lot art auctions that had become a veritable Melbourne institution. Fine art was amalgamated with a jewellery and decorative arts department and in July 2002, Leonard Joel introduced the first of its Monthly Art Auctions, offering 300 to 400 lots in the mid-price range; in actuality, withdrawing from the competition for quality paintings. The effective end of Leonard Joel's art sales has arguably contributed to the end of the firm's outstanding profits and success.

Not only was Leonard Joel overtaken by Christie's and Sotheby's, but it relinquished its position as the third biggest player in the paintings market to Deutscher-Menzies. Deutscher-Menzies had replaced Leonard Joel as the most successful Australian-owned auction firm by mid-1999. According to Ingram, even Leonard Joel's old and profitable associations with trustees of estates were slowly being severed, as the other firms were offering highly competitive deals.[43] In early 1998, prior to the take-over of Lawson's, the Menzies Group had offered to buy Leonard Joel's 'business and goodwill' for a reputed $3 million, to no avail.[44]

In the aftermath of Christie's withdrawal from the Australian market, Leonard Joel opened Joel Fine Art in Armadale, Melbourne to target once again the top end of the paintings market through both private treaty sales and auctions. It will be worthwhile to track the success of this new venture.

Phillips/Shapiro Auctioneers

Phillips International Auctioneers and Valuers is the third largest art auction house in the world after Christie's and Sotheby's and was one of the four major Georgian auction houses. Although Christie's and Sotheby's began arriving in Australia from the late 1960s, Phillips took much longer to establish a branch in Australia, possibly owing to its traditionally more docile approach to marketing and the absence of a high profile or brand. Christopher Weston, who owned Phillips for a few decades, retired and sold his 96 per cent holding of the company in 1996. His brother, Bill Weston, the Managing Director of H.E. Foster & Cranfield, 'a niche financial auctioneer dealing in life insurance policies and reversionary interests in trusts', then obtained a 20 per cent share of Phillips. Twenty per cent was bought by Phillips' management and 60 per cent by the Bank of Scotland and 3I, a venture capital group.[45] 3I revamped the organization, renovating the buildings and revising staffing and then sold it almost two years later 'for a very substantial profit' to LVMH (Louis Vuitton, Moet Hennessy).[46] They decided to revamp Phillips, once again, into an auction house that was even 'more boutique than Sotheby's or Christie's' and concentrating on the top end of the market.[47] This was to be a major change for Phillips, which had traditionally been more egalitarian than Christie's and Sotheby's.

Andrew Shapiro began his career in the art auction industry around 1974 in his hometown of Philadelphia, attaining an art history and historical preservation degree before working for Samuel T. Freeman, America's oldest auction house (founded in Philadelphia in 1805). He worked his way up the business ladder before moving to New York and joining Phillips in 1982, where he established its 20th Century Design Department. Shapiro worked for Phillips in New York until about 1988, before moving to Australia, where he was approached by the then owner of Phillips, Christopher Weston, and asked whether he would like to co-ordinate the firm's Australian operations.

Three Phillips ex-employees — presumably Robert Bradlow (Melbourne), Patrick Bowen (Perth) and Alison Harper (Sydney) — who had married Australians and were living in Australia in the 1980s, became Phillips' Australian representatives. Phillips gained its initial presence in Australia in about 1988 with the ambition of sourcing European art to sell in the London salerooms. The representative offices operated for a number of years and Shapiro revamped Phillips' Australian operations when he was appointed Managing Director in 1995. The firm thus really launched itself in Australia with its pioneer auctions of 20th Century Design, Shapiro's specialty, with the inaugural 20th Century Design auction held on 6 May 1996.

Phillips' Malcolm Enright sale on 2 May 1999 at Artspace in The Gunnery, Sydney demonstrated the popularity of art auctions and the success of selling contemporary art through this medium; this sale was held a few years after Sotheby's unsuccessful contemporary art sales and a year prior to Christie's establishment of a contemporary art department. Enright, a Brisbane creative director, sold 106 lots at The Gunnery, while 71 works from his study collection were sold by silent auction, with absentee bids only. According to one report, works sold at the public auction obtained more than $230,000.[48]

Enright was a charismatic collector who had supported contemporary Australian artists, such as Robert Macpherson and Jenny Watson, since the 1970s. The top price at the sale was achieved by Ken Whisson's *Blue Tourer* July–August 1975, which fetched $36,000, against an estimate of $20,000–$30,000. According to Shapiro, 'it was the first sale which affirmed contemporary art as a possibility for the auction industry'.[49]

From 10–12 August 1999, Phillips sold the decorative arts collection of Lord Alistair McAlpine, an English aristocrat who made his fortune in Australia. The sale included Gothic Revival furniture, porcelain, silver and also numerous paintings, most notably those by Sidney Nolan. The Nolan paintings included *Blackboys [Xanthorrhoea australis]* (1945); *Portrait of Lord Thorneycroft* (1979); and *Notes for Oedipus II* (1975). Other Australian artists represented in the collection included Sali Herman, Charles Blackman and Robert Dickerson. The contents had been housed in Bishop's House in Perth, McAlpine's former residence, although the auction was held at the S. H. Ervin Gallery at the National Trust in Sydney.

Phillips' Australian branch evolved into Shapiro Auctioneers in November 2001, when the board of LVMH deaccessioned their auction house interests, offering a management buy-out. Phillips merged with the art dealership, de Pury & Luxembourg, in 2001, who then acquired a controlling share of the firm in 2002 and the remaining interest in 2003. The buy-out of Phillips' Australian branch was announced on 18 November 2001 and Shapiro Auctioneers was launched, trading under their new banner the following day. A contemporary article observed that 'The sale [of Phillips] is part of a long-expected rationalisation of the Australian auction industry which is suffering from an acute competition for stock by too many operators in a very focused market'.[50]

Goodmans/Bonhams & Goodman

Michael Reid noted in 1997 that 'The mid-level auction houses are the engine room of the art auction market. Because they do not have the same capacity to promote their sales as the big houses, their prices are often a better reflection of the true state of the market'.[51] In spite of its mid-level status, Goodmans, which was established in 1994, held an extremely successful auction of contemporary art in Double Bay, Sydney on 31 March 2003, *The Jack & Isabella Klompé Collection — Australian and International Modern and Contemporary Art*. Tim Goodman thought that this was the biggest single-owner collection of modern and contemporary art to be sold in Australia.[52]

The collection belonged to Isabella Klompé and her late husband Jack and comprised 360 lots, which they had acquired principally from artists' solo exhibitions. The consignment might ordinarily have gone to one of the bigger multinational firms; however, the lower overheads associated with Goodmans would yield a greater profit. The Klompé collection represented the first occasion on which the works of many contemporary artists had entered the auction sphere and records were set for a number of artists, including Keith Looby, whose *Letter to Art Master* (1984) sold for $24,465. This was three times the auction estimate, as well as an Australian auction record. Overall, the sale prices doubled the estimates and 90 per cent of lots were sold by volume.[53]

Following the success of the Klompé sale, in August 2003, Goodmans, which already had affiliations with Leonard Joel, entered into a joint venture with the illustrious London firm, Bonham's. The Chairman of Bonham's, Robert Brooks, said of the move that 'Together, Bonhams and Goodmans [sic] will be a formidable force, ideally placed to compete for business at the highest level'.[54] Tim Goodman is the controlling shareholder in the new firm; minority holders include New Zealand's Mowbray Collectables, as well as Bonham's, which allows resources to be shared under a licensing agreement.

Early in 2005, Bonhams & Goodman merged with Bruce's of Adelaide, which was founded by Theodore Bruce in 1878, and it was announced in October 2005 that it was also taking over the boutique Sydney firm of Stanley & Co. The latter's founder, Dalia Stanley, remained in the capacity of a senior specialist. Horizontal integration could prove beneficial to Bonhams & Goodman, who had a turnover of $27 million in 2004. As events unfold there may be further rationalization of the Australian art auction market, with Bonhams & Goodman potentially moving onto a higher level on the art auction rung, having opened an office in South Yarra, Melbourne after Christie's departure.

Deutscher-Menzies

Deutscher-Menzies was established in 1998 and successfully rivalled the Christie's/Sotheby's duopoly of the Australian art auction market. Its very establishment is revealing about the extent to which art auction houses dominate the Australian marketplace and the mutability of the hierarchy.

Chris Deustcher, 'the Joseph Brown of his generation', was a highly respected and established art dealer.[55] He began his career as a dealer in 1975 and in the mid-1980s his dealership was turning over more than Christie's, with an annual turnover of at least $10 million. The recession of the late 1980s and early 1990s resulted in the forced closure of Deutscher's contemporary art gallery in Fitzroy (Deutscher Brunswick Street), as well as his other gallery in Carlton (Deutscher Fine Art) and the loss of his home. Speculation over Deutscher's self-confessed dire financial difficulties was rife, with Deutscher saying that by 1997, although he was still trading, it was a struggle and the business was debt-ridden.[56] By this stage he had already met Rod Menzies, his client, and Menzies proposed that they open a 'third auction house'.[57] Deutscher's initial response was disbelief that the market could support another firm, but after due consideration he agreed to undertake the enterprise.

Reid thought that 'Deutscher's move shows prescience. By analysing the overseas art market, one begins to understand the shifting sands of fine art distribution'.[58] The establishment of the new auction house and Deutscher's career change signifies the importance of auction sales as a preferred means of buying and selling art. Reid further claimed that 'The dealer-to-auctioneer move is a product of structural change in the international fine art market [owing to the recession]. The major multinational auction houses have been eating into the dealers' retail market for years'.[59] The auction houses had rallied against the impact of the recession by improving their marketing and client services and adding the retail market to their traditional repertoire of wholesale.

Deutscher-Menzies planned from the outset to hold four sales annually — three in Melbourne and one in Sydney — and to equal the turnover of Christie's and Sotheby's. Although Deutscher-Menzies initially operated from Melbourne, there was a move to hold more auctions in Sydney after the success of its first Sydney sale in March 2002 and concomitant with the gradual shift of the art market from Melbourne to Sydney. Deutscher-Menzies perceived a need to abolish the art auction market's traditional hibernation period of November to May, based on the fact that in London and New York the art market is bustling during that period and that Sydney has increasingly been a strong market. By holding a March auction it avoided buyer fatigue. The March sale in Sydney not only provides Deutscher-Menzies with an early and sizeable amount of revenue but also momentum for its next sale, with pictures continuing to flow in. Moreover, Sumner said that '60 per cent of what Sotheby's was selling when I was there [in the mid-late 1990s] was to New South Wales buyers, even though the auctions were in Melbourne'.[60]

Other Major Art Auction Houses

The original focus for the firm was on paintings, with sculpture and print media being embraced at later auctions, but the intention was always to be a fine art specialist. Sue Hewitt was Director of Paintings in New South Wales and its first auctioneer. However, that business relationship was short-lived and Anita Archer became Deutscher-Menzies' auctioneer. When Archer joined Deutscher-Menzies in 1998, she was the only employee to have any auction experience, having completed the one-year course at Sotheby's and having worked at Gregson Flanagan's and Bob Gregson's Auctions. After Deutscher-Menzies' inaugural auction, Archer was asked to work as its business administrator. Six weeks later, after conducting a successful charity auction at the Ballarat Fine Art Gallery, she was offered the position of auctioneer permanently. Archer is a rarity amongst the patriarchal confraternity of auctioneers and someone 'who has come to challenge Mr Roger McIlroy of Christie's as the master of the auction bon mot'.[61]

Deutscher-Menzies was a scrupulously planned enterprise. Nevertheless, owing to the staff's inexperience in the auction arena, early sales were reputedly chaotic in comparison with those of the multinationals. The first sale on 20 April 1998, which garnered $2.5 million, was criticized because of the uncertainty surrounding whether works had actually sold or not, compounded by the fact that successful bidders' numbers were not always confirmed verbally.[62] Nonetheless, Sasha Grishin said that the inaugural catalogue 'set a new standard in commercial auction catalogues, while the display in the Malvern show rooms [sic] looked more like a museum art exhibition than the usual crowded auction jumble sale'.[63]

Ironically, Deutscher-Menzies mimics practices employed by Sotheby's and Christie's overseas, many of which have not been adopted by their local firms. Menzies, himself an avid art collector and regular attendee of auctions in London and New York, has transferred his observations of international auction practices to his local enterprise; for example, sending Anita Archer and Vivien Anderson, its then Aboriginal art consultant, to America to watch international auction techniques at Christie's and Sotheby's in about 2000.

Deutscher-Menzies attempted, almost from the start, to adopt a more aggressive marketing stance and business approach than that traditionally used. Deutscher confessed that he used Sotheby's as a model for practices including obtaining and selling paintings and the strictly methodical, price-sensitive order of catalogue layouts.[64] Deutscher-Menzies has also been 'very target oriented' and Menzies had always intended to obtain auction results which fell between those of Christie's and Sotheby's.[65]

Deutscher proposed to pay vendors 'faster than the multinationals'; late arrival of cheques and auction catalogues had 'dogged' his dealership enabling dealers like Denis Savill, who has the ability to write a cheque instantly, to remain competitive.[66] This, as well as a reward programme, competitive commissions, a personalized service, flexible payment options and improved relations with dealers aimed to give Deutscher-Menzies the competitive edge over, not only its fellow auction houses, but also over art dealers. Menzies commented in 1998 that 'Internationally – and increasingly here – auctions have become social occasions...they are also great theatre. We'll be enhancing this...'[67] Archer confirmed that, despite the advent of telephone bidding, attendance figures at Deutscher-Menzies' art auctions are increasing and it is essential to book seats owing to demand.[68]

Auction houses overseas have been providing a wide array of financial services to their clients for some time. Emulating this trend, Deutscher-Menzies has offered guarantees of a minimum sale price and advances in order to secure works. However, this has not become general practice in Australia and it is worth noting that privately-owned companies like Deutscher-Menzies have the flexibility to adopt practices that public companies cannot. Deutscher maintains that guaranteeing has worked 'brilliantly' and that, in the worst-case scenario, Menzies would legally purchase the painting, paying the buyer's premium, so that the auction house still obtains the 'prestige of the sale' and it is this which is its most competitive asset.[69] Deutscher notes further that guarantees are only offered for 'special paintings' and the firm does not purchase paintings to sell at auction, despite accusations of multifarious iniquities and manipulations.[70] The practice of purchasing stock has not been favoured by Christie's and Sotheby's and is generally unpopular for providing the auctioneer with 'too much control over the sale'.[71]

Deutscher-Menzies' autonomy has been advantageous in enabling it to make instantaneous decisions and to have complete control over every facet of the organization. Deutscher said that 'the big difference in our business is we are perceived as being owner-operators...people are actually dealing with the principal in the business, whereas [with] the other [auction houses]...they are dealing...[with] an outpost employee for an international organization'.[72] The international collusion scandal and concomitant negative publicity plaguing Christie's and Sotheby's actually worked in favour of Deutscher-Menzies, reinforcing its local roots in contrast to the uncertainty surrounding the future ownership of the multinationals.

In August 1998, Deutscher-Menzies made its 'first published attempt to introduce sophisticated international incentives to the Australian market' when it gave John Schaeffer advances based on reserves for three works he had consigned to the firm.[73] However, two of the works did not sell and this meant that Deutscher-Menzies had to try and find buyers for them or take back the difference from Schaeffer. Works that are guaranteed are meant to be designated as such in the catalogues and Deutscher-Menzies has disclosed in catalogues whether the firm has a vested interest in any of the works. This practice of the auction house or auction house principals has characterized the firm since its inception, with claims in the popular press that Menzies frequently both buys and sells at Deutscher-Menzies auctions.[74] This could account for high clearance rates at some Deutscher-Menzies and Lawson-Menzies sales and may occasionally be a result of providing guarantees on works.

Catalogues were initially organized in chronological order, but this practice has been replaced with structuring the catalogue to control the rhythm of the auction. This is a departure from a curatorial sequence to a more business-oriented one, as modelled by Sotheby's in its catalogues, and which ensures that the more popular modern and contemporary works are not relegated to the end of the sale. Deutscher-Menzies announced on 17 April 2001 that it was intending to include in its catalogues works by artists who were not well known in order to 'promote Australasian artists commensurate with their art historical significance'.[75] This is very much the act of a dealer or curator, rather than a traditional auctioneer.

Deutscher-Menzies did not initially come into direct opposition with the extant duopoly as it started to carve out a new market and build a clientele of new buyers, rather than poaching from the existing clientele of the other auction houses. Deutscher introduced a number of clients, mainly buyers, from his extensive list of contacts from his art dealing days and Menzies expanded the client base substantially through his contacts in the horse racing industry, as Menzies is himself a horse breeder. These new clients were principally responsible for making numerous purchases at Deutscher-Menzies sales from the very beginning, benefiting the industry by increasing the overall number of buyers frequenting auctions. Nevertheless, the major auction houses were in direct competition for stock.

The Menzies Group made a second failed attempt, through private negotiations, to buy Leonard Joel from the Joel family in mid-1998 for a reputed $3 million.[76] This signalled from an early stage that Menzies was interested in cornering the market, particularly the high end thereof. The acquisition of Leonard Joel would have been particularly beneficial for the Menzies Group, providing access to its existing infrastructure and networks. However, Deutscher-Menzies has demonstrated that it could compete successfully without Leonard Joel's goodwill and business.

Roger McIlroy said in 1998 that the establishment of a new auction house would result in a diminution of stock and that Christie's would take the new competition 'very seriously indeed'.[77] However, he continued with the comment that a small, locally-owned firm would flounder in the face of the multinational domination of the art market, saying that 'It's an adventuresome move and I don't really see how they're going to compete with companies like us who have offices in 120 countries.'[78] Nonetheless, Deutscher-Menzies has succeeded in rivalling the strong hold that the multinationals have had on the Australian market. Its third auction (in 1998) totalled $3 million, putting it on par with Christie's and Sotheby's and at the end of this first operational year, Deutscher-Menzies had already attained what Reid refers to as 'first-rung status', along with Christie's and Sotheby's.[79] Moreover, in May 2000, Deutscher-Menzies obtained the highest amount ever at a single auction by a locally-owned auction house, with the sale realizing $5.35 million. Deutscher-Menzies superseded Christie's and Sotheby's for the first time in November 2000, claiming higher turnovers than its competitors.

Sotheby's Chairman, Justin Miller, said that, although the introduction of a 'high profile competitor' always has a negative effect on a firm's ability to gather quality stock — citing the example of the Lowenstein Sharp sale of November 2002, for which Deutscher-Menzies successfully outbid Sotheby's — Sotheby's business had been sustaining a period of growth from 2000–2002.[80]

Anita Archer believes that Christie's and Sotheby's had become too complacent and passive and that it took Deutscher-Menzies to raise standards through competition.[81] Deutscher-Menzies has been heavily influenced by New York practices, while Christie's and Sotheby's have always relied on 'brand identification'.[82] However, because Christie's Australian performance had been inconsistent, Christie's had begun to 'smarten up its act', adopting a more 'proactive' approach, prior to the disclosure that a new auction house was being established.[83] Ingram noted at the time that Christie's highly-marketed August 1998 sale 'must consolidate the hold of multinationals on the Australian auction market and the art resale trade as a whole'.[84] Nonetheless, since then, Deutscher-Menzies, through an aggressive pursuit of the marketplace, has successfully challenged this multinational domination.

The establishment of Deutscher-Menzies in 1998 could be viewed as a response to the dominance of auction houses in the Australian art market and its establishment has pre-empted responses in the market of its own. Deutscher-Menzies achieved art auction sales of $22 million in 2005, positioning it in second place behind Sotheby's on $33 million. The Australian art auction market was worth $93 million that year, with Deutscher-Menzies selling 24 per cent of the market by value. The end of Deutscher's involvement in Deutscher-Menzies and the subsequent founding of Deutscher and Hackett in 2006 will have further ramifications for the art auction market in Australia.

In this study we have observed the waxing and waning fortunes of art auction houses, with a particular focus on Christie's and Sotheby's. There is a common expression in the art market that Sotheby's are dealers trying to be gentlemen and that Christie's are gentlemen trying to be dealers. While maintaining a long-standing rivalry and different styles, the firms also share some commonalities, hence the 'Christoby's' tag. They have both cast off the pejorative connotations of being a plebeian means to dispose of second-hand goods and imbued themselves with prestige by refining the art of paintings auctions and adding panache to what is essentially the business of salesmanship. Despite Christie's recent withdrawal, the multinationals have become entrenched in the psyche of the Australian art market. They displayed the establishment dates of their parent bodies with reverence and pride, relying on their pedigree, which they re-established in Australia through assiduous marketing. The fate of current art auction houses in Australia will warrant monitoring, particularly that of Sotheby's. Since Christie's departure, there has been speculation that Sotheby's may follow suit.

Another intriguing — and recurring — trend is the sale of contemporary art at auction. According to Eugene Thaw:

> ...the 'hottest' of all art market commodities today, as always in the past, are the big names of contemporary art. Common sense must warn us, therefore, that soon others will become the big names, with only a small fraction of today's high-fliers surviving at all, and only a fraction of that fraction surviving with increased value.[85]

Collecting tastes are constantly evolving, as is technology. Future studies might well focus on the auction of new media, such as digital video, perhaps via internet auctions, which are demonstrating good results, even for the sale of relatively expensive art. Observing how the market restructure and collecting trends unfold will provide exciting opportunities for analysis and future studies. I hope that this book paves the way, as there are many avenues worthy of pursuit.

ENDNOTES

[1] The Art Newspaper, *The Art Newspaper — Guide to Art Auctions Worldwide — First Edition*, 2002.

[2] Terry Ingram, 'F. R. Strange throws down the gauntlet', *Australian Financial Review*, 15 July 1971, p.8.

[3] Charles Nodrum, taped interview with the author, Melbourne, 24 October 2002.

[4] Geoff K. Gray, 'Auctions and Grays', Geoff K. Gray (Holdings) Limited, *Annual Report*, 1969.

[5] Christopher Dawson, 'Going, going, gone at Grays', *Sydney Morning Herald*, 26 June 1971, p.7.

[6] Terry Ingram, 'Chocolate and orange, and Gray all over…', *Australian Financial Review*, 1 July 1971, p.8.

[7] Ingram, 'Chocolate and orange, and Gray all over…', p.8 and Charles Nodrum, taped interview with the author, Melbourne, 24 October 2002.

[8] Charles Nodrum, taped interview with the author, Melbourne, 24 October 2002.

[9] Geoff K. Gray, *Auction Sale of Australian Paintings Including 'The Darrel [sic] Lea Collection'*, Sydney, 13 February 1974.

[10] Terry Ingram, 'Dobell's "Wangi Boy" brings record $70,000', *Australian Financial Review*, 14 February 1974, p.8.

[11] Geoff K. Gray, *'The Darrel [sic] Lea Collection'*.

[12] This was according to Hodgson in Alan Farrelly, 'Art Boom and Bust: Part 2 — Why Ron Hodgson updated to art', *Sunday Sun*, 18 July 1974, p.13, 14.

[13] Ingram, 'Chocolate and orange, and Gray all over…', p.8.

[14] Jenny Dickerson, interview with the author, Sydney, 19 November 2002 and Helen James, 'Eye for an original', *The Herald* (Melbourne), 20 April 1968, p.26.

[15] William S. Ellenden, 'Reminiscences of an Auctioneer', *The Australasian Antique Collector*, 20th ed., 1980, p.126.

[16] Ellenden, 'Reminiscences of an Auctioneer', p.126.

[17] Peter Cochrane, 'Dueling Gavels', *Good Weekend Magazine*, 18 November 1989, p.57.

[18] Michael Redmond (possibly – unattributed in magazine), 'Lawson's – Yesterday, Today and Tomorrow', *The Australian Antique Collector*, 24th ed., July-December 1982, p.93.

[19] Terry Ingram, 'Lindsays, Drysdales fetch top prices at Sim Rubensohn sale', *Australian Financial Review*, 29 June 1973, p.10.

[20] Bruce Stannard, 'Collector sells his antiques for $500,000', *The Australian*, 30 June 1973, p.1.

[21] Ellenden, 'Reminiscences of an Auctioneer', pp.125–33.

[22] Carl Ruhen, *The Auctioneers: Lawsons – The First 100 Years*, Ayers and James Heritage Books and James R. Lawson Pty Ltd, Sydney 1984, p.136 and Stannard, 'Collector sells his antiques for $500,000', p.1.

[23] Ruhen, *The Auctioneers*, pp.11–12.

[24] Ruhen, *The Auctioneers*, p.136.

[25] Lawson's, <www.lawsons.com.au/ia.html> [16/07/2001].

[26] Antonia Williams, 'Playing Houses', *Sydney Morning Herald*, 2 August 2001, p.5.

[27] Sharon Verghis, 'Rivalry raises the bidding stakes', *Sydney Morning Herald*, 15 April 2003, <www.smh.com.au/articles/2003/04/14/1050172532114.html> [17/07/2003].

[28] Peter Fish, 'Relaunched kid on the block', *Sydney Morning Herald*, 6 November 2002, Money, p.10.

[29] Lawson-Menzies, 'Lawson-Menzies appoint new CEO', no pagination.

[30] Jon Dwyer, taped interview with the author, Melbourne, 23 October 2002.

[31] Roger Dedman, *Christie's Australian Art Market Movements Handbook*, Christie's, Victoria 2002, p.11.

[32] Terry Ingram, 'Quirky cataloguing of copies could confuse future buyers', *Australian Financial Review*, 28 July 1988, p.32.

[33] Charles Nodrum, taped interview with the author, Melbourne, 24 October 2002.

[34] Jan McGuinness, 'There's an art in buying art', *The Bulletin*, 11 July 1989, p.40.

[35] Author unknown, 'Graham and Warren Joel will sell your jewels or your junk', *Sydney Morning Herald*, Good Weekend, 9 November 1985, p.78.

[36] Robert Rooney, 'A stillness and silence', *The Australian*, 21–22 November 1987, Weekend Magazine, p.12.
[37] Geoff Maslen, 'Still Going, Going, Gone', *The Age*, 24 March 1994, p.9.
[38] Rooney, 'A stillness and silence', p.12.
[39] Quoted in Maslen, 'Still Going, Going, Gone', p.9.
[40] Author unknown, 'Graham and Warren Joel will sell your jewels or your junk', p.78.
[41] Jon Dwyer, correspondence with the author, 13 August 2003 and Geoff Maslen, 'Old hand to lead auction house revival, *The Age*, 6 December 2002, p.4.
[42] Kate Joel, taped interview with the author, Melbourne, 25 October 2002.
[43] Terry Ingram, 'Joel's grand renaissance plan suffers change of art', *Australian Financial Review*, 9 July 1999, p.23.
[44] Ingram, 'Joel's grand renaissance plan suffers change of art', p.23.
[45] Michael Reid, 'Phillips takes a gamble', *The Weekend Australian*, 21–22 February 1998, p.4.
[46] Andrew Shapiro, taped interview with the author, Sydney, 30 August 2002.
[47] Andrew Shapiro, taped interview with the author, Sydney, 30 August 2002.
[48] Sandra McLean, 'Flags fly at Enright sale', *Courier Mail*, 11 May 1999, no pagination.
[49] Andrew Shapiro, taped interview with the author, Sydney, 30 August 2002.
[50] Terry Ingram, 'Management Buyout at Art Auctioneers', *Australian Financial Review*, 20 November 2001, p.6.
[51] Michael Reid, 'All hyped up', *The Weekend Australian*, 22–23 November 1997, p.4.
[52] Goodmans, 'Hats off! Klompe Collection of Contemporary Art to be Auctioned', media release, undated [obtained 28 April 2003].
[53] Much of this paragraph on the Klompé sale was first published in Shireen Huda, 'The Power of Provenance – single-owner collections and recent art auction trends', *Australian Art Review*, issue 2, July–October 2003, pp.98–9.
[54] Geoff Maslen, 'Upping the ante', *The Age*, 25 August 2003, <www.theage.com.au/articles/2003/08/22/1061529323877.html?from=storyrhs> [23/10/2005].
[55] Jan McGuinness, 'Who are the Dealers?', *The Bulletin*, 11 July 1989, p.41.
[56] Chris Deutscher, taped interview with the author, Melbourne, 3 October 2002.
[57] Chris Deutscher, taped interview with the author, Melbourne, 3 October 2002.
[58] Michael Reid, 'Deutscher Menzies – Moving to a new house', *The Weekend Australian*, 14–15 February, 1998, p.4.
[59] Reid, 'Deutscher Menzies – Moving to a new house', p.4.
[60] Paul Sumner, partially taped interview with the author, Sydney, 19 November 2002.
[61] Terry Ingram, 'Unrelenting demand for the big picture at new auction', *Australian Financial Review*, 8 March 2002, p.10.
[62] See Terry Ingram, 'Lack of practice grounds the eagle', *Australian Financial Review*, 23 April 1998, p.24.
[63] Sasha Grishin, 'New auction house bids for its place', *The Canberra Times*, 4 May 1998, p.7.
[64] Chris Deutscher, taped interview with the author, Melbourne, 3 October 2002.
[65] Chris Deutscher, taped interview with the author, Melbourne, 3 October 2002.
[66] Terry Ingram, '"Deutschmen" promises speedy payments', *Australian Financial Review*, 5 February 1998, p.29.
[67] McCulloch, 'Reputations under hammer', p.24.
[68] Anita Archer, interview with the author, Melbourne, 25 November 2002.
[69] Chris Deutscher, taped interview with the author, Melbourne, 3 October 2002.
[70] Chris Deutscher, taped interview with the author, Melbourne, 3 October 2002.
[71] Terry Ingram, 'Deutscher-Menzies goes on exceptional buying spree', *Australian Financial Review*, 16 December 1999, p.26.
[72] Chris Deutscher, taped interview with the author, Melbourne, 3 October 2002.
[73] Terry Ingram, 'Running for cover loses its appeal', *Australian Financial Review*, the fin, 15–16 August 1998, p.13.

[74] Michael Reid, 'New boy breaks fresh ground', *The Weekend Australian*, 18–19 April 1998, p.4 and Michael Reid, 'New auction player needs to lift its game', *The Weekend Australian*, 22–23 August 1998, p.4.

[75] Deutscher-Menzies, 'Feast of Modern Masters + Uncovered Treasures', media release, 17 April 2001, <www.deutschermenzies.com/press/press/170401.html> [18/08/2003].

[76] Michael Reid, 'Bid rebuffs fail to blunt new force', *The Weekend Australian*, 25-26 July 1998, p.4.

[77] McCulloch, 'Reputations under hammer', p.24.

[78] McIlroy quoted in McCulloch, 'Reputations under hammer', p.24.

[79] Michael Reid, 'Runaway prices cap strong year', *The Weekend Australian*, 12–13 December 1998, p.4.

[80] Justin Miller, taped interview with the author, Sydney, 3 September 2002.

[81] Anita Archer, interview with the author, Melbourne, 25 November 2002.

[82] Anita Archer, interview with the author, Melbourne, 25 November 2002.

[83] Terry Ingram, 'Star-studded auction in new venue', *Australian Financial Review*, 20 August 1998, p.31.

[84] Ingram, 'Star-studded auction in new venue', p.31.

[85] Eugene Thaw, 'Beauty on the Block', *The New Republic*, 11 November 1985, quoted in Watson, *From Manet to Manhattan*, p.471.

Sources

Interviews and Oral Histories

Archer, Anita, auctioneer, Deutscher-Menzies, interview with the author, Melbourne, 25 November 2002

Bleakley, Robert, founder of Sotheby's Australia, taped interview with the author, Canberra, 28 November 2002

Clark, Jane, Deputy Chairman, Sotheby's Australia, taped interview with the author, Melbourne, 23 October 2002

Clark, Jane, Deputy Chairman, Sotheby's Australia, telephone conversation with the author, 2 August 2002

Dedman, Roger, author of *Christie's Australian Art Market Movements Handbook*, partially taped interview with the author, Melbourne, 2 October 2002

Deutscher, Chris, Executive Director, Deutscher-Menzies, taped interview with the author, Melbourne, 3 October 2002

Dickerson, Jenny, former manager of art department, Geoff K. Gray, interview with the author, Sydney, 19 November 2002

Dwyer, Jon, former head of paintings department, Leonard Joel, correspondence with the author, 13 August 2003

Dwyer, Jon, former head of paintings department, Leonard Joel, taped interview with the author, Melbourne, 23 October 2002

Fraser, Mark, then Head of Australian Art Department, Sotheby's Australia, taped interview with the author, Melbourne, 21 October 2002

Hewitt, Sue, former senior employee and auctioneer, Christie's Australia, taped interview with the author, Sydney, 2 September 2002

Joel, Kate, management consultant, Leonard Joel, taped interview with the author, Melbourne, 25 October 2002

Larkin, Annette, Head of Contemporary Art Department, Christie's Australia, taped interview with the author, Canberra, 5 September 2002

McClelland, Joan, former Melbourne representative, Christie's Australia, taped interview with the author, Melbourne, 2 October 2002

McIlroy, Roger, Chairman and Managing Director, Christie's Australia, taped interview with the author, Melbourne, 21 October 2002

Marshall, Christopher, convenor of the *Art and the Market: Then and Now* course at the University of Melbourne, interview with the author, Melbourne, 22 October 2002

Maslen, Geoff, art market analyst, *The Age*, correspondence with the author, 28 November 2002

Miller, Justin, Chairman, Sotheby's Australia, taped interview with the author, Sydney, 3 September 2002

Nodrum, Charles, former Manager of Melbourne office, Christie's Australia, taped interview with the author, Melbourne, 24 October 2002

Reid, Michael, art market analyst, *The Australian*, taped interview with the author, Sydney, 30 August 2002

Sayers, Andrew, Director, National Portrait Gallery, interview with the author, Canberra, 24 July 2002

Shapiro, Andrew, Managing Director, Shapiro Auctioneers, taped interview with the author, Sydney, 30 August 2002

Sumner, Paul, Chief Executive Officer and Managing Director, Lawson-Menzies, *curriculum vitae* provided to the author, 14 August 2003

Sumner, Paul, Chief Executive Officer and Managing Director, Lawson-Menzies, partially taped interview with the author, Sydney, 19 November 2002

Thomas, David, Director, Valuations and Research, Deutscher-Menzies, taped interview with the author, Melbourne, 3 October 2003

Van den Bosch, Annette, author of PhD thesis on *The Art Market since 1940* (University of Sydney 1989), interview with the author, Melbourne, 24 October 2002

Sources

Art Auction Catalogues and Brochures

Christie's

Christie's, Australian, International and Contemporary Art, Melbourne, 6–7 May 2003

Christie's, Australian, International and Contemporary Paintings, Melbourne, 27–28 November 2001

Christie's, Christie's — John Glover: Mount Wellington and Hobart Town from Kangaroo Point, Melbourne, Australia, 27 November 2001, sale brochure, 4 pages (gatefold)

Christie's, Christie's Contemporary Art, Sydney 13.08.00, Sydney, 18 August 2000

Christie's, The Harold E. Mertz Collection of Australian Art, Melbourne, 28 June 2000

Christie's, Australian and European Paintings, Melbourne, 23–24 November 1998

Christie's, Australian and European Paintings, Sydney, 17–18 August 1998

Christie's, The James Baker Collection of Contemporary Australian Art, Brisbane, 2–3 March 1996

Christie's, Australian and European Paintings, Prints and Photographs, Melbourne, 6–7 December 1994

Christie's, The Dallhold Collection, Melbourne, 28 July 1992

Christie's, The Collection of Sir Leon and Lady Trout, Everton House, Everton Park, Brisbane, Queensland, Australia, Brisbane, 6–7 June 1989

Christie's, The Dr John L. Raven Collection, Sydney, 13 September 1984

Christie's, Australian Historical and Contemporary Paintings, Drawings and Prints with some European Paintings and Prints, Melbourne, 19 June 1978

Christie's, Australian Natural History, Historical, Traditional, Contemporary and European Prints, Sydney, 29 September 1976

Christie's, Australian Historical and Contemporary Paintings, Drawings and Sculpture also European Paintings and Sculpture, Sydney, 3 October 1973

Christie's, The Major Harold De Vahl Rubin Collection of Australian Drawings and Paintings, Part 2, Sydney, 2 October 1973

Christie's, The Major Harold De Vahl Rubin Collection of Australian Drawings and Paintings, Part 1, Sydney, 4 October 1972

Christie's, Australian Historical and Contemporary Drawings and Paintings and Some European Paintings and Sculpture, Melbourne, 14–15 March 1972

Christie's, Catalogue of Australian Historical and Contemporary Drawings and Paintings and some European Paintings and Sculpture, Sydney, 5–6 October 1971

Christie's, Catalogue of Australian Historical and Contemporary Drawings and Pictures and Sculptures, Melbourne, 11–12 March 1971

Christie's, Christie's in Australia – Australian Historical and Contemporary Drawings and Paintings, Sydney, 24 September 1969

Deutscher-Menzies

Deutscher-Menzies, The Lowenstein Sharp Collection of Contemporary Australian Art, Melbourne, 11 November 2002

Deutscher-Menzies, Australian & International Fine Art Auction, Melbourne, 28–29 August 2002

Deutscher-Menzies, The Sydney Auction — Australian & International Fine Art, Sydney, 5 March 2002

Deutscher-Menzies, Modern Masters + 19th & 20th Century Australian and International Art, Melbourne, 9–10 May 2001

Deutscher-Menzies, Australian Modern Masters + 19th & 20th Century Australian and International Fine Art, Melbourne, 3–4 May 2000

Deutscher-Menzies, 19th and 20th Century Australian & International Paintings, Sculpture & Works on Paper, Melbourne, 10 August 1998

Deutscher-Menzies, 19th and 20th Century Australian Paintings, Sculpture and Works on Paper, Melbourne, 20 April 1998

Gemmell, Tuckett & Co.

Arthur Tuckett & Son and W. H. Gill's Fine Art Society, The Baldwin Spencer Collection of Australian Pictures and Works of Art, Fine Art Society's Galleries, Melbourne, May 1919, Melbourne, 19–21 May 1919

Gemmell, Tuckett & Co., Catalogue of the Magnificent Oil Paintings and Water-Colour Drawings Collected by the late Sir Thomas Fitzgerald, C. B., Melbourne, 24 September 1909

Gemmell, Tuckett & Co., Catalogue of the Beautiful and Costly Art Furniture, Marble Statuary, Real Bronzes, Art Treasures, Oil Paintings, Water Colour Drawings, Fine Old Engravings, &c., Collected by Sir George Verdon, K. C. M. G, C. B., Melbourne, 1 June 1891, Art Pamphlet 52(7)

Gemmell, Tuckett & Co., Fine Collection of Oil Paintings, Sketches, Artists' Materials, &c., of the Late G. F. Folingsby, Director of the National Gallery of

Victoria, and Master of the Painting School, Including also Fine Examples by Mrs Clara Folingsby, Melbourne, 18 March 1891, Art Pamphlet 40(16)

Gemmell, Tuckett & Co., Invitation to an 'Exhibition of Pictures By Fd [sic] McCubbin, Arthur Streeton, and Tom Roberts', Melbourne, 3 December 1890, Art Pamphlet 75(4)

Gemmell, Tuckett & Co., Catalogue of Herr Kahler's Beautiful Oil Paintings & Pastels, to be sold by Gemmell, Tuckett & Co. at their New Art Gallery Wednesday 7th May, 1890, Melbourne, 7 May 1890

Gemmell, Tuckett & Co., An Artist's Sanctuary – Catalogue Raisonne of the Contents of Herr Kahler's Studio Comprising A Matchless piece of Tapestry from Gobelins – Oil Paintings and Pastels – Carvings in Ivory and Wood – Brussels Lace – Ecclesiastical Robes – Antique Weapons, Girdles, Enamels – Antiquities and Curios All of which are perfectly unique of [sic] their kind to be sold by auction by Messrs. Gemmell, Tuckett & Co. In the Studio, No. 19 Elizabeth Street South, on Thurs 20th Feb at twelve o'clock, Melbourne, 20 February 1890

Gemmell, Tuckett & Co., Catalogue of the Magnificent Collection of Oil Paintings and Water-Colour Drawings – The Property of J. R. Tuckett, Esq., Melbourne, 27 October 1886, Art Pamphlet 58(4)

Gemmell, Tuckett & Co., Catalogue of Paintings in Water-Colour, Melbourne, 26 August 1885, Art Pamphlet 74(4)

Gemmell, Tuckett & Co., Catalogue of a Valuable Collection of Cabinet and Gallery Pictures by Eminent Masters, also a Collection of Engravings, including the Musee Francais and Musee Royal (Atlas size), A few lots of Photographs, a large quantity of Violin and other music, and a Small Library of Books, Containing some valuable works, the whole collected by Mr Joseph Griffiths, who is leaving the Colony, Melbourne, 22 May 1868

Geoff K. Gray

Geoff K. Gray, Australian and European Paintings, Sydney, 14 September 1987

Geoff K. Gray, Auction Sale of Australian Paintings Including 'The Darrel [sic] Lea Collection', Sydney, 13 February 1974

Geoff K. Gray, A Catalogue of Fine Art containing Works of Leading Australian Artists and Selections of Overseas Artists from the famous Voss Smith Collection of Melbourne, Sydney, 14–15 November 1962

Hamilton & Miller

Hamilton & Miller, Two Day Fine Art Sale – Rare Books, Fine Porcelains and China [sic] Marbles, Bronzes, Crystal, Objets d'Art, Paintings, Antique and Period Furnitures [sic], Table Wines, Camperdown, Sydney, 11–12 September 1975

Lawson's

James R. Lawson, The Emmanuel Margolin Collection of 18th & 19th Century Furniture, Clocks, Porcelain, Silver, Carpets, Tapestries and Other Objects of Art, 'Barford', Bellevue Hill, Sydney, 18–19 August 1980

James R. Lawson, Catalogue of Mr. Sim Rubensohn's Collection of Fine and Rare Art Effects, Kelvin Park, Dural, 26–29 June 1973

James R. Lawson, Catalogue of The Norman Schureck Collection of Valuable Pictures, Sydney, 27–28 March 1962

James R. Lawson, Catalogue of Mr S. Rubensohn's Collection of Magnificent Antique and Period Furniture Superb Art Treasures and Valuable Pictures, Sydney, 18–20 November 1947

James R. Lawson, Mr William Barclay's Collection of Magnificent Pictures, Sydney, 4 May 1937

James R. Lawson, Catalogue – Mr Leonard Dodds [sic] Collection of Valuable Pictures, Sydney, 22 November 1927

James R. Lawson, Catalogue of the W. A. Little Collection of Valuable Pictures including Important Oil Paintings, Water Colour Drawings and Etchings by Eminent English and Continental Artists, Sydney, 23 November 1926

James R. Lawson, Catalogue of the W. A. Little Art Collection Comprising: Rare Old English and Continental China, Sydney, 16–18 November 1926

James R. Lawson, Mr Leonard Dodds' Collection of Valuable Pictures, Sydney, 31 January 1922

James R. Lawson, Catalogue of the Eedy Collection, Sydney, 11 October 1921

James R. Lawson, Catalogue of J. T. Hackett's Art Collection, Sydney, from 17 September 1918

Lawson-Menzies

Lawson-Menzies, Australian and International Paintings – Works on Paper and Contemporary Art, Sydney, 29–30 October 2002

Leonard Joel

Leonard Joel, Australian, British, New Zealand and European Historical and Contemporary Paintings, Watercolours, Drawings and Graphics, Melbourne, 12–13 April 1989

Leonard Joel, 'Leonard Joel – Twenty Years at the Malvern Town Hall', in Australian Paintings – Australian, British, New Zealand and European Historical and Contemporary Paintings, Watercolours, Drawings and Graphics, Melbourne, 4–5 November 1987.

Leonard Joel, The Hans Heysen Collection, including works by eminent Australian and Overseas artists, Melbourne, 18–19 June 1970

Leonard Joel, The George Page-Cooper Collection – Historical Australian Paintings – Old Masters, Bronzes, etc, Melbourne, 21–22 November 1967

Leonard Joel, The Charles Ruwolt Collection of Australian Paintings, Melbourne, 17 November 1966

Phillips

Phillips, The Bishops House Collection, Sydney, 10–12 August 1999

Phillips, 20th Century Art and Design Featuring the Malcolm Enright Collection of Contemporary Art and Important Aboriginal Art, Sydney, 2 May 1999

Phillips, Selected Paintings, Furniture, Decorative and Asian Arts, Silver and Jewellery, Sydney, 26 July 1998

Phillips, 20th Century Design, Sydney, 6 May 1996

Sotheby's

Sotheby's, Aboriginal Art, Sydney, 28–29 July 2003

Klingender, Tim, 'View From Sotheby's', in Sotheby's, Aboriginal Art, Sydney, 28–29 July 2003, p.2

Sotheby's, The John McCaffrey Collection of Kimberley Art, Sydney, 28 July 2003

Sotheby's, Fine Australian and International Paintings, Melbourne, 26 November 2002

Sotheby's, The Fairfax Corporate Collection of Australian Paintings, Sydney, 17 November 2002

Sotheby's, Art from the Kerry Stokes Collection Including Works Formerly in the Orica Collection, Sydney, 26 August 2002

Sotheby's, The Collection of Mr and Mrs René Rivkin, Sydney, 3 June 2001

Sotheby's, Aboriginal Art, Melbourne, 26–27 June 2000

Sotheby's, Important Aboriginal Art – including property from the Louis A. Allen Collection, Melbourne, 29 June 1998

Sotheby's, Avant Garde Art and Design, Melbourne, 10 November 1997

Clark, Jane, 'View from Sotheby's', in Sotheby's, Aboriginal and Tribal Art – including property from the Dorothy Bennett Collection, Selected Works from the Holmes à Court Collection, Heytesbury, the Barnett Collection at Columbia University, the Hornshaw Collection of Oceanic Art, the Erkkila Collection of New Guinea Artefacts, Sydney, 9 November 1997

Sotheby's, The Decorator and Connoisseur Including the Mrs L. Voss-Smith Collection, Melbourne, 29 September 1997

Sotheby's, Fine Australian and European Paintings, Drawings, Prints, Photographs and Sculpture including works from the D R Sheumack Collection and the Len Voss Smith Collection, Melbourne, 25–26 August 1997

Sotheby's, 'Aboriginal Art Achieves Record Prices', in Fine Australian and European Paintings, Drawings, Prints, Photographs and Sculpture including works from the D R Sheumack Collection and the Len Voss Smith Collection, Melbourne, 25–26 August 1997

Sotheby's, Important Aboriginal Art, Melbourne, 30 June 1997

Sotheby's, Fine Tribal Art and Aboriginal Bark Paintings, Sydney, 27–28 October 1996

Sotheby's, Fine Contemporary and Aboriginal Art, Melbourne, 28 November 1995

Sotheby's, Fine Tribal Art and Aboriginal Paintings, Sydney, 19 November 1995

Sotheby's, Contemporary and Aboriginal Art including the Properties of: Mrs Anne Urban and Ms Shirley Urban, Dr Joy Kinslow-Harris, Melbourne, 18 June 1995

Sotheby's, Fine Australian Paintings and Sculpture, Drawings, Prints and Photographs and European Paintings, Prints and Sculpture, Sydney, 4–5 December 1994

Sotheby's, Fine Australian Paintings and Sculpture, Drawings, Prints and Photographs and European Paintings, Prints and Sculpture including the Collection of Mrs Una Fraser, Melbourne, 22–23 August 1994

Sotheby's, Fine Tribal Art, Sydney, 28 November 1993

Sotheby's, Contemporary Art, Melbourne, 24 October 1993

Sotheby's, Modern and Contemporary Paintings, Drawings, Sculptures and Prints including works from the Budget Collection and Paintings and Drawings from the Collection of Peter Nahum, Melbourne, 27 September 1992

Sotheby's, Fine Australian Paintings – European Paintings, Drawings, Prints and Books including Paintings by Conrad Martens from part of The Dallhold Collection and Books from the Holmes à Court Collection, Melbourne, 23 August 1992

Sotheby's, 143 works from the Museum of Contemporary Art, Brisbane, Melbourne, 21 June 1992

Sotheby's, 100 Works from the Museum of Contemporary Art, Brisbane, Melbourne, 16 June 1991

Sources

Sotheby's, Contemporary Australian Paintings and Works on Paper, Melbourne, 7 April 1991

Sotheby's, Australian Aboriginal, Melanesian and South Seas Tribal Art, Melbourne, 28 November 1989

Sotheby's, Fine Australian Paintings including Important Colonial Furniture, Silver and The J. and J. Altmann Art Reference Library, Melbourne, 14 August 1989

Sotheby's, Fine Australian Paintings including the Dr John L. Raven Collection of Important Colonial Paintings, Melbourne, 17 April 1989

Sotheby's, Fine Australian Paintings – John Glover, 'The Bath of Diana, Van Diemen's Land', 1837, Melbourne, 17 April 1989

Sotheby's, Fine Australian Paintings and Books, Sydney, 17 November 1988

Sotheby's, The George Cowlishaw Collection – Australian Paintings, Drawings and Watercolours, English and European Furniture and Works of Art, St Ives, Sydney, 10 November 1984

Sotheby's, Catalogue of the Cowlishaw Collection of Early Australian Colonial Books and Paintings, Sydney, 16–17 October 1984

Sotheby's, Australian Aboriginal and Melanesian Works of Art, Sydney, 13 October 1983

Sotheby's, Oriental Decorative Works of Art, from the Holt Collection and Other Owners, Sydney, 13 October 1983

Sotheby's, Catalogue of Australian and European Paintings and Oriental Ceramics and Works of Art, Melbourne, 23 March 1983

Sotheby Parke Bernet, The George Ortiz Collection of Primitive Works of Art, London, 29 June 1978

Sotheby's, Catalogue of Paintings and Drawings from the studio of Sir William Dobell, The Property of the Sir William Dobell Art Foundation sold by order of the trustees, Sydney Opera House, Australia, 19 November 1973

Exhibition Catalogues

Blaffer Gallery, *Legends and Landscape in Australian art: a selection of paintings from the Harold E. Mertz collection*, essay by Robert Hughes, exhibition catalogue, Blaffer Gallery, University of Houston 1986

Centre Georges Pompidou, *Magiciens de la terre: Centre Georges Pompidou, Musee national d'art moderne, La Villete, la Grande Halle*, exhibition catalogue, Editions du Centre Pompidou, Paris 1989

Clark, Jane and Bridget Whitelaw, *Golden Summers – Heidelberg and Beyond*, exhibition catalogue, National Gallery of Victoria 1985

Deutscher Fine Art, *Brett Whiteley: the graphics 1961–1992*, Malvern, Victoria 1995

Deutscher Fine Art, *A Century of Australian women artists 1840s–1940s*, essay by Victoria Hammond, Malvern, Victoria 1993

Edwards, Deborah, *Robert Klippel: catalogue raisonne of sculpture*, Art Gallery of New South Wales, Sydney c.2002

Eisler, William and Bernard Smith, *Terra Australis: the furthest shore*, exhibition catalogue, Art Gallery of New South Wales, International Cultural Corporation of Australia, Sydney 1988

Holden, Robert, 'Fine Art Exhibitions and Collectors in Colonial Sydney, 1847–1877', in McDonald, Patricia R, and Barry Pearce, *The Artist and the Patron – Aspects of Colonial Art in New South Wales*, exhibition catalogue, 2 March – 1 May 1988, Art Gallery of New South Wales, Sydney 1988, pp.161–7

Kerr, Joan, 'Views, Visages, Invisibility – Themes in the Art of Colonial New South Wales', in McDonald, Patricia R. and Barry Pearce, *The Artist and the Patron – Aspects of Colonial Art in New South Wales*, exhibition catalogue, 2 March – 1 May 1988, Art Gallery of New South Wales, Sydney 1988, pp.15–22

Lane, Terence, *Vienna 1913: Josef Hoffmann's Gallia apartment*, exhibition catalogue, National Gallery of Victoria, Melbourne 1984

Laverty, Colin, *Pastures and Pastimes: an exhibition of Australian racing, sporting and animal pictures of the 19th century*, the Victorian Ministry for the Arts, Melbourne 1983

McDonald, Patricia R. and Barry Pearce, *The Artist and the Patron – Aspects of Colonial Art in New South Wales*, exhibition catalogue, 2 March – 1 May 1988, Art Gallery of New South Wales, Sydney 1988

Madigan, Richard A., Ross K. Luck and Harold E. Mertz, *The Australian Painters 1964–1966 – Contemporary Australian Painting from the Mertz Collection*, exhibition catalogue, Griffin Press, Adelaide 1966

National Art Gallery of New South Wales, *Norman Schureck Loan Exhibition – A Selection of Paintings from his Collection*, National Art Gallery of New South Wales, Sydney, June 1958

National Art Gallery of New South Wales, *Sir W. Baldwin Spencer's Collection*, National Art Gallery of New South Wales, Sydney, December 1916

Pearce, Barry and Hendrik Kolenberg, *William Dobell: the painter's progress*, The Art Gallery of New South Wales, exhibition catalogue, 1997

Philip Bacon Galleries, *Aspects of the Trout Collection*, exhibition catalogue, Brisbane 1989

Rosenthal, Michael and Martin Myrone (eds), *Gainsborough*, with contributions from Rica Jones et al., exhibition catalogue, Tate, London 2002

Savill Galleries, *Savill Contemporary*, Sydney, 15 June – 12 July 2003

Smith, Geoffrey, *Arthur Streeton, 1867–1943*, National Gallery of Victoria, Melbourne 1995

Smith, Sydney Ure, *Art of Australia, 1788–1941: an exhibition of Australian art, held in the United States of America and the Dominion of Canada, under the auspices of the Carnegie Corporation*, Museum of Modern Art, New York 1941

Sutton, Peter (ed.), *Dreamings: the Art of Aboriginal Australia*, exhibition catalogue, Viking, Ringwood, Victoria 1988

Electronic Sources

Author unknown, 'Christie's Australia reverts to representative office', *State of the Arts*, 20 March 2006, <www.stateart.com.au/sota/news/default.asp?fid=4052> [04/04/2006]

Author unknown, 'Physical Deconstruction', *New York Times*, 14 March 2003, <http://www.nytimes.com/2003/03/14/arts/design/14INSI.html?ex=1049215911&ei=1&en=d420db4da8c429f2> [21/03/2003]

Author unknown, 'Phillips sells Australian House', *Maine Antique Digest*, February 2002, <www.maineantiquedigest.com/articles/feb02/shap0202.htm> [08/11/2002]

Auctioneers and Agents (Amendment) Act 1992, <www.legislation.nsw.gov.au> [26/05/2003]

Four Corners programme, Australian Broadcasting Corporation (*ABC*), 'Rogue's Gallery', aired 10/05/1999, transcript obtained from <www.abc.net.au/4corners/stories/s25145.htm> [23/03/2000]

Bennett, Will, 'Art sales: smart move', *The Telegraph* (London), <www.telegraph.co.uk/arts/main.jhtml?xml=%2Farts%2F2001%2F09%2F10%2Fbawb10.xml&secureRefresh=true&_requestid=363969> [15/01/2003]

Berry, Jamie, 'Aboriginal art at record highs', *The Age*, 30 July 2003, <www.theage.com.au/articles/2003/07/29/1059244620062.html> [08/08/2003]

Christie's, <www.christie's.com/history> [15/09/2000]

Christie's, <www.christie's.com/history/beyond.html> [15/09/2000]

Christie's, <www.christie's.com/history/expertise.html> [15/09/2000]

Environment Australia, <www.ea.gov.au/heritage/awh/movable/refused.html> [26/05/2003]

Samuel T. Freeman, <www.freemansauction.com> [15/05/2003]

Getty Museum, <www.getty.edu/cgi–bin/getty_print.pl> [07/03/2003]

Gibson, Joel, 'Aboriginal art auction record', *Sydney Morning Herald*, 30 July 2003, <www.smh.com.au/articles/2003/07/29/1059480341808.html> [30/07/2003]

Gome, Amanda, 'Family advice helps an auctioneer put his troubles behind him', *Business Review Weekly*, extract of an article in the hard copy of *Business Review Weekly* magazine, 25 May 1998, <www.brw.com.au/content/250598/brw01.htm> [14/07/2000]

The Grays Group (including Gray Eisdell Timms), <www.graysonline.com.au/about/AU/default.asp> [13/06/2003]

Hills, Ben, 'Art Forgery – A brush with fame', *Sydney Morning Herald*, 18 July 1998, <www.smh.com.au/news/9807/18/features/features2.html> [17/03/2000]

Lawson's, <www.lawsons.com.au/about.html> [16/07/2001], prior to new management

Lawson's, <www.lawsons.com.au/ia.html> [16/07/2001], prior to new management

Lawson-Menzies, 'Emily Masterpiece From Holt Collection Unveiled for the First Time In Lawson~Menzies $4.8M Aboriginal Art Auction', undated, <http://www.lawsonmenzies.com.au/EmilyMasterpieceFromHolt CollectionUnveiled.html> [08/02/07]

Leonard Joel, <http://www.ljoel.com.au> [08/07/2002]

Maslen, Geoff, 'Aboriginal art heads overseas', *The Age*, 27 July 2005, <http://www.theage.com.au/news/arts/art-heads-overseas/2005/07/26/1122143839680.html> [08/02/2007]

Maslen, Geoff, 'Curators seek bans to halt exodus of Aboriginal art', Museum Security Network mailing list, date of article, 23/06/2000, date of email, 25/06/2000

National Portrait Gallery, London, <www.npg.org.uk/live/d10684.asp> [07/03/2003]

Protection of Movable Cultural Heritage Act 1986, <http://scaleplus.law.gov.au/html/pasteact/0/309/top.htm> [26/05/2003]

Royal Holloway College, University of London, 'The Royal Holloway Collection – The Legacy of Thomas Holloway (1800–83)', <http://www.rhul.ac.uk/Visitors-Guide/picture-gallery.html> [05/09/2003]

Rutherford Pearls and Rutherford Fine Jewellery, <http://www.welcome-to.com/Australia/Melbourne/Retail_Theratheartnewspaperpy/Watches_&_Jewellery/Rutherford> [02Retail/06/2003]

Skinner Inc., <www.skinnerinc.com> [28/07/2003]

Smith, James, 'Descriptive Sketch of Victoria – Melbourne – The City – Part 2', in *Picturesque Atlas*, <http://www.geocities.com/toby_meares/040.htm> [17/12/2002]

Sproule, James, 'Many happy returns? Some good reasons why not to buy art for profit', *The Art Newspaper*, <www.theartnewspaper.com/news/article.asp?idart=8572> [15/05/2002]

Stadelsches Kunstinstitut, <www.staedelmuseum.de/Gemalde/Deutsche_des_Barock/ deutsche_des_barock.html> [14/05/2003]

Verghis, Sharon, 'Rivalry raises the bidding stakes', *Sydney Morning Herald*, 15 April 2003, <www.smh.com.au/articles/2003/04/14/1050172532114.html> [17/07/2003]

Media Releases

Australian Competition and Consumer Commission (ACCC), 'ACCC concludes investigation into allegations of unlawful conduct in art markets', media release, 10 December 2002, <http://203.6.251.7/accc.internet/digest/view_media.cfm?RecordID=896> [02/04/2003]

Australian Competition and Consumer Commission (ACCC), 'Allegations of Unlawful conduct in Art Markets', media release, 8 December 2001, <http://203.6.251.7/accc.internet/media/search/view_media.cfm?RecordID=539> [11/11/2002]

Australian Competition and Consumer Commission (ACCC), 'Auctioneers must provide clear GST information: ACCC', media release, 13 December 2000, <http://203.6.251.7/accc.internet/media/search/view_media.cfm?RecordID=203> [11/11/2002]

Christie's, 'More Mertz for your money in Melbourne at Christie's August Australian & International Paintings Auction', media release, 8 August 2000

Christie's, 'Christie's first Sydney auction of contemporary art set to top $1 million at the Museum of Contemporary Art', media release, 19 July 2000 <www.christies.com/departments/ast/press/details.cfm?press=85> [15/09/2000]

Deutscher-Menzies, 'Deutscher-Menzies achieved number 1 status in the Australian Fine Art Auction market in May 2001 with a sales result of 6.4 million accompanied by superior clearance rates', media release, 9 June 2001, <www.deutschermenzies.com/press/press/090601.html> [16/07/2001]

Deutscher-Menzies, 'Feast of Modern Masters + Uncovered Treasures', media release, 17 April 2001, <www.deutschermenzies.com/press/press/170401.html> [18/08/2003]

Deutscher-Menzies, 'Australian Owned Auction House Sponsors *Federation: Australian Art and Society 1901–2001*', media release, 17 March 2001, <www.deutschermenzies.com/press/press/170301.html> [07/05/2002]

Goodmans, 'Hats off! Klompe Collection of Contemporary Art to be Auctioned', media release, undated, obtained from Goodmans 28 April 2003

Lawson-Menzies, 'Charles Blackman painting sets company record for Lawson-Menzies', media release, October 2002, <www.lawsonmenzies.com.au/pr1.html> [24/02/2003]

Lawson-Menzies, 'Lawson-Menzies announce two year plan to establish the leading Australian-owned auction house in Sydney', media release, <www.lawsons.com.au/pr3.html> [24/02/2003]

Lawson-Menzies, 'Lawson-Menzies appoint new CEO', media release, September 2002, <www.lawsonmenzies.com.au/pr2.html> [24/02/2003]

Sotheby's, 'Australian Art expert Jane Clark appointed to the Board of Sotheby's Australia', media release, 30 June 1995 [Sotheby's archives, Art Gallery of New South Wales library]

Sotheby's, 'Two new appointments to the board of Sotheby's Australia', media release, June 1990 [Sotheby's archives, Art Gallery of New South Wales library]

Newspaper and Journal Articles

Author unknown, 'Library claims earliest Cook portrait find', *Australian Broadcasting Corporation (ABC) News*, 2 June 2003, no pagination

Author unknown, 'Australia's 50 Most Collectable Artists', *Australian Art Collector*, issue 23, January–March 2003, pp.51–77

Author unknown, 'A picture of a fair price', *The Canberra Times*, 12 December 2002, p.11

Author unknown, ''Rigged sale' inquiry', *Sunday Mail*, 9 December 2001, p.22

Author unknown, 'NGA buys into history', *The Canberra Times*, 28 November 2001, p.12

Author unknown, 'Glover find may tip $2.3m', *Herald-Sun*, 20 November 2001, p.53

Author unknown, 'Masterpiece returns home', *Daily Telegraph*, 3 November 2001, p.13

Author unknown, 'Australia's 50 Most Collectable Artists', *Australian Art Collector*, issue 15, January–March 2001, pp.57–98

Author unknown, 'New chums clean up', *The Age*, 14 December 2000, no pagination

Author unknown, 'Australia's 50 Most Collectable Artists', *Australian Art Collector*, issue 11, January–March 2000, pp.59–96

Author unknown, 'Fake art case told of balcony tussle', *The Age*, 14 October 1999, p.A2

Author unknown, 'Diary', *The Age*, 1 July 1999, p.5

Author unknown, 'Australia's 50 Most Collectable Artists', *Australian Art Collector*, issue 7, January–March 1999, pp.27–65

Author unknown, 'Soon parted', *Australian Financial Review*, 7 July 1998, p.59

Author unknown, 'Autumn Auctions: House by House Wrap Up', *Australian Art Collector*, issue 5, July–September 1998, p.58

Author unknown, 'The Sherman-Wright Collections Australian Art Index', *Australian Art Collector*, issue 5, July–September 1998, p.22

Author unknown, 'Artwatch — Sotheby's on the move', *Australian Jewish News – Sydney Edition*, 4 April 1997, p.29

Author unknown, 'Art courses sponsored', *Inner Western Suburbs Courier*, 28 January 1997, no pagination

Author unknown, 'Investment: Sotheby's Australia – Auction of Aboriginal Art', *The View*, Issue 6, 1997, pp.68–9

Author unknown, 'Bond was over the art market cliff and treading thin air', *Sydney Morning Herald*, 27 August 1996, p.28

Author unknown, 'Art on the menu', *Sydney Morning Herald*, 22 September 1995, p.14

Author unknown, 'From art to real estate', *Waverly Gazette*, 23 February 1993, p.43

Author unknown, 'Auction Update – Australia's First Major Contemporary Art Sale 'Resounding Success', *Antique Trader*, 15 July – 15 August 1991, p.76

Author unknown, 'Australian art – a world market', *Australian Antique Trader*, January/February 1989, pp.12–14

Author unknown, 'Local student joins Sotheby's', *Hawkesbury Courier*, 21 January 1988, no pagination

Author unknown, 'Sotheby's achieve record prices', *The Age*, 24 February 1987, no pagination

Author unknown, 'Graham and Warren Joel will sell your jewels or your junk', *Sydney Morning Herald*, Good Weekend, 9 November 1985, pp.76–81

Author unknown, Untitled, article begins with 'Mr Leonard Voss Smith...', *Australian Financial Review*, 21 March 1980, p.39

Author unknown, 'Obituary – Sim Rubensohn – a leader in the advertising world', *Sydney Morning Herald*, 2 March 1979, p.8

Author unknown, 'Christie's appoint woman director', *The Canberra Times*, 10 February 1977, p.14

Author unknown, 'Auction gamble starts again', *Australian Financial Review*, Fine Arts Feature, 5 April 1976, pp.4–5

Author unknown, 'New gallery head', *The Advertiser*, 27 February 1976, p.3

Author unknown, 'SA art gallery gets new director', *News*, Adelaide, 26 February 1976, no pagination

Author unknown, 'Dobell "disliked" his Wangi Boy', *Sydney Morning Herald*, 15 February 1974, p.3

Author unknown, 'At 1973's Auctions...Lindsay dominated watercolour market', *Sydney Morning Herald*, 7 January 1974, p.8

Author unknown, 'Lindsay works popular at 1973 auction sales', *Sydney Morning Herald*, 3 January 1974, p.4

Author unknown, 'Dobells auctioned', *Australian Financial Review*, 20 November 1973, p.48

Author unknown, 'Contents of Dobell studio for sale', *The Canberra Times*, 30 July 1973, p.6

Author unknown, 'For the Collector – Auction sale: $28,000 paid for a Drysdale', *Sydney Morning Herald*, 29 June 1973, p.12

Author unknown, 'For the Collector – Rarest antiques up for auction', *Sydney Morning Herald*, 22 June 1973, p.10

Author unknown, 'Auction could help artists', *The Herald* (Melbourne), 9 May 1973, p.9

Author unknown, 'Remarkable Rubensohn collection for auction', *Sydney Morning Herald*, 2 May 1973, p.16

Author unknown, 'Dobell art auction cancelled', *The Northern Territory News* (probably), 2 November 1972, p.5 [from biographical files on Sir William Dobell, National Library of Australia]

Author unknown, 'How Christie's builds an art market', *The National Times*, Money Talks section, 2–7 October 1972, p.45

Author unknown, 'Australian flavour 'hopeless' factor in art', *Sydney Morning Herald*, 31 July 1972, p.12

Author unknown, 'Dobell's Dobells', *Australian Financial Review*, 12 August 1971, p.32

Author unknown, 'Auctioneers compete to sell Dobells', *Sydney Morning Herald*, 19 March 1971, p.8

Author unknown, 'Auctioneer loses at his own game', *Sunday Australian*, 14 March 1971, p.3

Author unknown, 'Recent Art Auctions', *Art and Australia,* 6(4) March 1969

Author unknown, Untitled, *The Advertiser* (Adelaide), 28 February 1968, p.4

Author unknown, 'Recent Art Auctions', *Art and Australia,* 6(2) September 1968

Author unknown, 'Record city art sale', *The Age*, 23 November 1967, p.3

Author unknown, '$16,000 for painting he has never seen', *The Age*, 17 February 1966, no pagination

Author unknown, 'The Art Plantations – How gallery directors cultivate the boom', *Nation*, 16 October 1965, pp.15–16

Author unknown, 'William Dobell chooses his favourite Dobells', *Sydney Morning Herald*, 20 June 1964, no pagination

Author unknown, Untitled, *Sydney Morning Herald*, 16 July 1962, p.58

Author unknown, 'Interest from Overseas', *Sydney Morning Herald*, 16 July 1962, p.58

Author unknown, 'Art for Money's Sake', *The Bulletin*, 7 April 1962, p.5

Author unknown, '£50,000 auction: artist got £600', *Daily Telegraph*, 28 March 1962, p.1

Author unknown, 'Snobs! – Dobell's in the fashion', *Daily Mirror,* 28 March 1962, p.3

Author unknown, 'Art auction besieged', *Daily Mirror*, 27 March 1962, p.2

Author unknown, 'Dobell works submitted at auction sale', *The Sun,* 26 March 1962, no pagination

Author unknown, 'What price a Dobell?', *Woman's Day with Woman*, 26 March 1962, p.3

Author unknown, 'Early Dobell for Art Gallery', *Sydney Morning Herald*, 16 March 1962, no pagination

Author unknown, 'He was among the first to recognise Dobell's talent', *Sun-Herald*, 11 February 1962, no pagination

Author unknown, 'Old Masters: New Plans', *Sydney Morning Herald*, 3 February 1962, no pagination

Author unknown, 'Sydney Bequest to Israel University', *Sydney Morning Herald*, 2 February 1962, no pagination

Author unknown, 'Art Criticism Causes Stir – Public Heeded Our Expert's Warning – Auctioneer's Abuse of Critic Failed to Keep up Prices', *Daily Telegraph*, late edition, 5 May 1937, p.1

Author unknown, 'Art Critic Issues Warning to Buyers – Questions the Claims Made in Catalogue of Today's Big Sale – Doubts if Gainsborough and Reynolds Painted Pictures Credited to Them', *Daily Telegraph*, late edition, 4 May 1937, p.1, 6

Author unknown, Untitled, *Daily Telegraph Pictorial*, 22 February 1928, p.8

Author unknown, 'The Man of the Week – A King in his Kingdom', *Smith's Weekly*, 27 November 1926, p.2

Author unknown, 'The Man of the Week – Knight of the Hammer', *Smith's Weekly*, 23 October 1920, p.2

Author unknown, 'Hackett Art Collection – Trinkets from Royal Harems', *The Sun*, 20 September 1918, p.6

Author unknown, 'Sale of Hackett Collection', *The Sun*, 19 September 1918, p.5

Author unknown, 'Porcelain and Pictures', *The Sun*, 18 September 1918, p.5

Author unknown, 'Hackett Art Collection – Pictures, Porcelain and Ivories – Red Cross to Share Proceeds', *The Sun*, 17 September 1918, p.5

Author unknown, Untitled, *Australasian Art Review*, 1 July 1899, no pagination

Author unknown, Untitled, *Table Talk*, no. 304, 17 April 1891, p.5

Author unknown, Untitled, *Table Talk*, 19 December 1890, p.2

Author unknown, Untitled, *Table Talk*, 14 March 1890, p.5

Author unknown, Untitled, *Argus*, 17 June 1889, p.6 col.5

Author unknown, Untitled, *Table Talk*, no. 207, 7 June 1889, p.5 col.1

Author unknown, Untitled, *Sydney Morning Herald*, 25 June 1884, p.15

Author unknown, 'The Tariff on works of Art', *Princeton Review*, March 1884, pp.141–53

Author unknown, Untitled, *The Illustrated Sydney News*, 9 June 1883, p.3 col.3

Author unknown, Untitled, *The Illustrated Sydney News*, 14 April 1883, no pagination

Author unknown, Untitled, *Sydney Morning Herald*, 2 September 1861, p.2

Author unknown, Untitled, *Sydney Morning Herald*, 19 August 1861, p.8

Author unknown, Untitled, *Sydney Morning Herald*, 13 August 1861, p.8

Author unknown, 'The Greenoaks Collection', *Sydney Morning Herald*, 5 August 1861, p.5

Author unknown, Untitled, *Sydney Morning Herald,* 30 July 1861, p.5

Author unknown, Untitled, *Sydney Morning Herald,* 26 July 1861, p.5

Author unknown, Untitled, *Sydney Morning Herald,* 23 July 1861, p.2

Author unknown, Untitled, *Sydney Morning Herald*, 20 July 1861, p.8

Author unknown, Untitled, *Sydney Morning Herald,* 17 July 1861, p.2

Author unknown, Untitled, *Sydney Morning Herald,* 13 July 1861, p.5

Author unknown, 'The Fine Art Exhibition', *Illustrated Journal of Australasia*, Melbourne, January 1857, p.26

Author unknown, Untitled, *Argus*, 1 February 1855, p.5 col.6

Author unknown, Untitled, *Sydney Morning Herald*, 17 February 1854, no pagination

Author unknown, Untitled, *Sydney Morning Herald,* 29 May 1849, p.3 col.2

Author unknown, Untitled, *Bell's Life in Sydney*, 14 April 1849, p.2 col.2

Author unknown, Untitled, *The Australian*, 7 October 1841, p.2

Albert, Jane, 'Farmhouse art find worth $1m', *The Australian*, 14 February 2001, p.7

Anderson, Robert C., 'Paintings as an Investment', *Economic Inquiry*, 12(1) March 1974, pp.13–26

Atherton, Bruce, 'FED – Weak dollar aids Aboriginal art boom', *Australian Associated Press*, 18 January 1999, no pagination

Auty, Giles, 'An Australian Constable', *Courier Mail*, 1 October 2001, p.10

Baker, Godfrey, 'Do I hear $48 million?', *Good Weekend*, 5 September 1998, pp.46–48

Baker, Russell, 'Record year for auction houses', *Australian Business*, 16 August 1989, pp.30–1

Barnes, Allan, 'An 8000 per cent dividend in 25 years – There's a real ART in this business', *Sunday Telegraph*, 8 April 1962, p.17

Barrowclough, Nikki, 'The art of the marketplace', *Belle*, August/September 1987, pp.26–9

Barry, Paul, 'Bond's lost Captain Cook stranded without a sale', *Sydney Morning Herald*, 9 June 2000, p.4

Barton, Mairi, 'Crown attacks extra privileges', *The West Australian*, 4 September 1997, p.3

Barton, Mairi, 'Little-known trader who rivaled the high-flyers', *The West Australian*, 4 September 1997, p.3

Baumol, William J., 'Unnatural Value: Or Art Investment as Floating Crap Game', *The American Economic Review*, Papers and Proceedings of the Ninety-Eighth Annual Meeting of the American Economic Association, 76(2) May 1986, pp.10–14

Bellamy, Louise, 'The new collectors', *The Age*, 25 November 2002, The Culture, p.1, 3

Bellamy, Louise, 'Art for investment's sake', *The Age*, 4 December 2000, no pagination

Bellamy, Louise, 'Past Masters', *The Age*, 28 August 2000, p.6

Bellamy, Louise, 'Artistic Merit', *The Age*, 8 May 2000, p.6

Bellamy, Louise, 'Art for love and/or money', *The Age*, Money and Investment, 30 November 1998, p.4

Benhamou-Huet, Judith, 'E-Business and Art Business', *Art Press*, no. 245, April 1999, p.14

Benhamou-Huet, Judith, 'Buren, Richter, Christie's et Sotheby's – The Artist and the Auction House', *Art Press*, no. 241, December 1998, p.14

Benjamin, Roger, 'Aboriginal Art: Exploitation or Empowerment?', *Art in America*, vol. 78, July 1990, pp.73–81

Black, Eileen, 'Practical Patriots and True Irishmen: The Royal Irish Art Union 1839–59', *Irish Arts Review Yearbook*, vol.14, 1998, pp.140–6

Bloch, E. Maurice, 'The American Art-Union's Downfall', *The New-York Historical Society Quarterly*, 37(4) 1953, pp.331–59

Bogais, Jonathan, 'Australian Art – It's a local thing', *Australian Art Collector*, issue 1, July–September 1997, pp.18–19

Bonyhady, Tim, 'Buying power under the hammer', *Sydney Morning Herald*, 19 August 2000, Spectrum, p.9

Boreham, Gareth, 'Bond's art millions won't make a dent in debt pool', *The Age*, 15 May 1992, p.5

Brearley, David, 'Raiders of the lost art', *The Australian*, 4 April 2000, p.14

Brewster, Richard, 'Rare Australian Art to Tip Sales Over $6m', *The Age*, 20 April 2002, p.39

Brown, Penny, 'Gallery in clear on Glover buy', *The Australian*, 11 December 2002, p.2

Burke, Janine, 'Celebrating a Century of Lost Art', *The Age*, 8 June 1993, p.19

Burns, Mona, 'The artist and the painting', *Pix*, 30 June 1962, pp.10–11

Cadzow, Jane, 'How the Meek Inherited the Trout Millions', *Sydney Morning Herald*, Good Weekend, 6 May 1989, pp.30–35

Campbell, Lance, 'David moves to Carrick Hill', *The Advertiser* (Adelaide), 1 December 1983, p.2

Canon-Brookes, Peter, 'Cultural Terrorism', *Museum Management and Curatorship*, no. 13, March 1994, pp.73–4

Castle, Ray, 'Norman Schureck dies – Australian art loses great patron', *Daily Telegraph*, 10 August 1962, no pagination

Castle, Ray, 'Goes to the Art Auction and Comes Away Musing: Money-wise, Dobell was not in the picture', *Daily Telegraph*, 28 March 1962, no pagination

Clabburn, Anna, 'Stripes and squares animate landscape carnival', *The Australian*, 10 November 2000, p.40

Clark, Jane, 'Under the Hammer – 20 (in auction years)', *artonview*, Spring 2002, pp.62–3

Clark, Kenneth, 'The Value of Art in an Expanding World', *The Hudson Review*, 19(1) Spring 1966, pp.11–23

Cochrane, Peter, 'We have ways of making you *spend*', *Sydney Morning Herald*, 15 August 1995, Arts, p.15

Cochrane, Peter, 'Auction record for Koori painting', *Sydney Morning Herald*, 19 June 1995, p.2

Cochrane, Peter, '"Diana" at home in NGA', *Sydney Morning Herald*, 7 June 1994, p.24

Cochrane, Peter, 'From homegrown blockbusters to the saleroom', *Sydney Morning Herald*, 26 April 1994, p.24

Cochrane, Peter, 'Old patter sells tribal lots', *Sydney Morning Herald*, 29 November 1993, p.2

Cochrane, Peter, 'Bid goodbye to the bust', *Sydney Morning Herald*, 22 April 1993, p.11

Cochrane, Peter, 'Govt ban depletes black art auction', *Sydney Morning Herald*, 29 November 1989, no pagination

Cochrane, Peter, 'Dueling Gavels', *Good Weekend Magazine*, 18 November 1989, pp.54–67

Cochrane, Peter, 'The art of market 'correction'', *Sydney Morning Herald*, 18 August 1989, p.18

Cook, Margaret, 'School days: Tim Klingender', no newspaper title recorded, 25 March 1997, no pagination [from Sotheby's archives, Art Gallery of New South Wales library]

Coslovich, Gabriella, 'Art sails off to USA', *The Age*, 30 June 1999, no pagination

Coster, Peter, 'The lost art of profit', *The Weekend Australian*, 14–15 April 1990, p.23

Crawford, Ashley, 'Caveat Emptor – Let the Buyer Beware', *Australian Art Collector*, issue 23, January–March 2003, pp.86–7

Crawford, Ashley, 'Dealer – Charles Nodrum: Countercyclical Charles', *Australian Art Collector*, issue 22, October–December 2002, pp.76–8

Crawford, Ashley, 'Art as investment', *The Herald* (Melbourne), 17 April 1989, no pagination

Crisp, Lyndall, 'Robert Bleakley is sold on primitive collections', *The Australian*, 13 August 1981, p.10

Crowe, David, 'eBay takes on swish auctioneers', *Australian Financial Review*, 2–3 October 1999, p.18

Crowe, David, 'Net gets a slice of the auction', *Australian Financial Review*, 12 May 1999, p.15

De Vries-Evans, Susanna, 'When Dallhold hit the canvas...', *The Bulletin*, 10 March 1992, pp.54–5

Dale, Brian, 'Rubensohn preview – Collection of 40 years to go under auctioneer's hammer', *Australian Financial Review*, 1 June 1973, p.42

Daly, Martin, 'News Extra – Sale of the Century', possibly *The Age* [no newspaper title recorded], 5 July 1997, pp.A19–22 [from Sotheby's archives, Art Gallery of New South Wales library]

Daplyn, A. J., 'Art Notes', *Australasian Art Review*, 1(4) 1 June 1899, pp.12–15

Daplyn, A. J., 'Art Notes', *Australasian Art Review*, 1(3) 1 May 1899, p.14

Davis, Douglas, 'The Billion Dollar Picture?', *Art in America*, 76(7) July 1988, pp.21–23

Dawson, Christopher, 'Going, going, gone at Grays', *Sydney Morning Herald*, 26 June 1971, p.7

Debelle, Penelope, 'Golden Summers gave way to chill for this curator', *The Age*, 7 May 1994, News Extra, pp.5–6

Debelle, Penelope, 'When oils are not just oils', *The Herald*, 21 June 1990, p.9

Decker, Andrew, 'Anatomy of an auction', *ARTnews*, 94(5) May 1995, pp.134–7

Decker, Andrew, 'Christie's: The Public and the Private', *ARTnews*, 94(5) May 1995, p.45

Dedman, Roger, 'Does Death Sell?', *Australian Art Collector*, issue 1, July–September 1997, pp.78–9

Duigan, Virginia and Robert Milliken, 'Joe Brown and the Great Art Robbery', *The National Times*, week ending 20 January 1979, p.11

Ede, Charisse, 'Vic – Christie's auction set to break several records', *Australian Associated Press*, 23 November 2001, no pagination

Ellenden, William S., 'Reminiscences of an Auctioneer', *The Australasian Antique Collector*, 20th edition 1980, pp.125–33

Evans, Bob, 'Making a bid for the arts market', *Sydney Morning Herald*, 22 November 1991, p.4

Farrelly, Alan, 'Art Boom and Bust: Part 2 – Why Ron Hodgson updated to art', *Sunday Sun*, 18 July 1974, p.13, 14

Farrelly, Alan, 'Director's aim for Newcastle gallery', *Morning Herald* (Newcastle), 30 September 1965, no pagination

Fidell-Beaufort, Madeleine, 'A Measure of Taste: Samuel P. Avery's Art Auctions, 1864–1880', *Gazette des Beaux-Arts*, no. 100, September 1982, pp.87–9

Fink, Lois Marie, 'French Art in the United States, 1850–1870 – Three Dealers and Collectors', *Gazette des Beaux-Arts*, ser. 6E vol. 92, September 1978, pp.87–100

Fish, Peter, 'C20 design to go with the Dresser', 15 October 2005, *Sydney Morning Herald*, <www.smh.com.au/news/money/c20-design-to-go-with-the-dresser/2005/10/14/1128796705782.html> [23/10/2005]

Fish, Peter, 'Relaunched kid on the block', *Sydney Morning Herald*, 6 November 2002, Money, p.10

Fish, Peter, 'Foreign buyers go dotty over Aboriginal art', *Sydney Morning Herald*, 18 August 2000, Money, p.6

Fish, Peter, 'Primitive Urges', *Sydney Morning Herald*, 2 October 1996, p.5

Fisher, Catherin, 'The hype and hope of auctioneering', *The Age*, 22 August 1994, p.17

Fitzgerald, Michael, 'Urban man heeds call of the tribal', *The Age*, 25 July 1990, p.3

Fleming, David, 'Immaculate Collections, Speculative Conceptions', *Museum Management and Curatorship*, no.10, 1991, pp.263–72

Fortesque, Elizabeth, 'Builder a major gallery player', *The Daily Telegraph*, 1 October 1999, p.54

Fortescue, Elizabeth, 'The *fine art* of rivalry', *The Daily Telegraph*, 23 November 1996, pp.34–5

Fortescue, Elizabeth, 'Fee squabble hits auctions', *The Daily Telegraph Mirror*, 11 May 1991, p.112

Fraser, William, 'McAlpine's house lot up for sale over three days', *Australian Financial Review*, 15–16 May 1999, no pagination

Frey, Bruno S. and Werner W. Pommerehne, 'Is art such a good investment?', *The Public Interest*, Spring 1988, pp.79–86

Frost, Andrew, 'Sotheby's Premium', *Australian Art Collector*, issue 18, October–December 2001, pp.76–8

Frost, Andrew G., 'Autumn Auctions: New Players Drive Boom', *Australian Art Collector*, issue 9, July–September 1999, pp.22–4

Frost, Andrew G. (probably), 'Australian Modernism at auction – Swings & Roundabouts', *Australian Art Collector*, issue 8, April–June 1999, p.90

Frost, Andrew G., 'Tim Storrier: Master of Illusion', *Australian Art Collector*, issue 4, April–June 1998, pp.46–9

Frost, Andrew G., 'Hammer Heads', *Australian Art Collector*, issue 2, October–December 1997, pp.26–9

Fry Tony, and Anne-Marie Willis, 'Aboriginal Art: Symptom or Success?', *Art in America*, July 1989, pp.108–16, 159–163

Le Grand, Chip, 'Aboriginal art gem tipped to fetch $25,000', *The Australian*, 16 June 1995, p.4

Gibbs, Stephen, 'Art auction boss retires', *North Shore Times*, 24 March 1993, no pagination

Gill, Raymond, 'Arkley widow hits out at auction houses', *The Age*, 12 August 2000, p.10

Gimpel, René, 'Art as commodity, art as economic power', *Third-Text*, no. 51, Summer 2000, pp.51–5

Gleadell, Colin, 'Auction Trends in the Eighties', *Art International*, vol. 9, Winter 1989, pp.72–75

Goddard, Julian, 'Cautious bidding in Perth', *Art Monthly Australia*, October 1990, p.30

Goddard, Steven H., 'Brocade Patterns in the Shop of the Master of Frankfurt: An Accessory to Stylistic Analysis', *Art Bulletin*, LXVII September 1985, pp.401–17

Gora, Bronwen, 'The rebel in Sotheby's new "tribal" art chief', *Sunday Telegraph*, 22 October 1989, no pagination

Grant, Daniel, 'Is there recognition after death?', *American Artist*, 51 (540) July 1987, pp.70–3

Green, Nicholas, 'Dealing in Temperaments: Economic Transformation of the Artistic Field in France During the Second Half of the Nineteenth Century', *Art History*, 10(1) March 1987, pp.59–78

Greenwood, Helen, 'Modern Lovers', *Sydney Morning Herald*, 2 May 1996, p.8

Grishin, Sasha, 'Garry Shead – Amazed and Amused', *Australian Art Collector*, issue 14, October–December 2000, pp.78–82

Grishin, Sasha, 'New auction house bids for its place', *The Canberra Times*, 4 May 1998, p.7

Hadley, Ann, 'Christie's first woman auctioneer', *The Sun* (Sydney), 22 October 1976, p.49

Hamilton, John, 'Briefing', *The Age*, 14 September 1967, p.4

Hawley, Janet, 'Alternative Values', *Sydney Morning Herald*, Good Weekend, 26 November 1994, p.16

Hay, John, 'Our man at Christie's', *The Herald* (Melbourne), 16 February 1970, p.4

Heartney, Eleanor, 'Artists vs. the Market', *Art in America*, 76(7) July 1988, pp.27–33

Heller, Ben, 'The "Irises" Affair', *Art in America*, vol. 78, July 1990, p.53

Henning, Edward B., 'Patronage and Style in the Arts: A Suggestion Concerning their Relations', *Journal of Aesthetics and Art Criticism*, 43(4) June 1960, pp.464–471

Hernon, Fran, 'Selling "snobbism" at Sotheby's', *Daily Telegraph*, magazine, 31 October 1987, p.31

Hetherington, John, 'Australian Art Enters a Boom At Home and Abroad', *The Age*, Literary Supplement, 2 February 1963, p.17

Hickie, David, Sophie Gordon and Matt Coyte, 'Crime Czars move into Art', *Australian Art Collector*, issue 3, January–March 1998, pp.84–97

Hinch, Derryn, 'Robert Hughes rampant – New York, he says, is not America', *Sydney Morning Herald*, 1 July 1972, p.18

Hoad, Brian, 'Playing the Art Market', *The Bulletin*, 27 July 1968, pp.28–33

Holden, Robert, 'Sydney International Exhibition of 1879', *Art and Australia*, 17(3) 1980, pp.280–82

Holgate, Ben, 'Recesssionists: A New Trend in the Art Market', *Sunday Age*, 15 December 1991, p.10

Hollis, Patsy, 'Denis Savill: Big Bear for a Bull Market', *Australian Art Collector*, issue 2, October–December 1997, pp.52–5

Holyoake, Mary, 'Melbourne Art Scene – Part 2: Introduction to the 1850s', *Art and Australia*, 17(2) 1979, pp.138–9

Holyoake, Mary, 'Melbourne Art Scene from 1839 to 1859', *Art and Australia*, 15(3) 1978, pp.289–96

Holyoake, Mary, 'Art Unions – Catalysts of Australian Art', *Art and Australia*, 12(4) 1975, pp.381–4

Hubble, Ava, 'Robert Bleakley: Dealer with a Difference', *Australian Art Collector*, issue 4, April–June 1998, pp.36–40

Hubble, Ava, 'Switzerland discovers our missing Captain Cook', *Sydney Morning Herald*, 29 July 1993, p.1

Huck, Peter, 'Robert Bleakley – In full flight', *Panorama*, August 1987, pp.38–40

Huda, Shireen, 'The Power of Provenance – single-owner collections and recent art auction trends', *Australian Art Review*, issue 2, July–October 2003, pp.98–9

Huda, Shireen, 'International or Insular? – Internationalization, Australian art and the market', *Australian Art Review*, issue 3, November 2003–February 2004, pp.100–101

Huda, Shireen, 'Over-priced, Under-appreciated', *Australian Art Review*, issue 6, November 2004–February 2005, p.25

Hughes, Robert, 'Sold!', *Time Australia*, 4(48) 27 November 1989, pp.60–4, 67

Hurrell, Bronwyn, 'The great art dot con', *The Daily Telegraph*, 3 February 2001, p.65

Hurrell, Bronwyn, 'Possum art forgery case goes to trial', *The Advertiser*, 15 July 2000, p.3

Hurtado, Shannon Hunter, 'The Promotion of the Visual Arts in Britain 1835–1860', *Canadian Journal of History*, 28(1) 1993, pp.59–80

Hutak, Michael, 'The New Guard at Auction', *Australian Art Collector*, issue 21, July–September 2002, pp.59–60

Hutak, Michael, 'Black market clash', *The Bulletin*, 21 November 2000, p.100

Hutak, Michael, 'Dealers get ready for the good times to roll', *Sydney Morning Herald*, 22 March 1994, p.20

Hutak, Michael, 'It's seating room only at new Oxford St cinema', *Sydney Morning Herald*, 28 August 1993, p.15

Ingram, Terry, 'A short history of Christie's in Australia', *Australian Art Collector*, issue 37, July–September 2006, pp.98–100

Ingram, Terry, 'A lasting impression of the Australian art world', *Australian Financial Review*, 23 March 2006, pp.44–5

Ingram, Terry, 'Christie's bids Australia farewell', *Australian Financial Review*, 15 March 2006, p.3

Ingram, Terry, 'Bonhams joins Goodman to establish local presence', *Australian Financial Review*, 21 August 2003, p.65

Ingram, Terry, 'Big works lose out', *Australian Financial Review*, 31 July 2003, p.57

Ingram, Terry, 'Fire fails to catch at auction of Desert artists' work', *Australian Financial Review*, 29 July 2003, p.4

Ingram, Terry, 'Auction chief trades places', *Australian Financial Review*, 17 July 2003, p.8

Ingram, Terry, 'Bidets bucketed', *Australian Financial Review*, 22 May 2003, p.64

Ingram, Terry, 'Medal dents presale barrier', *Australian Financial Review*, 22 May 2003, p.65

Ingram, Terry, 'Dealer syndicate pays $486,000 for Olsen', *Australian Financial Review*, 15 May 2003, p.65

Ingram, Terry, 'Snap!', *Australian Financial Review*, 15 May 2003, p.65

Ingram, Terry, 'News – Briefs', *Australian Financial Review*, 8 April 2003, p.8

Ingram, Terry, 'Alliance Unstuck', *Australian Financial Review*, 13 February 2003, p.58

Ingram, Terry, 'Auction house rescue lands in court', *Australian Financial Review*, 6 February 2003, p.10

Ingram, Terry, 'Corporate funk hits the rostrum', *Australian Financial Review*, 30 January 2003, p.49

Ingram, Terry, 'Badgery to head Cromwell's Auctioneers', *Australian Financial Review*, 16 January 2003, p.43

Ingram, Terry, 'Young artists overtake baby boomers', *Australian Financial Review*, 30 December 2002, p.4

Ingram, Terry, 'Art Crowd frets till the cows come home', *Australian Financial Review*, 12 December 2002, Supplement, p.11

Ingram, Terry, 'All at sea – Christie's left floundering after taking a punt', *Australian Financial Review*, 28 November 2002, p.65

Ingram, Terry, 'Memories of boom times', *Australian Financial Review*, 21 November 2002, p.65

Ingram, Terry, 'Art Gallery of NSW gets in early for Fairfax painting', *Australian Financial Review*, 15 November 2002, p.4

Ingram, Terry, 'Animal attraction Herd instinct turns contemporary', *Australian Financial Review*, 14 November 2002, p.73

Ingram, Terry, 'Losing one's memorabilia', *Australian Financial Review*, 7 November 2002, p.65

Ingram, Terry, 'Lawson-Menzies cuts old ties', *Australian Financial Review*, 31 October 2002, p.65

Ingram, Terry, 'Whiteley widow says burn fake paintings', *Australian Financial Review*, 30 October 2002, p.7

Ingram, Terry, 'Feline Inspiration is less than purr-fect', *Australian Financial Review*, 28 September 2002, p.34

Ingram, Terry, 'In the Frame', *Australian Financial Review*, 27 September 2002, p.72

Ingram, Terry, 'Hungry dealers set the pace', *Australian Financial Review*, 12 September 2002, p.65

Ingram, Terry, 'Smart Art – Two histories of the Kellys are fodder for thought', *The Weekend Australian Financial Review*, Smart Money, 7–8 September 2002, p.34

Ingram, Terry, 'Prize collection a coup for Deutscher-Menzies', *Australian Financial Review*, 5 September 2002, p.56

Ingram, Terry, 'A Purrfect picture', *Australian Financial Review*, 5 September 2002, p.56

Ingram, Terry, 'Beware black diamonds: GST shock at Stokes' big sell-off', *Australian Financial Review*, 29 August 2002, p.64

Ingram, Terry, 'Auctioneer seeks a touch of class', *Australian Financial Review*, 22 August 2002, p.73

Ingram, Terry, 'Auction house revamp', *Australian Financial Review*, 15 August 2002, p.65

Ingram, Terry, 'Shoot-out of the Ned Kellys as auctioneers go gangbusters', *The Weekend Australian Financial Review*, Smart Money, 10–11 August 2002, p.35

Ingram, Terry, 'Cool and Jazzy – Striking up the new Lawsons brand', *Australian Financial Review*, 1 August 2002, p.57

Ingram, Terry, 'You're history – Exported heritage under the hammer', *Australian Financial Review*, 25 July 2002, p.53

Ingram, Terry, 'Counter-cyclical Madonnas: the power of primitive', *The Weekend Australian Financial Review*,Smart Money, 20–21 July 2002, p.34

Ingram, Terry, 'A Brief History of Art', *Australian Art Collector*, issue 21, July–September 2002, pp.102–3

Ingram, Terry, 'Unrelenting demand for the big picture at new auction', *Australian Financial Review*, 8 March 2002, p.10

Ingram, Terry, 'Colonial Art Find Fetches Just $1.79m', *Australian Financial Review*, 28 November 2001, p.3

Ingram, Terry, 'Management Buyout at Art Auctioneers', *Australian Financial Review*, 20 November 2001, p.6

Ingram, Terry, 'Christie's shuts up shop', *Australian Financial Review*, 9 August 2001, p.40

Ingram, Terry, 'Going, going…up: why pre-sale auction estimates can cost you lots', *Australian Financial Review*, 9 June 2001, no pagination

Ingram, Terry, 'Sotheby's chief for Olympia', *Australian Financial Review*, 24 May 2001, no pagination

Ingram, Terry, 'Deutscher-Menzies makes up ground on the big two', *Australian Financial Review*, 17 May 2001, no pagination

Ingram, Terry, 'Mertz lifts Christie's to No 1', *Australian Financial Review*, 11 January 2001, p.17

Ingram, Terry, 'Bumper art offering for end of the year', *Australian Financial Review*, 16 November 2000, no pagination

Ingram, Terry, 'Theme auction snubbed', *Australian Financial Review*, 14 September 2000, p.22

Ingram, Terry, 'When AM means "after Mertz"', *Art and Australia*, 38(2) 2000, pp.288–9

Ingram, Terry, 'Rites of passage', *Australian Financial Review*, 31 August 2000, p.21

Ingram, Terry, 'Dead artists headline contemporary sale', *The Weekend Australian Financial Review*, Smart Money, 19–20 August 2000, p.38

Ingram, Terry, 'Cook portrait gets taken to the cleaners', *Australian Financial Review*, 9 August 2000, p.5

Ingram, Terry, 'Mertz may have done better with Sydney real estate', *Australian Financial Review*, 15 July 2000, p.38

Ingram, Terry, 'Tjupurrula painting sets record price of $486,500', *Australian Financial Review*, 27 June 2000, p.2

Ingram, Terry, 'Sotheby's reclaims top spot with Bridal March', *Australian Financial Review*, 4 May 2000, p.39

Ingram, Terry, 'Boil the Pot and Skin 'Em Alive', *Australian Art Collector*, issue 12, April–June 2000, pp.94–6

Ingram, Terry, 'Mertz collection could tax interest in other sales', *The Weekend Australian Financial Review*, Smart Money, 11–12 March 2000, p.43

Ingram, Terry, 'Mertz may yet fund Old Masters', *Australian Financial Review*, 2 March 2000, p.36

Ingram, Terry, 'Cutting edge art on ball-bearings', *Australian Financial Review*, 16 December 1999, p.26

Ingram, Terry, 'Deutscher-Menzies goes on exceptional buying spree', *Australian Financial Review*, 16 December 1999, p.26

Ingram, Terry, 'If history is missing you may not get the full picture', *Australian Financial Review*, 9 October 1999, p.38

Ingram, Terry, 'Sotheby's not going tribal in November', *Australian Financial Review*, 23 September 1999, p.30

Ingram, Terry, 'Sales of the Century: Sydney Harbour and the Bush Are Tops', *Art and Australia*, 37(2) 1999, pp.270–75

Ingram, Terry, 'Summer surprise – Record sales for auctions and galleries', *Art and Australia*, 36(4) 1999, pp.546–7

Ingram, Terry, 'Wall Power – Art that's making it in the late 1990s', *Art and Australia*, 36(3) 1999, pp.394–5

Ingram, Terry, 'Full gallop to the auctions', *Australian Financial Review*, 2 September 1999, p.34

Ingram, Terry, 'Oddlots', *Australian Financial Review*, 2 September 1999, p.34

Ingram, Terry, 'Sotheby's doubles earnings', *Australian Financial Review*, 13 August 1999, no pagination

Ingram, Terry, 'Some risqué offerings from a Goodman', *Australian Financial Review*, 29 July 1999, no pagination

Ingram, Terry, 'Joel's grand renaissance plan suffers change of art', *Australian Financial Review*, 9 July 1999, p.23

Ingram, Terry, 'That Magic Four Letter Word...Fake!', *Australian Art Collector*, issue 9, July–September 1999, pp.84–5

Ingram, Terry, 'Sales highlight our booming art market', *Australian Financial Review*, 13 May 1999, p.37

Ingram, Terry, 'Modern art brushes up well second time around', *Australian Financial Review*, 7 May 1999, p.24

Ingram, Terry, 'Art – Even a trained eye can't pick fact from fiction', *Australian Financial Review*, 6 March 1999, p.36

Ingram, Terry, 'Wemyss hopes for a killing with collectibles on the net', *Australian Financial Review*, 5 February 1999, no pagination

Ingram, Terry, 'From Here to Obscurity', *Australian Art Collector*, issue 7, January–March 1999, pp.66–9

Ingram, Terry, 'Smart Art', *Australian Financial Review*, 30 December 1998, p.19

Ingram, Terry, 'Things are not always as they seem in the auction room', *Australian Financial Review*, 24–28 December 1998, p.33

Ingram, Terry, 'Shoe boxes of ephemera find a market in cyberspace', *The Weekend Australian Financial Review*, 21–22 November 1998, p.40

Ingram, Terry, 'Business as usual since Dwyer's adieu', *Australian Financial Review*, 19 November 1998, p.29

Ingram, Terry, 'A Cautionary Tale of Art Booms Past', *Australian Art Collector*, issue 6, October–December 1998, pp.62–4

Ingram, Terry, 'Art consultants back in the picture', *Australian Financial Review*, 27 August 1998, p.22

Ingram, Terry, 'Star-studded auction in new venue', *Australian Financial Review*, 20 August 1998, p.31

Ingram, Terry, 'Art houses take a hammering during a year of turmoil', *The Weekend Australian Financial Review*, the fin, 15–16 August 1998, pp.12–3

Ingram, Terry, 'Running for cover loses its appeal', *The Weekend Australian Financial Review*, the fin, 15–16 August 1998, p.13

Ingram, Terry, 'Christie's poach former Joel's expert for new art position', *Australian Financial Review*, 15 July 1998, no pagination

Ingram, Terry, 'Family out of the picture after 75-year art alliance', *Australian Financial Review*, 10 July 1998, no pagination

Ingram, Terry, 'Lack of practice grounds the eagle', *Australian Financial Review*, 23 April 1998, p.24

Ingram, Terry, 'Sotheby's warns against heritage changes', *Australian Financial Review*, 16 April 1998, p.44

Ingram, Terry, 'Australia Goes to Auction…Offshore', *Australian Art Collector*, issue 4, April–June 1998, pp.70–4

Ingram, Terry, 'Show goes on with some welcome levity', *Australian Financial Review*, 23 April 1998, p.25

Ingram, Terry, 'Obsessions with rarities', *Art and Australia*, 36(2) 1998, p.251

Ingram, Terry, 'New auction house makes its D-mark as era comes to an end', *Australian Financial Review*, 12 February 1998, p.43

Ingram, Terry, 'Bill gives his best to Ballarat', *Australian Financial Review*, 5 February 1998, p.28

Ingram, Terry, '"Deutschmen" promises speedy payments', *Australian Financial Review*, 5 February 1998, p.29

Ingram, Terry, 'Deutscher Deals in Sydney Representative for New Venture', *Australian Financial Review*, 3 February 1998, p.4

Ingram, Terry, 'Art of survival calls Sotheby's founder', *Australian Financial Review*, 13 January 1998, p.4

Ingram, Terry, 'From Rembrandt to Roberts – Great Saleroom Moments', *Australian Art Collector*, issue 3, January–March 1998, pp.56–9

Ingram, Terry, 'Oddlots – Christie's departure', *Australian Financial Review*, 30 October 199_? [from Sotheby's archives, Art Gallery of New South Wales library]

Ingram, Terry, 'Australia loses out as Klimt fetches record sum', *Australian Financial Review*, 16 October 1997, no pagination

Ingram, Terry, 'Mobile phone king makes an Aboriginal connection', *The Weekend Australian Financial Review*, 4–5 October 1997, Smart Money, p.37

Ingram, Terry, 'Copyright squeeze on art', *Australian Financial Review*, 18 September 1997, p.52

Ingram, Terry, 'Equilibrium restored', *Art and Australia*, 35(2) 1997, pp.254–55

Ingram, Terry, 'Black Market', *Art and Australia*, 35(1) 1997, pp.126–7

Ingram, Terry, 'In Tasmania, It's a Mild Colonial Buy', *Australian Financial Review*, 11 September 1997, p.32

Ingram, Terry, 'Collecting art – A Socially Respectable Activity', *Art and Australia*, 34(1) Spring 1996, pp.106–7

Ingram, Terry, 'A brace of bids from the beret', *Australian Financial Review*, 28 August 1997, p.33

Ingram, Terry, 'Dobell's Irish Youth reaches $266,500', *Australian Financial Review*, 26 August 1997, p.6

Ingram, Terry, 'Sotheby's wins war of the "widow's mite"', *Australian Financial Review*, 24 July 1997, p.41

Ingram, Terry, 'Sydney favoured for tribal gathering', *Australian Financial Review*, 19 September 1996, p.33

Ingram, Terry, 'The lesser of two cities', *Artlink*, 14(3) Spring 1994, p.19

Ingram, Terry, 'Tribal art makes a comeback', *Australian Financial Review*, 2 December 1993, no pagination

Ingram, Terry, 'Sydney art sale defies gravity, says big spender', *Australian Financial Review*, 1 December 1993, no pagination

Ingram, Terry, 'Auction house in spotlight', *Australian Financial Review*, 25 November 1993, no pagination

Ingram, Terry, 'Commission rise rocks art market', *Australian Financial Review*, 22 November 1993, no pagination

Ingram, Terry, 'Cook portrait on convoluted voyage', *Australian Financial Review*, 12 August 1993, p.28

Ingram, Terry, '$1.5m agreed for Cook portrait', *Australian Financial Review*, 3 August 1993, p.2

Ingram, Terry, 'An ill wind that blows no good', *Art and Australia*, 30(3) Autumn 1993, pp.392–3

Ingram, Terry, 'Art sale dot test', *Australian Financial Review*, 11 February 1993, p.30

Ingram, Terry, 'Levy gap stirs art sale rivals', *Australian Financial Review*, 5 January 1993, no pagination

Ingram, Terry, 'Colonial art sets the pace', *Art and Australia*, 30(2) Summer 1992, pp.248–9

Ingram, Terry, 'Fine-art rivalry puts Sotheby's in black, Christie's in red', *Australian Financial Review*, 4 August 1992, no pagination

Ingram, Terry, 'Christie's wraps up Alan Bond collection', *Australian Financial Review*, 15 May 1992, p.9

Ingram, Terry, 'Sotheby's takes its cue from Lawson's', *Australian Financial Review*, 28 November 1991, no pagination

Ingram, Terry, 'Sweating it out as auction climate changes', *Australian Financial Review*, 30 November 1989, p.55

Ingram, Terry, 'Sotheby's profit down', *Australian Financial Review*, 23 November 1989, no pagination

Ingram, Terry, 'Art sales business reaches its reserve', *Australian Financial Review*, 16 October 1989, no pagination

Ingram, Terry, 'Melbourne's great expectations', *Australian Financial Review*, 24 August 1989, no pagination

Ingram, Terry, 'A Splash for Diana's Bath', *Australian Financial Review*, 20 April 1989, p.41

Ingram, Terry, Untitled, *Australian Financial Review*, 14 March 1989, p.10

Ingram, Terry, 'Sotheby's moves into real estate', *Australian Financial Review*, 24 February 1989, no pagination

Ingram, Terry, 'Sotheby's lifts profit, dividend in Australia', *Australian Financial Review*, 27 October 1988, no pagination

Ingram, Terry, 'Quirky cataloguing of copies could confuse future buyers', *Australian Financial Review*, 28 July 1988, p.32

Ingram, Terry, 'Auction success can be mixed blessing for the art trade', *Australian Financial Review*, 26 July 1988, no pagination

Ingram, Terry, 'Art market pioneer, Len Voss Smith, dies', *Australian Financial Review*, 10 March 1988, no pagination

Ingram, Terry, 'Art trade discovers life after Sotheby's', *Australian Financial Review*, 13 August 1987, p.32, 33

Ingram, Terry, 'Bond believed buyer of Flinders portrait', *Australian Financial Review*, 8 April 1987, p.2

Ingram, Terry, 'Gift of paintings softens the image of rugged Sir Leon', *Australian Financial Review*, 25 May 1978, p.16

Ingram, Terry, 'Appointment to fine art auction firm', *Australian Financial Review*, 9 February 1977, p.7

Ingram, Terry, 'Storrier and Wallis – a faded fashion', *Australian Financial Review*, 15 January 1976, p.10

Ingram, Terry, 'The bidders at Christie's show which industries are prospering', *Australian Financial Review*, 30 October 1975, p.25

Ingram, Terry, 'Christie's: no Grosz expectations', *Australian Financial Review*, 16 October 1975, p.14

Ingram, Terry, 'Christie's sale not quite an "unmitigated disaster"', *Australian Financial Review*, 10 October 1974, p.29

Ingram, Terry, 'Estates with works of art come under Govt scrutiny', *Australian Financial Review*, 6 June 1974, p.33

Ingram, Terry, 'A quality collection is still possible', *Australian Financial Review*, 26 April 1974, p.47

Ingram, Terry, 'Dobell's "Wangi Boy" brings record $70,000', *Australian Financial Review*, 14 February 1974, p.8

Ingram, Terry, 'Art boom echoed Poseidon', *Australian Financial Review*, 27 December 1973, pp.18–19

Ingram, Terry, 'Paintings Reached Peak in 1973', *Australian Financial Review*, 27 December 1973, p.18

Ingram, Terry, 'Darrell's Dobells to test the market', *Australian Financial Review*, 18 December 1973, p.1, 6

Ingram, Terry, 'Dobell prices uneven', *Australian Financial Review*, 22 November 1973, p.42

Ingram, Terry, 'Pre-Hollywood epics of Alma-Tadema get a re-run', *Australian Financial Review*, 22 November 1973, p.42

Ingram, Terry, 'New York auctioneer offers five-year guarantee', *Australian Financial Review*, 27 September 1973, p.36

Ingram, Terry, 'The "steal" that wasn't', *Australian Financial Review*, 27 September 1973, p.36

Ingram, Terry, 'Art now attracts a religious respect', *Australian Financial Review*, 20 September 1973, p.39

Ingram, Terry, 'Price and Prejudice interest in mammoth Dobell sell-out', *Australian Financial Review*, 13 September 1973, p.36, 39

Ingram, Terry, 'Who wants a dead landlord, even if it is a Dobell?', *Australian Financial Review*, 3 September 1973, p.10

Ingram, Terry, 'Lindsays, Drysdales fetch top prices at Sim Rubensohn sale', *Australian Financial Review*, 29 June 1973, p.10

Ingram, Terry, 'Where there's a will there's a way – Dobell's Opera House auction', *Australian Financial Review*, 1 November 1972, p.1, 11

Ingram, Terry, 'Robert Hughes on local art – The high cost of chauvinism', *Australian Financial Review*, 31 July 1972, p.1, 7

Ingram, Terry, 'Artist, teacher, prophet', *Australian Financial Review*, 17 February 1972, p.11

Ingram, Terry, 'Christie's explores new areas', *Australian Financial Review*, 13 January 1972, p.24

Ingram, Terry, 'A German romantic in a hostile land', *Australian Financial Review*, 13 January 1972, p.24, 27

Ingram, Terry, 'The Gentle Art of Persuasion', *Australian Financial Review*, 2 December 1971, p.11, 35

Ingram, Terry, 'Dobell's "Night of the Pigs" to NSW Gallery', *Australian Financial Review*, 8 October 1971, p.3

Ingram, Terry, 'The generations gap is still a dampener on cultural growth', *Australian Financial Review*, 27 July 1971, p.2

Ingram, Terry, 'UK art dealers scent Aust pay dirt', *Australian Financial Review*, 26 July 1971, p.1, 5

Ingram, Terry, 'F. R. Strange throws down the gauntlet', *Australian Financial Review*, 15 July 1971, p.8

Ingram, Terry, 'Chocolate and orange, and Gray all over...', *Australian Financial Review*, 1 July 1971, p.8

Ingram, Terry, 'Why Christie's and Sotheby's are here', *Australian Financial Review*, 4 July 1969, p.6

James, Bruce, 'Sotheby's eyes the future', *Australian Business Monthly*, February 1993, pp.84–6

James, Colin, 'Bond painting moved', *Herald-Sun*, 3 April 2000, p.9

James, Graeme and John Rolfe, 'Market Trends – Art: super idea', *Daily Telegraph*, 21 November 2000, p.41

James, Helen, 'Eye for an original', *The Herald* (Melbourne), 20 April 1968, p.26

Jope-Slade, R., 'An Australian Quartette', *Magazine of Art*, vol. 1, 1890, no pagination

Kavanagh, John, 'A collage of art successes', *Business Review Weekly*, 12 January 2001, no pagination

Kavanagh, John, 'Dream time to the big time', *Business Review Weekly*, 18 August 2000, p.57

Kavanagh, John, 'Contemporary art offers rewards', *Business Review Weekly*, 19 November 1993, p.98

Kavanagh, John, 'Art sales recovering but remain far from well', *Business Review Weekly*, 15 May 1992, p.96

Kelleher, Leonie, 'Our Public collections: Community resources or realisable assets?', *Art Monthly Australia*, no. 99, May 1997, pp.6–9

Kelly, Philippa, 'Women at auction', *Art Monthly Australia*, no. 150, June 2002, pp.5–7

Kerr, Joan, 'Colonial Ladies' Sketchbooks', *Art and Australia*, 17(4) 1980, pp.356–62

Kerr, Joan, 'Sydney International Exhibition 1879,' *Art and Australia*, 17(3) 1980, pp.234–5

Klein, Rachel N., 'Art and Authority in Antebellum New York City: The Rise and Fall of the American Art-Union', *The Journal of American History*, 81(4) 1995, pp.1534–61

Klemperer, Paul, 'Auction theory: A Guide to the Literature', *Journal of Economic Surveys*, 13(3) July 1999, pp.227–86

Klingender, Tim, 'Important Aboriginal Art', *Sotheby's preview*, London, May 1997, pp.30–1

Lancashire, Rebecca, 'Portrait of Mrs William Bligh', *The Age*, 12 August 1996, p.5

Lawson, Valerie, 'How the great navigator finally found his way back home', *Sydney Morning Herald*, 12 August 2000, p.1

Leane, Ted, 'Sue Hewitt – Australia's only woman auctioneer?', *People*, 29 September 1977, p.17

Lester, Libby, 'Christie's vs Sotheby's', *Sunday Herald*, 18 November 1990, no pagination

Little, W. A., *Sydney Morning Herald*, business advertisement, 21 September 1915, p.4

Lufkin, Martha, 'The ring cycle', *The Art Newspaper*, 8(72) July–August 1997, p.54

Lynch, Paul, 'Lone collector nets choice of Trout sale', *The Australian*, 7 June 1989, p.3

Macdonald, Marion, 'The New Spectator Sport', *The Bulletin*, 14 October 1972, pp.40–41

Mackay, Ian, 'Youthful image of our gallery's new director', *The Advertiser* (Adelaide), 27 February 1976, p.4

Mackay, Mary, 'For a mere five guineas, Carl would paint you in next to the Governor', *Sydney Morning Herald*, 24 December 1983, no pagination

McCaughey, Patrick, 'Dangerous dumping of Dobells', *The Age*, 9 November 1973, p.2

McClelland, Joan, 'Melbourne's April Harvest – Art keeps pace with stock market boom', *Art and Australia*, 37(1) September–November 1999, pp.112–3

McClelland, Joan, 'Art at auction', *Art Monthly Australia*, no. 104, October 1997, pp.28–9

McCulloch, Alan, 'Dream home – well almost', *Herald* (Melbourne), 13 March 1971, p.6

McCulloch-Uehlin, Susan, 'Galleries ecstatic at art bargain', *The Australian*, 28 November 2001, p.3

McCulloch-Uehlin, Susan, 'Clear fortune awaits Glover's obscured view', *The Australian*, 23 November 2001, p.3

McCulloch-Uehlin, Susan and Ben Holgate, 'Art on his sleeve for $1m "tap on shoulder"', *The Australian*, 1 May 2001, p.5

McCulloch-Uehlin, Susan, 'Auction spotlight falls on Sotheby's', *The Australian*, 5 May 2000, p.17

McCulloch-Uehlin, Susan, 'Dealers, police advise art buyers beware at auction', *The Australian*, 11 October 1999, p.3

McCulloch, Susan and Michael Reid, 'Art-breaking decision to end century of family ties', *The Australian*, 10 July 1998, no pagination

McCulloch, Susan, 'Exports caught in the Act', *The Australian*, 26 June 1998, p.15

McCulloch, Susan, 'Reputations under hammer', *The Weekend Australian*, 14–15 February 1998, p.24

McCulloch, Susan, 'Going, Going…Gone??', *The Australian Magazine*, 19–20 April 1997, pp.18–22

McCulloch, Susan, 'Body of origin', *The Weekend Review*, 18–19 November 1995, no pagination

McDonald, Annabelle, 'Students to brush up on picking art fakes', *The Australian*, 4 May 2005

McGillick, Paul, 'Sure, Aboriginal art is trendy. But you've got to ask: is it worth buying and is it any good?', *The Weekend Australian Financial Review*, the fin, 20–21 September 1997, pp.16–7

McGuinness, Jan, 'Benefits of recession', *The Bulletin*, 26 March 1991, no pagination

McGuinness, Jan, 'There's an art in buying art', *The Bulletin*, 11 July 1989, pp.38–40

McGuinness, Jan, 'Who are the dealers?', *The Bulletin*, 11 July 1989, pp.41–2

McLean, Sandra, 'Flags fly at Enright sale', *Courier Mail*, 11 May 1999, no pagination

Makin, Jeff, 'Autumn auctions signal art market boom', *Australian Art Collector*, issue 5, July–September 1998, pp.54–7

Maslen, Geoff, 'Price-fixing is still out, says ACCC', plus another article on same page, undated [possibly 1995], no newspaper title recorded, presumably *The Age*, no pagination [from Sotheby's archives, Art Gallery of New South Wales library]

Maslen, Geoff, 'Upping the ante', *The Age*, 25 August 2003, <www.theage.com.au/articles/ 2003/08/22/1061529323877.html?from=storyrhs> [23/10/2005]

Maslen, Geoff, 'Mark Fraser Sotheby's Supremo', *The Age*, 13 May 2003, p.A3

Maslen, Geoff, 'Old hand to lead auction house revival', *The Age*, 6 December 2002, p.4

Maslen, Geoff, 'The star of the show sells in a silent night for bids', *The Age*, 27 November 2002, p.3

Maslen, Geoff, 'Young tyros attack art market', *The Age*, 13 November 2002, p.6

Maslen, Geoff, 'Balancing the books – hammer falls on record of friendship', *The Age*, 11 November 2002, p.5

Maslen, Geoff, 'Blackman, Boyd, Maguire swell Menzies' coffers', *The Age*, 1 November 2002, p.5

Maslen, Geoff, 'New front in war between auction houses', *The Age*, 23 October 2002, p.3

Maslen, Geoff, 'New front opens in battle of salerooms', *Sydney Morning Herald*, 18 October 2002, no pagination

Maslen, Geoff, 'ACCC inquiry into Glover painting sale', *The Age*, 16 September 2002, p.4

Maslen, Geoff, 'Contemporaries coming into their own as prices seesaw', *The Age*, 10 September 2002, p.4

Maslen, Geoff, 'A nervy flutter at the salerooms', *The Age*, 2 September 2002, p.5

Maslen, Geoff, 'When it comes to auctions, Furphy has the big picture', *The Age*, 27 March 2002, p.6

Maslen, Geoff, 'Going, Going, (almost) Gone to Sydney', *The Age*, 12 March 2002, p.4

Maslen, Geoff, 'Agreement reached on copyright cost', *The Age*, 7 March 2002, no pagination

Maslen, Geoff, 'Public Interest?', *The Age*, 12 December 2001, no pagination

Maslen, Geoff, 'Joel auction house closes art section', *The Age*, 30 November 2001, p.7

Maslen, Geoff, 'From Beaux-arts to faux arts', *The Age*, 30 May 2001, no pagination

Maslen, Geoff, 'Von Guerard landscape resurfaces after 131 years', *Sydney Morning Herald*, 14 February 2001, p.16

Maslen, Geoff, 'Auction plan: let the dealer beware', *Sydney Morning Herald*, 9 February 2001, p.14

Maslen, Geoff, 'Auction house survives US parent's cash crisis', *Sydney Morning Herald*, 6 February 2001, no pagination

Maslen, Geoff, 'Final art auctions start under a cloud', *The Age*, 11 November 2000, p.14

Maslen, Geoff, 'Every day of the web…', *The Age*, Review, 28 September 2000, no pagination

Maslen, Geoff, 'Records tumble as art auctions spark clamor', *The Age*, 1 July 2000, p.21

Maslen, Geoff, '$20m Saleroom Bonanza – Fine art turnover hits all time high…', *Australian Art Collector*, issue 13, July–September 2000, pp.42–4

Maslen, Geoff, 'Frequent buyer points', *Sydney Morning Herald*, 4 April 2000, p.13

Maslen, Geoff, 'Getting a piece of the auction', *Sydney Morning Herald*, 9 February 2000, no pagination

Maslen, Geoff, 'Queen of the auction room', *The Age*, 2 December 1998, p.20

Maslen, Geoff, 'Art is alive with the sound of bidding', *The Age*, 20 November 1998, p.16

Maslen, Geoff, 'Auctions to declare unsold lots', *The Age*, 2 May 1998, Business, p.1, 2

Maslen, Geoff, 'Dealers hurt but not beaten by auctions', *The Age*, 16 August 1997, p.B1, B2

Maslen, Geoff, 'Boom time for art auctions', *Sydney Morning Herald*, 23 August 1996, no pagination

Maslen, Geoff, 'Auctioneers make a bid for the big spenders', *The Age*, 15 April 1996, p.B1, B3

Maslen, Geoff, 'Going, Going, *Strong*', *Good Weekend*, 23 December 1995, pp.24–26

Maslen, Geoff, 'Bond paintings come back on the market', *Sydney Morning Herald*, 21 November 1995, p.15

Maslen, Geoff, 'Going once, twice, three times…sold to the owner?', *The Canberra Times*, 8 May 1994, no pagination

Maslen, Geoff, 'Still Going, Going, Gone', *The Age*, 24 March 1994, p.9

Maslen, Geoff, 'Sotheby's raises auction buyer's commission to 15 per cent', *The Age*, 4 November 1992, p.5

Maslen, Geoff, 'Art buyers settle only for the best', *The Age*, 29 August 1992, p.13

Maslen, Geoff, 'Bond's art remnants sold off', *Sydney Morning Herald*, 24 August 1992, p.4

Maslen, Geoff, 'Alan Bond's rise and fall traced in art', *The Age*, 22 August 1992, no pagination

Maslen, Geoff, 'Bond's art collection sells for $5.5 million', *The Age*, 29 July 1992, p.3

Maslen, Geoff, '60 works from Bond's art collection for auction tonight', *The Age*, 28 July 1992, p.5

Maslen, Geoff, 'Fine art's boom and bust', *The Age*, 3 January 1991, no pagination

Maslen, Geoff, 'Salerooms scramble for market', *A–Z Antiques*, Summer 1990, pp.65–6

Maslen, Geoff, 'Glover Intrigue', *The Age*, 11 October 1989, no pagination

Maslen, Geoff, 'Art market flushed with rude health', *The Age*, 20 April 1989, no pagination

Maslen, Geoff, 'Growth of a super salesman', *The Age*, 26 March 1988, p.6

Maslen, Geoff, 'Values can vary at the whim of fashion', *The Age*, 1 February 1988, Money Extra, p.2

Maslen, Geoff, 'The art of the auction', *The Age*, 18 November 1987, p.3

Meagher, David, 'Hand-in-Glover', *Australian Financial Review*, 26 October 2001, p.84

Meagher, David, 'Shapiro Fashions a Niche', *Australian Financial Review*, the fin, 24 October 1998, p.3

Menadue, Peter, 'Art cleaned out collector, and now he'll clean up', *The Australian*, 13 September 1984, p.3

Miller, Steven, 'Deaccessioning – Sales or Transfer?', *Museum Management and Curatorship*, no. 10, 1991, pp.245–53

Minogue, Dennis, 'Hughes attacks our myths', *The Age*, 7 December 1974, p.15

Montias, J. M., 'On Art and Economic Reasoning', *Art in America*, 76(7) July 1988, pp.23–7

Morgan, Joyce, 'Christie's boss puts polish on tarnished name', *Sydney Morning Herald*, 12 July 2001, p.14

Morgan, Joyce, 'Controversial art trots triumphantly from the park', *Sydney Morning Herald*, 12 October 1999, p.2

Morgan, Patricia, 'World will bid for a painter's hoard', *The Advertiser* (Adelaide), 11 August 1973, p.25

Morris, Christine, 'Police fear stolen masterpieces burnt', *The Age*, 7 April 1979, p.5

Munro, Thomas, 'The Marxist Theory of Art History: Socio-Economic Determinism and the Dialectical Process', *Journal of Aesthetics and Art Criticism*, 43(4) June 1960, pp.430–45

Murdoch, Lindsay and Tom Jacob, 'Police find stolen art', *The Age*, 10 September 1979, p.1

Museums Association, *Museums Journal*, London, September 1991

Naidoo, Manika, 'Million-dollar sale bucks the trend on a slow night for traditional art', *The Age*, 24 August 1999, p.5

Nicklin, Lenore, 'The images of Joseph Brown: patriotic migrant made good', *The Bulletin*, 19 March 1985, pp.56–60

Nodrum, Charles, 'Weak at the moment', *Art Monthly Australia*, May 1990, pp.26–7

Nuding, Gertrude Prescott, 'Reflections on Art Market Analysis', *Apollo*, February 1990, pp.110–114

Nuding, Gertrude Prescott, 'Showbiz?', *Apollo*, November 1989, pp.321–27, 363

Nuding, Gertrude Prescott, 'Saleroom Practice', *Apollo*, July 1988, pp.34–41

O'Brien, Mary, 'Treasures in the Attic', *A–Z Antiques*, Winter 1989, pp.112–14

O'Grady, Desmond and Vic Worstead, 'Investment in Art – A Sound New Business', *The Bulletin*, 14 April 1962, pp.13–16

Oliphant, Jo, 'Auction's success seals MOCA move', *The Courier Mail*, 19 June 1991, p.36

Owens, Susan, 'From the outback to Manhattan', *The Weekend Australian Financial Review*, the fin, 30 September – 1 October 2000, p.5

Palmer, Roderick, 'It's going to be quite a month for sales', *The National Times*, 2–7 October 1972, p.26

Pearson, Christopher, 'Recognition as an arbiter of an artist's worth', *Australian Financial Review*, 24 November 1997, p.21

Pearson, Lynn Stowell, 'Stolen Art Alert', *IFAR Reports*, 7(7) September 1986, p.10

Petersen, Don, 'Heritage Lost', *The Courier-Mail*, Great Weekend, 3 June 1989, p.1, 2

Plant, Simon, 'At her bidding', *Sun*, 6 May 1994, no pagination

Pos, Margaretta, 'Prime purchase under investigation', *Hobart Mercury*, 15 December 2001, p.38

Pos, Margaretta, 'Van Gogh record makes investors hungry for a share of art market', *Hobart Mercury*, 4 April 1987, no pagination

Price, Jenna, 'Painting over the bubble that burst', *The Canberra Times*, 20 July 1996, p.C4

Prout, John Skinner, 'The Fine Arts in Australia', *Art-Union*, vol. 10, 1848, p.332

Ratcliff, Carter, 'The Marriage of Art and Money', *Art in America*, July 1988, pp.76–84, 145, 147

Redmond, Michael (possibly – unattributed in magazine), 'Lawson's – Yesterday, Today and Tomorrow', *The Australian Antique Collector*, 24th ed., July–December 1982, pp.91–3

Reid, Michael, 'From broadest canvas of heartlands', *The Australian*, 16 July 2003, no pagination

Reid, Michael, 'Must bid to slash fake sales at a stroke', *The Australian*, 30 April 2003, no pagination

Reid, Michael, 'Christie's does a Lazarus in $7.6m sale', *The Australian*, 21 May 2003, no pagination

Reid, Michael, 'All our own work', *Australian Art Review*, issue 1, March–June 2003, p.64

Reid, Michael, 'After the boom, a time to buy', *The Australian*, 14 December 2002, p.42

Reid, Michael, 'No nudes is good nudes as auction fatigue sets in', *The Australian*, 7 December 2002, p.36

Reid, Michael, 'One good churn creates a bother', *The Australian*, 21 September 2002, p.36

Reid, Michael, 'Auctions bask in warm bid glow', *The Weekend Australian*, 31 August – 1 September 2002, p.38

Reid, Michael, 'Cash cow wranglers ride to move 'em out', *The Weekend Australian*, 24–25 August 2002, p.42

Reid, Michael and Kimberly Needham, 'Fine art auctioneers paint themselves out of a corner', *The Australian*, 24 April 2002, p.28

Reid, Michael, 'Sold! Oh, hang on, here's a higher bid', *The Australian*, 9 March 2002, p.36

Reid, Michael, 'Glover lovers see big picture', *The Australian*, 1 December 2001, p.37

Reid, Michael, 'Full sales, come Hull or high water', *The Australian*, 24 November 2001, p.35

Reid, Michael, 'Individual fortunes Top 5 single-owner collections...', *The Australian*, 23 November 2001, p.19

Reid, Michael, 'Buyout for Phillips', *The Australian*, 19 November 2001, p.33

Reid, Michael, 'Beware the auction ramp-up', *The Australian*, 25 November 2000, p.37

Reid, Michael, 'Mertz triggers a stampede for quality', *The Australian*, 1 July 2000, p.45

Reid, Michael, 'Auction house staff going, going...gone', *The Australian*, 9 June 1999, p.5

Reid, Michael, 'Export rule shakeup', *The Weekend Australian*, 20–21 March 1999, p.4

Reid, Michael, 'Auction room intrigues distort true sale values', *The Weekend Australian*, 6–7 March 1999, p.4

Reid, Michael and Susan McCulloch, 'Art dealers puzzled by 20–year rule', *The Australian*, 25 January 1999, p.17

Reid, Michael, 'Sotheby's brings down gavel on boom year', *The Australian*, 19 January 1999, p.21

Reid, Michael, 'Runaway prices cap strong year', *The Weekend Australian*, 12–13 December 1998, p.4

Reid, Michael, 'Lawsons sends pathfinder north to establish a beachhead', *The Australian*, 21 November 1998, no pagination

Reid, Michael, 'New auction player needs to lift its game', *The Weekend Australian*, 22–23 August 1998, p.4

Reid, Michael, 'London search turns up fresh stock', *The Weekend Australian*, 22–23 August 1998, p.4

Reid, Michael, 'Bid rebuffs fail to blunt new force', *The Weekend Australian*, 25–26 July 1998, p.4

Reid, Michael, 'Phillips offers prizes', *The Weekend Australian*, 25–26 July 1998, p.4

Reid, Michael, 'Aboriginal collection comes home', *The Weekend Australian*, 20–21 June 1998, p.4

Reid, Michael, 'Auction houses show off shopfronts', *The Weekend Australian*, 30–31 May 1998, p.4

Reid, Michael, 'Modern paintings the best movers', *The Weekend Australian*, 9–10 May 1998, p.4

Reid, Michael, 'New boy breaks fresh ground', *The Weekend Australian*, 18–19 April 1998, p.4

Reid, Michael, 'Phillips takes a gamble', *The Weekend Australian*, 21–22 February 1998, p.4

Reid, Michael, 'Deutscher Menzies – Moving to a new house', *The Weekend Australian*, 14–15 February 1998, p.4

Reid, Michael, 'When age is an advantage', *The Weekend Australian*, 24–25 January 1998, p.4

Reid, Michael, 'All hyped up', *The Weekend Australian*, 22–23 November 1997, p.4

Reid, Michael, 'Sotheby's gives ground to end war with dealers/Out of the picture', *The Australian*, 8 November 1997, no pagination

Reid, Michael, 'Mixed results for top traders', *The Australian*, 4 July 1997, p.11

Reid, Michael, 'Budding connoisseurs bid for knowledge', *The Weekend Australian*, 11–12 January 1997, p.63

Reid, Michael, 'A public hanging can perk up art world', *The Australian*, 7 December 1996, p.68

Reid, Michael, 'Newcomers shake grip of Sotheby's, Christie's', *The Weekend Australian*, 7–8 September 1996, p.72

Reid, Michael, 'Race for fresh stock as fine art auction industry hots up', *The Australian*, 10 August 1996, p.60

Robinson, John Martin, 'The Origins of Bonhams – A foundation in print-selling', *Apollo*, 138(380) October 1993, pp.42–44

Robinson, Michael F., 'Art and Money – Deaccessing the accessible in exchange for the inaccessible', *Connoisseur*, no. 220, September 1990, pp.132–6

Robotham, Michael, 'Claws out in bitter art feud', *Sunday Telegraph*, 20 November 1988, p.44

Rooney, Robert, 'A stillness and silence', *The Australian*, 21–22 November 1987, Weekend Magazine, p.12

Rosenbaum, Lee, 'How permanent is the permanent collection?', *ARTnews*, 89(5) May 1990, pp.190–7

Rowbotham, Jill, 'The art dealer who is not bound with tradition', *The Herald*, 6 November 1989, p.13, 15

Ruberti, Federico, 'Too much to do with investment', *The Art Newspaper*, 9(83) July–August 1998, p.37

Russell, Matthew, 'Aboriginal art weaves magic prices on world stage', *Sydney Morning Herald*, 20 June 1997, possibly p.10

Ryan, Colleen and Kate McClymont, 'Bond's trail leads the art world to the first of our missing explorers', *Sydney Morning Herald*, 18 June 1994, p.1, 34

Safe, Georgina, 'Painter mocks arts council bull', *The Australian*, 20 June 2003, p.6

Safe, Georgina, Susan McCulloch-Uehlin, and Michael Reid, 'A masterpiece undercut', *The Australian*, 8 December 2001, pp.1–2

Safe, Georgina, 'Long-lost $2m Glover to come home', *The Australian*, 18 August 2001, p.7

Safe, Georgina and Ben Holgate, 'The deal of the art', *The Australian*, 6 January 2001, p.22

Sampson, Annette, 'Rising Stars – Sotheby's bids up', *Australian Business*, 11 November 1987, pp.96–7

Saville, Margot, 'Collectibles', *The Weekend Australian*, 15–16 December 1990, no pagination

Saville, Margot, 'Collectibles', *The Weekend Australian*, 8–9 September 1990, no pagination

Saw, Ron, 'No longer a boom at the top – Artists now share the jackpot', *Mirror* (Sydney), 5 June 1964, no pagination

Scheding, Stephen, 'James Howe Carse', *Art and Australia*, 17(1) September 1979, pp.72–6

Schroder, Philippa, 'Pictures offer good returns for the wary', *The Canberra Times – Sunday Times*, 5 July 1998, p.9

Simon, Robin, 'Editorial – Let the buyer be wary', *Apollo*, no. 348, February 1991, pp.76–7

Simpson, Cheryl, 'Cultural Heritage on the Move: Significance and Meaning', *Law in Context*, 14(2) 1996, pp.45–67

Smith, Jan, 'Auction by satellite fails to get off ground', *The Australian*, 27 June 1968, p.4

Stanford, Jon, 'Returns to Australian Contemporary Art 1972–1989', *Art and Australia*, 30(4) 1993, pp.532–3

Stannard, Bruce, 'Collector sells his antiques for $500,000', *The Australian*, 30 June 1973, p.1

Steene, Mark, 'Dealer accused of art fraud', *The Advertiser* (Adelaide), 13 October 1999, p.3

Stein, John Picard, 'The Monetary Appreciation of Paintings', *The Journal of Political Economy*, 85(5) October 1977, pp.1021–1036

Stratford, Deborah, 'The Changing Role of the Auction House', *Orientations*, 30(3) March 1999, p.126

Stretton, Rowena, 'Art and artifice: the pitfalls and pleasures of Aboriginal paintings', *The Weekend Australian Financial Review*, the fin, 29–30 August 1998, pp.2–3

Stretton, Rowena, 'Sotheby's targets the designer generation', *Australian Financial Review*, 22 August 1997, p.16

Stretton, Rowena, 'Bleakley takes punt on Eco development', *Australian Financial Review*, 8 June 1994, p.5

Stretton, Rowena, 'The art gulf war', *The Bulletin*, 19 March 1991, no pagination

Stretton, Rowena, 'The art of making money', *The Bulletin*, 8 January 1990, pp.88–91

Stretton, Rowena, 'Seminar to look at the art of buying', *The Weekend Australian*, 19–20 September 1987, p.32

Strickland, Katrina, 'Odd Lots', *Australian Financial Review*, 10 August 2006, p.45

Strickland, Katrina, 'As the 10th anniversary of indigenous art auctions looms...', *Australian Financial Review*, Australian Financial Review Magazine, 30 June 2006, p.26

Tay, Miranda, 'Importance of being earnest', *The Age*, 11 February 1995, no pagination

Thomas, Daniel, 'Creative Displacements – Three Art Dealers: Georges Mora, Rudy Komon, Joseph Brown', *Art and Australia*, 30(4) Winter 1993, pp.481–7

Thomas, Laurie, 'Dobells dominate $500,000 Australian art sale', *The Australian*, 1 October 1971, p.3

Thomas, Martin, 'Bond's art collection tipped to fetch $5m', *The Australian*, 13 July 1992, p.3

Thorncroft, Antony, 'The Art Market – Papering over the cracks', *Apollo*, 132(343) September 1990, pp.174–7

Timms, Peter, 'Artnotes: National', *Art Monthly Australia*, no. 107, March 1998, p.31

Titmarsh, Mark, 'Stand By Me – The Rise of the Art Dealer in Australia', *Australian Art Collector*, issue 5, July–September 1998, pp.36–9

Tribe, David, 'Household name turns 250', *Sydney Morning Herald*, 30 November 1994, no pagination

Trioli, Virginia, 'Art in the open market', *The Age*, 30 September 1994, p.11

Turner, Brook, 'An authentic market', *The Australian Financial Review Magazine*, Undated, possibly 1999, pp.12–15

Uzanne, Octave, 'The Hotel Drouot and Auction Rooms in Paris Generally, Before and After the French Revolution', *The Connoisseur*, vol. 3, May–August 1902, pp.235–242

Van den Bosch, Annette, 'What is a Good Reputation Worth? Changing Definitions of the Artist', *Art and Australia*, 30(3) 1993, pp.355–63

Van den Bosch, Annette, 'A Taste for the New – Corporate Art Collections, Museums and the Art Market in the United States and Australia', *Art and Australia*, 30(2) Summer 1992, pp.226–37

Van den Bosch, Annette, 'The Market for Contemporary Australian Art: The Formative Years', *Art and Australia*, 29(3) 1992, pp.316–24, 392

Vincent, Steven, 'Online or Flatline?', *Art & Auction – Special issue: Online or Flatline? Taking the Pulse of the Internet Art Market*, 22(10) Summer 2000, pp.74–81

Waldren, Murray, 'Crooke's paradise', *The Australian Magazine*, 6–7 June 1998, pp.28–32

Walker, R. W., 'Insider trading under investigation', *ARTnews*, October 1985, p.19

Ward, Peter, 'Christie's v Sotheby's – A very civil war', *The Australian Magazine*, 4–5 July 1992, pp.16–25

Warneminde, Martin, 'The truth about Picasso and the goldfish', *The Bulletin*, 19 November 1991, pp.42–6

Washington, David, 'Plug pulled on Diana's Bath export', *The Advertiser* (Adelaide), 5 October 1989, p.1

Watson, Bronwyn, 'Glover painting may bring auction record', *Sydney Morning Herald*, 9 February 1989, p.2

Watson, S. and A. S. Cocks, 'A bigger market for all?', *The Art Newspaper*, 9(82) 1998, pp.51–52

Webster, Mary Hull, 'The Battle of Art and Money', *Artweek*, 29(15) May 1998, p.12

Weiss, Philip, 'Selling the Collection', *Art in America*, no. 78, July 1990, pp.124–31

White, Judith, 'Australia's Most Wanted', *Australian Art Collector*, issue 1, July–September 1997, pp.30–3

Widdicombe, Ben, 'Dramatic growth for Internet auctions', *Australian Art Collector*, issue 9, July–September 1999, p.31

Widdicombe, Ben, 'Growth locks in – Saleroom gets muscular', *Australian Art Collector*, issue 8, April–June 1999, pp.27–8

Wilcox, Alexandra, 'Canvassing Sydney pays off', *The Age*, 9 March 2002, p.5

Wild, Dorian, 'First impressions are good', *Sun Herald*, 9 April 1989, p.138

Williams, Antonia, 'Playing Houses', *Sydney Morning Herald*, 2 August 2001, p.5

Williams, Antonia, 'Men for all seasons', *Sydney Morning Herald*, 10 June 1999, p.8

Williams, Antonia, 'Affairs of the Art', *Sydney Morning Herald*, 17 September 1998, p.8

Williams, Antonia, 'Salesroom challenge', *Sydney Morning Herald*, 12 February 1998, p.7

Williams, Pamela, 'Sotheby's sale will be final judge', *Business Review Weekly*, 17 November 1989, pp.51–2

Wilson, Marshall and Jamie Fawcett, 'Family Bond', *Courier Mail*, 25 March 2000, p.23

Wood, Danielle, 'Star attraction', *Sunday Tasmanian*, 4 November 2001, p.5

Woodroofe, W., 'On Collecting', *The Antiquarian Gazette*, 17 December 1910, no pagination

Woolford, Don, 'Glover comes home, but can Tassie afford it?', *Australian Associated Press*, 2 November 2001, no pagination

Wyld, Ben, 'Over $2m Expected for Glover Masterpiece', *Sydney Morning Herald*, 16 November 2001, p.5

Yaman, Ebru, 'Sotheby's accuses art dealers of subterfuge', *The Australian*, 28 April 1997, no pagination

Zemel, Carol, 'What Becomes a Legend Most', *Art in America*, 76(7) July 1988, pp.88–92, 151

Books

Author unknown, *The First Gallery in Paddington – the Artists and Their Work Tell the Story of the Rudy Komon Art Gallery*, Edwards & Shaw, Sydney 1981

Author unknown, *Twice Round the Block, Or A Visit to the Auction Rooms, of Sydney*, anonymous pamphlet, 1840s, Mitchell Library, Sydney

Abbott, Graham and Geoffrey Little (eds), *The Respectable Sydney Merchant – A.B. Spark of Tempe*, Sydney University Press, Sydney 1976

Adams, Brian, *Portrait of an Artist: A Biography of William Dobell*, Vintage, Milson's Point, New South Wales 1992

Adorno, Theodor and Max Horkheimer, 'The Culture Industry: Enlightenment as Mass Deception', in *Dialectic of Enlightenment*, Continuum, New York 1993

Adorno, Theodor, 'Culture Industry Reconsidered', in *The Culture Industry: Selected Essays on Mass Culture*, Routledge, London 1991

Allen, Louis A., *Time Before Morning – Art and Myth of the Australian Aborigines*, Crowell, New York 1975

Allingham, E. G., *A Romance of the Rostrum: being the business life of Henry Stevens, and the history of thirty-eight King street, together with some account of famous sales held there during the last hundred years*, compiled by E.G. Allingham; with a preface by the Right Honorable Lord Rothschild, F.R.S., London 1924

Alpers, Svetlana, *Rembrandt's Enterprise: The Studio and the Market*, University of Chicago Press, Chicago 1988

Altman, Jon, *The Aboriginal Arts and Crafts Industry: Report of the Review Committee, July 1989*, Australian Department of Aboriginal Affairs, Australian Government Publishing Service, Canberra 1989

Anderson, Patricia, *Art + Australia: Debates, Dollars & Delusions*, Pandora Press, Sydney 2005

Andrews, Keith, *Adam Elsheimer: Paintings–Drawings–Prints*, Phaidon, Oxford 1977

Arnau, Frank, *The Art of the Faker – Three thousand Years of Deception*, trans. J. Maxwell Brownjohn, Little, Brown and Company, Boston and Toronto 1961

Ashton, Julian, *Now Came Still Evening On*, Angus & Robertson, Sydney 1941

The Art Newspaper, *The Art Newspaper – Guide to Art Auctions – Worldwide*, First Edition, 2002

Australian Dictionary of Biography, Melbourne University Press, Melbourne, published from 1966 onwards

Ballou, Maturin Murray, *Under the Southern Cross*, Houghton, Mifflin 1890 (third ed.)

Barnard, Alan, *Visions and Profits – Studies in the Business Career of Thomas Sutcliffe Mort*, Melbourne University Press, Melbourne 1961

Barnet, Sylvan, *A Short Guide to Writing About Art*, Tufts University, United States 2003 (seventh ed.)

Berger, John, *Ways of Seeing*, Penguin, London 1972

Bleakley, Robert, *African Masks*, Thames and Hudson, London 1978

Bonyhady, Tim, *Images in Opposition — Australian Landscape Painting 1801–1890*, Oxford University Press, Melbourne 1985

Bourdieu, Pierre, *The Field of Cultural Production: Essays on Art and Literature*, ed. and intro by Randal Johnson, Polity Press, Cambridge 1993

Bourdieu, Pierre, *Distinction: A Social Critique of the Judgement of Taste*, trans. Richard Nice, Routledge and Kegan Paul, London 1984

Brigstocke, Hugh, *William Buchanan and the 19th Century Art Trade: 100 Letters to His Agents in London and Italy*, Paul Mellon Centre for Studies in British Art, London 1982

Bonython, Kym, *Ladies' Legs and Lemonade*, Rigby Adelaide 1979

Bowness, Alan, *The Conditions of Success: How the Modern Artist Rises to Fame*, Walter Neurath Memorial Lectures, Thames and Hudson, London 1989

Brodsky, Isadore, *Sydney Looks Back*, Angus and Robertson, Sydney 1957

Baudrillard, Jean, 'The Precession of Simulacra', in Wallis, Brian (ed.), *Art After Modernism – Rethinking Representation*, The New Museum of Contemporary Art, New York 1984

Candy, Philip C., and John Laurent (eds), *Pioneering Culture: Mechanics' Institutes and Schools of Arts in Australia*, Adelaide 1994

Cassady, Ralph, *Auctions and Auctioneering*, University of California Press, Berkeley 1967

Chapel, Jeannie, *Victorian Taste – The Complete Catalogue of Paintings at the Royal Holloway College*, foreword by Jeremy Maas, A. Zwemmer Ltd, London 1982

Christie's, *Christie's Australian Art Sales Index 1969–1974*, Christie, Manson & Woods (Australia) Ltd, Double Bay c.1974

Conklin, John E., *Art Crime*, Westport 1994

Cooper, Jeremy, *Under the Hammer: the Auctions and Auctioneers of London*, Constable, London 1977

Craig, Edward D., *Australian Art Auction Records*, Ure Smith, Sydney, published from 1975 onwards

De Chantilly, Marc Vaulbert, 'Property of a Distinguished Poisoner: Thomas Griffiths Wainewright and the Griffiths Family Library', in Myers, Robin, Michael Harris and Giles Mandelbrote (eds), *Under the Hammer: Book Auctions since the Seventeenth Century*, British Library, London 2001, pp.111–142

Dedman, Roger, *Christie's Australian Art Market Movements Handbook*, Christie's, Victoria 2002

Dobson, Rosemary, *Focus on Ray Crooke*, University of Queensland Press, Queensland 1971

Ellis, Aytoun, *The Penny Universities, a History of the Coffee-houses…*, Secker & Warburg, London 1956

Engelbrecht-Wiggans, Richard, Martin Shubik and Robert M. Stark, *Auctions, Bidding and Contracting: Uses and Theory*, New York University Press, New York 1983

Faith, Nicholas, *Sold: the Rise and Fall of the House of Sotheby*, Macmillan, New York 1985

Falk, Peter, *Who Was Who in American Art*, Sound View Press, Connecticut, 1985

Freedberg, David, *Iconoclasts and their Motives*, Gary Schwartz, Maarsen, The Netherlands 1985

Furphy, John, *Australian Art Sales Digest: a Survey of Australian Sales of Art at Auction from 1988 to 1995*, Acorn Antiques, Armadale, Victoria 1996 ed.

Galbally, Ann and Margaret Plant (eds), *Studies in Australian Art*, Department of Fine Arts, University of Melbourne, Melbourne 1978

Geoff K. Gray, *Auctions and Grays*, Geoff K. Gray (Holdings) Limited, Annual Report, 1971

Geoff K. Gray, *Auctions and Grays*, Geoff K. Gray (Holdings) Limited, Annual Report, 1969

Germaine, Max, *Artists and Galleries of Australia*, Craftsman House, Roseville, New South Wales 1990 (rev. and enl. 3rd ed.)

Gimpel, René, *Diary of an Art Dealer*, Farrar, Straus & Giroux, New York 1966

Grampp, William D., *Pricing the Priceless: Art, Artists and Economics*, Basic Books, New York 1985

Grishin, Sasha, *Garry Shead: Encounters with Royalty*, Craftsman House, North Ryde c.1998

Grishin, Sasha, *Garry Shead: the D. H. Lawrence Paintings*, Gordon and Breach Arts International, East Roseville 1993

Hansard, Commonwealth Parliamentary Debates, House of Representatives, 27 November 1985

Harris, Michael, 'Newspaper Advertising for Book Auctions before 1700' in Myers, Robin, Michael Harris and Giles Mandelbrote (eds), *Under the Hammer: Book Auctions since the Seventeenth Century*, British Library, London 2001, pp.1–14

Hauser, Arnold, *The Sociology of Art*, trans. Kenneth J. Northcott, Routledge and Kegan Paul, London 1982

Hauser, Arnold, *The Social History of Art*, Routledge and Kegan Paul, London 1962, 4 vols.

Heathcote, Christopher, *A Quiet Revolution – The Rise of Australian Art 1946–1968*, Text Publishing Company, Melbourne 1995

Herbert, John, *Inside Christie's*, St. Martin's Press, New York 1990

Herbert, John (ed.), *Christie's Review of the Year 1970–71*, Hutchinson of London, London 1971

Herrmann, Frank, *Sotheby's: Portrait of an Auction House*, Chatto & Windus, London 1980

Herrmann, Frank, *The English as Collectors – A Documentary Chrestomathy*, Chatto & Windus, London 1972

Herodotus, *History*, trans. A.D. Godley, William Heinemann Ltd., London 1975, 4 vols.

Hoff, Ursula, *European Paintings before 1800*, National Gallery of Victoria, Melbourne 1961

Hogrefe, Jeffrey, *'Wholly Unacceptable' – The Bitter Battle for Sotheby's*, Harrap, London 1986

Holden, Robert, *Photography in Colonial Australia – The Mechanical Eye and the Illustrated Book*, Hordern House, Sydney 1988

Hughes, Robert, 'Art and Money', given as the first Harold Rosenberg Memorial Lecture at the University of Chicago, 1984 in Robert Hughes, *Nothing If Not Critical – Selected Essays on Art and Artists*, Alfred A. Knopf, New York 1991, pp.387–404

Hughes, Robert, *Nothing If Not Critical – Selected Essays on Art and Artists*, Alfred A. Knopf, New York 1991

Ingram, Terry, *A Matter of Taste – Investing in Australian Art*, William Collins Publishers, Sydney 1976

Johnson, Heather, *The Sydney Art Patronage System 1890–1940*, Bungoona Technologies Pty Ltd, Grays Point, New South Wales 1997

Keen, Geraldine, *Money and Art: A Study Based on the Times-Sotheby's Index*, G. P. Putnam's Sons, New York 1971

Klemperer, Paul (ed.), *The Economic Theory of Auctions*, Edward Elgar, Cheltenham, United Kingdom 2000, 2 vols.

Lacey, Robert, *Sotheby's – Bidding for Class*, Little, Brown and Company, London 1998

Learmount, Brian, *A History of the Auction*, Barnard and Learmount, Great Britain 1985

Lhotsky, John, 'Australia, in its historical evolution', *The Art Union*, July 1839, pp.99–100, included in Bernard Smith, (ed.), *Documents on Art and Taste in Australia – The Colonial Period 1770–1914*, Oxford University Press, Melbourne 1975, pp.71–6

Long, Sydney, 'The Trend of Australian Art Considered and Discussed', *Art and Architecture* (Sydney), January 1905, included in Bernard Smith, (ed.), *Documents on Art and Taste in Australia – The Colonial Period 1770–1914*, Oxford University Press, Melbourne 1975, pp.263–8

Longden, Reginald, *An Antiques Saga*, R. Longden, Adelaide 1991

Lumby, Catharine, *Tim Storrier: the Art of the Outsider*, Craftsman House, St. Leonards, New South Wales c.2000

McAfee, R. Preston and John McMillan, 'Auctions and Bidding', in Paul Klemperer, (ed.), *The Economic Theory of Auctions*, 2 vols, United Kingdom 2000, vol. 1, pp.159–198

McCulloch, Alan, *Encyclopedia of Australian Art*, Allen & Unwin, St. Leonards, New South Wales 1994 (3rd ed.)

Mandelbrote, Giles, 'The Organization of Book Auctions in Late Seventeenth-Century London', in Robin Myers, Michael Harris and Giles Mandelbrote (eds), *Under the Hammer: Book Auctions since the Seventeenth Century*, British Library, London 2001, pp.15–50

Marillier, H.C., *Christie's 1766 to 1925*, Constable & Company Ltd, London 1926

Martorella, Rosanne, *Corporate Art*, Rutgers University Press, New Brunswick and London 1990

Maslen, Geoffrey, *For Pleasure and Profit – A Guide to Collecting in Australia*, Brooks Waterloo, South Melbourne 1988

Mercier, Louis Sebastien, *Tableau de Paris*, Amsterdam 1783

Meyer, Karl, *The Art Museum: Power, Money, Ethics*, Morrow, New York 1979

Milgrom, Paul R. and Robert J. Weber, 'A Theory of Auctions and Competitive Bidding', in Paul Klemperer, (ed.), *The Economic Theory of Auctions I*, Edward Elgar, Cheltenham UK, Northhampton MA, c.2000, 2 vols, pp.1089–1091

Minchin, Jan and Roger Butler, *Thea Proctor: the Prints*, Resolution Press, Glebe, New South Wales 1980

Montias, John Michael, *Artists and Artisans in Delft: A Socio-Economic Study of the Seventeenth Century*, Princeton University Press c.1982

Moore, William, *The Story of Australian Art – From the Earliest Known Art of the Continent to the Art of To-day*, Angus & Robertson Ltd, Sydney 1934, 2 vols.

Morley-Fletcher, Hugo and Roger McIlroy, *Christie's Pictorial History of European Pottery*, Phaidon, Oxford 1984

Moulin, Raymonde, *The French Art Market*, trans. Arthur Goldhammer, Rutgers University Press, New Brunswick c.1987

Mulvaney, D. J., and J. H. Calaby, *'So Much That Is New' – Baldwin Spencer, 1860–1929 – A Biography*, Melbourne University Press, Carlton, Victoria 1985

Mundy, Lt. Colonel Godfrey Charles, *Our Antipodes: or, Residence and Rambles in the Australasian Colonies, with a Glimpse of the Gold Fields*, Richard Bentley, London 1852, 3 vols., (second ed., rev.)

Murphy, Bernice, *Museum of Contemporary Art: Vision & Context*, Museum of Contemporary Art, Sydney 1993

Myers, Fred R., *Painting Culture: the Making of an Aboriginal High Art*, Duke University Press, London 2002

Myers, Robin, Michael Harris, and Giles Mandelbrote (eds), *Under the Hammer: Book Auctions since the Seventeenth Century*, British Library, London 2001

Oxford English Dictionary, Clarendon Press, Oxford, 1978 (repr.)

Pears, Iain, *The Discovery of Painting: the Growth of Interest in the Arts in England 1680–1768*, Yale University Press, London 1988

Pepys, Samuel, *The Diary of Samuel Pepys*, transcribed by M. Bright from the shorthand manuscript in the Pepysian Library, Magdalene College, Cambridge, with editions by H.B. Wheatley, London, G. Bell, London 1946

Phillips, *Phillips 1796–1996*, London c.1996

Quartermaine, Peter, 'The Lost Perspective: Australian Photography in the Nineteenth Century', in Peter Quartermaine, (ed.), *Readings in Australian Arts – Papers from the 1976 Exeter Symposium*, University of Exeter, Exeter 1978, pp.1–15

Quemin, Alain, *Les commissaries–priseurs: la mutation d'une profession*, Paris c.1997

Reid, Michael, *How to Buy & Sell Art*, Allen & Unwin, Sydney 2004

Reitlinger, Gerald, *The Economics of Taste – The Art Market in the 1960s*, Barrie and Jenkins, London 1970, vol. 3

Reitlinger, Gerald, *The Economics of Taste – The Rise and Fall of Objets d'Art Prices since 1750*, Barrie & Rockliff, London 1963, vol. 2

Reitlinger, Gerald, *The Economics of Taste – the Rise and Fall of Picture Prices 1760–1960*, Barrie & Rockliff (Barrie Books Ltd) London 1961, vol. 1

Rivett, Collinridge, *The Art Union Story and Old Parramatta*, Art in Parramatta Series, limited edition, New City Press, Parramatta 1953

Ruhen, Carl, *The Auctioneers: Lawsons – The First 100 Years*, Ayers and James Heritage Books and James R. Lawson Pty Ltd, Sydney 1984

Sello, Gottfried, *Adam Elsheimer*, C. H. Beck, München 1988

Shubik, Martin, 'Auctions, Bidding and Markets: An Historical Sketch', in Richard Engelbrecht-Wiggans, Martin Shubik and Robert M. Stark (eds), *Auctions, Bidding and Contracting: Uses and Theory*, New York University Press 1983, pp.33–52

Smith, Bernard, 'Art Marketing in Sydney 1970-1975', in Peter Quartermaine, (ed.), *Readings in Australian Arts – Papers from the 1976 Exeter Symposium*, University of Exeter, Exeter 1978, pp.74–83

Smith, Bernard (ed.), *Documents on Art and Taste in Australia – The Colonial Period 1770–1914*, Oxford University Press, Melbourne 1975

Smith, Bernard, *Place, Taste and Tradition – a Study of Australian Art since 1788*, Ure Smith Pty Limited, Sydney 1945 (first ed.)

Smith, Charles W., *Auctions – The Social Construction of Value*, University of California Press, Berkeley, Los Angeles 1990 (reprint)

Smith, James, *Herr Kahler's celebrated historical picture of 'The Lawn at Flemington on Cup Day' with a biographical sketch of the artist*, McCarron, Bird & Co., c.1889

Sotheby's Australia Ltd and John Dixon & Co. Pty Ltd, *The Cowlishaw Collection of Early Australian Colonial Books and Paintings*, Darlinghurst, New South Wales 1984

Thomas, Daniel, *Outlines of Australian Art: the Joseph Brown Collection*, Harry N. Abrams, New York 1989 (3rd ed.)

Towner, Wesley, *The Elegant Auctioneers*, completed by Stephen Varble, Hill & Wang, New York 1970

Tyrrell, James R., *Old Books, Old Friends, Old Sydney*, Angus and Robertson, Sydney 1952

Turner, Jane (ed.), *The Dictionary of Art*, Macmillan, London 1996, vol. 2

Van den Bosch, Annette, *The Australian Art World: Aesthetics in a Global Market*, Allen & Unwin, Sydney 2005

Vaughan, Gerard, 'The Armytage Collection: Taste in Melbourne in the late nineteenth century', Galbally, Ann and Margaret Plant (eds), *Studies in Australian Art*, Melbourne 1978, pp.36–44

Watson, Peter, *Sotheby's: Inside Story*, Bloomsbury, London 1997

Watson, Peter, *From Manet to Manhattan – The Rise of the Modern Art Market*, Random House, New York 1992

Whitley, W. T., *Artists and their Friends in England 1700–1799*, London 1928, 2 vols

Wolff, Janet, *The Social Production of Art*, Macmillan, Houndmills, Basingstoke 1993

Wraight, Robert, *The Art Game Again!*, Leslie Frewin of London, 1974

Unpublished Theses

Bayer, Thomas Michael, Money as Muse: The origin and development of the modern art market in Victorian England. A process of commodification, PhD thesis, Tulane University, 2001

Berryman, James, Field to Fieldwork: the exhibition catalogue and art history in Australia, PhD thesis, Australian National University, 2005

Bolas, Gerald Douglas, The Early Years of the American Art Association, 1879–1900, PhD thesis, The City University of New York, 1998

Brown, Timothy Richard, The Language of Public Service and Private Interest in France: the Vexed Case of the Paris Auctioneers, 1750–1848, PhD thesis, Department of History, Stanford University, August 2000

Chiba, Kathryn, Dr Joseph Brown: Dealing in Cultural Capital, MA thesis, University of Melbourne, 1999, 2 vols

Holden, Robert, Aspects of Art Collecting and Patronage in Colonial New South Wales, Honours thesis, University of Sydney, 1981

Leiboff, Jacklyn Marett, Reconstructing the Role of Cultural Significance in the Protection of Movable Cultural Heritage Act 1986 (Cth), PhD thesis, Griffith University, November 2004

Phillips, Dimity, Impressions of distance: a study of women printmakers practising in regional Australia 1993–2003, PhD thesis, Australian National University, 2005

Prothero, Barry, Four Young Artists and a Dealer: a study in the Manufacture of Value, essay submitted in partial fulfilment of a B.A. (Hons) in Fine Arts, University of Sydney, 1976

Schibeci, Lynn Frances, The London auction market and the commodification of English Taste, 1766–1823, PhD thesis, Northwestern University, 1999

Stansfield, Mary, Show & Tell – The Melbourne Galleries, 1945–1995. A Survey with Studies, MA thesis, University of Melbourne, 1996

Van den Bosch, Annette, The Art Market since 1940 – A Model of the Relationships between Key Players and the Interactions Between Aesthetic and Financial Values, PhD thesis, Department of Fine Arts, University of Sydney, June 1989, 2 vols

Unpublished Papers

Huda, Shireen, 'The Impact of Auction Houses on the Commodification of Contemporary Australian Art', unpublished paper, delivered at the Australian National University, Canberra, 28 October 1999

Huda, Shireen, 'Art and the Ethics of Collecting in the Twentieth Century – The Politics of Deaccessioning', unpublished Honours seminar paper, Australian National University, Canberra 1997

Huda, Shireen, 'The History of Collecting: Art and War, Art and Revolution – Art as a Socio-political Weapon', unpublished Honours seminar paper, Australian National University, Canberra 1997

Sayers, Andrew, unpublished floortalk on the John Webber portrait of Captain Cook, delivered at the National Portrait Gallery, Canberra, 11 August 2002

Shoemaker, Adam, 'From Embassy to 'Embarrassment': Debates over Indigenous Cultural Property in the Public Sphere', unpublished paper, delivered at the *Art and Human Rights Conference*, Canberra, 10 August 2003

Van den Bosch, Annette, 'The Role of Art Auctions in the integration of national art worlds in the global market and its effects on contemporary artists', unpublished conference paper, delivered at *The Economics of Art Auctions* workshop, held by the International Center for Art Economics (ICARE), Venice, 17–18 January 2002

Velthuis, Olav, 'Promoters and parasites – An Alternative Explanation of Price Dispersion on the Art Market', unpublished conference paper, delivered at *The Economics of Art Auctions* workshop, held by the International Center for Art Economics (ICARE), Venice, 17–18 January 2002

Index

A Secret, 46
Aboriginal and Torres Strait Islander, 71, 112, 124
ACCC, 141, 143-44
After the Bath, 34
Agnew, 12, 23
Agnew & Son, 12
Albers, Adolf, 49
Allingham, E. G., 10
Alton Towers, 41-42
American Art Association, 12, 151
Anderson, Patricia, 2
Ansell, Robert, 21
Art and Art Treasures Exhibition, 136
Art Gallery of New South Wales, 49-50, 54, 61-62, 64, 88, 97, 136, 140, 143
Art Gallery of South Australia, 78, 143
Art Gallery of Western Australia, 113, 134
Art House, 2
Art in Australia, 47, 49
Art of Australia, 1788–1941, 70
art resale royalty, 66, 118
Art Union Act, 35
art unions, 33, 35, 37
Artemis, 26
Arthur Tuckett & Son, 47
artists, 1-2, 4-5, 11-12, 16, 19, 21, 33, 35-37, 39-41, 43, 47-50, 60-61, 63-64, 66-69, 71-72, 84, 87, 89, 93-94, 96-99, 103, 114, 117-18, 123-24, 131, 138-41, 162-63, 167
Artists and Galleries of Australia, 150
Ashton, Julian, 49
Asia Society Galleries, 112
Aspects of the Trout Collection, 92
Associated Auctioneers, 126
Attalus, 7
Attwood, Thelma, 91
auctioneers, 1, 7-8, 10-12, 15-16, 19, 23, 28, 30, 34, 37-40, 42-43, 55-57, 59-60, 62, 68, 72, 80, 91-92, 105, 108, 125-26, 132-33, 145, 149, 153-54, 156-58, 165
Auctioneers and Agents Act 1941, 132-33
Auctions (Bidding Agreements) Act 1927, 15

Australian Art Auction Records, 124, 130
Australian Art Collector, 130
Australian Art Sales Index 1969–1974, 124
Australian Broadcasting Corporation, 85
Australian Commercial Galleries Association, 123
Australian Competition and Consumer Commission, 141
authenticity, 1, 12, 30, 34-35, 39, 59-60, 72, 94, 106, 123, 131, 133
Avery, Samuel P., 12

Bacon, Philip, 92
Badgery, 153, 155-56
Baker, Samuel, 10, 28
Baldwin Spencer, Sir Walter, 5, 47-50, 60, 64, 67, 69, 93, 159
Ballarat Gallery of Painting Art Union, 36
Ballou, Maturin Murray, 38
Barclay, William, 59-60, 72
Barlow, Montague, 15, 24, 79
Batten, Jan, 136
Beauchamp and Rocke, 39
Beckford, William, 27
Belle Ile, 92
BHP Billiton, 98
Bladin sale, 98
Bleakley, Robert, 80, 86, 90, 92-93, 105-109, 112, 123, 125, 127, 129, 131-32, 134-36, 138-39
Blum, Irving, 4
Bond, Alan, 30, 94-95, 109-110, 158
Bonhams & Goodman, 4, 117, 149, 163
Bonyhady, Tim, 97
Bonython Gallery, 86
Bonython, Kym, 96
bought-in, 15, 29, 124
Bowness, Sir Alan, 4
Boy Sunbathing, 104
Boyd, Arthur, 66, 72, 78, 86-87, 99, 129, 138
Brack, John, 97, 143
Bradley, Newton & Lamb, 43
Brame, Hector Gustave, 12
Breton, Jules, 13-14
Brodsky, Isadore, 38, 88
Brown, Joseph, 93-94, 98, 164

Bruce's of Adelaide, 163
Burge, 98
Bush Idyll, 143
Buttsworth, John, 94
buyer's premium, 3, 7, 30, 91, 94, 97, 108, 123, 132-34, 143, 155 166
buying-in, 123-26

Capon, Edmund, 140
Carfrae & Bland, 39
Carnegie Corporation, 70, 96
Carrington, Lord, 91
Catherine the Great of Russia, 11
Caz Gallery, 112
Chevalier, Nicholas, 33, 112
Chiba, Kathryn, 99
Chippendale, 79
Christensen, Allan, 113
Christie's, 1, 2-5, 12, 19, 21-24, 26-30, 40, 46, 55, 61, 64-66, 69-73, 77-81, 84-95, 97-99, 103-104, 106-110, 113, 117, 123-27, 129-34, 139-40, 143, 145, 149-53, 155-69
Churcher, Betty, 110
Clark, Jane, 34, 48, 129
Clark, Stanley, 29
Cock, Christopher, 10
Coffee House, 9-10, 15
Coles Myer, 98
collectors, 1,-2, 4, 11-12, 24, 28-29, 33-34, 40, 42-43, 49-50, 60, 68, 70-72, 77, 79, 84-85, 87-90, 93-96, 98, 104-104, 107, 116-19, 123, 127, 130, 138-41, 144, 150-52, 155, 158
Colnaghi, Martin, 27
colonial, 28, 33-38, 40, 43, 45, 51, 64, 67-69, 84, 90, 94-95, 138, 158
commissaires-priseurs, 8
commission, 2, 7, 10, 21, 30, 33, 35-36, 47, 66, 85, 93-94, 97-98, 103, 119, 123, 125-26, 128, 132-35, 141, 165
Conditions of Sale, 16, 30, 39, 59, 69, 135
Condon, Christopher, 134-35
contemporary, 2, 4-5, 7, 12-13, 19, 35, 42-43, 47, 60, 64, 66, 68, 70-71, 86, 96, 108, 112-14, 116-18, 123-24, 140, 155, 158, 162-64, 167, 169

Cooper, Jeremy, 2, 11
Cornes, Don, 145
Corrozet, Gilles, 8
Courbet, 12, 63
Craig, Edward D., 124
Cupid and Psyche, 144

Daily Telegraph, 59, 60
Daily Telegraph Pictorial, 56
Dallhold, 94-95, 109-10
Darrell Lea, 64, 152
Davidge, Christopher, 91
de Wees, Adrian, 11
dealers, 1, 2, 4-5, 11-13, 15-16, 19, 27, 29-30, 33-36, 40, 42, 55-56, 58, 61-62, 64, 66, 70-72, 84-85, 87-88, 90, 94, 96-97, 99, 106, 109, 117, 119, 123, 126-27, 130-34, 139-41, 143, 145, 151, 158, 162, 164-66, 168
Debenham Coe, 26
Decoration & Co., 55
Dedman, Roger, 127
Derby Day, 43
Deutscher-Menzies, 2, 4, 46, 78, 97-98, 116, 129, 134, 143, 149, 155-57, 160, 163-68
Diggins, Lauraine, 113
Dighton, Robert, 21, 23
Dobell, Sir William, 60-66, 70-71, 84, 87-89, 99, 103-104, 106, 113, 152-53
Dodds, Leonard, 49-50
Dreamings, 112
Drysdale, Russell, 63, 66, 78, 84, 87, 89, 99, 154
Durand-Ruel, Paul, 12
Dürer, 9
Duveen, Joseph, 24

Edmiston's, 26
Elkingtons of London, 41
Ellenden, William, 56, 71, 153-54
Elsheimer, Adam, 81, 83-84
Elstub, Warren, 72, 151
Emus in a Landscape, 84
Encyclopedia of Australian Art, 78
English Method, 9
Enright, Malcolm, 162

F. R. Strange, 4, 149-50
Faith, Nicholas, 15
fake, 13, 16, 124-25, 131-32
Feeding Time, 95
Floyd, Jo, 78-80, 86
Fonthill Abbey, 27

Gainsborough, Thomas, 21-23, 25, 42, 55, 59
Gambart, Ernst, 12
Garrick, David, 21
Gemmell, Tuckett & Co., 34, 38-40, 43, 45, 66
Geneva, 26
Geoff K. Gray, 4, 55, 64, 72, 88, 131, 149-50, 152
Germaine, Max, 106, 150
Gilbert, George, 39
Gill's Fine Art Society's Galleries, 47
Gilmore, Dame Mary, 62, 88
Glover, John, 7, 43, 134-35, 137, 140-44
Gold Rush, 34, 37
Golden Summer, Eaglemont, 48
Goldschmidt, 26, 29
Goodmans, 4, 97, 133, 149, 155, 163
Gowing, Denis, 104
Grampp, William, 4
Graphic, 23
GraysOnline, 152
Greenoaks, 40, 42
Grimwade, Arthur, 61
Grishin, Sasha, 165
Groth, Peter, 153
GST, 97, 134
guarantees, 29-30, 57, 59-60, 72, 106, 131, 166-67

Hackett, James T., 58-59
Hallinan, Peter, 117
Hals, Frans, 24
Hamilton Palace, 24
Hannen, Guy, 78-79
Harris and Ackman, 55
Heathcote, Christopher, 66
Heller, Ben, 3
Henshaw, John, 78-79, 87, 89, 124, 126
Herbert, John, 26, 29, 77, 90, 99
Herodotus, 7, 19
Hewitt, Sue, 77-79, 81, 87, 90-93, 165
Heysen, Hans, 47-49, 58, 67, 158-59
Hilder, J. J., 48-49
Hoffmann, Josef, 81
Hogarth, William, 16
Hogrefe, Jeffrey, 1
Holden, Robert, 40, 41, 43, 45
Holyoake, Mary, 37
Hood, Robin Vaughan, 33
Hughes, Robert, 3, 71-72, 89-90, 99
huissiers-priseurs, 8
Huntington, Collis P., 13
Hutchinson, Sir Walter, 78

Impressionist, 12, 23, 29-30, 62, 84, 94, 131
inch of candle, 9
Indigenous, 99, 105, 118, 135
Ingram, Terry, 37, 69, 77, 94, 97, 103, 105, 116, 118, 130, 132-33, 149, 152, 160, 168
International Association of Auctioneers, 155
international style, 80
investment, 2, 3, 5, 40, 48, 50, 55, 58, 60, 63, 66-67, 70, 89, 93, 99, 106, 130, 139, 154
Irises, 30

J. Paul Getty Museum, 21-22

Kahler, Carl, 5, 43-47
Kirby, Thomas, 13
Klimt, Gustav, 81-82
Klingender, Tim, 113, 116, 118-19
Klompé, 163
Kluge, John, 112
Kneller, Sir Godfrey, 27
Kngwarreye, Emily Kame, 114
Koekkek, 34
Komon, Rudy, 62, 64, 66

La Graffinade, 15
Lacey, Robert, 130
Lambert, George, 47-48

Langford, Abraham, 10
Lawson's, 2-4, 50, 55-60, 62, 66, 70, 72, 88, 91, 97, 130-31, 133, 145, 149-58, 160
Lawson-Menzies, 4, 117, 149, 153, 156-57, 167
Le Garçon au Gilet Rouge, 29
Learmount, Brian, 2, 7, 133
Legends and Landscape in Australian art, 96
Leigh, George, 16, 28
Lely, Sir Peter, 11, 38
Leonard Joel, 3-4, 55, 66-69, 72, 84, 92, 94-95, 131, 134, 149, 155, 157-61, 163, 167
Leslie, James B., 91
Little, William Augustus, 42, 57-58
Lloyd Jones, Charles, 88, 155
London, 2, 4-5, 8-11, 13, 15-16, 19, 21-22, 26-27, 29-31, 33-34, 40-43, 55, 57-58, 61, 64, 69-72, 77-81, 84-87, 90-94, 99, 103, 105-10, 114, 116, 118, 125-26, 130-32, 136, 139, 144, 150-51, 153, 156-57, 161, 163-65
London style, 80
Long, Edwin, 19-20
Longden, Reginald, 103
Love Story, 113, 119
Lowenstein Sharp, 168
Lucius Cecilius Iucundus, 7
Lucius Mummius, 7

MacDonald, J. S., 59-60
Magiciens de la Terre, 113
Manby, Thomas, 11
Margolin, 155
Martens, Conrad, 36, 42, 90
Maslen, Geoff, 130
McAlpine, Lord Alistair, 162
McCaffrey, John, 118
McClelland, Joan, 77-78, 140
McCubbin, Frederick, 40, 48, 67, 69, 95, 143-44
McIlroy, Roger, 80, 90-94, 98, 110, 131, 165, 167
McInnes, W. B., 47-49, 67
Mead, Dr Richard, 28
Meadmore, Clement, 72

mechanics' institutes, 33, 36
Melbourne, 3, 5, 26, 29, 33-34, 36-40, 43, 45-48, 50, 55, 66-69, 72, 77-80, 85-88, 90-91, 94-95, 98, 103-104, 107-108, 112-14, 116-19, 124, 129-30, 132-34, 136, 138, 140-41, 144-45, 149, 158, 160-61, 163-64
Mellon, Paul, 29
Mercier, Louis Sebastien, 8, 13
Mertz, 95-98, 143
Messum's Fine Art, 157
Miller, Justin, 119, 127, 131, 133, 168
Millington, Edward, 10, 13, 15-16
Mineing, 9
Montreal, 26
Moore, William, 48
Mora, William, 116
Morgan, James Pierpont, 23
Mort, Thomas Sutcliffe, 28, 38, 40-43
Mossgreen Auctions, 157
Mount Wellington and Hobart Town, 140, 142-43
Movable Cultural Heritage Act 1986, 116, 134-35
Mundy, Lt. Colonel Godfrey Charles, 38

Namatjira, Albert, 87
Nash, David, 105
National Gallery of Australia, 84, 109-10, 113, 135, 141, 143-44
National Gallery of Victoria, 40, 47-48, 59, 81, 97, 129 141, 143
National Library of Australia, 109
National Portrait Gallery, Canberra, 88, 110
Nero, 7
Nevill Keating Fine Art, 94, 98, 109
New York, 5, 12, 16, 26, 28-31, 71, 80, 85, 87, 93, 103, 106, 109, 112, 114, 116, 118, 125, 131-32, 144, 151, 161, 164-65, 168
Ngurrara Canvas I, 118
Nicholson, Sir Charles, 38
Nodrum, Charles, 80, 106, 151
Nolan, Sidney, 63, 66, 86-87, 97, 138, 162
Northwick, 27, 41-42, 77

O'Connell, Maurice Charles Philip, 36
Ortiz, 105
outroping, 9

Page-Cooper, George, 67-70, 72
Paris, 8, 13, 16, 26, 43, 58, 87, 89, 113, 118-19
Parke-Bernet, 29-30, 80 131, 151
Parkes, Henry, 40
Paterson, Samuel, 10
Perth, 34, 37, 90, 110, 118, 138, 144, 161-62
Pfaff, Pinschof and Co., 43
Phillips, 4, 19, 26-27, 41, 92, 97, 130, 149, 156, 161-62
Pinault, Francois, 26
Pizzi, Gabrielle, 119
Port Phillip Herald, 39
Portrait of Captain James Cook RN, 108-109, 111
Portrait of Georgiana, The Duchess of Devonshire, 23, 25
Portrait of Hermine Gallia, 81-82
Portrait of James Christie, 21-22
potboilers, 34
Properties, Stock and Business Agents Act, 133
provenance, 19, 39, 42, 59, 68-69, 79, 93-95, 114, 117, 127-28, 131
Purves, Stuart, 123

Queensland Art Gallery, 93, 97, 113, 143

Raven, John, 90
referrals, 123, 125-26
Reid, Michael, 2, 130, 163-64, 168
Reitlinger, Gerald, 11, 128
Rembrandt, 9, 11, 37-38, 41
reserve, 15, 29, 39, 57-58, 79-80, 84, 105, 108, 123-27, 141, 166
Reynolds, Sir Joshua, 21, 39, 59
rings, 13, 15-16, 143-44
Robert Holmes à Court Collection, 34, 114, 117
Robert L. Godfrey Auctions, 154
Roberts, Tom, 40, 48, 50, 67
Rooney, Robert, 158-59

Royal Holloway, 19
Rubens, 8-9, 24
Rubensohn, Sim, 70, 154
Rubin, Major Harold Du Vahl, 62, 64, 70, 88-89
Ruhen, Carl, 2, 56, 62, 64, 155
Rutherford, Bruce, 103
Ruwolt, Charles, 67, 70, 155

Sabine, Patricia, 144
Salute to Five Bells, 104
Savill, Denis, 97, 165
Sayers, Andrew, 110
Schaeffer, 98, 110, 166
scholarship, 1, 67, 70, 72, 80, 130
Schureck, Norman, 5, 55, 60-66, 70-71, 88-89, 99, 139, 154, 159
Seney sale, 13
Settled Lands Act, 24
Settler's Camp, 34
Shapiro Auctioneers, 4, 149, 161-62
Shubik, Martin, 8
sleeper, 80-81, 124
Smart, Thomas Ware, 28, 40, 42-43
Smith's Weekly, 56-57
social status, 1, 56, 92, 145
Sotheby's, 1-5, 10, 15-16, 19, 23-24, 26-31, 34, 55, 65-66, 69-70, 72-73, 77-80, 84-86, 88-95, 97, 99, 103-10, 112-14, 116-19, 123-36, 138-40, 143, 145, 149-53, 155-69
speculation, 3, 139
Spencer, Sir Walter Baldwin, 5, 47-50, 60, 64, 67, 69, 93, 159
Spowers, William, 77-79, 85-86, 88, 90, 125
St Helena Questions the Jew, 81, 83
Stadelsches Kunstinstitut, 84
Stanley, Dalia, 163
Staples, Charles Raymond, 34
Stowe, 23
Streeton, Sir Arthur, 5, 34, 40, 47-50, 67-69, 135
sub hasta, 7
Suddenly Everything Happened, 157
Sumner, Paul, 139, 156-57, 164
Sunday Telegraph, 64

Sunflowers, 92
Sutherland, Kathie, 91
Sydney, 3, 5, 26, 33-34, 36-38, 40-42, 47, 49, 55-59, 61-62, 64, 71, 77-81, 85-86, 88-91, 94, 97-99, 103-104, 107-109, 118, 129-30, 132-33, 139, 144, 149-52, 155-56, 159, 161-64

Tasmanian Museum and Art Gallery, 141, 144
Tate Gallery, 4, 70
Tate Modern, 81
Tattersall, Richard, 21
Taubman, A. Alfred, 30, 106
Terra Australis: the Furthest Shore, 110
The Advertiser, 99
The Australian, 78, 130, 141
The Babylonian Marriage Market, 19-20
The bath of Diana, 134-37
The Betting Ring at Flemington, 43
The Bulletin, 61-62, 72
The Christ Child as the Good Shepherd, 21
The Dead Landlord, 89, 104
The Derby Day at Flemington, 43-45
The Hull Trinity House, 108-09
The Lawn at Flemington on Melbourne Cup Day, 43
The Munich Burgher's Daughter, 46
The Night of the Pigs, 88
The Ruinous Tendency of Auctioneering, 16
The Sex Kitten, 104
The Story of Australian Art, 48
Titian, 9, 38
Tjakamarra, Michael Nelson, 113
Tjapaltjarri, Clifford Possum, 113, 119
Tjupurrula, Johnny Warangkula, 95, 114-15, 118
Tokyo, 26, 31
Trade Practices Act 1974, 143-44
Traill, Jessie, 159
Trout, 92-94
Tyrrell, James, 57

Uluru (Ayers Rock), 118
Une Nuit De Canicule, 158
United States, 2, 13, 94, 97
University of Texas, 96-97

Upwey Landscape, 98

Van den Bosch, Annette, 2, 72
Van Dyck, 9
van Ludik, Lodewyck, 11
Vasari, Giorgio, 7
von Guérard, Eugene, 33, 36, 84, 94-95
Voss Smith, Len, 77-79, 84, 86

Wallis, Henry, 33
Walpole, Horace, 21, 27
Walter Bradley & Co., 38
Walton, Parry, 11
Wangi Boy, 61, 64-65, 152
Water Dreaming at Kalipinypa, 95, 114-15, 118
Waterhouse, David, 134-35
Watson, Peter, 2
Webber, John, 108-109
Weinberg, 29
Whitechapel Galleries, 70, 78
Whiteley, Brett, 72, 96-97, 138
Wilkie, Joseph, 33
Wilson, Peter, 28-30, 89, 104-105, 123
Woods, Thomas, 19, 23
Wymark, Charles, 154

www.ingramcontent.com/pod-product-compliance
Lightning Source LLC
Chambersburg PA
CBHW040545220526
45473CB00017B/3032